"PROVOCATIVE AND CHALLENGING . . . he displays on every page a quirky, wide-ranging intelligence."
—*Washington Times*

"From time to time a book appears that is such a brilliant critique of accepted wisdom that it is a landmark. This book deserves that status." —*Calgary Herald* (Canada)

"A MASTERFUL AND ENJOYABLE DEBUNKING OF THE PRETENSIONS OF CRYSTAL GAZERS."
—*Publishers Weekly*

"Max Dublin not only shows how misleading futurologists' prophecies are, but also lucidly explains how and why they are incurably simple-minded, dangerous and amoral. Dublin has his wits about him. If we attend to what he says, we can keep ours too."
—Jane Jacobs, author of
The Death and Life of Great American Cities

"An antidote to contemporary credulity." —*Booklist*

"Adroitly surveys the whole realm of predictions."
—*Seattle Times*

MAX DUBLIN is a Research Fellow at the University of Toronto. He was educated at the University of Chicago and received his Ph.D. from Harvard University. *Futurehype* is his first book. He currently lives in Toronto.

MAX DUBLIN

FUTUREHYPE

THE TYRANNY OF PROPHECY

A PLUME BOOK

PLUME
Published by the Penguin Group
Penguin Books USA Inc., 375 Hudson Street, New York, New York 10014, U.S.A.
Penguin Books Ltd, 27 Wrights Lane, London W8 5TZ, England
Penguin Books Australia Ltd, Ringwood, Victoria, Australia
Penguin Books Canada Ltd, 10 Alcorn Avenue, Toronto, Ontario, Canada M4V 3B2
Penguin Books (N.Z.) Ltd, 182-190 Wairau Road, Auckland 10, New Zealand

Penguin Books Ltd, Registered Offices: Harmondsworth, Middlesex, England

Published by Plume, an imprint of New American Library, a division of Penguin Books USA Inc.
Previously published in a Dutton edition.

First Plume Printing, June, 1992
10 9 8 7 6 5 4 3 2 1

The following are used by permission:

Robert Aldridge, First Strike! The Pentagon's Strategy for Nuclear War *(Boston: South End Press), 1983.*

Herman Kahn and B. Bruce-Briggs, Things to Come: Thinking about the 70s and 80s *(New York: Macmillan), 1972*

Alan Turing, "Computing Machinery and Intelligence," in Alan Ross Anderson, Minds and Machines *(Englewood Cliffs, N.J.: Prentice-Hall), 1964.*

 REGISTERED TRADEMARK—MARCA REGISTRADA

LIBRARY OF CONGRESS CATALOGING-IN-PUBLICATION DATA
Dublin, Max, 1947-
    Futurehype : the tyranny of prophecy / Max Dublin.
      p.   cm.
    Originally published: New York : Dutton, 1989.
    ISBN 0-452-26800-1
    1. Forecasting.   I. Title.
CB158.D83   1992
303.49—dc-20   91-45916
                             CIP

Printed in the United States of America
Original hardcover design by Steven N. Stathakis

FOR MY PARENTS
ROSE AND MORRIS

ACKNOWLEDGMENTS

Research for this book was begun during the year I was appointed as the first Institute Fellow at the Ontario Institute for Studies in Education in Toronto. I am indebted to Malcolm Levin, Dwight Boyd, George Geis and Ian Winchester for offering me collegial hospitality at that time and in ensuing years. For useful research leads and/or comments on the manuscript I would like to thank John Briner, Phoebe Chytiri, Mary Damianakis, Gina Feldberg, Michael Fullan, Trevor Hancock, Jane Jacobs, Robert Kuttner, David Levine, Orlando Patterson and James Rosenfield. Special thanks to Isabelle Gibb of the Institute library. I am also indebted to Nancy Anderson, Robert Bick, Deanne Bogdan, Niall Byrne, John Eisenberg, Michael Laing, Elizabeth McLuhan, Richard Rockefeller and Harold Troper who have, at different stages in the book's development, given me the yin and yang of moral support; and I am particularly grateful to my auditors in Cambridge, John Bowles, John Carey, Janet Levoff, Andrew Morvay, Nita Sembrowich and

Siki Cat, for giving me some needed encouragement and feedback at a crucial stage in the writing. Finally, I want to thank Iris Skeoch, Kevin Mulroy and Mitch Horowitz of Penguin Books, whose editorial feedback has substantially contributed to the book's improvement, and Morton Mint who saw the merits of this book while it was still at an early stage of development. Chapters seven and eight, in slightly different form, were first delivered as lectures at the Coolidge Center for Environmental Leadership and at the Center for Society Technology and Values, respectively.

Events, by definition, are occurrences that interrupt routine processes and routine procedures; only in a world in which nothing of importance ever happens could the futurologist's dream come true. Predictions of the future are never anything but projections of present automatic processes and procedures, that is, of occurrences that are likely to come to pass if men do not act and if nothing unexpected happens; every action, for better or worse, and every accident necessarily destroys the whole pattern in whose frame the prediction moves and where it finds its evidence.

—HANNAH ARENDT, *On Violence*

. . . most of the research now going on about the future tends to advocate further increases in the institutionalization of values . . .

—IVAN ILLICH, *Deschooling Society*

We [Devils] want a man hag-ridden by the Future—haunted by visions of an imminent heaven or hell upon earth—ready to break [God's] commands in the Present if by so doing we make him think he can attain the one or avert the other—dependent for his faith on the success or failure of schemes whose end he will not live to see. We want a whole race perpetually in pursuit of the rainbow's end, never honest, nor kind, nor happy *now* but always using as mere fuel wherewith to heap the altar of the Future every real gift which is offered them in the Present.

—C.S. LEWIS, *The Screwtape Letters*

CONTENTS

FUTUREHYPE

. . . the Erewhonians are a meek people, easily led by the nose, and quick to offer up common sense at the shrine of logic.

—SAMUEL BUTLER

PROLOGUE:
THE POWER OF PROPHECY

The impetus to write this book originally came from the desire to shed some light on a number of troubling contradictions that were impressed on me a few years ago while I was working as a government consultant. At that time, I was hired to help a special task force to complete a unique report, the sort of long-range planning document which modern-day corporate executives and bureaucratic officials, aping their military counterparts, like to call a *strategic plan.* Because long-range planning is today closely integrated with forecasting, while working for this task force I was eventually asked to take a hard look at what our different types of prophets have to say about the future.

Predicting the future has become so integral to the fabric of modern consciousness that few people feel compelled to question it, and fewer still feel the need to defend it. And yet, in surveying the landscape of modern prophecy, it was shocking to discover how much of what even our most respectable prophets have to say about the future is blatantly false, that is, either deeply flawed intellectually, or morally questionable, or both. It is true that their predictions and visions are logical, up to a point, but when you look at them closely, many of even the most respectable prophecies today still fly in the face of common sense and/or common decency. And there seem to be no real people in these visions of the future, no real life in the rich and sometimes puzzling way in which we experience it—only banal abstractions of life and neat little caricatures of people.

Since it is obvious that our prophets and our prophetic leaders in government, in the media and in industry have a powerful impact on our lives, and since so much of what they say turns out to be false, in the end I found myself thinking more and more not so much about *what* they have to say, but *how* they say it. I became concerned about the nature of their appeal, the techniques and rhetoric that make our prophets credible and persuasive, and also about how prophecy shapes our world and how we think about the future. The more I learned about modern prophecy, and the more I thought about the role our prophets have come to play in the development of our world, the more contradictions I discovered, and the more striking—and troubling— did these contradictions appear.

The first of these contradictions to strike me, and perhaps the one that really got me going on this book, goes something like this: on the one hand, a great many present-day prophets—perhaps John Naisbitt, one of the current lions among pop futurologists, is most prominent among these—have proclaimed that present trends allow for almost endless possibilities for developing the world of the future; on the other hand, however, many of the same futurologists—and Naisbitt is noteworthy here too—also take great pains to explain to their followers that the world of the future will only be *thus and so*. And sometimes they even go on to warn that those who are not willing to prepare for this specific future, or for a short list of possible futures, will run into any number of difficulties and dangers, and perhaps be hopelessly left behind. As Naisbitt himself has put it in this somewhat benign, but ultimately rather patronizing warning:

"Trends tell you the direction the country is moving in. The decisions are up to you. But trends, like horses, are easier to ride in the direction they are already going. When you make a decision that is compatible with the overarching trend, the trend helps you along. You may decide to buck the trend, but it is still helpful to know it is there."[1]

Endless possibilities, but very few real choices—unless, of course, you are willing to run the risks and pay the costs of "bucking trends."

Not everyone has such a respectful, if not worshipful, view of trends. George Orwell, who many people have mistakenly considered to be a prophet, was actually, in his time, a severe detractor of modern prophets, and especially of trend-chasers like Naisbitt.[2] In a long essay about James Burnham, a prominent American futurologist and trend-follower of his time, Orwell cast a very different light on trend-chasing when he made the following criticism of Burnham's political predictions: "The prediction that Russia would gang up with Japan against the U.S.A. was written early in 1944, soon after the conclusion of a new Russo-Japanese treaty. The prophecy of Russian world conquest was written in the winter of 1944, when the Russians were advancing rapidly in eastern Europe while the Western Allies were still held up in Italy and northern France. It will be seen that at each point Burnham is predicting *a continuation of the thing that is happening*." (emphasis in original)[3]

However, Orwell's critique went much further than merely pointing out the intellectual fallacy of "predicting a continuation of the thing that is happening." Orwell argued that this way of thinking was the consequence of a moral failing. He wrote: "The tendency to do this is not simply a bad habit, like inaccuracy or exaggeration, which one can correct by taking thought. It is a major mental disease, and its roots lie partly in cowardice and partly in the worship of power, which is not fully separable from cowardice."[4] Later in this critique Orwell went on to elaborate how our experience teaches us that such predictions are false and to describe how the worship of power works in political prophecies, but his observations are generally applicable to all sorts of prophecies, not only the political ones. He wrote:

Power worship blurs political judgement because it leads, almost unavoidably, to the belief that present trends will continue. Whoever is winning at the moment will always seem to be invincible. . . . This habit of mind leads also to the belief that things will happen more quickly, completely, and catastrophically than they ever do in practice. The rise and fall of empires, the disappearance of cultures and religions, are expected to happen with earthquake suddenness, and processes which have barely started are talked about as though they were already at an end. . . . The slowness of historical change, the fact that any epoch always contains a great deal of the last epoch, is never sufficiently allowed for. Such manner of thinking is bound to lead to mistaken prophecies, because, even when it gauges the direction of events rightly, it will miscalculate their tempo. Within the space of five years Burnham foretold the domination of Russia by Germany and of Germany by Russia. In each case he was obeying the same instinct: the instinct to bow down before the conqueror of the moment, to accept the existing trend as irreversible.[5]

It might be nice to think that the differences between how Orwell and Naisbitt think about trends are merely intellectual, a gentleman's disagreement to be sorted out over drinks at the club: one thinks trends are to be exploited; the other thinks this amounts to worshipping the conqueror of the present moment. But the reason that this and the other contradictions of modern prophecy that I will be discussing in this book are *not* merely intellectual is that predictions are not merely exercises of the mind. Predictions have power: there is no rhetorical or propaganda device more powerful than prophecy. Predictions do not simply describe the world—they *act* on it. How do they do this? For one thing, predictions are seldom neutral, seldom merely descriptive. Usually predictions—even weather forecasts—are also prescriptive; they contain a strong element of advice and warning. The advice and warning inherent in Naisbitt's forecasting are not unique in modern prophecy—in fact, they are quite characteristic of it—but often the advice is much stronger, and the warning more dire, than those I quoted above.

But even when predictions have no advice or warning built into them, they still act powerfully on their audiences because they naturally function in the same way that promises do in the sense that they create expectations, and there is no question but that people will act on the basis of these kinds of expectations. But false predictions—and, as I will show in this book, most predictions, except for the most obvious and short-range ones do, in fact, turn out to be false—are like false promises, that is to say, they act like lies. And false predictions are destructive in the same way that lies are because, when uttered with conviction, they disarm and inspire us and put us into false positions. Furthermore, these false positions, like all false positions, encourage us to act in ways we never would if we really understood where we stood and what we were doing, in ways that are typically self-defeating.

There are all sorts of self-defeating things that false predictions may encourage us to do, but usually the false positions into which they put us will be a result of the fact that, because of the promise inherent in a prediction, we will act irresponsibly to the present. Acting irresponsibly to the present can take many forms. False predictions can lead us to abandon something of the present—something that we have known, valued, understood and lived with over the years, and something that is still worthwhile and viable if only we would continue to give it the effort and attention it deserves—in favor of something "better" that we neither know, nor value, nor yet properly understand but which, we are told, will be a great good in the future. And sometimes we abandon not just one but many things for the sake of the one that is yet to be, for this is often the nature of "building the world of the future." From the railroads in our transportation system, to the humanities in our education system, to innumerable viable industries we hasten to dissociate ourselves from worthwhile endeavors that enrich our lives in large part because their demise has been predicted and we do not want to be "left behind." Or we hasten to associate ourselves with questionable, sometimes dangerous, but in any case unproven endeavors simply because their rise has been predicted. When you think about it, it is extraordinary what we are willing to relinquish in the world of the present in order to usher in what our prophets tell us will be the world of the future—and, what is much the same thing, what we neglect for the same reasons. But the rashness and destructiveness of this kind of lemming-like behavior is seldom apparent to us because our prophets lead us to believe that to follow them is to do something brave and good. They tell us that the thing of the future is better than the thing of the past and present—or at least it is the next necessary step—and the panic, simple-mindedness and vain self-assurance which they inspire make us behave irresponsibly.

These facts were vividly brought home to me in a disturbing story I heard when I was working on an oral history project in Jamaica, a number of years before I began analyzing the thinking of our modern prophets. The story was an account of an episode in Jamaican history that occurred during the early part of this century in one of Kingston's outlying districts called August Town. In 1920 a prophet by the name of Bedward, who was based in August Town, began to preach all over Jamaica, predicting the end of white rule and his direct ascent with his followers to heaven. Bedward's message was that World War I and a major earthquake, which happened also to have occurred at that time, were signs that his prophecy was about to be fulfilled. He urged the people to give up their worldly goods and follow him. And, perhaps to his credit as a sincere, though deluded, prophet, he was very precise in his predictions. He predicted that he would make his ascent exactly at a certain time on December 31, 1920. Many people believed him. Many people—even many whose recent ancestral memory included landless slavery—sold or gave their land away, left their homes, donned white robes and gathered with him in August Town. Even the whites took this prophecy seriously. Shortly before the fateful day the Kingston *Gleaner* reported:

Yesterday there was great excitement at the Railway. Every train brought in a large number of people, men, women and children all bound for August Town. But they came from Colon as well, on a steamer travelling across seas to see their "Lord of August Town" ascend. In King Street all tram-cars travelling to Hope Gardens were besieged by men, women and children, some infants in arms, others hardly able to help themselves, but they were all bundling in with their clothes, baskets and fowls. All have sold out to come up and see the Lord and Master do the disappearing trick. There are still more to come.[6]

But they did not see Bedward do the "disappearing trick." Instead they saw him use the characteristic delaying tactics that the cult-prophet employs when his predictions fail to materialize. A few days before the day of his predicted ascent Bedward resorted to high drama: he swung one of his female followers from a tree to see if her faith was strong enough to make her fly, but when she failed to learn to fly he proclaimed it was too weak. When the predicted day of ascent finally arrived—but without the predicted result—he naturally pushed the date forward and kept doing so until the month of May. But these postponements could do nothing for his followers, many of whom had given up their land and livelihood, had given up everything for the promise of something better—in this case nothing less than heaven. Some were eventually arrested for vagrancy. Most of them were too ashamed to return to their homes, so they settled there in August Town, and some of their descendants live there to this day.†

This incident in Jamaica's history certainly was not earthshaking, but though it occurred as part of a fleeting religious movement and may sound somewhat droll, it is still

† When I was told this story, the narrator and I stood before a beautiful poinciana tree that insisted on growing defiantly amidst the rubble on which this wretched community was built. The poinciana tree seemed to me to be a reminder of the verdant tropical bush which is so abundant in the rural areas these people had abandoned to follow their false prophet. But not everyone has the ability to remember, for better or for worse, that which has been lost or abandoned. For example, when literacy is relinquished, one loses, even within a single generation, a great deal of the ability to remember and appreciate what was lost.

quite symbolic of our rather more secular lives. Though we live today in a world whose self-image is decidedly secular, we still have our civil religions, based largely on technology, money and power. The Bedwardite vignette represents in miniature and in stark relief the widespread, sometimes subtle, but often profound effect of prophecy on our lives. Predictions are capable of harmfully misleading not only relatively small groups of people, like Bedward's followers, but entire societies and even whole civilizations—and sometimes in the most monumental and decisive ways. Wars have been started on the basis of prophecy, and so have economic and social movements, large and small.

Because it is capable of influencing us this way, modern prophecy, in all of its different manifestations, should be considered a force in its own right—a force which, like all sources of power, is liable to be abused. It does not merely monitor the development of our civilization, as futurologists like John Naisbitt like to claim it does, but actually shapes it, often in decidedly harmful ways. By saying this, however, I have a great deal more in mind than the now commonplace observation that polling often affects the outcome of elections or, for example, that Naisbitt's futurological boosterism has given extra impetus to the growth and economic development of Tampa, Florida, which he predicted would be one of the "cities of the future." The effect of prophecy on a society is much more powerful than this. Because of its power, there is, and always has been, a great deal of manipulative, exploitative and destabilizing potential in prophecy—and often this is precisely what false prophecy is all about. Of course it can also be about simple foolishness. During the course of this book I will describe a number of prophecies of our time that have been either manipulative or foolish, and sometimes both. In each case it will be obvious how the prophecy feeds on and appeals to the worse parts of our nature. What should also be clear is the extent to which prophecy in our time, though often claiming on the basis of science to be an objective business which transcends any system of values or ethics, nevertheless still plays a highly value-ridden part in our political and economic debates. However, while claiming to be objective and scientific, modern-day prophecy merely uses the mantle of science to strengthen and legitimate itself while masking its ideological content.

It is characteristic of science, in its quest for objectivity, to exclude and avoid ethical considerations. Therefore it is natural for modern prophecy, which has scientific pretensions, to do the same thing. But a prophecy with scientific pretenses, and especially one which on this basis often manages to avoid or mask ideological and ethical issues rather than facing them head-on, is a disturbing development in the history of the world. There have always been false prophets, but before scientism began to obscure ethical questions by claiming to transcend them, all forms of prophecy were deeply and explicitly grounded in ethical thinking, for the simple reason that they were a part of religious practice. Prophets were spiritual leaders and foretelling the future was only one part of the extremely complex roles they played in their nations and societies. One only has to recall the prophets of ancient Greece and Israel during what may be regarded as the golden age of prophecy to realize how integral this grounding used to be.

Consider, for example, the role that prophecy played in the life and times of King Oedipus of Thebes.[7] We are all familiar with the bare bones of this story. A young man kills a stranger, who turns out to be his father, and through a series of quirks becomes king and marries another stranger, who turns out to be his mother. For commiting these crimes he dooms himself to a miserable destiny of blindness and exile. What is interesting, however, is how all of this is revealed, for the most important work of revelation is left to a prophet by the name of Tiresias. Tiresias, the famous blind prophet of Oedipus's kingdom of Thebes, far from thrusting himself into the political fray, as our modern prophets like to do, was actually at the outset a very reluctant oracle. In fact, when first questioned by Oedipus, Tiresias was adamantly unwilling to talk. He knew the truth would eventually come out, that it would bring doom to his king and shame to the city, and so the prophet preferred not to be the one to break this terrible news. Describing his predicament, Tiresias himself says in Sophocles's version of this story, "Alas, how terrible is wisdom when/It brings no profit to the man that's wise!"[8]

But Oedipus, true to character, immediately became incensed with Tiresias for this reluctance. It was only at this point, when Oedipus had once again displayed his famous temper, that Tiresias hinted at all of the crimes that would eventually be revealed. Ultimately it was Oedipus's temper, now brandished at Tiresias himself, that reminded the prophet of the original source of this tragedy, the earlier occasion when Oedipus had lost his temper and killed another old man during an altercation on the road, a stranger who turned out to be his father. "You blame my temper," the prophet reproached King Oedipus, "but do not see / your own that lives within you."[9]

In the end, when Tiresias was forced to reveal the source of present misery and to foretell the coming doom of King Oedipus, he did so by way of a moral chastisement. Tiresias did not merely glibly predict the future for Oedipus, he did it in the context of raising explicit moral issues. He not only predicted that horrible things were in store for Oedipus but he also explained that it was the King's own reprehensible behavior that had doomed him. Tiresias indicted Oedipus in the harshest way possible by maintaining that it was nothing less fundamental than Oedipus's own character, his unruly temper, that had shaped his destiny. Character is destiny said Tiresias to King Oedipus; I predict that all of these horrible things will happen to you and they will happen as a consequence of the way you have lived your life.

Like Tiresias, most of the Old Testament prophets also chastised the Children of Israel, reminding them of their moral shortcomings. In the case of the Hebrew prophets, however, the prophecy-cum-chastisement took a somewhat different form: the call of the prophet was often an exhortation to the Israelites to better themselves so that they would be worthy of the great destiny that had been prepared for them, so that it would not be delayed by their undesirable behavior. Moses, the first and greatest of these prophets, forced them to wander through the desert for forty years to expiate their sin and prepare themselves for their destiny. Elijah, in his turn, called upon them to live a more spiritual life, and Isaiah censured them for materialism and land-grabbing.† Isaiah said, "Woe to those who add house to house/and join field to field/until everywhere belongs to them/and they are the sole inhabitants of the land." (Isaiah, 5:8).

In a sense the *foresight* which these ancient prophets possessed was fundamentally part of their more general and profound *insight* into human nature. It was a vehicle for making an honest and open moral argument about the future. There have always been charlatans in the prophecy business, but moral intelligence based on a profound understanding of the complexity of human nature has always been an integral part of true prophecy. In modern prophecy, however, this is hardly the case. Trendiness and the managerial/technological juggernaut that drives most modern forecasting generally have little if anything to do with ethics. Elijah predicted of the Children of Israel, "You will be a light unto the nations." Today our prophets are just as likely to predict, "You will sell computer chips, or armaments or banking services to the nations."

Typically, the only thing that is left of a moral argument in the prophecy of our times is lip service to progress and a great deal of the power of prediction to make us act is based on the rhetoric of progress. However, contrary to popular conceptions—conceptions which are often promoted by futurologists themselves for obvious self-serving reasons—prediction has very little, if anything, to do with progress. In fact, in our time prediction has often acted as a hindrance to real progress. This is true because, first of all, governments often use rosy predictions as a mechanism for avoiding coming to grips with the intractable problems of the present. A great deal of time, energy and money is spent making and fostering these kinds of predictions—and the often foolish interventions that are based on them—instead of taking responsibility for the present situation and tackling the

† Nowhere is the power of prophecy more evident than in the history of the Jewish people. On the positive side, the prophecy of the return to the promised land served as a binding force to preserve the Jewish culture and identity and to sustain the Jewish people for millennia. However on the negative side it also acted, and tragically acts to this day, as one of the main legitimating reasons behind the claim that is made by some sectors of Israeli society to the right of permanent occupation of the territories that were captured during the Six Day War.

problems at hand. Second, and perhaps more important, predictions often retard progress: when one speaks of progress it is important to be specific because we do not all agree on what it is, and because progress in one area often means regress in another. For example, although the arms race is now presumably over, its progress was characteristically based on predictions of future military superiority or a future state of "parity." Since the end of World War II this kind of futuristic propaganda served as an excuse for constantly postponing the talks and negotiations that were necessary to create progress in peace.†

Divorced from the progressivism of earlier periods, prophecy has also largely lost what was left, as recently as the turn of this century, of the moral and ethical basis for gazing forward. Because of this rupture we have developed an ethic about forecasting that is often self-serving but ethically indifferent. Fitting ourselves into a vulgar Darwinian definition of our humanity, in following our false prophets we are always "adaptive" and "exploitative" creatures rather than morally purposive ones. Therefore we are not so much concerned about what the future will be because, on the basis of our values, we want it to be a certain way, rather we want to know what the future will be because we think this is the only way we can protect ourselves and perhaps take advantage of it. Worse than this, many people have come to think that the future must be good merely because it is the next step, because it is there, because the next step is said to be inevitable. In our time false prophecy consistently substitutes the ethic of inevitability for the ethic of responsibility. What this amounts to—instead of futuregazing tied to truly progressive thinking—is a bland, pervasive, sterile and rather mechanical *futurity*. The future is the place to go to and we should want to go there simply because it is the next place to go.

† In spite of the fact that the cold war has largely died down, the end of the arms race is greatly exaggerated: in spite of the disarmament treaties of the last few years new weapons systems are still scheduled to come on board until the end of the century. A conference of NATO defense ministers in April 1990 issued a communique that the Alliance will continue to adhere to its first strike policy because they are unwilling to relinquish a policy that has supposedly served them so well in the past. This is a typical incidence in which "clinging to the past" is called "looking to the future."

Because it so often puts us into false positions and encourages us to make blind bargains, prophecy today has become an instrument for violating the very future it claims to predict, and which it sometimes even claims to protect. It creates an attenuation of the many possible futures that actually *can* be for the sake of the future that, in the mind of the usually self-appointed prophet, *should* be. Even those of our prophets like Naisbitt, who flutter the banner of endless possibilities use it only as a hook, as a rhetorical device and as a distraction from the limited choices, from the very narrow road, along which they are encouraging us to follow.

Therefore the real issues that are raised by the role of modern prophecy in our lives have ultimately to do with the relationship between the virtual infinity of real possibilities for development which exist compared to the few that are presented and promoted by our prophets. These are ultimately issues about freedom, growth, diversity and fulfilment. A certain course of development may be "logical" to a certain extent—even pathological developments and the transformations and transactions of decline follow a logical course—but it is never "in the nature of things," that is, it is never the only logical way to go. There is nothing inherently logical about the way we are developing now or the way the world has ever developed. Development is now and has always been an interplay between our values and the many possibilities contained in the world before us, and, contrary to a great deal of conventional wisdom, it has always been more of an improvised and creative rather than planned affair. We are continually impoverishing and betraying both our present and our future by following the narrow and ultimately restrictive paths that are pointed out by our present-day prophets. We are constantly impoverishing ourselves by abandoning what we value and have mastered in favor of what we do not yet even understand. Thereby we destroy the richness and diversity of our skills and resources: the very tools that could ensure that our futures are at least as rich as the present, and might even help us to adapt to the real world that will unfold for us.

Even true science, whose power is based on its predictive capabilities, has discovered many areas in which it is incapable of making predictions, but outside of the realm of true science there are very few neutral predictions in this world. In fact, since predictions are often heavily laden with the values of our prophets, when we buy into the world which they project before us—and thereby help make their prophecies self-fulfilling—we fulfill not ourselves but them. Fulfilling the visions of the prophets of our time has meant not only buying into banal technological utopias, but also into their vain fantasies of controlling everything from recessions to nuclear wars.

The pathological strain in modern prophecy is as broad as it is deep. It might be nice to think that it is restricted to the so-called lunatic fringe, but who can distinguish the mainstream from the lunatic fringe if a prominent politician like Henry Kissinger has envisioned that we could control nuclear wars using the psychological precepts of game-theory, while a distinguished computer scientist like Edward Feigenbaum imagines that one day we will be able to solve the problem of loneliness by using robot companions?†

In today's world we are witnessing a deadening convergence of purposes. This convergence is putting all of us in jeopardy because not only, as the saying goes, are the nations of the world all rushing to put all of their developmental eggs in one basket, they are also all trying, as much as possible, to put them into one and the same basket. There are many sources for this unhealthy convergence, but modern prophecy is undoubtedly one of the most powerful. In the long run, individual and national development which is not truly open-ended—ready both to preserve what has already been mastered and continues to be valued, as well as to pursue an infinite variety of possibilities, and not merely the ones our prophets claim to see so clearly—is bound to be dead-ended. A rich civilization—one that is masterful in a great variety of present endeavors and not merely dreaming about

† So much has futurology become woven into the fabric of our culture, now it is indeed often difficult to distinguish establishment futurology from the kind that is popularized in the media. Members of the Board of Directors of *The Futurist,* which is a pop-futurology magazine with a large following, include: former U.S. Secretary of Agriculture, Orville Freeman; former U.S. Secretary of Health, Education, and Welfare, John Gardner; former Secretary of Defense and President of the World Bank, Robert McNamara; and former Chairman of the U.S. Atomic Energy Commission, Glenn T. Seaborg.

how well it will do in the future based on one or two new ones—is one that takes an immeasurable amount of time and patience to attain; once it is relinquished, even for a relatively short period of time, it is immeasurably difficult to regain. There is a great deal of talk about decline today, especially with respect to the superpowers. Although their obituaries are rather premature, one thing the superpowers do have in common—one might call it their common enemy from within—is that they have both been particularly susceptible to the propaganda of prophets who have persistently narrowed their field of vision.

Since what is always at stake in our relationship with our prophets is nothing less than what we want to become, and since the very act of prediction has the power to influence what we will become, the questions we must pose for ourselves in this relationship are these: Will we make our own choices, or will we accept the ready-made ones with which they present us, and based on which, if they are leaders in positions of power, they often act in our behalf? Will we buy into their dreams, or will we assert the right that is the precursor to real growth, the right to dream our own dreams?

Dreaming our own dreams, that is, pursuing a diverse and rich economic and cultural development, may appear to be a luxury in our time when we are possessed by the need to predict the future in order to be purposive in conquering it. In fact it is not a luxury but one of the most compelling of necessities. It is necessary because of the diversity it promotes. It is one of the few things that can keep our civilization diverse enough so that, as time unfolds, we retain choices through the skills and knowledge that we have preserved and developed by continual cultivation.

As to our modern prophets themselves, all of the earlier ages of prophecy would have been ashamed to own up to them. The reader will not find an Isaiah, a Tiresias, or even a Cassandra or Merlin among them, but he will find, insofar as they have any moral conviction, that they are constantly inviting us to worship the ancient idol of "progress." But this is only an empty piety because the sticky and complex debate about what progress at this or any other point in time might actually mean is an issue for which they have neither the moral intelligence nor, usually, even the *patience* in which to engage. They legitimate this idol worship and make it respectable by cloaking themselves in the mantle of science, even though they are not true scientists. They also sometimes claim to be humanists, but this claim is also hollow. In fact, most of the prophets of our time have no deep tradition to draw upon or with which to ground themselves in their extremely ambitious and influential enterprise. C.S. Lewis has said of such actors that they are "merely modern . . . the severities both of abstraction and of high human tradition have passed them by."[10] Yet what is most remarkable about them, but not surprising given the nature of their training, is how impressionable they are. Though a great many of them are simply wide-eyed technophiles or mechanical extrapolators, some are obviously fools and charlatans. And, though the self-interest and the quest for power are self-evident in some modern prophets, in others these motives are disguised in self-righteous disclaimers about the public interest.

Self-interest and the quest for power: this, of course, is what false prophecy is and always has been about. But I hope it will be obvious by the end of this book that I have written it not merely to demonstrate how banal, simple-minded, and self-serving many of the most influential of our present-day prophets are. Some of that will be necessary as I go along, but my main purpose is to help make my readers more alive to the real possibilities, to the real variety of choices we can make to shape our present—and ultimately, of course, our future—according to the way we want to live, not according to the way others, in the guise of prophecy, say we ought to live. In the end, I shall be arguing that there are better vehicles than prophecy, not only for deciding where we want to go, but for affecting individual growth and social, economic and cultural development. These ways pertain to an ethic of responsibility that insists on the necessity of making the most of the present, in mastering its challenges in our personal, corporate and national lives. By elucidating the role that prophets play in our society and in our lives, by explaining their motives, their ideology and the aspects of our psychology that make us want to listen to them, it is my hope that this book will help people to become more thoughtful and critical about where we are going and why we are going there.

NOTES

1. John Naisbitt, *Megatrends* (New York: Warner Books, 1982), p. xxxii.
2. It may surprise those who have only read his fiction to learn that Orwell wrote a powerful diatribe against futurology, because he himself dabbled in prophecy for many earlier years. For example, even as late as 1945 Orwell predicted, wrongly as it turned out, that Churchill and the Conservatives would win the post-war general election. Perhaps it was because he himself so often made mistaken predictions that Orwell rethought the prophecy issue. If one reads his papers one learns that *1984* was written not so much to serve as a prediction of future society, but rather as a critique of the present society in which he lived, a speculation of what could happen if it continued its present course. The propagandized state, the state on a permanent war footing, the state which insistently intrudes on private life, was already going strong in Orwell's time and, due to the effects of World War II and its immediate aftermath, was particularly evident in 1948, when Orwell finished this novel. (The title of the book, of course, is simply a reversal of the last two digits of the year when it was completed. He had earlier toyed with the idea of calling the book *The Last Man in Europe.*) Unfortunately, using the device of future projection to gain a critical perspective on the present can now be seen, with hindsight, to have been a questionable practice on Orwell's part. Having finally passed the monumental year whose number he used for the title of this book, the sad irony is that so many people treat it as a test that has been passed—it has come and gone and was not nearly as bad as Orwell is said to have predicted it would be in his fiction—in spite of the fact that all of the major criticisms implicit in the novel have been increasingly vindicated over time.
3. George Orwell, "James Burnham and the Managerial Revolution," in *Collected Essays, Journalism and Letters* (New York: Harcourt Brace Jovanovich, 1968), vol. 4, pp. 172–173.
4. Orwell, p. 173.
5. Orwell, p. 174.
6. Quoted by Martha Beckwith in *Black Roadways* (New York: Negro University Press, 1969), p. 169. Beckwith actually met Bedward just before his predicted ascent. I have drawn on her classic and reliable version to refresh my memory and validate the stories I heard personally many years later.
7. It is a great pity that the story of Oedipus has been reduced in the modern popular imagination to the deeply colored and rather narrow psychological interpretation given to it by Freud. As interesting as Freud's tale of father/son rivalry and juvenile eroticism may be, the original story, as it is told in the literature of ancient Greece, is far richer, more subtle and grounded in a more complex morality.
8. Sophocles, *Oedipus the King* (trans. David Grene), in *Greek Tragedies* (Chicago: University of Chicago Press, 1973), Volume 1, p. 123.
9. Sophocles, p. 124.
10. C.S. Lewis, *That Hideous Strength* (London: Pan Books, 1983), p. 109.

1

PROPHECY AS PROPAGANDA

It has always been compelling to think about the future—it is, after all, the repository of our hopes and vision. But the future is also the repository of our fears because it raises monumental questions: What will become of us and our descendants? Will we be fulfilled or depleted by the lives we are going to live? Will we succeed or fail? In our time, an unusually large and ever growing number of people will readily admit to an anxious concern about these questions and about what the future may bring. In fact, it is not too much to say that we are living at a time when a pervasive concern about the future has become no less than an obsession. This obsession has many sources, but undoubtedly it stems mainly from an almost universal unease about the present, based both on its failures and on its general lack of stability. Therefore most people, even those who by the terms of the entire history of the world are doing very well, nevertheless still feel at risk, in jeopardy; they feel that the future may hold something unpleasant in store for them in the form of a loss or undesirable change in their economic, social, or personal lives.

And yet, though anxiety about the future is particularly pronounced in our time, it is certainly not a new or extraordinary phenomenon. It has occurred many times throughout history whenever social, economic, political and technological changes have altered generally stable relationships and thus produced a climate of instability. René Dubos has observed that "There have always been timid souls who believed that adaptation to the future would be difficult, painful, and perhaps impossible. . . . In 1575, four centuries before the phrase 'future shock' was coined, there was published in Paris a small book† by an author who worried . . . about the disturbances caused by the new knowledge and technologies of his time, and even more about what was in store for the future."[1] So even though we may be inclined to convince ourselves that our times are unique and wholly unprecedented, pervasive anxiety about the future has recurred so often in history, and has been so common at *all* times, that it should be regarded as part of the human condition.

This is not to say, however, that this anxiety does not present its problems. Not only does apprehension about the future take its toll on our emotions, it also makes us vulnerable; we are as easily victimized by it as by any other of our fears. There have always been those who are ready— even eager—to play on our apprehensions about the future, and sometimes even to capitalize on them.

Forever feeding our anxiety about the future are words—words coming from the mouths of our modern-day prophets and carelessly repeated by opportunistic and impressionable journalists, academics, advertisers and politicians, some of whom like to play the role of prophet themselves. Prophecy makes good press. We are forever being told by the media that some sort of fad or recent development will be *the wave of the future,* or *megatrend.* We are told that one particular factor will make or break the economic future of a given nation, be it that vague and peculiar abstraction "competitiveness," which is currently being ban-

† *De la Vicissitude ou Variété des Choses dans l'Univers,* by Louis Le Roy.

died about in the United States; free trade with the United
States, which is presently the favorite panacea/bogeyman in
my own country, Canada; or enterprise zones, which have
recently played a similar role in China. Most countries have
their own version of the magic formula that will be decisive.
We are also constantly being told that some recent medical
discovery will lead, in the not too distant future, to the cure
for the most endemic health problems, and many of us want
to believe this, in spite of the fact that the cures for cancer,
cardiovascular disease, mental illness and other complex syndromes seem to be incessantly receding into the horizon.
And we are constantly being sent on chases after the professions of the future—communications, computer programming, investment banking—only to find the market rather
overcrowded when we finally arrive in it, or to discover that
we never really wanted to do that kind of work in the first
place. Yet, no matter how many wild-goose chases we are
sent on, we are ever eager for the hunt.

But whatever else we may believe of all these words
about the future, many people find at least this much inescapable: that the present rate of change is unprecedented in
the history of the world. From this often repeated assertion
we conclude that we should all be preparing ourselves to live
in revolutionary futures, futures which will occur within our
very own lifetimes. Yet the merits and flaws of these revolutionary futures are seldom discussed so much as is their
inevitability.

Many of those who listen to the pronouncements and
read the literature produced by our futurological gurus feel
that significant changes are indeed *inevitable* and will produce the future difficulties or traumas that everyone would
naturally want to avoid. But a great many of those who follow
our modern-day prophets have also come to feel that, if we
can predict now what the future will be like, we will be able
to *control* it, or at least prepare for it in advance by anticipatory actions consisting mainly of avoiding dangers and/or
securing our present position. (These are the types of measures which, according to the conventions of military strategy,
are commonly referred to as *defensive*.) Others—it is difficult
to know whether we should call them optimists or oppor-
tunists—follow our prophets in the hopes of enhancing their

own positions by capitalizing on insights about the inevitable transformations that are supposed to be in store for us. (These would be considered *offensive* measures according to the conventions of military strategy.)

When thinking of the future in these ways, *control* is always the objective. We play a sort of cat-and-mouse game with the future: we act as if it has a life of its own, one which is quite separate from the lives we are living in the present and somehow malevolent and threatening, somehow opposed to us. In our desire to control the world of the future, we are constantly trying to outwit, outmaneuver, or at least adapt to it—before it even exists.

The masters of this peculiar game are, of course, those who are also most likely to play on our apprehensions about the future: our prophets. They not only predict but talk a great deal about *controlling* the future. John von Neumann, one of the fathers of computer science, made a number of predictions about computers in his time. One of these was that by the present time computers would have made weather data so manageable and manipulable, and would thereby have enhanced our knowledge about the weather so greatly, that we would not only be masters at predicting it, we would also be able to control it. Though this was a false prediction, at least theoretically von Neumann was right about controlling the future with the help of predictions. Within limits and under certain conditions, scientists can indeed make predictions about natural phenomena. And sometimes, with clever interventions in the natural order, they can also bring about certain outcomes. The sustained nuclear reaction upon which atomic energy is based is the classic example of this. But to bring about predictable outcomes in the natural order, two conditions are necessary. First, that order must be profoundly understood, and second, the intervention must be doable. The reason that even today, in the future von Neumann was trying to predict, we can still forecast weather only four or five days in advance and do little if anything to change it, is that neither of these conditions has yet been met with respect to the weather system, even with the help of tremendous computing power. Though it is far more accessible to our unaided senses, the weather system is even more incomprehensible and—in spite of clever fantasies of elab-

orate cloud seeding—also far more difficult to control than
the subatomic system. And of course human civilization—
that is, the human system with its social, economic and technological components—though in some ways tied to the natural order, is even still more complicated and difficult to
control than the weather system because it is also subject to
the irrational aspects of human nature as well as to free will.

Because of its extraordinary complexity and deep-seated
irrationalities, predictions about the human order, outside
of the shortest time frame, and beyond those having to do
with the most fundamental biological imperatives, are usually wrong. They are wrong because, even today, they are
usually no more than simple linear projections, or what Orwell called "a continuation of the thing that is happening."
Typically, the "thing that is happening" eventually slows
down or stops happening entirely or changes its meaning in
our lives; really remarkable changes are seldom if ever predicted. Consider the remarkable, yet unpredictable, developments that have occurred even since the end of the last
World War: the rise of Japan as the leading economic power;
the huge hole that has developed in the ozone layer; the
appearance of the AIDS virus; President Sadat going to Je-
rusalem; the rise to power in the Soviet Union of a radical
reformist like Gorbachev and the ensuing liberation of Eastern Europe. Not one of these unpredictable yet earth-
shaking developments has even the least bit of a "continuation of the thing that is happening" flavor, so when one
considers them, one cannot help but wonder why we are so
enthralled by these "more of the same" predictions when
they are, in the present, not very enlightening and, in the
long run, invariably wrong.

A brief look at prophecy in the oil industry, which has
characteristically been of the most straightforward linear variety, will provide at least the beginning of the answer to
this last question, and should also serve as the beginning of
the answer to a more general question: Why do we persist
in accepting prophecies that are more intricate than the
"more of the same" variety but just as unenlightening and
ultimately just as false?

For the last two decades the oil industry has tried very
hard to predict the future price of oil in order to gauge what

sorts of revenues they could expect in the future, and thereby know how much money could be profitably invested for acquisition, exploration and development. During consecutive stages in this period of time, the forecasters in this industry have developed five different predictive consensuses.[2] We are still waiting to see how well the fifth of these will fare, but as far as the first four are concerned, they have all proven to be dead wrong.

The pre-1971 "more of the same" consensus predicted that oil prices would remain stable, with the expectation that prices would fluctuate by no more than mere pennies for the indefinite future. This predictive consensus was damaged by the rise of OPEC in 1971, and completely devastated by the oil embargo of 1973.

The second consensus, which lasted from 1974 to 1977, actually contained two variations, one of which originated in North America, and the other in Europe and Japan. In other words, there were two somewhat different "more of the same" predictions based on different experiences and perspectives of what "the same" really meant. The point is, however, that they were both in the same ballpark and, in the end, they both proved to be wrong. The difference between them, however, is revealing about how this kind of forecasting really works and what it means. The North American version was more optimistic than its Euro-Japanese counterpart. The reason for this is that it relied on related predictions that effective technological fixes in the form of economical substitutes for oil from shale and coal tar would be developed in a reasonable amount of time. The Europeans and Japanese, however, were more pessimistic about the prospects of beating the cartel in the future through technological innovation or by any other means. Yet in spite of this divergence, both versions of this particular predictive consensus complied with Orwell's characterization of "a continuation of the thing that is happening." As Cambridge Energy Research Associates have observed: "North American optimism was based on confidence in technology and experience of abundant resources, while Europe's pessimism was rooted in a history of resource constraints. Europeans had not only lived through shortages during World War II but had also experienced an 'energy crisis' in the late 1940s.

The Japanese were even more conscious of their resource dependence and vulnerability than the Europeans. Economic and resource 'dependence' was a new experience for North Americans, and more likely to be regarded as an aberration. For Europeans, it was the normal state of affairs. For the Japanese, it was a fact of life."[3]

In the end, however, both versions of this predictive consensus failed to anticipate the true strength of OPEC in pushing up prices. Therefore, both of these predictions were shattered by facts, and in 1977 the North American and Euro-Japanese oil price forecasts once again completely merged to project a huge price rise based on an oil crunch which was to occur around 1985. It did not occur around 1985, but occurred instead in 1979 with the fall of the Shah of Iran and the Iranian Revolution.

New predictions were again required, so in 1980 a fourth predictive consensus was developed which foretold that prices would continue to rise sharply for an indefinite period with "OPEC in the driver's seat." This consensus was also shattered in 1982 when an unexpected oil glut began to develop in the global oil market, effectively eroding OPEC's strength and pushing down prices, which finally collapsed in 1986.

Each of the first four predictive consensuses of the last two decades was shattered in turn by unpredicted events and was consequently replaced by the next. There is no reason to expect that the fate of the fifth, and present, predictive consensus, which prophesies OPEC's comeback sometime in the next four years, will be any different. If it does turn out to be correct, however, this will not be the result of its being more accurate; it will be because it is more vague and contingent than the others.†

The above analysis is not meant as a wholesale condemnation of forecasting in the oil industry. On one level, one cannot help but empathize with oil industry executives who feel they must rely on such forecasts to make their investment decisions. During the four-year period between 1980 and

---

† At the time this book is going to press, oil prices are again rapidly rising, but not because of an OPEC comeback, as the most recent consensus predicted, but because of the Persian Gulf crisis. What long-term effect this conflict will have on oil prices is, of course, unpredictable.

1983, 375 public oil and gas companies spent $227 billion to acquire properties and conduct exploration and development.[4] The expenditure of such large sums of money is nerve-wracking, to say the least, and, though industry executives have learned that price predictions are invariably wrong, they use them anyway.

They use them anyway because they feel the need to use *something*. The function of this type of prediction, in light of its persistent failure, is ultimately rather political if we look at it in the context of the corporate culture in which it plays its part. In the large modern corporation, prediction often serves the function of legitimating decisions; and the power of this function, and its consequences, should not be underestimated. Decisions must be justified, they must be based on *something*, preferably on something rational. But if something rational is not available—and this is more often the case than is usually admitted—then they must be based on something that at least *appears* to be rational. And, because of the nature of corporate culture, through a process of information exchange and corroboration, all predictions, that is, all appearances of rationality, fairly rapidly become one; they all converge into consensuses like the ones I described above.

The best position in corporate culture, especially with respect to prediction, is, of course, to be right when everyone else is wrong; from this may come the greatest rewards and the greatest amount of satisfaction. Second best is to be right along with everyone else. But if one is going to be wrong, then it is better to be wrong in the same way that everyone else is wrong rather than in a different way; at least then, when the moment of reckoning comes, this shows that you are capable of consulting with and listening to your colleagues, and everyone can feel foolish together, in a collegial fashion. It is not for nothing that one Canadian oil price forecaster has said, "Oil price forecasters make a flock of sheep look like independent thinkers."[5]

Beyond its questionable ability to forge unfounded consensuses and justify corporate decisions, there might appear to be little, if anything, to concern us about the role that price forecasting plays in the oil industry. In a sense, this type of forecasting should not even be called prophecy, or even prediction, for it is no more than a form of monitoring. Much like weather forecasting, another form of monitoring which uses a time frame that extends only slightly forward from the present, it may sometimes be mildly useful; often it is not. If all prediction were to be viewed from this perspective, there would be little to say about it. But this perspective is far too narrow to explain the deeper role of modern prophecy. The fact of the matter is, that a great deal of futurology—be it in the form of prediction, forecasting, or scenario writing—far from being no worse than mere speculation that basically harms only the speculators involved, often plays a destructive role in the world by justifying harmful political decisions.

It is one thing for the shareholders in the major oil companies to periodically squander what is presumably discretionary wealth in making speculations based on predictions of the future prices of oil. But consider the all too typical case of a country like Mexico. Mexico has engaged in a similar sort of oil price speculation and has in recent history planned a great deal of its development on the expectation of revenues based on these same predictions. Mexico nationalized its oil industry in 1938 under the leadership of then President Lázaro Cárdenas, but the speculation did not really begin until the mid-1970s, when President José López Portillo decided to strongly tie the economic development of the entire country almost exclusively to the development of newly discovered vast oil reserves. He thereby made economic development heavily dependent almost solely on the accuracy of predictions of future oil prices. In the ensuing period, not only did buoyant predictions legitimate a lack of discipline in labor, and among corporate and bureaucratic spenders, but, more generally, the kind of thinking that stemmed from embracing such predictions encouraged the development of a lopsided supply- or resource-based economy. Expectations of future oil revenues also legitimated national borrowing of over $100 billion during this period; of course the banks were as culpable as the government in financing all of these deals. When these predictions proved to be false, the 1986 collapse in prices resulted in a drop in government revenues of no less than 25 percent! In the wake of this calamity, the plans for economic development that were being promoted in 1988 from some political quarters in Mexico advocated measures no less drastic than the repudiation of large parts of the national debt.[6]

Mexico's basing its development policy on oil price predictions, in spite of their historical unreliability, is not unusual, since this is what macro-economic theory encourages one to do. But prediction of one sort or another is almost always at the heart of policy, and not just economic policy. Most policies—aside from the kind which are no more than mere posturing—are designed to bring about or respond to future developments: either a bad outcome is to be avoided or mitigated, or a good one is to be attained. It is not at all uncommon for a well articulated policy paper, based on a hopeful or fearful prediction and laden with a vast quantity of ideological blustering, to set the tone for debate and influence policy direction for a generation or more. And because the rhetoric of prediction is so powerful, it can often effectively close off the possibility of truly open debate for an entire era.

In modern times, grandiose and sweeping predictions have even served as the justification for policies affecting other countries and other people. For example, strenuous ideological prophecy was used to justify American territorial expansionism starting in the middle of the nineteenth century, some of which, incidentally, had a powerful impact on Mexico. In 1845 the American editor and author John L. O'Sullivan wrote an article in the *United States Magazine and Democratic Review* in which he predicted that in a hundred years time, that is by 1945, the population of the United States would grow to 250 million or more. Here, in a piece appropriately called "Annexation," he coined the powerful and famous prophetic term "manifest destiny" to legitimate the expansionist policy that he felt was justified by his prediction; he argued that it was the "fulfillment of our manifest destiny to overspread the continent allotted by Providence for the free development of our yearly multiplying millions."[7] O'Sullivan's prediction, with its disregard for the rights of native populations and other sovereignties, is a good example of a prophecy that has been sundered from any moral basis, or, perhaps more accurately, the extent to which morality, and even God, were reduced to the precepts of what O'Sullivan liked to think were natural laws. Later, appealing at once to the laws of both God and science, he wrote: "Texas has been absorbed into the Union in the inevitable fulfillment of the general law which is rolling our population westward; the connexion of which with that ratio of growth in population which is destined within a hundred years to swell our number to the enormous population of *two hundred and fifty millions* (if not more), is too evident to leave us in doubt of the manifest design of Providence in regard to the occupation of this continent." (emphasis in original)[8]

To late-twentieth-century ears, which are used to hearing policy pronouncements with questionable motivations and consequences made in more obscure and equivocal language, O'Sullivan's words are truly searing. Yet even more remarkable than this is the rest of the ideological baggage which accompanied this prophetic rhetoric. It was not enough that the population should grow and occupy the continent: all of the extra room, in this influential visionary's mind, was destined only for one kind of American, the white Anglo-Saxon. He wrote: "In the case of California . . . the Anglo-Saxon foot is already on its borders. Already the advance guard of the irresistible army of Anglo-Saxon emigration has begun to pour down upon it, armed with the plough and the rifle."[9] Not surprisingly, then, another part of O'Sullivan's vision was that, if and when America's slaves should be emancipated, they should also be deported to South and Central America so as not to pollute the Anglo-Saxon stock that was destined to populate the northern hemisphere. O'Sullivan stated:

> . . . It is undeniably much gained for the cause of the eventual voluntary abolition of slavery, that it should have been thus drained off towards the only outlet which appeared to furnish much probability of the ultimate disappearance of the Negro race from our borders. The Spanish-Indian-American populations of Mexico, Central America and South America, afford the only receptacle capable of absorbing that race whenever we shall be prepared to slough it off—to emancipate it from slavery and

(simultaneously necessary) to remove it from the midst of our own. Themselves already of mixed and confused blood, and free from the "prejudices" which among us so insuperably forbid the social amalgamation which can alone elevate the Negro race out of virtually servile degradation, even though legally free, the regions occupied by those populations must strongly attract the black race in that direction; and as soon as the destined hour of emancipation shall arrive will relieve the question of one of its worst difficulties, if not absolutely the greatest.[10]

One cannot overestimate the force of this prophetic propaganda. The doctrine of manifest destiny was used as an argument of legitimation for expansionism at first only by Democrats, but eventually the policy crossed party lines and was later also used by Whigs and Republicans. It was used for half a century to justify the annexation of Texas, California and Oregon, and ultimately repeated in debates about Alaska, Guam and Cuba. And there is no question, had the opportunity arisen, that it would also have been used to legitimate the annexation of Canada, because, according to O'Sullivan's prophecy, this was to be the last step before a vast and purely Anglo-Saxon North America would be able to defy the rest of the world. But obsession with grandiose future outcomes based on presently promulgated policies was certainly not a passing mood in the development of American political culture. As in other great nations, prophecy has been the spur that has driven on politicians with grandiose world views.

In the second half of this century, probably no politician has been as obsessed with and conscious of the future as Henry Kissinger. One of his former colleagues at Harvard has therefore remarked that the former secretary of state "can always be counted upon to utter commonplaces in the tone of prophetic revelation."[11] And, remembering his tenure as national security adviser and secretary of state under President Nixon, another American historian has observed that Kissinger's career during this period was based largely on a prophetic

style of manipulation and deception.[12] Perhaps these judg-
ments are somewhat harsh, but during a political career that
has now spanned more than thirty years, prophecy has certainly been one of the hallmarks of Kissinger's rhetoric, and
the role of the prophet seems to have long been part of his
own self-image. In his very first book, as if penning the stage
directions for his own controversial career, Kissinger wrote:
"The statesman is . . . like one of the heroes of classical
drama who has had a vision of the future but who cannot
transmit it directly to his fellow man and who cannot validate
its 'truth.' "[13]

Recently—perhaps sobered by the contentiousness of
his career, but also, apparently, smitten by the recurrently
popular ethic of managerialism—Kissinger wrote, in an article about Soviet-American arms negotiations, that "statesmanship consists, in large part, of foreseeing and managing
the *inevitable*." (emphasis added)[14] Such a statement may
be very compelling on the surface, but exactly what does it
mean?

The ethic of inevitability, which is so attractive to politicians like O'Sullivan and Kissinger, is perhaps the greatest
rhetorical device used by prophetic politicians. However,
unlike O'Sullivan, one thing that Kissinger certainly did not
spell out in his article—and what present-day prophets who
finally do get down to such bald terms seldom do spell out—
is why a certain course of events or actions should be *inevitable*. And what is more important is that those, like Kissinger, who choose to speak with a prophetic voice in our
time seldom say why a particular way of managing a certain
development is preferable to any other. Management and
inevitability are attractive to prophets because they have a
neutral tone. But nothing is inevitable, and management is
not a neutral activity: it does not merely order things, it
makes them happen. And usually, when management works
as it is intended to, it makes things happen in a very certain
way.

The sense of the inevitable, which is so strong in the
pronouncements of policy-making prophets like O'Sullivan
in the last century and Kissinger in ours, does not work in
the same way for everyone. Historians who, with the benefit
of hindsight, can try to be objective seldom, if ever, make

the assertion that a certain course of events was inevitable.†
But more important, though the rhetoric of inevitability may
sound prescient in the mouth of the prophet, ultimately it is
part of the rhetoric of cynicism and/or defeatism; yet it is a
powerful device for closing and stifling debate, and can be
used to legitimate the most questionable self-interested long-
range goals or projects.

Needless to say, Kissinger and many other politicians
use prophecy this way. Indeed, the last part of the article
from which his pronouncement of inevitability was quoted
is full of point-by-point prescriptions based on what he believed the Reagan administration should do to respond to
certain proposals which Mr. Gorbachev had then put forth
with respect to arms control in light of the American strategic
defense initiative. Aside from the fact that some of Kissinger's prescriptions were based on questionable assumptions,
in the end they were all rather constrictive. They constrained
the entire debate about Star Wars to the leaden framework
of cold war thinking which Kissinger himself had so long
labored to promote. This is typical. Talk of an inevitable
future always aborts most open discussion of real options,
and at the same time narrowly defines both the range of
choice and the type of activity in which it is said one can
engage to solve the problems at hand.

It is distressing that so much future-thought is so full of
a sense of the inevitable because there is an enormous
amount of evidence, from the variety of arrangements and
developments ongoing around the world, to indicate that
there is a great deal of scope for people, as individuals and
as nations, to shape their own destinies without deferring to
so-called inevitabilities. The variety of life-styles, cultures,
social structures and economies that exist even under similar
conditions is so great that one cannot help, when one takes
thought, but balk at easy talk of the inevitable.

† But many futurologists are so enamored of the notion of inevitability that they
use it even in their occasional analysis of the past as well as of the future. For
example, in the typically vulgar way in which futurologists analyze history, Stanley
Lesse, a prominent medical futurologist, writes, "Historic records show that cultures that fail to heed the challenges of social and technologic shift *inevitably* sink
into a morass of darkness and *inevitable* oblivion." (emphasis added) (Stanley
Lesse, *The Future of the Health Sciences*, New York: Irvington Publishers, 1981,
p. 13.)

However, inevitability is not the only rhetorical device used by our modern-day prophets. Often complementing the ethic of inevitability in prophetic rhetoric has been another of *boldness,* as if, once one is sure of what the future will be, the best behavior is to dash right for it. Some futurologists have even made a virtue out of the boldest kinds of forecasts, as if there is virtue in the forecast itself and bolder implies braver and therefore better. In fact Jerrold Maxmen, an American health futurologist, has gone so far as to assert: "While some forecasters appear to lack imagination, others actually seem to fear it . . . even though *all of the necessary facts are available,* the would-be prophet cannot see that they point to an inescapable conclusion. . . . This unwillingness to accept the *inevitable consequences of available facts* is what so often leads to excessively conservative forecasts." (emphasis added)[15]

One certainly could not accuse the Mexican government of relying on conservative forecasts when it based its entire lopsided and overheated economic development on traditionally unreliable predictions of the future price of oil. But in recent times there is perhaps no more troubling reminder of the questionability of radical economic interventions based on bold but mistaken forecasts than the adverse economic consequences which have followed in the United States as a result of the economic policies—perhaps one should say economic adventurism—of the Reagan administration.

A great deal has been written about Reaganomics from the perspective of economic theory. The theory of supply-side economics, which was the driving force behind Reagan's massive intervention in the American economy, was dignified by its promoters as being a subtle economic theory, but vilified by its detractors as "voodoo economics." But whatever else one may say about it, in the end Reagan's version of supply-side economics was little more than a mess of bad predictions. It predicted that tax cuts would put more money into the pockets of consumers and corporations. It predicted that the consumers would then save, spend, or invest this extra money: savings would provide capital for investment while at the same time spending would create demand and stimulate the economy. It also predicted that corporations would invest their own tax savings and the tax savings of individuals (which they could readily borrow from banks) in ventures that would create jobs. Jobs would be created not only for the middle classes, but also for the lower classes through a mechanism known as "trickle-down." And finally, the theory of supply-side economics predicted that, in the end, all of this favorable economic activity would generate additional tax revenue which would make up for the shortfall created by the cuts and pay for increased defense spending, which was being promoted at the same time.

It is now painfully obvious that only one of the above predictions has come true: when the government cut taxes some consumers, particularly those in the higher tax brackets, and many corporations did indeed have more money to dispose of—and the government had less. Since *control* is the underlying assumption of such future-minded interventions, it is notable that this last eventuality was the only part of the future scenario which the government, by its own decision-making and behavior, could and did control. By now it is all too familiar how the many decisions, large and small, that the government could *not* predict or control were made; these are the decisions that have created the present adverse economic situation in the United States and, because of America's pivotal role in the world economy, ultimately in the whole world.

During the 1980s in the United States investment and savings actually went down, and though there was a great deal of spending in certain sectors of the economy and in certain geographical regions, its form was not terribly encouraging. Car and home purchases went down during the 1980s because these particular items kept going out of the reach of more and more consumers in spite of the much touted prosperity. Many taxpayers who received rebates, and consumers in general, spent their extra cash on foreign goods thus stimulating not the economy of the United States so much as those of Japan and West Germany, and thereby contributing to the increase in the American balance of payments deficit. Others invested in non-stimulating items like real estate and art. All too many corporations, in turn, decided to spend their extra cash not on ventures which would create long-term employment, but on non-stimulating take-overs; the effect was to create some jobs, many of them temporary in the financial services industry which works on these deals, but also to destroy many long-term or permanent jobs in others. At the same time corporations doing the takeovers created for themselves a great deal of long-term, often unmanageable debt. However, given the climate which the Reagan administration created by cutting taxes and boosting defense spending, why should consumers and corporations necessarily have acted differently? Why, outside of acting in their own interests, should any of the players in the economic game have acted in such a way as to make Reagan's predictions of good economic outcomes into self-fulfilling prophecies?

In the end, the point about Reagan's economic predictions is that they were too simplistic to be believable; they were based on a caricature of how the American economy works, not on a profound understanding. They were based, in other words, on the manipulation of a single simple variable, not on a broad-based concerted and complex effort. In free societies people and corporations make their own decisions and serve their own ends. No matter what the economic theories may be predicting that they should be doing at any given time, they will behave according to their own complex purposes. It is the sum of individual decisions, large and small, which make a world—not a grand theory like supply-side economics which predicts it will be thus and so. Why should the decisions of the people of an extremely heterogeneous and individualistic nation like the United States conform to the shape of a U-curve (the famous Laffer curve which justified the Reaganomic predictions), an S-curve, or any other overly simple way of predicting extremely complex behavior? It is remarkable how many predictions are made even by our most "sophisticated" prophets on the basis of mechanistic and monolithic views of the nature of society and of the nature of individual and collective decision-making. And yet it was these groundless economic predictions that made the Reagan administration's decision to cut taxes and increase spending seem credible and legitimate at the time that it was made.

In the end, the supply-side forecasting of the Reagan

administration simply legitimated what has turned out to be
an enormous and destructive intervention in the American
economy. It is true that this intervention was not the only
factor to cause the decline which has become noticeable at
the end of the 1980s—when Reagan began to implement his
economic policies, many of the factors that have been contributing to this decline were already in place. However,
Reagan's policies did hasten it and make it critical—and
much more intractable—when more sensible policies, policies that did not rely on an abstract, remote and mechanistic
theory, could have delayed, averted, or perhaps even reversed these trends.

But the point of all these observations is not merely that
the predictions upon which supply-side economics was based
have proven in the long run to be wrong, and that serious
harms have accrued as a consequence of acting on them.
This scheme was wrong from the very first day: not only was
it wrong as a prediction, it also acted as a false promise. The
American people and government were put into a false position and thereby encouraged to behave badly by, among
other things, spending money which they did not have, and
which they groundlessly expected to have only at some time
in the future: they were encouraged to live dishonestly.† It
is true that it took awhile for the effect of this type of dishonest living to become abundantly clear, but the effect was
there from the first day that the government, facing a shortfall in tax revenue because of the cuts it had imposed, had
to borrow the money from the bank, that is, from American
and foreign savers. Of course Americans have a strong streak
of common sense and are not more inherently dishonest than
any other people, but Reagan's predictions acted as a sort
of spell. During this period, Americans thought that they
were living honestly by accumulating debt, but they were in
fact deluding themselves. They were deluding themselves
because they had been lied to by means of the false prophecy
of the Reaganomic economists. This is the nature of the false
position that America now finds itself in due to heeding the
false promises inherent in the Reaganomic predictions.

† In this context it is important to note that the American spending spree on foreign
goods was actually encouraged by another bit of falseness, that is, the Reagan
administration's policy of propping the U.S. dollar above its natural level.

While it may be true that a people always get the government they deserve, it is also true that the government they get shapes the behavior of the people they represent. The folly of the American people during this period reflects not so much their fecklessness as the power of prediction to corrupt people by suspending their common sense and incredulity and encouraging them to behave poorly.

Many Americans are now feeling very sober about their economy and its long-term prospects now that the much-vaunted future has arrived. During the 1980s the national debt rose to 180 percent of GNP compared to 137 percent during the three decades before that. Foreigners also own a vast number of financial and tangible assets in the United States which they have bought with their surplus trade dollars. The stability of the American economy now depends as much on the common sense and goodwill of foreigners as on the virtues of Americans. In recent years, in spite of the proven bankruptcy of grand economic theories to predict major developments, Americans are still trying to control their economy by prediction. Since inflation is a recurrent bugbear, influential economists are constantly predicting that it can be controlled through engineered recessions. For example, in 1988, Albert Wojnilower, a forecaster who works as a senior economic adviser at First Boston Corporation advocated the following prescription: "After six or seven years of expansion it seems to me we will be doing quite well if there's a recession in the second half of 1989. The recession lasts about a year, and unemployment goes to eight, nine, ten percent and then goes down again. I don't believe recessions are therapeutic, but sometimes they are unavoidable."[16] Wojnilower and other financiers, like Peter Peterson, who wrote a celebrated article on this topic in the *Atlantic,* seem to believe, as Henry Kissinger does, that they can both foresee the inevitable and manage it. The inevitable, in this case, is runaway inflation; managing it means an engineered recession. Wojnilower believes recession is the only way to control the inflation which he predicts will get out of hand as long as unemployment remains low and too many people have money in their pockets. Prophets like Wojnilower who foresee inevitabilities always have prescriptions for managing them in mind. In this case they want to *manage* the so-called inevitability of inflation by raising interest rates to create a *controlled* recession that will dampen inflation.

The narrowness of Wojnilower's vision is quite obvious. Why is inflation inevitable? Theoretically, inflation is the result of too many dollars chasing after too few goods. Our experience with inflation in the early 1980s suggests that there is more to inflation than this theory will allow, but insofar as this theory is correct, Wojnilower has chosen to look at only one side of this equation: the many dollars in people's pockets chasing after goods. What about the availability of goods? The fact of the matter is that America in particular and the world in general are now, just as these predictions of inflation are being made, experiencing a surplus of most goods, including those in greatest demand: most minerals, including oil, in the absence of a crisis like the one presently taking place in the Persian Gulf, food and textiles. So why raise interest rates to avoid the inflation that is by no means inevitable? Once one gets past the rhetoric of inevitability there are, of course, alternative courses to an engineered recession that the United States could pursue. William Greider has argued that, alternatively, America should try to get out of its economic difficulties by creating a policy that promotes growth, not contraction. America could thus pay its debts by creating new wealth and not through the austerity which will adversely harm the most helpless members of society.

Given the scope of action which can be taken in response to economic problems, it is disheartening to recall that while America was working itself into a tight corner by following Reagan's false economic prophets, Prime Minister Thatcher of England was also insisting to her fellow countrymen— while ever increasing numbers of them, especially outside of the London region, were being driven by her economic policies onto the rolls of the unemployed—that "There is no other way." When a leader says "such and such a course is inevitable," or, "there is no other choice," they mean to sound high-minded: "this suffering is necessary, and is to be endured for the sake of a better future for all"; or, "this

situation is in the nature of things, part of the world order."
Yet such an attitude is tyrannical.

Many actions which are taken by governments and large
corporations and justified on the basis of predictions of future
conditions are tyrannical. First, any adaptation in the present
time made in anticipation of conditions which are predicted
for the future is bound to contribute towards making these
predictions into self-fulfilling prophecies. How could it be
otherwise? To cite a now somewhat tired example from the
height of the auto-industrial period, if one builds superhigh-
ways on the basis of the prediction of increased demand for
them, automobile manufacturers will find it easier to sell cars
because of the ongoing expansion of the highway system and
demand will indeed increase. This is all very well if that is
the direction a nation wants to go and undoubtedly many
nations, even in this "age of information," would not mind
having a robust auto-industrial economy. However, in the
case of an economy that is willing to accept an increased rate
of unemployment rather than an increased demand for cars,
the legitimating nature of prediction becomes reprehensible.
Yet many governments, with the telling exceptions of Sweden, Japan, Austria and a few others, act as if there is no
choice but to adapt to this "inevitable" future.[17]

To illustrate this point in greater detail I will briefly
describe some developments which have occurred during the
last fifteen years or so in the economies of Sweden and Denmark. These developments demonstrate how effective societal wilfulness, as opposed to accepting inevitabilities or
pursuing grand schemes, can be in shaping national destiny.[18]

In 1973, at the beginning of the recessionistic period
which we are still in, the social policy-makers of both Sweden
and Denmark made divergent decisions about how to deal
with the projected "inevitable" rise in the tide of youth unemployment, and took divergent actions to implement them.
The Swedish government, always believing rising unemployment to be unacceptable, decided, in spite of the worldwide economic downturn, to try to retard and minimize
unemployment as much as possible by continuing to
strengthen what economists call an employment policy. In
the depth of this recession, the American economist Robert

Kuttner described the measures taken by the Swedish government to minimize unemployment: "The parent labor board spends about 12 billion Swedish crowns a year, or some 2 percent of Sweden's GNP, creating jobs. The board not only sponsors relief work; it subsidizes retraining and relocation costs for the unemployed, and runs the workshops for the handicapped. It can even stockpile goods in order to help manufacturers through short-term economic downturns, and it can invest capital in new ventures."[19]

The government of Denmark, on the other hand, has been unwilling—some would argue, unable—to tamper with the labor market. It decided instead only to maintain existing programs designed to mitigate the adverse effects of unemployment, and therefore maintained its rich variety of social and economic support programs which fall under the rubric of what is commonly called a welfare policy.

By 1983, ten years after these countries headed along their divergent roads, Denmark's unemployment rate had grown to 10.4 percent while that same year Sweden, during the worst part of the recession, experienced 3.4 percent unemployment compared to a European average of over 10 percent. The costs of implementing both types of approaches has been, and continues to be, much the same. The real difference between these two divergent social and economic policies lies not in costs but in consequences for the people involved and, like all really existential differences, is therefore immeasurable. Presumably the Danish government felt unable to respond to the rising tide of unemployment in any other way, but during this period the people of Denmark, having arrived at the future which their government believed to be acceptable for them, have been voting with their feet by emigrating in greater numbers.

By planning a welfare as opposed to an employment policy, Denmark and many other western countries have painted themselves into an existential corner. A society with a higher rate of unemployment has become the norm for these countries: programs are entrenched, patterns have been set, money that might have been committed for job maintenance and creation has instead been committed to transfer payments. And now, several years later, the scope for maneuvering is rather less. The world economy and individual national economies are no longer very forgiving. Of all of the bad planning that goes on in this world, the kind that is most debilitating in the long run is the kind that the late Professor Herbert Marcuse of Brandeis University had in mind when he said that planning limits choice.[20] Preemptively limiting choice in planning is equivalent to the ethic of inevitability in prediction. The kind of planning that Marcuse had in mind was reflected in Reagan's economic policy in the sense that it squeezed America into an economic corner in which economic choices are now limited and/or made by foreigners. It should be contrasted with the kind of planning that Sweden has chosen to do, the kind that enriches the context which makes development possible and thereby maintains or even expands the realm of choice. After all, should Sweden now decide, for reasons that are almost impossible to imagine, to go the route of subsidizing leisure rather than employment opportunities, it can much more easily do so than can Denmark change its course.[21]

Reagan's debilitating—it is yet too early to say whether it will turn out to be disastrous—economic planning highlights another way in which the future, as ultimate realm of simple solution to complex and difficult problem, is used to falsely enhance the present.[22] Any behavior, no matter how reckless, can be justified in the present if a future solution is posited. Present accumulation of massive debt has been said to be acceptable—as long as prosperity is predicted so that, presumably, future generations can repay the debt with spare cash; use of nuclear reactors in the present is also supposed to be all right—as long as it is supposed that in the future there will be a solution to the problem of waste disposal. In this way, the unknown and unknowable are used by one generation to betray the next. This development, so characteristic of our time, is profoundly disturbing and rather ironic because planning for the well-being of the future generation used to be considered one of the virtues of the present generation. Today, this process is all too often perverted so that the future generation is systematically betrayed by the present one.

One certainly could not accuse Reagan of having used conservative forecasting in legitimating his supply-side economic plan; in fact he even tried to make a virtue of the radical nature of his interventions in the American economy while predicting the boldest and best outcomes. But whether his motives were based on foolishness, as some of his detractors have argued, or cynicism, as the more outspoken ones have held, it is tragic that in making his moves Reagan did not make the important distinction between bravery and recklessness. Aristotle pointed out in his *Ethics* that it is recklessness that is the opposite of cowardice, whereas bravery, the real virtue in all of this, is the golden mean between these two extremes. What the reckless forecasting of the Reagan administration has taught us during the last decade is that it is the ability to distinguish between recklessness and bravery that is the true mark of the statesman today, not a sense of the inevitable, as politicians like Kissinger would have us believe.

The virtue of statesmanship is not to "foresee the inevitable and manage it" as Kissinger has contended—and certainly not with false and self-serving predictions. The virtue of statesmanship is to bring out the best in people by creating a political culture, like that of Sweden, that makes them act responsibly. Acting responsibly always means taking into account the bigger picture; acting in the present and acting in a consistent, disciplined and sustained way. Greider's suggestion that America solve her fiscal problems through expanded growth is certainly more attractive from the perspective of the vulnerable unemployable than is Wojnilower's prescription of a recession. But both rapid growth and rapid contraction are dangerous courses because they are hard to control: the former can lead to a so-called overheated economy and runaway inflation, while the latter can spiral down to long-term depression. Neither is as desirable as the kind of stability that comes from consistent, responsible behavior in the present. This responsibility has nothing to do with ideology. Sweden and Japan, which both have a political culture which is geared towards making the population act responsibly, are on different sides of the political spectrum, the former being more to the Left, while the latter is more to the Right. It is the coherence of their culture and not wilful abandonment to grand schemes for the future that is guiding them forward.

Talk of the inevitable by our prophets is both insidious and powerful, and when abused, as it usually is, is tyrannical. When we hear it, we would do well to ask ourselves: What does the promoter of a particular inevitable scenario have at stake in having it realized? What do they have to gain? And, perhaps more importantly, because there is no such thing as a neutral future, what do other, undoubtedly more helpless members of our society, have to lose?

The tyranny of prophecy very often lies in the fact that it inspires us, as Orwell has said, to act out of fear or a desire for power (in economics this is called greed). It therefore brings out the worst in us. And although such prophecy may not always be a wilful act of manipulation per se, it acts as though it is, inspiring us to abandon our common sense and our best virtues for those which the false and self-serving prediction tell us will help us to succeed or survive. Aristotle wrote in his *Politics* that, on the contrary, government leadership should be such that it brings out the best in people. Irresponsible prophecy brings out the worst: it brings out the exploitative forces of greed, abandonment and neglect. And, ultimately, tyrannical prophecy leads to the denial of individual meaning and fulfilment, because if one acts so as to make such prophecies self-fulfilling, one is acting to bring about the fulfilment of the prophet, not of oneself.

In this century prophecy has been playing on our anxiety about the future in all sorts of ways. Twenty to twenty-five years ago prophecy was, for the second time this century, in what sociologists would call its charismatic stage. In the United States, popular futurologists like Herman Kahn, Alvin Toffler and Buckminster Fuller were at the height of their popularity and had managed to capture both the public, private, individual and corporate imaginations. Toffler played on our fears by telling us how difficult it would be to cope in an ever more rapidly changing world; Fuller played on our hopes by telling us we could solve all of our problems by clever design; and Kahn played on our nerves by talking about nuclear war in the most bloodless, academic way. In

France, Bertrand de Jouvenal had established the journal called *Futuribles,* in which he began to publish a sort of Michelin Guide to the future—places to go, places to avoid—in the form of speculative essays. Futurologist bureaucrats like Ervin Laszlo and Amadou-Mahtar M'Bow (the latter was later to be disgraced) were rapidly working their way up through the well-funded international agencies; futurist societies were springing up all over the world and holding conventions from Oslo to Tokyo. In spite of a plethora of serious problems and conflicts, the world was generally a much more genuinely optimistic place then, and futurology was, in a way, part of the optimism that pervaded it. But though it was a part of this optimism, it certainly was not the basis for it.

Though its profile at present may be somewhat lower than it was then, futurology is now more pervasive than ever. And modern prophecy has also entered a new phase, which sometimes makes its effects more subtle. Like all charismatic movements, it has finally become institutionalized and rationalized, has become a given, a presence, an essential part of our corporate and bureaucratic life and culture, as well as of our personal lives.

Our world is full of advisers that function much the same way as the government task force for which I worked, but often in ways that are not nearly so bureaucratically equivocal. We have all heard by now of the thousands of newsletters published by business forecasters. Some of these are a form of monitoring and serve as a security blanket, but many have encouraged serious hiccups in the stock market in recent years, and some even contributed to the panic that led to the crash of 1987. When the next crash comes, they will undoubtedly also help it along. More important, however, is the fact that many analyses of the stock market crash of October 1987 have concluded that it was caused by the instability created by "futures" trading. If the stock market is at all rational some of its rationality has been based on its operation in real time, that is present time, with all of the necessary corrective feedback loops this entails. Futures trading, which in America has largely been fueled by the more speculative traders who are based in Chicago, has only

served to unground and undermine a system that is often
excessively abstracted and little enough grounded in reality.†

Beyond the minor industry of purveying "privileged"
knowledge about the future in the form of newsletters, most
large private corporations now use futurologists as consultants, or even have them on permanent staff. Futurologists
are to be found advising the highest levels of government,
including heads of state, all over the world, both East and
West. Futurologists are "in," they are now, like the court
astrologers of old, an integral part of our culture. They are
no longer the irrepressible starry-eyed children they were in
the 1960s. They are seasoned consultants and bureaucrats,
plying the leaden seas of the so-called rationalism that today
encroaches upon every nook and cranny of our culture and
society. Our anxiety about the future has naturally enhanced
the position of our prophetic politicians, and of our futurologists and forecasters—they have the map of the future,
they will tell us how to get there.

All of this frenzied prophetic activity is carried out in
the name of progress and necessity, or inevitability. George
Orwell has remarked about progress: "If each epoch is as a
matter of course better than the last, then any crime or folly
that pushes the historical process forward can be justified.
Between, roughly, 1750 and 1930 one could be forgiven for
imagining that progress of a solid, measurable kind was taking place. Latterly this has become more and more difficult
. . ."[23] We have certainly seen enough crimes and folly committed in our time for the sake of the future in the name of
progress and its handmaiden, inevitability. In this chapter
alone I have mentioned dispossession of land, transfer of

† Futures trading is typical of novel schemes that give advantage to interest groups
but are rationalized as being in the public interest. Many revolutions are like this,
but in the case of futures trading the victims are blamed for not being able to
master the computer technology that makes this trading possible. In a critique of
futures trading in *The New Republic,* James Cramer has noted "the current debate
always begins with the inevitability of a product that is less than a decade old, and
instead gets diverted to remedies about how to live with increased volatility that
futures cause." But he rightly maintains that "the debate isn't about technology,
it's about capital. If the investors in stocks had the same amount of buying or
selling power as the users of the computers, and if the users of computers had to
be bound by the rules against bear raids, we would be proud to embrace the new
technology. But that's not the case." (James J. Cramer, "Basket Case," in *The
New Republic,* November 13, 1989.)

wealth from the poor to the rich, borrowing beyond means and forced unemployment. The prophecies upon which all of these policies were based were false, not only intellectually but, more important, morally. That is why we can properly speak of the tyranny of prophecy.

It may be difficult to say which prophecies are false and may do us harm but it is possible to do so if we take thought; usually it takes more courage than wisdom to figure it out. Most false prophecies fly in the face of common sense, common decency, or both. They ask us either to prepare for something that will not happen; not prepare for something that is bound to happen in the expectation of miraculous (read technological) redemption; persist in something that is foolish, fatally flawed; or neglect something good and worthwhile because we are told we will not need it in the future. And one does not need an elaborate fantasy in order to escape reality: the simplest lie will do if it serves the purpose of deflecting our attention from it. Even the overwhelming costs of failed economic predictions do not seem to bring home to us the general weakness of economic theory. After giving a long account of failed economic development plans in both the Third World and the West that have relied on false economic predictions, Jane Jacobs observed that: "Failures can help set us straight if we attend to what they tell us about realities. But observation of realities has never, to put it mildly, been one of the strengths of economic development theory."[24] If you are going to escape the responsibility of reality, what does it matter what ship you use? The ship can be the most prosaic thing in the world. A simple linear projection, which is the substance, even today, of a vast amount of forecasting, with all of its apparent simplicity, sterility, and lack of emotion, will serve well as a lie.

So why do we follow our prophets? We can understand some of the irrational reasons simply by looking at the origins and meaning of trends. It is impossible to say where these eruptions we call trends actually come from, but it would be wrong to assume that they necessarily come from the best part of our nature, and undoubtedly they often come from quirky, perverse or even pathological aspects of our subconscious, aspects which want to be exalted or to play. Therefore we should take to heart Orwell's caution against bowing down to the conqueror of the moment, not only because, as he himself observes, at the moment of conquest it is impossible to gauge how far or how fast he will go, but also because the conqueror, that is, the present trend, may not be such an admirable thing in the first place.

Every period produces trends which tend to have a certain tone or flavor; in our time, this flavor tends to be rationalistic. I say rationalistic rather than rational because the technological juggernaut that drives most modern trends pertains only to a part of reason, its tendency to reduce problems to their simplest components, its reductionist aspect, rather than to the whole thing.

It has been said that most modern visions are caricatures of reality. This is true because it is in the nature of caricature both to oversimplify and to represent an exaggerated aspect of a larger reality as the whole thing. (What greater caricature of reality is there than the straight line epitomized by the linear projection that is so dear to the futurist's heart.) In the nineteenth century, humorists like the Frenchman Albert Robida used caricature to satirize modern trends. It is a sign of the humorlessness of our time that we take these future-minded caricatures seriously.

The danger in following our modern visionaries and thereby contributing to the fulfilment of their prophecies is two-fold. If we fail to fulfill their visions, we will have wasted a great deal of money, time and energy in trying to realize them. If we succeed, however, then we diminish our humanity precisely to the degree that we do succeed by squeezing it into one corner of our souls, that corner which I have just called rationalistic.

Actually, the part of our nature which drives trends while wearing the mask of reason appeals to highly irrational elements. Orwell has rightly ascribed the elements of fear and worship of power to modern futurity but more generally, the psychology of trend-chasing is mob or horde psychology. All of these irrational elements are laid bare in the trends which erupt in the fashion industry. Here we can also see the self-interested and exploitative roles played by the prophets of that industry, who are commonly and shamelessly called trend-setters. When we see individuals suspending their judgment and deluding themselves in order to squeeze or bend their natures in the service of following fashion trends, we rightfully find the spectacle pathetic, but we little appreciate the degree to which this same nature-bending phenomenon occurs in our institutions, in politics and in business.

Modern prophecy taps into every aspect of the modern consciousness: how we think about most of our problems, the psychological and ideological trappings of our souls. And the influential false prophets of our time are like bad psychotherapists who go into practice because of an endless and unresolved fascination with their own neurosis, and encourage their patients to ceaselessly play with theirs rather than face reality and take responsibility for their lives. Therefore the study of modern prophecy is not only a study of what we are becoming, but of what we are. In the next two chapters I will explore this psychological and ideological soul, and in the following four, my case studies, I will show how this plays itself out in vital and particularly vulnerable areas of our existence, how we defend ourselves, how we replace ourselves, how we preserve ourselves, and how we treat the world of nature. In the final chapters I will offer alternative ways of approaching the problem of the future, of what we are going to become.

NOTES

1. René Dubos, *Beast or Angel: Choices that Make Us Human* (New York: Scribner, 1974), pp. 119, 122.
2. The following analysis is drawn from Cambridge Energy Research Associates (CERA) and Arthur Andersen & Co., *The Future of Oil Prices: The Perils of Prophecy* (Cambridge and Houston, 1984).
3. CERA et al., p. 13.
4. Arthur Andersen & Co., *Oil & Gas Reserve Disclosures: Survey of 375 Public Companies, 1980–1983* (Houston, 1984), cited in CERA et al., pp. 1–2.
5. CERA et al., p. 8.
6. See Daniel Yergin, "Taming the Dinosaur," in *The New Republic* (July 4, 1988), pp. 17–20.
   Of course Mexico has not been the only nation in our time that has based its plans for economic development on simple-minded projections; after all, simple-minded projections are the primary product of macro-economic theory in our times. No one has summarized the all too familiar panorama of foolishness better than Jane Jacobs, who observed: "Khrushchev, visiting the United Na-

tions, banged his shoe on the table and foretold a Soviet economy that by 1975 would overtake America's and thereafter proceed to 'bury' the West. In the United States, Presidents Kennedy and Johnson and their advisers not only assumed, as most Americans did, that the country's high productivity and economic supremacy were assured far into the future; they also assumed that the fiscal measures they were using to fine-tune the economy were going to eliminate even its jiggles: no more depressions, and soon no more recessions." She continues: "Poor countries on the fringes of Europe were anticipating great prosperity when it came their turn to join the European community and share in supplying its huge, integrated and safely wealthy markets. . . . People and rulers in backward countries, including those that had just won independence from colonial rule or were struggling to do so, expected professionally drawn up development schemes to engineer prosperity and progress for them too. Their expectations were fully shared in countries financing development schemes with loans or gifts." But what was the result of these grandiose predictions and the expectations they created? "We think of the experiments of particle physicists and space explorers as being extraordinarily expensive, and so they are. But the costs are as nothing compared with the incomprehensibly huge resources that banks, industries, governments and international institutions like the World Bank, the International Monetary Fund and the United Nations have poured into tests of macro-economic theory." (Jane Jacobs, *Cities and the Wealth of Nations: Principles of Economic Life*, London: Viking, 1985, pp. 3–6.)

7. John L. O'Sullivan, "Annexation," in *United States Magazine and Democratic Review* (July–August 1845), p. 5.
8. O'Sullivan, p. 7.
9. O'Sullivan, p. 9.
10. O'Sullivan, p. 7.
11. Richard Pipes, "Why the Soviet Union Thinks It Could Fight and Win a Nuclear War," in *Commentary* (July 1977), p. 24.
12. Frederick Siegel, *Troubled Journey* (New York: Hill and Wang, 1984).
13. Henry Kissinger, *A World Restored: Metternich, Castlereagh and the Problems of Peace, 1821–1822* (Boston: Houghton Mifflin, 1973).
14. Henry Kissinger, "My Reply to Mr. Gorbachev," London *Observer*, (September 8, 1985). Kissinger has a great deal at stake in the present arms-control negotiations since, as I will demonstrate in Chapter Four, his earlier prescriptions, based on his own predictions, significantly contributed to the nuclear arms build-up. His view of the statesman as forecaster/manager is in sharp contrast to that of Hannah Arendt who has written, on the contrary, that "Proudhon's passing remark, 'The fecundity of the unexpected far exceeds the statesman's prudence,' is fortunately still true. It exceeds even more obviously the expert's calculations." (*On Violence*.)
15. Jerrold Maxmen, *The Post-Physician Era: Medicine in the Twenty-first Century* (New York: John Wiley & Sons, 1976), p. 10.
16. Cited by William Greider in "The Shadow Debate on the American Economy," in *Rolling Stone* (July 14–28, 1988), p. 86.
17. In this context I cannot help but recall that towards the end of the last recession when I was working as a consultant to my strategic planning task force in the Government of Ontario, one of the big issues that came up then was how the Education Ministry should respond to the prediction of ever increasing rates of unemployment, especially among youth. Since one of the functions of the education system is to prepare youth for the world of work, my task force felt that it was in a quandary as to how to plan for this much touted eventuality. One solution that some members of the group toyed with was that we may have to change our education system to prepare youth for "involuntary leisure" rather

than for work. And it should be borne in mind that in adopting this strategy, or at least, for the moment, paying lip service to it, the task force was following the lead of the Council of Europe which around that time was also publishing papers advocating similar policies, in response, apparently, to the alarming rise of youth gangs in many European cities.

18. The following account is drawn from Robert Kuttner, "Trials of Two Welfare States," in *The Atlantic Monthly* (November 1983), pp. 14–20.

19. Kuttner, p. 16.

20. Herbert Marcuse, *Eros and Civilization: A Philosophical Inquiry into Freud* (Boston: Beacon Press, 1966).

21. Even in Sweden, where the government has adopted a policy of trying to avoid unemployment rather than one which more or less accepts it as inevitable as in the case of Denmark and Canada, one finds futurological thinking in a similar, though more insidious, vein. In addressing the unemployment problem in a recent publication, a committee of futurologists in the Swedish Secretariat for Futures Studies came to the conclusion that, "In order for this [future workplace] equation to balance in terms of employment, working hours will have to be reduced and *some continued increase will be required in the public sector . . .* full employment without a reduction of working hours *and an enlargement of the public sector* does not appear to be a realistic target." (emphasis added) (Secretariat for Futures Studies, *Time to Care*, Oxford: Pergamon Press, 1984, p. 240.) Reduce the length of the work week—fine. But why should the public sector be the one to take up the slack? Instead of planning to play the role of employer of last resort, why should not the government of Sweden, with probably the most sophisticated job creating and retraining apparatus in the world, not create conditions so that the private sector, rather than the public one, take up the slack in the fight against rising unemployment? However the irony of members of the public sector advocating a future expansion of their own area of the economy seems to have entirely escaped this committee of planners and futurologists. This is the sort of thinking that exists behind "managing the inevitable"—and this is the sort of thing that often passes for planning today.

22. In a celebrated article that analyzes many of the time bombs that have been put in place in America because of a dishonest regard for the future, Peter G. Peterson has written: "We have, in addition, saddled ourselves with an informal debt of nearly $10 trillion in unfunded liabilities in Social Security, Medicare, and federal pensions. That astronomical figure is the difference between the benefits today's workers are now scheduled to receive and the future taxes today's workers are slated to pay for them. It amounts to a hidden tax of $100,000 on every American worker, and its toll will be exacted on our children." (Peter G. Peterson, "The Morning After," in *The Atlantic Monthly*, October 1987, p. 60.)

23. George Orwell, "Catastrophic Gradualism," in *Collected Essays, Journalism and Letters* (New York: Harcourt Brace Jovanovich, 1968), Volume 4, p. 17.

24. Jacobs, *Cities and the Wealth of Nations*, p. 7.

No plausible claim to intellectuality can possibly be made in the near future without an intimate dependence upon this new instrument [the computer]. Those intellectuals who persist in their indifference, not to say snobbery, will find themselves stranded in a quaint museum of the intellect, forced to live petulantly, and rather irrelevantly, on the charity of those who understand the real dimensions of the revolution and can deal with the new world it will bring about.

—EDWARD FEIGENBAUM

THE PSYCHOLOGY OF FUTUROLOGY

Susan Sontag once made an astute comment about photography that might well have been made about futurology, a field with which photography has a great deal in common: "Photography, which has so many narcissistic uses, is also a powerful instrument for depersonalizing our relation to the world; and the two uses are complementary. Like a pair of binoculars with no right or wrong end, the camera makes exotic things near, intimate; and familiar things small, abstract, strange, much farther away. It offers, in one easy, habit-forming activity, both participation and alienation in our own lives and those of others—allowing us to participate, while confirming alienation."[1] Sontag's observation might be disturbing for those who instinctively look at pictures with an uncritical eye, because it robs photography of much of its commonly presumed innocence, an innocence which is reflected in such popular sayings as "the camera never lies," and "one picture is worth a thousand words." But by questioning photography's superficial innocence Sontag has also shed light on the photographer's social role, ascribing a more active status, as "participator" and "alienator," than is usually attributed to him.

Sontag's insight is also disturbing in other ways that are relevant to both photography and prophecy. In a sense, she has asserted a social critic's version of Heisenberg's famous dictum that there is no such thing as pure observation because observation is itself a kind of *interference* or *intrusion;* the very act of observing changes the observer and/or the observed even while it is being performed. However, if observation is an *act* rather than a *happening,* then it is a moral act. It is moral because it entails both perspective and posture; it defines not only where the observer stands but how, by positioning himself, he would like to look at the world, and how he would like to make the world appear to himself and to others to whom he might be describing it. Unless it has no particular interest to you, you seldom simply look at something: you eye it, or you watch it at a safe distance, or you peek at it, or peer at it, or stare it down. You may even try, by your very act of observation, either to control or avoid it. In all observation there may be elements of directness, honesty, clarity, but there may also be elements of avoidance, condescension, worship.

The futurologist has much in common with the photographer because his enterprise is also highly selective and deeply interpretive by nature. And, insofar as present reality is so rich that it can never adequately be captured by observation, how much less so can future reality? All predictions, all "observations" of the future, are superficial, are snapshots *by nature and by necessity.* Consequently, they have built into them not only the limitations of distant perspective, but also opportunities for deception—of others as well as of oneself. Even where goodwill exists, these opportunities arise from unavoidable selectivity; in the absence of goodwill they arise from wilful or foolish misconstruction. Predictions, like snapshots, also have the ability to depersonalize the world because they are characteristically so abstract and general, and in this abstraction is contained a great deal of moral lassitude. It is all right, it seems, to predict a recession or rising interest rates, even if the act of prediction helps to bring these things about, because the harm that they cause is abstract, not meant to harm any particular person's future.

To a certain extent the biases and limitations of forecasting are also true of the social sciences in general. However, in the social sciences one can occasionally temper the distance; one can alter one's perspective by attempting to draw closer; one can drop theory and orthodox methodology by going out into the field to try to get an unmediated taste of raw reality. For example, if an economist observing the economy of the United States in the late 1980s were confused by the distant perspective given by aggregate statistics (statistics that do not reveal the particulars of its inner workings but post a number of seemingly healthy indicators like low unemployment, low inflation and relatively low interest rates), he might try to unpack this perspective by taking a closer look at certain details. If he did so he might find, for example, that the unemployment rate was deceptive because one-eighth of all employed persons were employed only part-time; or, if he looked at other data to try to determine the meaning of having a job he might learn that, in spite of high employment, an increasing number of those who had recently entered the job market had given up hope of ever owning their own homes. But futurology cannot make use of the kind of self-correction that comes from drawing closer, because its distance from its subject matter is part of its method, is part and parcel of the field itself. Futurologists are trapped in a distant observational outpost of their own contrivance. If they attempt to shorten the distance by shortening the time frame in which their predictions are made, they take the life out of them; their prophecy becomes less interesting because, as it is framed closer to the present time, it begins to lose the right to call itself prophecy. (What is so terribly prophetic about predicting that you are going to have lunch with a certain friend next week?) Furthermore, as one shortens the time frame even further, one is finally really working in the present, and one is reduced, ultimately, to monitoring it. Of course, studies of the present can be made to appear to be studies of the future—and very often they are—but only by being dressed up in futuristic blather. The true social scientist can alter his perspective by drawing closer because what he has ultimately fixed in his mind is reality;

the futurologist cannot draw closer even if he wishes to do so because what he has fixed in his mind is imaginary, it does not yet and may never exist.

Photography, at its worst, is undoubtedly superficial. But unlike photography, futurology, even at its best, does not have the redeeming feature of at least potentially being able to leave a somewhat honest record. While the photographer's psychological makeup includes, as Sontag has remarked, the elements of participation and alienation, the futurologist's includes distancing, avoidance, self-delusion and deception. In this sense, both photography and futurology are active participants in the cult of superficiality. They both freeze a minute part of the real or imaginary world, turn it into an icon and invite us not to question it but to pay homage—or even to worship it.

From the above remarks it should be clear that there is more to the psychology of prophecy than the cowardice and worship of power which Orwell found so striking. But the best way to get a deeper and more broadly based psychological understanding of why so much folly manages to maintain such a strong hold on our lives is to examine a few prophets in action to observe both what they do and why their appeal works. I will begin with one who is fairly contemporary but not current, so that it will be possible also to apply to him the "test of time."

Anyone who is interested in computers, especially if they are also interested in the field of artificial intelligence, should know something about the work of the logician Alan Turing, who, in the 1930s and 1940s, was one of this field's great theorists. In fact, like Einstein in the field of physics, Turing provided a great deal of direction and much of the theory which many scientists have spent their entire careers exploring. However, while Einstein was perfectly willing to let the chips fall where they may in the proving or disproving of his theories, Turing chose to assume the role of propagandist for his views, and what is particularly interesting about his role as a propagandist is that he played it by assuming the part of the prophet.

In 1950 one of the big burning questions in the field of artificial intelligence (AI) was "Can computers think?"—a question that still interests people today. In that year, Turing wrote a famous article called "Computing Machinery and Intelligence" in which he addressed this question in such an intriguing and compelling way that it set the tone of the discussion for most people who have raised it from that time to the present day. What is interesting about Turing's answer was that though the question was posed in the present tense, he chose to play the role of prophet and answer it for future time.

Since Turing was one of the most eminent logicians of our time it is not surprising that his argument appears on the surface to be completely logical; I will have to quote him at length to convey the logical flavor of his argument.[2] He started this paper by dismissing the question "Can computers think?" as too ambiguous to be meaningful. Instead he offered an alternative approach that worked as follows:

> I propose to consider the question "Can machines think?" This should begin with definitions of the meaning of the terms "machine" and "think." The definitions might be framed so as to reflect so far as possible the normal use of the words, but this attitude is dangerous. If the meaning of the words "machine" and "think" are to be found by examining how they are commonly used it is difficult to escape the conclusion that the meaning and the answer to the question, "Can machines think?" is to be sought in a statistical survey such as a Gallup poll. But this is absurd. Instead of attempting such a definition I shall replace the question by another, which is closely related to it and is expressed in relatively unambiguous words.[3]

Notice that Turing did not say why a question should be considered to be meaningless just because it is ambiguous. Is the question, "Do you love me?" which is always at least a little ambiguous, also therefore always meaningless? But let us follow his argument a little further to see what he proposes to be a more meaningful and appropriate question. Turing went on to deal with the question of whether machines can think in the following way:

The new form of the problem can be described in terms of a game which we call the "imitation game." It is played with three people, a man (A), a woman (B), and an interrogator (C) who may be of either sex. The interrogator stays in a room apart from the other two. The object of the game for the interrogator is to determine which of the other two is the man and which is the woman. He knows them by labels X and Y, and at the end of the game he says either "X is A and Y is B" or "X is B and Y is A." The interrogator is allowed to put questions to A and B thus:

C: "Will X please tell me the length of his or her hair?" Now suppose X is actually A, then A must answer. It is A's object in the game to try to cause C to make the wrong identification. His answer might therefore be:

"My hair is shingled, and the longest strands are about nine inches long."

In order that tones of voice may not help the interrogator the answers should be written, or better still, typewritten. The ideal arrangement is to have a teleprinter communicating between the two rooms. Alternatively the questions and answers can be repeated by an intermediary. The object of the game for the third player (B) is to help the interrogator. The best strategy for her is probably to give truthful answers. She can add such things as "I am the woman, don't listen to him!" to her answers, but it will avail nothing as the man can make similar remarks.

We now ask the question, "What will happen when a machine takes the part of A in the game?" Will the interrogator decide wrongly as often when the game is played like this as he does when the game is played between a man and a woman? These questions replace our original, "Can machines think?"[4]

From the above quotation it should be fairly clear that, as a psychologist, Alan Turing was a particular type of behaviorist, the kind that attributes a great deal of meaning to appearances, that is, to the external manifestations of psychological states. Therefore to him, on a certain level, people and computers could both be conveniently regarded as black boxes. To behaviorists it does not matter what goes on inside the box—we do not, perhaps cannot, know anyway—as long as what comes out is the same. Thinking—whatever it may actually be—and the imitation of thinking are, for all intents and purposes, the same thing by virtue of the fact that they produce the same result: a word or phrase, a symbol, a gesture, or an act.

For forty years now practitioners in the field of artificial intelligence have been trying to develop programs that, for different purposes and on different occasions, would enable computers to play the imitation game so well that what they "say," that is, their output, might not be easily distinguishable from what a thinking human being might say under the same circumstances. Presumably this great project will be completed when a program is produced that will enable a computer to play the imitation game on all occasions and for every purpose. At that point, computers into which this program is loaded will "think" even better than humans because—it is a commonplace by now—whatever it is that computers in fact do, they do it faster and with more data than do human beings.

Some scientists say this will never happen, others that it is just a matter of time. Who is right is not important here, and, in any case, unprovable one way or the other at present. What is important, however, is that Turing hedged his bets and assumed a fallback position on this issue, and here is where he played the part of the futurologist. Later in this same article he wrote: "I believe that in about fifty years' time it will be possible to program computers, with a storage capacity of about 10^9, to make them play the imitation game so well that an average interrogator will not have more than 70 percent chance of making the right identification after five minutes of questioning. The original question, 'Can machines think?' I believe to be too meaningless to deserve discussion. Nevertheless I believe that at the end of the century *the use of words and general educated opinion* will have altered so much that one will be able to speak of machines thinking without expecting to be contradicted." (emphasis added)[5]

This passage is worth examining closely because it reveals not only how Turing operated as a futurologist, but also how futurologists characteristically think about the issues of the future. The first thing that is noteworthy about it is simply that Turing chose to play the role of oracle, and that this could not help but be a rather self-serving thing to do under the circumstances. After all, Turing was in a field that had by 1950 already shown great promise of growth. It is the tendency of people in such fields to be their own promoters, and what better way to do this than by playing the role of prophet, by predicting that at some point in the not too distant future your field will be bigger and better than it is at present.[6] If enough people believe you and get involved in your project on the basis of this belief, your prophecy is bound to be self-fulfilling for this reason alone.

Second, Turing predicted that the battle over whether or not computers think will be won at the end of the century in one way or another, if not by facts, then by "the use of words." But notice that by making this prediction Turing was directly contradicting what he had said in the first passage we looked at when he stated: "If the meaning of the words 'machine' and 'think' are to be found by examining *how they are commonly used* it is difficult to escape the conclusion that the meaning and the answer to the question, 'Can machines think?' is to be sought in a statistical survey such as a Gallup poll. But this is absurd." (emphasis added) By making his prediction in these terms, Turing revealed here that, at least for some of its adherents, there is a hidden agenda behind the artificial intelligence movement, and that that agenda is to win, if nothing else, than the war with words by somehow or other changing the way people use them. Naturally, this moved the artificial intelligence project out of the realm of science alone and into the realm of politics. Notice too that although Turing was opposed to referring to common usage as a test for answering the question "Can computers think?" *at present,* he thought it would be perfectly all right to use this test *in the future* by which time, presumably, usage would have changed along with "general educated opinion." Characteristically, however, he did not say what he meant by educated opinion. In short, all of the ambiguity which he found so objectionable in dealing with this problem in *the present* would be perfectly acceptable in *the future,* especially because by then the artificial intelligence movement would have "general educated opinion" on its side.

Although words, if they are not used to make lies, do reflect reality, their relationship to reality is somewhat loose, and in a sense at any given moment in time we always have to create meaning anew with them. Generally speaking a prediction has little or no meaning if it relies for its fulfilment on a change in the deepest meaning of any of its key terms. For example, suppose that I, a man of modest means, were to predict that in twenty years time I would be a billionaire, meaning a man of extraordinary wealth. Suppose, too, that although in relative terms my wealth did not in fact increase during that period of time, the inflationary pace was such that at the end of it my assets were in fact worth a billion dollars. Technically speaking, with respect only to the superficial sense of its terms, the prophecy would be fulfilled but it would be a meaningless fulfilment. Similarly, and more to the point about prophecies about thinking, a hundred years ago the term literate had a meaning very different from the one we know now. In the late nineteenth century a literate person was one who not only could technically read and write but was also well-read, that is, a "literate" person then was what we might call a "cultured" person now. The accuracy of any prediction about literacy made at that time about the present would have to be judged in terms of the great shift in meaning of the term over the years. There is a substantive as well as a formal meaning to words and any prediction that does not pay attention to the substantive meaning of words is not so much a prediction of the real world but only about a change in the use of words, which can be brought about by propaganda as well as by a change in reality.

Ironically, almost forty years after Turing published this paper, in spite of the enormous amount of work that has been done by the vast army of researchers, theoreticians and programmers in the artificial intelligence movement to engineer hardware and write programs that enable computers to play the imitation game with increasing ability in certain controlled situations, very few people, except, perhaps, those working in the field of artificial intelligence, still find it appropriate to ask the question, "Can computers think?" But in historic movements sometimes one can only appreciate the true depth of irony with the benefit of hindsight. What I have in mind now is that by making these statements Turing was, perhaps unintentionally, setting the stage for Edward Feigenbaum, a present-day prophet of the artificial intelligence movement who has added a new twist to the debate by going so far as to define "educated," or at least "intellectual," in terms of computer literacy.

In 1983, thirty-three years after Turing's famous article was published, computers were definitely *in*. Artificial intelligence scientists are part of the establishment, software production and marketing are big businesses, and Feigenbaum, a Stanford University computer scientist and entrepreneur of AI software, in the inimitable style of the cult-prophet, writes that "no plausible claim to intellectuality can possibly be made in the near future without an intimate dependence upon this new instrument [the computer]." He then goes on to predict that "those intellectuals who persist in their indifference, not to say snobbery, will find themselves stranded in a quaint museum of the intellect, forced to live petulantly, and rather irrelevantly, on the charity of those who understand the real dimensions of the revolution and can *deal with* the new world it will bring about." (emphasis added)[7]

According to Feigenbaum, Turing's prophecy is so much on the way to being admirably fulfilled that, if we are to accept what he asserts, it is no longer the machines who are on trial but people—scoffers and disbelievers, those who have not bought into the new system and the new norms. Whether or not computers can think is no longer an issue for Feigenbaum. For him, the big question now is, "Can people who are computer-illiterate claim to be intellectuals?"

This is the gist of Feigenbaum's contention, but more absurd than its thrust is its tone. It is not enough merely to use these machines, we must become "intimately dependent" on them, and, if we do not, then our lives will become not merely peripheral, out of the mainstream, but "irrelevant." But most important, for all of the wonders these machines create, the world of the future will emphatically not become more benign, because we will not only have to live in it, we will have to *deal with it*. Feigenbaum's prediction contains the kind of smugness that characterized the worst kind of Victorian Darwinism, in which the dictum "survival of the fittest" was uttered not merely as a scientific principle, but as a war-cry. It proclaimed, and prophets like Feigenbaum continue to proclaim to this day, that only the fittest will survive—and the prophets, of course, are pleased to count themselves among their number.

But getting back to Turing, adopting ambiguity only when it suited his purposes was not the only rhetorical device he used when he played the role of prophet. A more important one was his willingness, when it suited his purposes, to oversimplify, sometimes even trivialize a problem and/or its related solution. Consider Turing's proposed test for determining whether computers will be able to think in the future. If the turn-of-the-century computer will, by imitation, have a "70 percent chance" of fooling the "average interrogator" for "five minutes," it will win the game, and all disbelievers will presumably be forced to conclude that computers can indeed think.

Why five minutes? Aristotle, who was also a behaviorist in the sense that he believed you could gain ethical knowledge only through experience of your own behavior, asked another difficult question in his *Nichomachean Ethics* nearly 2,500 years ago. He asked, "How can you tell if a person is happy?" but rather than the five-minute test, he applied another, rather more strenuous one. Aristotle, reflecting an ethic that was already long-standing in Greece by his time, asserted that we should not assume a person to be happy by observing his behavior for a period of less than the whole of his lifetime. He applied the lifetime rule by saying, in effect, that happiness is one of those things that cannot be defined by a brief experience, but only by a whole lifetime of activity and feeling.

The difference between Aristotle and Turing is not

merely one of degree—it is much more fundamental than that. It is the difference in their respective approaches to understanding the world. Turing, as a prophet trying to capture a complex reality, is very much the photographer. Clearly, for Turing, thinking is sort of a happening, a snapshot event. On the basis of this onetime event we are to presume that it can be sustained for a lifetime—or, at least it is the same as if it could be. Whereas to Aristotle happiness is a process, the appropriate evaluation and definition of which entails a lifetime of observation and deliberation. Turing, by projecting a very complex problem into the future, was able also to trivialize it by making it remote—so that his solution, his clever, trivial little test, might seem adequate to it.

The technique of trivializing a problem by projecting it into the future and then offering a trivial solution for understanding and resolving it is very common among futurologists of both the optimistic and pessimistic variety (although the latter, naturally, do not always get down to "solutions"). Trivialization is the futurologist's equivalent of the photographer's alienation. Of course it is sometimes also used in the present in order to give a sense of certainty where one does not really exist, as when physicians, for instance, will say a cancer has been cured if it goes into remission for five years, in spite of the fact that certain cancers are known to have incubation periods of more than twenty years. If your cancer returns after five years and, say, one month, then you are still said to have been *cured*—but, nevertheless, somehow or other you have it again.

Another good example of the trivialized solution to a previously trivialized problem comes from Professor Archie Bowen, a futurologist at Carleton University in Ottawa. Bowen has predicted the demise of middle managers by the year 2000 using the following foolish reasoning: "Today's manager, as such, I don't believe will exist in the year 2000. In fact, managers tend to feel that their jobs are relatively safe through this [computer] revolution. It's a comforting feeling. It's the comforting feeling that you might have if you were at the foot of an avalanche and you were looking the other way and didn't see it coming at you. *The role of the manager is merely to manipulate information and make decisions.* In most cases that function, as we have discussed earlier, is ideally suited to the computer and has already been taken over by the computer." (emphasis added)[8] From Professor Bowen's account it appears as if the chief requirement for using the futurologist's trivialization technique is ignorance about what one is talking about. For instance, the case could also be made—and quite persuasively nowadays—that university professors, like Professor Bowen himself, also play the role of middle managers in their own corporations. However, in spite of his eagerness to do so with other professions, it is difficult to imagine Professor Bowen predicting his own demise, that is, the demise of his own profession, or trivializing his own work as being no more than "merely manipulating information" and/or "merely making decisions."

Edward Feigenbaum also uses the trivialization trick later in the same book when he predicts the future uses of the computer in society. For example, suppose a problem of the future will be loneliness and anxiety among the elderly? In that case, predicts Feigenbaum, we will simply provide them with robot companions. Here is one of his visions:

> The geriatric robot is wonderful. It isn't hanging about in the hopes of inheriting your money—nor of course will it slip you a little something to speed the inevitable. It isn't hanging about because it can't find work elsewhere. It's there because it's yours. It doesn't just bathe you and feed you and wheel you out into the sun when you crave fresh air and a change of scene, though of course it does all of those things. The very best thing about the geriatric robot is that it *listens.* "Tell me again," it says, "about how wonderful/dreadful your children are to you. Tell me again that fascinating tale of the coup of '63. Tell me again . . ." And it means it. It never gets tired of hearing those stories, just as you never get tired of telling them. It knows your favorites, and those are its favorites too. Never

mind that this all ought to be done by human care-takers; humans grow bored, get greedy, want variety. (emphasis in original)[9]

But perhaps, upon reading this passage, the reader is thinking that this vision is not really so objectionable if one allows that Feigenbaum, from his own perspective, is probably describing a desperate remedy for a desperate situation. Though a human rather than a machine solution might be ideal, in the case of care of the elderly, given present values and trends, the human solution may no longer be feasible, and therefore we should perhaps not be too critical of the machine alternative. One might take some comfort in thinking that this was the reasoning behind Feigenbaum's prediction/proposal and that his attempts to make it sound attractive by praising its virtues are desperate attempts to make the unsavory seem palatable; but one would be mistaken in doing so. Feigenbaum's solution, far from being a desperate one, is actually characteristic of the psychology of futurology; it is an *ideal* solution, the solution of *choice*. It is corroborated by Richard Wolkomir, another American futurologist, in his account of the role that robot pets or pals will have in the future lives of all classes and categories of humans, not just the elderly:

If people already have trouble differentiating between their relationships with people and a machine, over the next decade or so, as we develop computers with ultrahigh-speed parallel processing, people may find conversations with a robot indistinguishable from talks with people . . . they may even find the machines to be preferable.

Here we are, hardly settled into our electronic cottages, and already the age of electronic pals is upon us. Androbot's Nolan Bushnell painted a comforting picture of future friendships when he introduced his diminutive (three foot tall) home robot. While you wiggle a video-game joystick, making your aluminum sidekick dance a jig, it will speak to you, sing your favorite songs, or whisper

Shakespearean sonnets in your ear—the very model
of a learned and entertaining soul mate. As Bushnell told reporters when he announced his new robot protégé: "We're talking about a someone, not
a something—a friend that would greet you after a
long day at the office."[10]

The question, of course, is not whether these machines, as
they are envisioned by futurologists and computer scientists
playing the role of prophet, will ever be perfected. Only time
will tell. The real point is, given the enormous confidence
these prophets have in the potential of this evolving technology to do and be just about anything, that their visions
are dominated by a certain tone: technology will only be
used in one way and not another; it will be used to pander
to our whims and vanity and not to promote the development
of our virtues. One can only assume that this tone reflects
the personalities of these prophets themselves because they
so ardently promote it, to the exclusion of countless feasible
others.

Feigenbaum, Wolkomir and many other modern prophets who belong to what might be called the "techno-romantic" school of futurology seem to be enamored not merely
of the technical fix, the technical solution to a human problem, but of a very particular type of technical fix, one which
places individual autonomy and control above social interaction. The point about the celebrated future with machines
that they describe above is not only that these devices will
be hypothetically accessible to all, but that they will entail
a sort of automated enshrinement of their owners' egos; in
this way they will, in a sense, fulfil certain individual needs,
but always in a banal sort of way. The issue that seems to
be of paramount importance to these futurologists is how to
achieve individual mastery of personal, isolated environments, and how to put the individual who owns the machine
at the commanding center of the environment in which he
lives. The type of mastery which they advocate, the only
type, it would appear, that seems feasible to their minds, is
a sort of petty mastery, like personalized stereo carried to
ever greater degrees. In the scenarios that they paint for us,

having one's personal whims and conceits satisfied is more important than having to deal with contrariness in others, or having to rub up against personalities that are different from one's own. In a word, these are future scenarios in which psychological avoidance is the name of the game.

No one has summarized the psychological makeup of the techno-romantic school of futurology better than Stewart Brand in his description of the research endeavors of the Media Lab at MIT, where, he reports, engineers actually claim to be going about the business of "inventing the future." Every research project is being designed to cater to the characteristic futurologist personality that craves isolation and control. Writes Brand: "Everything mentioned involves communications, empowers the individual, employs computers . . . and makes a flashy demonstration."[11] There is that sexy term "empower"; it is used so much today that you cannot help but wonder if it still has any meaning. Yet it must have some meaning because, if nothing else, it evokes the all too common psychological states of frustration and helplessness and implies a remedy for them. It is interesting, however, that although for millennia power has always had mixed connotations, implying a potential for both good and evil, the way the term is used here and the way it is now generally bandied about, it seems to imply that we are to believe that empowerment will always be an absolute good. Is it always good to empower your feet by driving everywhere in your car? or to empower your hand by putting a gun in it? What Brand's glorification of individual empowerment does not address are the issues of when, to what degree, and under what circumstances we should become empowered. If you examine their projects for solving social problems, the techno-romanticist solutions seem to imply that we should empower the banal side of our natures and thereby further shelter ourselves from the unpleasant aspects of reality; in effect, we should become more narcissistic, self-flattering, closed-minded. It is hard to imagine how humans who controlled their personal and business relationships by constantly interacting with machines this way could possibly develop their personalities or even their minds.

Yet, ultimately, it would be inaccurate to say that these

futurologists are completely oblivious to the darker side of human nature; their vision is not only to control the enemy from without, who often happen to be other ordinary humans, but also the one inside of us. However, as usual, the technique that they advocate for achieving this control is a mechanical one—automated decision-making, so that the individual may abdicate responsibility for his or her existence.

Roy Mason, another American futurologist, has published a scenario in which he depicts a day in the life of a family that will live in the super-automated house of the future, based on a prototype located outside of Orlando, Florida, called the Xanadu House. The most striking quality about the scenario he describes in this prophecy is that the house computer not only panders to the narrow vision and whims of its occupants, like the toys that Feigenbaum and Wolkomir describe so admiringly above, but that it even appropriates a great deal of simple day-to-day decision-making from its inhabitants. For example, the "master" of the house, as he is called in Mason's vision, decides to order a meal from the automated kitchen, but it happens to contain cholesterol and therefore may be harmful to his health. So the computer vetoes his request in this endearing little early morning breakfast scene:

> Johnny dashes into the kitchen just as his father is finishing his first cup of coffee. After hearty "good mornings," both go to the computer dietitian and punch in their breakfast orders for the autochef. Johnny's order of hot cakes, orange juice, and milk goes through with no trouble, but John Sr.'s scrambled eggs, bacon, and toast are quickly nixed for their high cholesterol count. He is forced to settle for an English muffin, orange juice, and another cup of coffee.[12]

And so, early in the morning in this ideally automated home of the future, the computer gets to play culinary tyrant with the "master" of the house—presumably, of course, for his own good. Actually, things are not quite as bad as that. Everyone knows that computers only do what they are programmed to do, and so Mason, unlike some other futurologists†—has also envisioned an override mechanism. Using this mechanism when ordering the evening meal, the master does manage to get a piece of chocolate cake, in spite of the computer's better judgment.

Mason's entire article reeks of a dim, if not dim-witted, view of human nature. In fact, one finds no humans in this story at all, only caricatures. Their foibles are petty—father and son are both reluctant to get out of bed, mother needs to be coaxed with "a gentle massage like thousands of tiny fingers"—and so are their strengths. If the characters in Mason's prediction of future domestic life remind one of anything, it is of comic strip characters like Dagwood and Blondie: the energetic, moderately intelligent woman who quietly craves a small amount of affection and/or attention; the reluctant but ultimately goodwilled and able father whose weakness is for food, not sex; and the children, a crude version of their parents. These people are safe to read about and, presumably, would be safe to live with if one could ever find them in the real world. The minor wrinkles in their personalities can readily be ironed out with clever appliances.

In writing of their visions, Feigenbaum, Wolkomir and Mason are basically acting as existential cheerleaders for the automated world they feel comfortable contemplating, and in which they would like us all to live in the future. But Mason's vision also points to an inevitable consequence of extreme mechanization and automated decision-making: the loss of individual freedom, including the freedom to make decisions and to make mistakes. And this last twist is not

---

† A speculation from the *Omni Future Almanac* is not nearly so equivocal about the virtues of automated decision-making. In fact it justifies this process in terms of utilitarian principles and "computer rights" of all things. Here is what the *Almanac* has to say about this issue: "The decision-making power of computers will become so awesome that a Computer Responsibility Act may have to be passed in the United States. A possible scenario: In 2035, some seven hundred fifty publicly assisted housing unit residents, deemed expendable by a civic energy balance maintenance computer, will be frozen in their homes. Many of the elderly will die. Upon examination and investigation, the computer will respond that its evaluation revealed that the community was better served by letting the individuals freeze than by saving energy in any other fashion. Resulting protests from computers over the dismantling of the offending machine may lead to negotiations on computer responsibility for such actions. The establishment of a computer court for dealing with ethical problems will be the result." (Robert Weil [ed.], *Omni Future Almanac*, London: Sidgwick & Jackson, 1982, p. 32.)

merely a novel idea which this author lacked the decency
to remove, it is an essential part of the psychology of
futurology.

The French futurologist François Hetman has given a
name to this aspect of future-think. He calls it "comprehensive guarantism," and not only does he think it is a reasonable thing to expect that everyone will want nothing more
than to live in an environment of maximum comfort and ego-
gratification, but he also thinks it logical that they will be
willing to give up freedom for the sake.[13] In an article written
in 1962 called "Well-being and Freedom in 1970," Hetman
predicted that the demand for well-being will increasingly
take the form of a categorical absolute. He also went on to
predict that it will be logical for people to sacrifice a great
deal, including their freedom, for a maximum amount of
comfort and safety. In his vision of the future, the greatest
ideal, in a pablum-seeking society, will be risk-free existence,
insurance against anything and everything that is the least
bit threatening or unpleasant. It follows that the greatest
"risk," death, is also on the list of things that futurologists
believe can be "avoided"—provided, of course, that one is
willing to give up *a certain amount of freedom.*

This last theme was taken up with a vengeance by American futurologist Grant Fjermedal in a book which he published in 1987 called *The Tomorrow Makers: A Brave New
World of Living Brain Machines.* From the title of this book
it is easy to guess that the research he did for it consisted of
interviews not with physicians and microbiologists, the traditional purveyors of immortality, but with computer-
scientists. The project that these scientists are working on is
to devise the techniques, software and hardware to make it
possible to transfer the "contents" of the human brain into
a computer, make several copies of "the file," put them into
robot bodies and thus make the human subjects both "immortal" and "multipresent" at the same time. Here is the
process, called "downloading," as it is described in an interview by Fjermedal with Hans Moravec, a senior research
scientist at Carnegie-Mellon University.

"That computer sitting next to you in the operating
room would in effect be your new brain. As each

area of your brain was analyzed and simulated, the accuracy of the simulation would be tested as you pressed a button to shift between the area of the brain just copied and the simulation. When you couldn't tell the difference between the original and the copy, the surgeon would transfer the simulation of your brain into the new, computerized one and repeat the process on the next areas of your biological brain. Though you have not lost consciousness or even your train of thought, your mind—some would say soul—has been removed from the brain and transferred to a machine," Moravec said. "In a final step your old body is disconnected. The computer is installed in a shiny new one, in the style, color, and material of your choice."[14]

If one ponders closely what Moravec is saying here, the arrogance of this vision is truly extraordinary, even considering that we are dealing here with a vision of the future (after all, even visions of the future have to have some continuity with the present). Here, of course, we have Turing revisited, but this time we have the imitation game in spades. Even supposing, for the sake of argument, that one of these clever surgeon robots could be constructed, how long will the person on the operating table be given to decide whether the "copy," the imitation of himself which is being constructed in an electronically-fitted box beside him, really is the same as the original, that is, really is the same as himself? Will we be asked to settle for a snapshot of reality in this case, too? Will "five minutes" do for this imitation game? Consider also some of the enormous assumptions behind this quest: first, that the mind or "soul" is actually located in the brain and only in that part of the body; and second, that the structure of the brain, if it could indeed be thoroughly analyzed, would be similar to and compatible with computer logic and circuitry, and could therefore be assimilated to it. As far as the second assumption is concerned, if anything can safely be said to be the case, the accumulating evidence seems to demonstrate that computer and brain structure are actually very different. Though we still know very little about this area, recent studies suggest that memory is located in the brain in a non-specific way, that is, memory that is lost by cutting out one part of the brain may later be regained in another. We do not yet know how this comes to be in human brains, but this simply does not happen with computer discs, as anyone who has had data erased from the memory of his or her computer will willingly testify. And yet the vision and project continue, as if these scientists could possibly know what they are doing!

Having read this account, the reader may also be wondering what will become of the human brain—and bodies!—after the downloading is completed. When Fjermedal asked Moravec about this he replied in a cavalier way: "You just don't bother waking it up again if the copying went successfully. . . . It's so messy. Humans have got so many problems that you might just want to have it retired. You don't take your junker car out if you've got a new one." This disdain for the body is rather common among the technologically moonstruck type of futurists. Professor Marvin Minsky of MIT, who is also working on aspects of this project, echoes sentiments similar to Moravec's later in the same article: "Why not avoid getting sick and things like that? . . . It's hard to see anything against it. I think people will get fed up with bodies after a while. Then you'll have another population problem. You'll have all the people of the past as well as all of the new ones."†

Disdain for the body is not a new thing in either eastern or western philosophy, but in the latter it was probably given its first articulate expression by Plato in his dialogue called the *Phaedo*. When reading the interviews in Fjermedal's article I could not help but remember similar remarks written by Plato in his dialogue about Socrates's last hours. The heart

† Perhaps through working with machines for so long Minsky seems to have developed a serious antipathy to living creatures. In 1980 he wrote, "Today, a successful biological science is based on energetics and information processing; no notion of 'alive' appears in the theory, nor do we miss it." (See Marvin Minsky, "Decentralized Minds," in *Behavioral and Brain Sciences* [1980] 3, p. 439.) In a way it might be nice if this absurd notion were true, then biological researchers could stop experimenting with live animals and the animal rights activists would no longer have to worry about this problem! Minsky is a future hypist par excellence. Later in the same article, to prove a fantastic point, he plays the part of the future historian and quotes, as evidence, an as-yet-unpublished journal of the future. Recognizing the absurdity of this kind of rhetoric he quickly concedes it to be a joke—but uses it again a few paragraphs later, this time without the concession.

of the passage that Fjermedal's article reminded me of goes like this:

> Surely the soul can best reflect when it is free of all distractions such as hearing or sight or pain or pleasure of any kind—that is, when it ignores the body and becomes as far as possible independent, avoiding all physical contacts and associations as much as it can, in its search for reality.
>
> That is so.
>
> Then here too—in despising the body and avoiding it, and endeavoring to become independent—the philosopher's soul is ahead of all the rest.[15]

Of course the ancient Greeks had no computers or thoughts of downloading in the sense that Moravec and Minsky mean it, but in the *Phaedo,* as in the world of these futurists, discarding the body is the preliminary step for achieving immortality, because they believed, or tried—as far as their at times fanatical addiction to pure reason would let them—to believe in the immortality of the soul. For them the body only obstructs the quest for immortality and creates discomfort, distraction, and distortions. The soul can be pure only when freed from the body, like the "soul" that these prophets predict will one day be constructed in the memory section of a computer.†

Since these present-day computer-scientist futurologists do not appear to believe in the immortality of the soul outside of its transfer into a computer, it follows that for them the height of tragedy would be to miss the boat for this technological type of immortality. Gerald Sussman, another MIT professor who is also working on aspects of the downloading project, has expressed this tragic sense in the following

---

† It is remarkable that some of the ancient Greek philosophers as well as these modern futurologist counterparts had so little appreciation for the positive aspects of inhabiting a human body: the sensuous nature of good health, the heightened consciousness stemming from the pleasures of the body, the contentment brought about by physical contact, hard work, and physical exertion. Obviously, this is the philosophy of old men whose bodies, through the debilitation of age, have progressively become a burden to them.

words: "Everyone would like to be immortal. I don't think the time is quite right but it's close. I'm afraid, unfortunately, that I'm in the last generation to die."

Disdain for the human body and the desire to mechanize it are particularly characteristic of present-day futurology. However, in spite of its roots in antiquity, this attitude is a real departure from the spirit of the end of the last century and the first half of this one. The cultural antecedents for futurist magazines like *Omni* were the hobbyist magazines like *Popular Mechanics* and *Electronics Illustrated,* which began to develop mass appeal and following just before World War I. Aside from offering a few do-it-yourself plans for the home tinkerer, their content, like that of their modern counterparts, was a mixture of science-fiction, popularized science and a panorama of curious discoveries from around the world. But in those days, Darwin's theory of evolution was still a very strong part of the popular imagination and so the progress of civilization was typically correlated with the belief that the human body would continue to evolve to an ever higher level. Ideally, supermachine and superman were seen as being complementary and, in a way, evolving together.

More to the point, however, these magazines were honestly aimed at average individuals who wanted to improve their lot in life. Their advertising content tells the whole story. Along with ads for correspondence courses in refrigerator- and radio-repairing—the vocations of the future of that time—were ones offering Charles Atlas's famous course for turning 97-pound-weaklings into "he-men." There is still some of that, of course, in the present-day ads for exercise machines and vitamins, but today's futurist magazines have a more narcissistic flavor than did their predecessors. But more significantly, in the area of mental activity, which is supposed to be so important in the present "age of information," most of the responsibility is abdicated to the machines, which are pictured as already having achieved supremacy in this area. In short, in the present-day vision of the future, the coevolution of humans with machines seems to have stopped with, ironically, the humans having been left behind.

There are any number of ironies in the visions of our

modern-day prophets but this is particularly true of the work of the artificial intelligence movement. Not surprisingly, many members of the artificial intelligence movement are also futurologists, and it is certainly from the work of this movement that many futurologists draw their inspiration. The affinity between futurologists and the "artificial intelligentsia" is only natural: they are both in the business of trying to reduce life problems to what they consider to be their essences, that is, to manageable bits. Futurologists do this by projection and computer scientists do it by imitation. In the world of science, as well as in the world of art, there is certainly room for both of these techniques—but they both entail a particular danger. The danger is in what might be lost in the process, that problems that are projected and objects that are imitated will be trivialized in the process. It takes a great deal of discipline and honesty to avoid this trivialization.

Joseph Weizenbaum, a distinguished MIT computer-scientist, is of a different ilk from those we have so far encountered. He is one member of the artificial intelligence movement who does have this discipline and consequently never makes more of what he has constructed than he rightfully should. But even this is not perfectly safe because his followers, who are less intelligent and less honest than he is, have seriously misconstrued his work. In his book, *Computer Power and Human Reason,* he laments just such an incident in his career.[16] A number of years ago he devised a program which he called ELIZA that could make a computer imitate a psychoanalyst, much in the manner of Turing's description at the beginning of his famous paper. Weizenbaum's purpose in writing this program, however, was to demonstrate the absurdity of such a device, to show how simplistic and inflexible it would be. But his reviewers thought it was wonderful—not an ironic gesture but a serious enterprise. It was widely praised and imitated and, even to this day, there is a demonstration of it for children at the Lawrence Hall of Science in Berkeley to show how clever computers can be at imitating psychiatrists. But the demonstration does not even mention Weizenbaum's intentions in constructing the program, his reservations about its potential misuse, or his misgivings about what it actually does do. This is how hungry we are today to trivialize our problems, even to our children, to reduce them to the nth degree in order to be able to claim mastery over them, no matter how petty that mastery may be, and it is this hunger for mastery on which our prophets play.

If one had to summarize the psychology of these futurologists, one would have to say that their main motivational force seems to be a quest for a petty sort of mastery. By projecting problems into the future and thus making them remote, they can then be made to appear masterable, or at least manageable, if by no other means than, as Turing has taught us, by the mere manipulation of words. The quest of modern prophets is also for a paltry kind of control: of others, that is, commandable machines that have taken the place of people, and of the self, when responsibility is delegated to machines so that decisions can be made automatically, without any self-struggle. Of course, generally speaking, mastery and control are not in and of themselves bad things. But we are not talking here about Rostropovich playing the cello. Rostropovich's mastery of the cello does not contain the element of mastery through alienation that seems to be so central to the psychology of so many futurologists, and it is certainly not geared towards enhancing his creature comfort.

The complementary tendency—to at once glorify small, tentative, or at least very limited accomplishments and trivialize even the greatest of challenges—is a strong one in futurology. Some might say it is a characteristic of optimists, but it is also a quality of fools. It is the foolishness of the child who, intoxicated by the initial easy but dramatic accomplishments of, say, beginning to learn a musical instrument or mastering any other serious skill, deludes himself into thinking that really significant mastery will come just as easily, just as quickly, and just as dramatically as these euphoric beginnings. Though such foolishness may be tolerable, and even becoming, in children, it is troubling, if not pathetic, in adults.

This is well illustrated in the vision which is presently being promoted by Stewart Brand. It is worth recalling that Brand used to be a sort of cult figure in the late 1960s and early 1970s. In 1968 Brand founded and edited a popular review of "tools for living" called the *Whole Earth Catalog*. It reviewed tools and technical manuals for gardening, farming, land use, shelter, light industry and craft. It also reviewed alternative communities and life-styles, all the sorts of things that we now call "New Age." It was a great coffee-table and bookstore-browsing book, and also served as a sourcebook for the "back to the earth" movement, which was then going strong.

Brand's review was also a source book for budding futurologists. It opened with a paean to Buckminster Fuller, reviewing all of his books and also those of other, more esoteric futurists. There was an obvious link between Fuller and the reviews of tools: Brand believed, as did Fuller, in salvation through design, that well-designed tools would make the future world a better place. Brand's catalogues characteristically addressed the minor problem of access to tools, but made short shrift of the major problem of how they are to be used.

It is easy to understand how Brand and Fuller were drawn by the paradigm of design: it is nothing if not seductive. Well-designed tools, furnishings, houses are often very life-enhancing, and anyone who has ever mastered anything knows that mastery is enhanced with proper tools. But ultimately the paradigm is very limited: how many tinkerers do we know who have exquisite tools yet hardly know how to use them, or conversely, can work wonders with inadequate tools, can make a cardboard cello sing and build a house with found material and basic hand-tools. Yet Brand really was thinking that these tools would of themselves create a more masterful future. In *The Media Lab: Inventing the Future at MIT,* his 1987 paean to tools-cum-vision of the future, he reveals the persistence of this belief and tells how, during a brief period in which his vision of the future seemed to him to have gone blank, far from inducing him to reassess its premises, this development simply threw him into an existential black hole: "Back in 1968 when I started an access-to-tools compendium called the *Whole Earth Catalog,* and for a few years following, I'd had a clear feeling for the 'future' and what to do about it. By the time I'd done half a dozen versions of the book, ending with a *Whole Earth*

Software Catalog in 1985, I had no idea whatever about futures and was operating strictly on reflex."[17]

Brand sadly came to the realization that he could not live with uncertainty about what the future held in store. So what did he do about it? He went to MIT for a few months to review the fanciest computer-enhanced communications tools on the planet and wrote a book about them. Yet, in his mind, this book is no mere review of tool development in progress; it is, in his own words, "about two media labs. It is about the specific five-story pile of equipment, academics, and ideas in eastern Massachusetts, and it is about the worldwide media laboratory in which *we are all likely to be experimenters for the rest of our lives.*" (emphasis added)[18]

It is difficult to say exactly what Brand means by this abstract and impersonal proclamation because, like most futurologists using high-falutin phrases, he characteristically does not explain what it means in his book. But what a nice egalitarian sounding phrase it is—until one considers its implications by trying to personalize it a bit. If we are *all,* in fact, experimenters in this lab, then who will be sweeping the floor and dishing out food in the cafeteria? After all, even in this age of inexpensive electronic equipment, this is a privileged existence that Brand is describing. Whose future was he really talking about? On the other hand, it is difficult to imagine what this vision might even mean. Would these tools, which can produce things like a customized newspaper, a customized television station and a robot secretary which knew its boss's whims and fancies, really be accessible to everyone? And if they were, should we regard them as the lowest common denominator, the highest common denominator, or the essence of our future egalitarian life on earth? Will we all really be working and playing with sophisticated communications devices for the rest of our lives? Will these devices really help us through our days; through our eating, bathing and sleeping; through our search for love, work, power; through our avoidance of love, work, power? All of us? Including, for instance, those who are now entering the work force in the fastest expanding sector, euphemistically called the hospitality industry, which is offering low-paying, low-tech jobs like waitressing, short-order cooking and dishwashing? All of us?

Brand at least managed to banish his uncertainty about the future and come up with an image he himself could easily live with on his tugboat in San Francisco Bay. After leaving MIT he wrote with great relief: "The Media Lab provided, finally, what I went for—a clear feeling of the future and some ideas about what to do about it."[19] And yet there is no statement in the entire book that explains what this "clear feeling of the future" really is, never mind what to do about it. What it *appears* to be, however, is a vision of the future as the realm where we will be able to objectify and depersonalize our existences. As it turns out, however, this is not a new vision for Brand, but an old one. A number of years ago Brand wrote: "To get a hand on your future you've got to get outside yourself, because only from outside can you see your space-time environment whole. One way is to identify out into another culture, Indian or whatever. . . . Another is to take Philip Wagner's trip into fascinated objectivity about earthly doings."[20] Fascinated objectivity: there certainly are many examples of this in Brand's book. Even in the last chapter, when he finally does make an attempt to sober up from his cheerleading mode, he writes about our future robot secretaries: "Programming these machines to match one's habits and preferences can be tiresome, but it's also usefully revealing. It forces you to be conscious about everything you would like the machine to do, which can be an opportunity to change habits while your mind is on them. Once the machines are programmed, you can be unconscious again and do what they're knowing, probably more, better, and easier than before . . ."[21] Whatever "fascinated objectivity" may be, one of the great feats that one will be able to accomplish in this future way of being will be to treat one's habits as if they are as easily programmable as a computer. This vision is certainly embarrassing to those of us who have trouble keeping even New Year's resolutions in the dreary present in which we are now living! But Brand is not merely talking about everyday personal habits which are fundamentally enough a part of character to be very difficult to change; he envisions no limits to how far design will be able to go to make us better future people. Later he writes in the same spirit: "Designing *ethical* robots is a long and interesting problem. We have enough trouble designing

ethical human beings. Maybe practicing on robots will help."
(emphasis in original)[22]

It must be very comforting to live on a tugboat in San
Francisco Bay and think that one is going to share a common
future, a common destiny, with a younger person who is
starting out their working life as a short-order cook, simply
on the basis that you may both—but on very different levels
and in very different ways—be using the same computer-
enhanced telecommunications system. But a telecommunications system is not a laboratory, and using it does not make
one an experimenter—unless, of course, one trivializes the
work of scientific experimentation. By espousing the pseudo-
egalitarianism which is implied by his electronic vision—the
computer as the great equalizer, the six-gun of the future—
Brand is, in the end, avoiding the real issue of how fundamentally different is the relationship of different classes of
users to technology, present, past and future.[23]

In the end, Brand's book tells us a great deal more about
the psychology of futurologists by what it leaves out than by
what it says, by its failure to address in any way the messy
developments of the present that, if allowed to continue, are
bound to play themselves out by creating future problems.
All of the mess is avoided just so that Brand can have a neat
and flashy tool-rich future to relate to.

Ironically, avoidance is a dominant element in the psychology of futurologists, just as, Susan Sontag has reminded us,
alienation is for photographers. After all, as the futurologists
gaze into the future they are not social actors or even, properly speaking, social observers of the scenes which they envision. Rather, given the unavoidably severe limits to their
perspective, they are basically social voyeurs, much as photographers sometimes are. But photographers at their best
are artists, trying to intrigue and suggest the possibilities of
life. Futurologists are not nearly so honest or modest. As
far as futurologists are concerned, it would be more accurate
to say that they are easily titillated by what they see—or
think they see—and in turn share their vision by trying to
titillate the rest of us. Because of the element of avoidance
in their posture, because they can never get close to what
they are pointing at, they do not have to be responsible to

it and can always perform their dramatic posing and pro-
posing at a safe distance.

It is often said of voyeurs that theirs is an act of offense
and aggression. In a way this is true, but it is also true that
theirs is an act of defense and avoidance. It is easy for voyeurs
to glorify what they see because with their little peeps they
can never truly understand it, they can never achieve the
often unglorious but truly substantive understanding—and
responsibility—which comes from real contact.

In the end, of course, it is not an optimistic but rather
a dim view of humanity that is reflected in the visions of a
great number of futurologists, even those who like to number
themselves among the optimists of the world. Most utopians
of the past, from Thomas More on down, have tried to
envision future conditions which would ennoble the soul. It
is a sad comment on our modern-day visionaries that they
are advocating future conditions in which the soul—their
own as well as those of others—will be systematically
avoided.

NOTES

1. Susan Sontag, *On Photography* (New York: Farrar, Straus and Giroux, 1973),
   p. 167.
2. Because it is one of the main themes of this book, the following analysis focuses
   narrowly on some propagandist elements that unfortunately made their way
   into Turing's thinking, but Turing's thought has already been seriously critiqued
   along a number of other lines by philosophers of science. Perhaps the most
   prominent, but not necessarily the most subtle, of these was launched in 1980
   by John Searle who argued that computers have syntax, that is, the ability to
   follow rules, but not semantics, the ability to understand what they mean. Along
   a similar line see also S.G. Shanker, "Wittgenstein versus Turing on the Nature
   of Church's Thesis," *Notre Dame Journal of Formal Logic* (1987), vol. 28, no.
   4, pp. 615–649, which highlights some important discrepancies between Turing's
   mathematics and the philosophical conclusions he attempted to draw from it,
   and "The Dawning of (Machine) Intelligence," *Philosophica* (1988), no. 2, pp.
   95–144, which elucidates the roots of Turing's philosophy of knowledge in
   behavioral psychology and demonstrates the mutually reinforcing errors in both
   which have been carried forward by cognitive science. In another vein, see
   Nicholas Georgescu-Roegen, *The Entropy Law and the Economic Process*
   (Cambridge, Mass.: Harvard University Press, 1971), especially pp. 1–94, which
   argues that it is impossible to express certain kinds of concepts in mathematical
   terms and therefore impossible for computers to "understand" them.
3. Alan Turing, "Computing Machinery and Intelligence," in Alan Ross Anderson, *Minds and Machines* (Englewood Cliffs, N.J.: Prentice-Hall, 1964), p. 4.
4. Turing, p. 5.

5. Turing, pp. 13–14.
6. A more recent example of self-promoting propaganda cum futurology in a "newer" field can be found in E.O. Wilson's preface to his book *Sociobiology,* in which he writes: "The conventional wisdom also speaks of ethology, which is the naturalistic study of whole patterns of animal behavior, and its companion enterprise, comparative psychology, as the central, unifying fields of behavior biology. They are not; both are destined to be cannibalized by neurophysiology and sensory physiology from one end and sociobiology and behavioral ecology from the other . . . I hope not too many scholars in ethology and psychology will be offended by this vision of the future of behavioral biology. It seems to be indicated both by the extrapolation of current events and by consideration of the logical relationship behavioral biology holds with the remainder of science. The future, it seems clear, cannot be with the ad hoc terminology, crude models, and curve fitting that characterize most of contemporary ethology and comparative psychology. Whole patterns of animal behavior will inevitably be explained within the framework, first, of integrative neurophysiology, which classifies neurons and reconstructs their circuitry, and, second, of sensory physiology, which seeks to characterize the cellular transducers at the molecular level." (E.O. Wilson, *Sociobiology,* Cambridge, Mass.: Harvard University Press, 1976, p. 6).
7. Edward Feigenbaum and Pamela McCorduck, *The Fifth Generation: Artificial Intelligence and Japan's Computer Challenge to the World* (London: Pan Books, 1984).
8. "The Future of Work: The Future Office" (videorecording), Toronto: TV Ontario, 1982.
9. Feigenbaum, p. 193.
10. Richard Wolkomir, "Robots at Home," in *Omni* (April 1983), p. 76.
11. Stewart Brand, *The Media Lab: Inventing the Future at MIT* (New York: Viking, 1987), p. 4.
12. Roy Mason, "A Day at Xanadu," in *Futurist* (February 1984), p. 20.
13. François Hetman, "Bien-être et liberté en 1970," in *Bulletin S.E.D.E.I.S.*, no. 811, *Futuribles* (February 10, 1962), no. 24.
14. Grant Fjermedal, "Surrogate Brains," in *Omni* (October 1986), p. 38.
15. Plato, *Phaedo* 65, c-d (trans. Hugh Tredennick), in *The Collected Dialogues of Plato* (Princeton, N.J.: Princeton University Press, 1961).
16. Joseph Weizenbaum, *Computer Power and Human Reason: From Judgement to Calculation* (Harmondsworth, England: Penguin, 1984).
17. Brand, p. xi.
18. Brand, p. xiii.
19. Brand, p. xvi.
20. Stewart Brand (ed.), *The Updated Last Whole Earth Catalog* (New York: Portola Institute, 1974), p. 9.
21. Brand, *The Media Lab,* p. 254.
22. Brand, p. 258.
23. See Edmund Sullivan, "The Computer as Equalizer," Ontario Ministry of Education, 1983.

Many have dreamed up republics and principalities which have never in truth been known to exist; the gulf between how one should live and how one does live is so wide that a man who neglects what is actually done for what should be done paves the way to self-destruction rather than self-preservation.
—MACHIAVELLI

3

THE IDEOLOGY OF FUTUROLOGY

Given his usually ponderous persona, it may surprise some readers to learn that no less prominent a politician than Winston Churchill was, in his time, smitten by the futurist bug. In 1932, while he was sitting as a member of the British Parliament and after he had already served a term as chancellor of the exchequer, he wrote a prophetic article which he published, of all places, in the hobbyist magazine *Popular Mechanics*. Here he speculated about what the world would be like fifty years from that time. Whatever its merits as prediction—it happens to have the usual unremarkable track record which characterizes "more of the same" projections—what is really interesting about Churchill's article is the fact that he packed a great deal of ideological baggage in with his futurology.

Near the beginning of this piece he took a couple of gratuitous swipes at the Soviet Communists; this is hardly surprising. More revealing than this assault is a vision that comes at the end of the article in which he predicts that man will eventually be able to produce test-tube babies. This, of course, was not such a remarkable prediction in itself, given the fact that, although the DNA code had not yet been cracked, man had forever been speculating about and searching for the essence of life in the laboratory, and the field of embryology had, even by that time, already yielded many of the precursors in thought and technique for achieving the feat of growing and manipulating fetuses *in vitro*. However, what was significant about Churchill's vision were some of its details: he imagined that the development of techniques for producing test-tube babies would naturally be accompanied by a program of what we would today call genetic engineering, but Churchill's genetic engineering was for very questionable purposes.

After setting the scene by making an ambiguous allusion to *R.U.R.*, a fantasy play about the invention of robots which was very popular at the time—were we to regard humans whose coming into being had been tampered with by their predecessors on earth as mere robots?—he wrote, "There seems little doubt that it will be possible to carry out the entire cycle which now leads to the birth of a child, in artificial surroundings. . . . Interference with the mental development of such beings, expert suggestion and treatment in the earlier years, *would produce beings specialized to thought or toil*." (emphasis added).[1] For Churchill, the prospect of future techniques for growing fetuses in the laboratory presented opportunities for intervention, but intervention of a certain kind, the kind of intervention that would not ameliorate, but rather would enhance the class differences which were, and to a great extent still are, so characteristic of English society. Never mind the evolutionary questionability of engendering humans who, like toy poodles, were to be genetically diddled into overspecialized niches. Never mind, either, the social and moral questionability of such interventions.

Churchill is not the only forecaster to use prophecy to make an ideological argument about class. Unfortunately it is a tradition of long standing. In 1798 the English economist Thomas Malthus published a famous treatise called *An Essay on the Principle of Population as it Affects the Future Improvement of Society*. In this pamphlet Malthus predicted what would today be commonly called a "doom and gloom" scenario of the "time-bomb" variety, much like the "limits to growth" type of predictions that were produced in the early 1970s by the Club of Rome. Malthus prophesied that, since the population, when unchecked, increases in geometric ratio (that is, like compound interest), whereas the food supply only increases in arithmetic ratio (like simple interest), the people of England would eventually starve. Malthus's pamphlet had many of the qualities of modern futurology. It relied on simple projection and on a mathematical model based on very questionable assumptions— Why should the population always continue to grow unchecked? Why should the rate of food production not increase more rapidly than it happened to be at the time the author was writing?—all of which were eventually proven to be unfounded. But more importantly, there was an explicit prescription contained in Malthus's prediction: that the lower classes restrain their rate of reproduction. It is now conventional wisdom among historians that this prescription vindicated the prejudices of the dominant elite of the society in which Malthus lived who wanted to blame the poor for their misery rather than take some of the responsibility for this situation on themselves.[2] This futurology was therefore imbued with self-righteous moralizing of a threatened elite.

Yet the ideological bias of such projected visions is not unusual in futurology; in fact, a close scrutiny of the prophecy business shows it to be extremely common. Ideology is not merely a by-product of certain kinds of prophetic vision. On the contrary, prophecy is a basic tool of ideology, Left or Right, East or West. In fact, attempts by one ideological camp to exert influence by "outprophesying" the other have been prominent centerpieces in ideological propaganda wars throughout recorded history; and of course the ultimate prophetic act in any ideological camp is naturally to predict its triumph over all others.

You do not have to go very far to demonstrate this: if you follow the now fading propaganda war between the competing ideologies of East and West, you can easily find some fascinating, and ultimately very revealing, skirmishes. For example, a few years ago the Soviet futurologist Georgi Shakhnazarov published a cutting diatribe in which he lam-

basted western futurology for being—bourgeois, of course—
but also, among other things, *unscientific*. According to
Shakhnazarov: "Futurology originated in the West as a specific academic discipline to provide an immediate alternative
to the Marxist-Leninist, communist ideas about the future
society. It was no natural offspring born at a point where a
new branch of science hives off from the general body of
knowledge. It was rather a peculiar hybrid artificially produced by the bourgeois social sciences . . . to meet a generously rewarded demand. Unlike any genuine science that
arrives at the truth at the end of the road, futurology has an
anteriorly posited result to which it must suit the facts."[3] It
may have gone largely unnoticed in the West—this certainly
was not a major Soviet propaganda offensive—but neither
was Shakhnazarov's diatribe a mere idle volley from the
Soviet propaganda machine. Why did he write it, and who
was he really addressing? After all, why should this Soviet
propagandist care whether western futurology is good, bad
or indifferent?

To understand why this was an issue for Shakhnazarov
and for his communist masters, it is necessary to consider
his work in context. Until recently, in the Soviet Union the
ideological machine was constantly working to legitimate
the state of political domination that existed there and in the
eastern bloc in general. The mere existence in the West of
a futurology which claimed to be scientific was bound to rub
against the Soviet ideological grain because futurology, of a
special sort, was a centerpiece of the Soviet ideological campaign. And because this Communist ideology had its roots
in Marxist political thought, futurology held a central position since even before the Russian revolution.

In writing this diatribe Shakhnazarov was working, in a
vulgar and rather technocratic sort of way, along two prominent lines in the tradition of Marxist political criticism. The
first is the persistent claim by Marxist theory that it is notable,
almost unique, for being *scientific*. And related to this claim
is another to the effect that Marx's thought contains powerful
insight into the nature of the world order—and insight which
emphatically includes a great deal of foresight. This second
strain is often referred to as the visionary or utopian aspect
of his thinking.

A little elaboration will help to explain how this relates to the concerns of this book. Very early in his writings Marx developed a specialized and very purposeful use of the word *scientific*. Marx used the term in various contexts often to contrast his own thought with that of other philosophers and social theorists. In Marx's critique, *science,* that is, his own work, was deemed to be more rational, more in touch with the true nature of things and with the logic inherent in that nature, than the "impoverished" philosophy of other theorists. By making this distinction Marx was both making a political move, in that he was trying to empower his own thought by elevating it above all others, and following the tradition which has been so powerful and persistent ever since the Enlightenment, the deification and worship of reason. So it was in this special, exclusive sense that Shakhnazarov was arguing that western futurology is not *scientific*. In the end, the implication in Shakhnazarov's book is that, since western futurology is not Marxist, almost by definition it cannot therefore possibly be *scientific*.[4]

As far as Marx's claim to special insight into the evolution of civilization is concerned, the story is similar. Marx's world view relied heavily on his penetrating analyses of economic, historical and political events, all of which he used in order to explain the evolving social, economic, and political order. He drew on his historical studies and analyses of current events to make broad predictions of future developments, all within the framework of the logical progression which he claimed he was uniquely able to discern. This way of thinking was particularly evident in his theory of revolution. One of the important features of Marx's theory of revolution was that it would proceed everywhere in logical, predictable stages. It is impossible to do Marx's usually rather thickety thinking justice here but, roughly speaking, in his scheme a stage of extreme discontent and contradiction was to be followed by another stage of violent overthrow of the existent regime; this was to be followed by a stage of legitimate domination called "dictatorship of the proletariat" during which new conditions and new social and economic relationships would be established; and this stage was ultimately to be followed by no political domination whatsoever, Marx's version of utopia, in which government of the sort we know now would no longer be necessary because of the so-called "withering" of the state into civil society. What is critical here, however, and what makes Marxist prophecy no different from many strains to be found in the West, is that this last stage exists always at some unknown point in the future and justifies the injustices, inconveniences and inequities which must be borne between now and then. Everything—including, in Marx's scheme, capitalism—is preparation for that stage. Everything points logically and *scientifically* in that direction. This was used to justify the recent state of affairs in the Soviet Union which entailed, among other things, constrained elections, domination of the state and individuals in the society by a single party, an elaborate policing system and all of the other all too familiar things that flow from Marx's prophecy. In short, the ruling party justified its domination not only on the basis of the status quo and its purported egalitarianism, but also, significantly, on the basis of insight—insight into the ultimate long-term good of the nation which was largely based on foresight into the future.

In this world view the non-Communist world remains full of contradictions because it has not yet reached its Communist phase. Not only is it full of inequity and injustice, but it remains subject to the irrationalities of capitalism usually epitomized by the surges and flutterings of the business cycle. However, upon surveying western futurology, Shakhnazarov's problem was that the largest and most prominent part of it also claims to be systematic and scientific in its analysis of world events, and also plays that game of political image management which specializes in evoking the future. In light of this fact, and in light of the ideological competition between East and West, which was based in large part on delineating *differences* between the two camps, the existence of the growing field of futurology in the West since the end of World War II, therefore, logically represented a threat. This threat was not to the physical Soviet state, of course, but to something very basic nevertheless: the Soviet persona, its very identity, which claimed, through its Marxist origins, to have a monopoly on scientific prophecy. If you consider the matter in this light, it is obvious that futurology would be one of those items to which the Soviets would have wanted to claim exclusive rights. The reasons are similar to those that motivated Marx to claim exclusive rights to the use of *science* in his political theory and, it must be added, similar to those that have led to the exclusive claim to political freedom which has so often been made for the West. Under these circumstances, therefore, how could the Soviet Union regard the rise of a so-called scientific futurology of the West with indifference?

Marxism is not the only ideology that relies heavily on a vision of the future. A well articulated vision of the future is the natural centerpiece of most ideological systems, especially those on the farther ends of the political spectrum. The reason this is so is that the extreme ideologies all envision the playing out of a great drama over time, and the final climax (the extreme ideologies always seem to go in for dramatic climaxes)—be it the "withering" of the state if it is an ideology of the Left, or some sort of breathtaking apocalypse in which the world will be destroyed and/or renewed if it is one on the Right—is always played out at some, usually unspecified, period in the future. A good example in recent years of the ideological right wing's use of prophecy to legitimate policy was the remark made by Reagan's former secretary of the interior, James Watt, who, when questioned about his department's policy to lease federal wilderness land for commercial development and exploitation, remarked that he saw no problem with deforestation because it would create a clearer view for the Messiah when He returned to redeem the earth in His Second Coming.

Politicians, who often view themselves as major actors in these great dramas, are always inordinately concerned with the final act. If they feel they have been major players in important decisions, they invariably want to have their judgment vindicated by the future; if they feel they are great leaders, they want future time to indicate that they knew exactly where to lead their people, even if their regime entails great hardship.† But more fundamentally, politics being

---

† When political leadership entails great hardship for the population, this must always be justified by an attractive or at least worthwhile future outcome, in which case the hardship is equated with making sacrifices for future generations. However, such leadership means that the leader be alienated from the people insofar as he does not share their burdens.

the tenuous business that it is, they are very concerned about their own personal futures. If they feel that they are an important part of the present status quo, they want to continue to be an important part of the status quo that is to come; they want to reproduce the present political order in such a way that no matter what else happens they will retain an important role in the political order of the future.

These different sorts of obsession with the future have long been a favorite preoccupation of politicians; in fact it is no exaggeration to say that at certain times they have been treated by politicians as a kind of religion. In the first century B.C the Roman senate would not make a move without first consulting the book of the Sibyl, a famous collection of prophecies made by a woman from Cumae. When this collection was destroyed by a fire in the Capitol in 83 B.C. the senators were unwilling to make any decisions until it had been replaced. It became so much a part of the established order that a group of conspirators led by Lentulus felt obliged to manufacture a set of rival ones, forgeries, to refute the official prophecies, much as opposition parties today publish rival policy papers and make rival predictions to discredit the official ones published by the government of the party in power to promote their own views. For the Roman senate, the publication of opposing prophecies was no small matter: these rival predictions were so threatening that Augustus had two thousand copies destroyed in 12 B.C Similarly, in Wales in 1406, laws were framed against "false prophecy" because there had been a great deal of divination that was said to be against the state. Today, of course, futurology think tanks like the Rand Corporation serve as the source of and repository for our current set of Sibylline papers. They are not, however, produced by an inspired woman— or inspired men for that matter. They are churned out by technocrats using the whole array of modern quantitative and qualitative projection techniques. But in the consciousness of the politicians who consult them, these papers serve the same function as the Sibylline papers did in Rome; they are, quite literally, a part of their secular religious practice.

Getting back to Shakhnazarov, though, of course he was right about western futurology. It is assuredly not a science. But it is no less of a science than was the futurology of the Soviet Union. In a sense, Shakhnazarov's diatribe was a modern-day symbolic equivalent of Augustus burning the rival prophecies of the Lentulus camp. But what is more important than this is that the *claim* to be scientific or systematic is a characteristic feature of much of the futurology of both East and West. It wears the mantle of science even though it cannot properly be said to be a real science itself. And we should bear in mind that this is no mere affectation; it serves several indispensable functions. First, not only does it distinguish futurology from the most questionable forms of forecasting like astrology, extrasensory perception and all of the other more esoteric forms of divination which flood our existential airwaves, but this characteristic use of scientism also serves the functions both of lending legitimacy to the tenuous business of prediction and of obscuring its hidden agenda. In short, the scientism of futurology serves as a mask for its inherent ideology.

This kind of legitimation is crucial to futurology's well-being. Since the predictions and prescriptions which futurologists make must somehow be made credible in the eyes of their audiences, it follows that a very good way to accomplish this has been to somehow associate their activity with science. Notwithstanding the growing skepticism and doubts about its uses, science retains the cachet of mastery and legitimacy. It remains deeply entrenched in our civil religion that scientists both know the nature of things and can effectively act on the world to make things happen. Not surprisingly, therefore, many futurists have gone very far in order to establish an association with science. They use scientific methods and techniques—whether or not it is meaningful or appropriate to do so—and above all they use a great deal of scientific or pseudo-scientific language. Even the term "futurology," which was coined by the German sociologist Ossip Flechtheim in 1942, serves the purpose of creating this association.[5]

We came across an example of the use of pseudo-scientific jargon in the last chapter when I introduced futurologist François Hetman's term, "comprehensive guarantism (*garantisme intégrale*)." Consider it again: clumsy, pretentious, and murky, but definitely containing an air of scientific *savoir faire*. Why use this phrase when one could just as easily, and far more clearly, have said something like "complete insurance"? The answer becomes immediately obvious as soon as you consider the phrase in context. This phrase is used to modify the word "existence." How could anyone use the whole phrase, "complete insurance against existence" without feeling foolish? Hence, "comprehensive guarantism."

Though perhaps they are no worse than futurologists from other countries, French futurologists have long been notable for inventing jargon. In the early nineteenth century the French utopian socialist Charles Fourier was particularly imaginative and colorful in this game. He liked to argue by what he called "analogy" and predicted that, in the harmonized world of the future, "anti-lions" would tame the world of nature, "anti-crocodiles" would shrink its domain and there would be a creature called a "great hen" which was to lay enough eggs to pay off the English national debt in six months. Would that there were a few such "great hens" around in our time, that is, Charles Fourier's future!

In order to give the reader a better taste of what is entailed in this game, here are a few more examples of the kinds of pseudo-scientific words and phrases that futurists regularly use. They are not nearly as colorful as Fourier's, but they make up for this by being a great deal more pretentious and absurd. It is impossible to resist making a few comments about them.

Futuro-Epistemology-Conceptology-Engineering. The Japanese futurist Yujiro Hayashi coined this phrase at a conference in 1967 in order to help the convenors classify their research of the future. It breaks down to the following three categories: *Futuro-epistemology* is the study of conditions under which one can gain an objective understanding of the future. *Futuro-conceptology,* on the other hand, is the conscious activity of mapping out desirable futures. And *futuro-engineering* describes a practical activity: applied research on means for implementing desirable futures. The first term seems to describe an impossibility. Under what conditions could one possibly gain an "objective" understanding of that which does not yet exist? Most scientists have enough trouble getting an "objective" understanding of things that are in front of their noses! But if you are going to lay claim to being scientific you have to claim to be objective, hence *futuro-epistemology*. The second term describes a prescriptive activity which, however, pretends to be derived from the nature of things. It suggests that the process of mapping out desirable futures is value free and scientific rather than being full of moral considerations. Whose desirable futures do these futurists have in mind? If the term meant negotiating or building consensus around desirable futures, then it might be acceptable as a political challenge, but mapping in this context is an evasion in the form of a pseudo-scientism. As to the third term, once one gets past the considerable hump of introducing an agenda of desirables, as one does in the second term, the means for getting them would fall into the realm of practical problem solving, engineering.[6]

Symbiosis. Here a common scientific word is appropriated and used in a characteristically uncommon and inappropriate way as follows: "It is clear that over the past century our relationship with it [the telephone] has grown more complex. Today we have a sort of symbiotic relationship with telephones. In tomorrow's society, the symbiosis, for better or worse will be even stronger." According to the *Oxford English Dictionary,* symbiosis is "the permanent union between organisms each of which depends for its existence on the other as the fungus and alga composing lichen." It is clear that either the author did not really understand the word—after all, telephones are not organisms, so what can it possibly mean to say they depend on humans—or, more likely, that he decided, by a mere wave of the futurologist's lexicographic wand, to elevate these appliances to the level of organisms in order to enhance his forecasting by glamorously associating it with the environmental movement. The hidden message: if you use your fancy telephone a great deal you will be developing a natural relationship with it and perhaps contributing to ecological stability.[7]

Ephemeralization. Probably Buckminster Fuller's most famous idea was that by using clever design we can do more with less. The word *ephemeralization,* which is supposed to describe that process, is obscure enough on the surface, but it is even harder to understand when he uses it in context, as in the following: "The progressive doing of more with less per each and every reinvested resource unit of energy M (matter), energy R (radiation) and I (intellect). Wealth is intellect harnessed in animate energy, tooled anticipatorily to automatically produce the forward metabolic regeneration of humanity. Ephemeralization is scientifically identifiable with anti-entropy; it is a product of the metaphysical conservation being more effective and coherent than physical entropy." Once you work out the pseudo-scientific babble, it should be clear that Buckminster Fuller, like many futurologists, belongs to the school of economic thinking that holds that material scarcity, as opposed to human nature, is the real economic problem. This passage is part of a larger argument that says that clever design will optimize the use of resources and eliminate scarcity, and thus eliminate the need for politics, a tool that humans have invented to deal with the issue of distribution under the conditions of scarcity. What Fuller is really implying in the above passage is that if we solve our technical problems, our human problems will simply fall into place.[8]

Basic Long-term Multifold Trend. Futurologist Herman Kahn made the less than profound observation that certain major trends are complex, interrelated and likely to continue for the long-term. He used this phrase as a sort of conceptual net into which to place these trends so he could, in a sense, call them his own. Included on his list are: worldwide industrialization and modernization; population growth; increasing the tempo of change; increasing capability of mass destruction; and accumulation of scientific and technical knowledge. Here we have a combination of stating the obvious without bringing any additional insight to it, and masking this by combining one's terms in an unfamiliar package. Kahn was a supreme master of packaging—was there ever a time when cultural change did not have to do with complex and interrelated events and phenomena?[9]

Disintermediation. Emerson would have used the term "self-reliance" instead, and we would all have immediately known what he meant. This other word, *disintermediation,* was invented by futurist Paul Hawken to describe a hiccup of a trend which occurred in most of the advanced industrial nations in the late 1970s and at the beginning of the 1980s. He noticed that during this period of high interest rates many investors were switching from stocks to bonds because of their higher rate of return. Because one can buy bonds directly at a bank without a broker, he shortsightedly saw this development as a trend to eliminate the middle-person, and cleverly called this process *disintermediation*. Meanwhile, a few years later, the stock market is bullish and not only are stockbrokers very much back in business, but banks are charging more for services and the financial services industry is growing rapidly. But before, during, and after this hiccup many people, mainly women, have continued to sew at home and thereby disintermediate the manufacturers of clothing— without even knowing they are in the business of disintermediation.[10]

These are but a handful of innumerable examples but, aside from giving the uninitiated reader a taste of what this business is all about, it should make my point abundantly clear. In spite of their pretension, once you master them, most of the ideas expressed by these terms are remarkably simple-minded. It is easy to see why futurologists desperately need the ballast of scientism in order to be taken seriously. In the end, their quasi-scientific terms are little more than fancy, obscure and sometimes wrong and/or inaccurate ways of naming very ordinary things.

The process of naming things, or the parts of them, in order to try to understand them is an activity which is as old as science itself. But when we name things with unnecessarily esoteric language, we do something more than simply try to understand them; we try to own them, we appropriate mastery of these things for ourselves alone and for the members of the group with whom we share this special language. This is unquestionably a political act because any group which can claim mastery over something that most people would also like to understand and control is in this way exercising dominance over them. In the last decade or so this fact has at least been recognized in the field of medicine, by many patients and some doctors, and so, thankfully, we now have a small movement to simplify medical terminology.

The question of domination brings us squarely into the realm of politics. The French sociologist Alain Gras has argued that futurology is basically a technique of political domination, and that it is intimately linked with the policy of ruling elites because its hidden agenda is the reproduction of domination.[11] It may not be fair to say this of all of futurology, but it is disconcerting how often themes of dominance and elitism emerge in this field. In the last chapter we had a taste of this in Edward Feigenbaum's raving about the rising class of computer technocrats—he calls them "intellectuals"—who will presumably come to dominate the life of the mind. Likewise Buckminster Fuller, who is usually more sober than Feigenbaum, nevertheless glories in talking about his influence on the decision-makers of the world.[12] Daniel Bell, on the other hand, has self-righteously proclaimed that the mandate of his group of futurologists, the Commission on the Year 2000, was to "widen the sphere of moral choices," while at the same time he has prescribed that the range of actors who should make these choices should be kept narrow and should consist primarily of intellectuals, the class of which he happens to be a part.[13] But no one has gloated more than Herman Kahn about the privileged position held by these advisers to the future-makers of this world. He has even prided himself on being duplicitous in his role of court astrologer, saying one thing to the general public and another to the powers that be:

> Two different perspectives can be used in future studies . . . [they] can be labeled *descriptive* (or *predictive*) and *normative* . . . descriptive forecasting is basically passive, merely attempting to record what the world will be like so that we may react to it.
>
> The normative perspective emphasizes changing the future in a desired fashion, making more likely *the good* and/or less likely *the bad*. . . . However, although descriptive forecasting may be useful in many fields where the outcome cannot be affected by choices today, decision makers are primarily concerned with normative forecasting. In practice, it is not possible to separate the two types completely. There are obvious constraints and limits on the ambition of any individual or institution that must be descriptively forecast before any normative forecast can be made. When working on

individual projects for agencies or organizations we put our primary emphasis on the "normative" approach, trying to delineate what options are open to decision makers and what can be the implications of their decisions; but when addressing a more general audience, as in this book, we emphasize the "descriptive" face of futurology, although normative aspects are certainly present. (emphasis added)[14]

One thing that can be said for Kahn is that his elitist pretensions were perfectly consistent with his normative vision of the world of the future. In an earlier book, it is remarkable how many techniques for population control are included in a neat list of one hundred—futurologists love to deal in round numbers—expected developments. These include:

Other new and possibly pervasive techniques for surveillance, monitoring, and control of individuals and organizations.
New and more reliable "educational" and propaganda techniques for affecting human behavior—public and private.
New and relatively effective counterinsurgency techniques (and perhaps also insurgency techniques).
Other genetic control or influence over the "basic constitution of an individual."[15]

Futurology is also used by corporate elites, not only to try to control the outside world, the *environment* as it is frequently called, but for control within the corporation and in infighting and competitions within the corporation itself. Two Dutch futurologists, Henk Becker and Joseph van Doorn, have observed that "futures research has become important for successful negotiations. A policy maker either uses the results of a futures research project to beat his opponents, or his opponents attack him by using futures research and he needs to have this kind of research available to hit back." They also remark that "futures studies must transform uncertainty into risk as much as possible. The

dynamics and complexity of the social systems which the
policy maker wants to control demand analytical instruments
that are able to consider the relative (unpredictability) of
the developments involved."[16] Even in our business corporations, which pride themselves on governing themselves
strictly on the basis of rationality, there is no rhetoric more
powerful than the often irrational rhetoric of prophecy, nor
any better tool for self-promotion or the promotion of one's
favorite policy ideas. And even when the acknowledged unpredictability of the outside world finally does leave corporation executives feeling uneasy, their anxiety can always be
assuaged by prophetic placebos.

Another sense in which futurology acts in the service of
social control was suggested by Ivan Illich, who has argued
that futurology promotes cultural convergence along technocratic lines. He has observed that "most of the research
now going on about the future tends to advocate further
increases in the institutionalization of values."[17] Given the
technocratic consciousness which so heavily permeates futurological thinking, this would almost be inevitable. As I
demonstrated earlier in my analysis of prediction in the oil
industry, wherever else one might find diversity and individuality of thought and values, it is not in this realm. In fact,
all too often one comes across an outright hostility to a
diversity of values, or even to values per se. Tohru Moto-
oka, head of the Japanese Fifth Generation project, has
asserted: "[Fifth Generation computers] will take the place
of man in the areas of physical labor, and, through the in-
tellectualization of these advanced computers, totally new
applied fields will be developed, social productivity will be
increased, and *distortions in values will be eliminated*." (emphasis added)[18] Both the "institutionalization of values" and
the "elimination of distortions" in them reflect a rhetoric for
which modern prophecy is always striving—the rhetoric of
consensus, that cool-headed and benign posturing so valued
in politics and economics because it leaves no room for dissent or criticism. Although the prophet often assumes a
harsh, stern face when he is issuing a warning, his mask of
preference is the serene face in which ideology always prefers
to appear in public, the unassailably benevolent and impenetrable face of the rhetoric of consensus.

But the consequence of institutionalizing values, or, as Tohru Moto-oka would have it, eliminating distortions in them, is that the number of what may generally be regarded as "reasonable" courses of action is seemingly diminished. More than this, if you take the narrowing of reasonable choices together with the narrowing of the numbers of actors that can make these choices—both being trends that futurology promotes—you have a simple recipe for elitist domination. There is a saying among strategic planners in the private sector that captures this idea nicely. It has a marked predatory flavor which goes, "plan or be planned for."[19] If you do not make plans and get others to go along, then you will have to go along with the plans that they make for their own benefit and for *you*. If this sounds like a form of corporate Darwinism, it should. Many of Darwin's more elitist followers in the late nineteenth century were ardent futurologists. They believed in hastening the process of natural selection through selective breeding in the interests of the upper classes, much the same as Churchill predicted we would do through genetic engineering. They believed too in what another author has called "the arrival rather than the survival of the species."[20]

In this context, the scientism of futurology serves another function: it neutralizes the opposition which may exist in the mind of a public with different values by appealing to transcendent values, the values of science. What are these values? The Greeks of antiquity equated science, which was then part of philosophy, with the pursuit of the truth, and equated truth, in turn, with the good. This idea, easy to believe then and attractive even now, has been perpetuated to this day. It accounts for part of the prestige of science, even though most of it is based on its power rather than its association with virtue. But if there ever was an easy relationship between truth and good, it has been lost from science today. It is a commonplace that scientific knowledge can be used for either good or evil. There is nothing inherent in logic or reason that leads to goodness or virtue—we are all familiar by now with the adage that the same process that made Ford efficient at building cars made Hitler efficient at killing people. However, today many scientists skirt this issue by saying that science is beyond good and evil—a stance that is probably what led the German philosopher Jürgen Habermas to remark that "technocratic consciousness reflects not the sundering of an ethical situation, but the repression of 'ethics' as such as a category of life."[21] Again, there is no better rhetoric than the prophet's favorite rhetoric of consensus for repressing ethics. All ethical issues are immediately repressed as soon as consensus is assumed.

One of Buckminster Fuller's last books, *Critical Path*, even tried to make a virtue of the sundering of ethics. He begins it with the incredible assertion, "It is the author's working assumption that the words *good* and *bad* are meaningless." This statement he justifies by the following childish line of reasoning: "This is based on science and not on opinion. In 1922 physicists discovered a fundamental complementarity of disparate individual phenomena to be operative in physical Universe. This was fundamentally amplified with the subsequent discovery of the always-and-only-different, always-coexisting proton and neutron which, with their always-coexistent electrons, positrons, neutrinos, and antineutrinos, are eternally intertransformable." (emphasis in original)[22] Fuller's method of sundering ethics is to neutralize them by using the simple but silly device of an analogy to chemistry. In his analogy, good and evil are treated like chemicals, acid and base, which combine and lose their original properties and identity when simply placed together in the same vial. Much of the book from which this quotation was taken is also devoted to touting his own simple-minded ideas about how to save humanity through efficient design (see *ephemeralization* on page 91). But all of this is placed in the context of a dispassionate "scientific" view of the world as a sort of test-tube experiment—perhaps it works, perhaps not. God exists in this world (indeed Fuller refers to Him as if they have a special relationship) but Fuller would have us believe that God is indifferent to the outcome of the experiment.

However, if you usher values out the front door, they have a peculiar habit of sneaking in again through the rear, and naturally they make a reappearance even in Fuller's scheme. Though God is indifferent, Fuller reminds us that we must be *truthful* if we are to make it in this world, especially when we are programming computers: "The nearest each of us can come to God is by loving the truth. If we don't program the computer truthfully with all the truth and nothing but the truth, we won't get the answers that allow us to 'make it.' "[23] Even setting aside the anthropomorphism of such a statement, what could Fuller possibly have meant by entreating us to be *truthful* when we program computers? Surely he meant nothing as trivial as entering our symbols and figures as precisely as we can. That would be the kind of imperative to direct perhaps at schoolchildren, and Fuller's concerns seem to go well beyond that. His exhortation reminds one of a memorable passage in Hannah Arendt's famous essay on truth-telling called "Lying in Politics." I shall quote it at length because it makes some penetrating points about what truth-telling might mean, and why it is antithetical to the field of futurology.

> Unlike the natural scientist, who deals with matters that, whatever their origin, are not man-made or man-enacted, and that therefore can be observed, understood, and eventually even changed only through the most meticulous loyalty to factual, given reality, the historian, as well as the politician, deals with human affairs that owe their existence to man's capacity for action, and that means to man's relative freedom from things as they are. Men who act, to the extent that they feel themselves to be the masters of their own futures, will forever be tempted to make themselves masters of the past, too. Insofar as they have the appetite for action and are also in love with theories, they will hardly have the natural scientist's patience to wait until theories and hypothetical explanations are verified or denied by facts. Instead, they will be tempted to fit their reality—which, after all, was man-made to begin with and thus could have been otherwise—into their theory, thereby mentally getting rid of its disconcerting *contingency*. Reason's aversion to contingency is very strong; it was Hegel, the father of grandiose history schemes, who held that "philosophical contemplation has no other intention than to eliminate the accidental." Indeed, much of the

modern arsenal of political theory—the game theories and systems analyses, the scenarios written
for imagined "audiences" and the careful enumer-
ation of, usually, three "options"—A, B, C—
whereby A and C represent the opposite extremes
and B the "logical" middle-of-the-road solution of
the problem—has its source in this deep-seated
aversion. The fallacy of such thinking begins with
forcing the choices into mutually exclusive dilem-
mas; reality never presents us with anything so neat
as premises for logical conclusions. The kind of
thinking that presents both A and C as undesirable,
and therefore settles on B, hardly serves any other
purpose than to divert the mind and blunt the judgment from the multitude of real possibilities. What
these problem-solvers have in common with down-
to-earth liars is the attempt to get rid of facts and
the confidence that this should be possible because
of the inherent contingency of facts. (emphasis in
original)[24]

Arendt's implied point—that the same sort of mentality that
will make a person a certain kind of historian will also make
him or her a typical futurologist—is not just fanciful. Although historians can try to maintain their integrity by at
least trying to be faithful to the always too elusive "facts"
which make up their palette, both professions concern themselves with a theoretical mastery of action and of events over
time. Amazingly, some futurologists even regard themselves
as historians of a sort. Therefore, Daniel Bell, who is considered the intellectual's futurologist, has made the all too
clever assertion that while historians are concerned with *retrospective history,* futurologists are concerned with something he calls *prospective history.* In coining the phrase
prospective history to describe what futurologists do, Bell
seemed to be trying to legitimate futurology, which was then
a newer and more vulnerable field, by associating it with
conventional history. In his foreword to futurologist Burnham Beckwith's book, *The Next Five Hundred Years,* Bell
wrote: "While it may be startling to think of looking ahead
five hundred years, one realizes that the great historians have

always taken periods of several hundred years to identify and explain the major social processes which lay behind the course of civilizations and empires. It took several hundred years for Christianity to become accepted in the Western world. Five hundred years is a period one takes, as Gibbon did, to deal with the decline of the Roman Empire. Five hundred years is a normal unit in the history of ancient Egypt and certainly of classical China. What Professor Beckwith is doing is writing *prospective* rather than *retrospective* history. This is his claim to novelty." (emphasis in original)[25] Novelty is the futurologist's favorite word. Yet there is nothing novel about Bell's analogy at all—it is simply absurd. Here we have the clever gazer into time: at one moment he sets his time-telescope to gaze at a point five centuries earlier; then he merely flips it around one hundred and eighty degrees and gazes at events that will occur five centuries later. In fact, Bell's characterization of the futurologist's profession brings to mind a discussion that Alice had on the other side of the looking glass:

"The rule is, jam to-morrow and jam yesterday—but never jam *today*."

"It *must* come sometimes to "jam today," Alice objected.

"No, it can't," said the Queen. "It's jam every *other* day: Today isn't any other day, you know."

"I don't understand you," said Alice. "It's dreadfully confusing!"

"That's the effect of living backwards," the Queen said kindly: "it always makes one a little giddy at first—"

"Living backwards!" Alice repeated in great astonishment. "I never heard of such a thing!"

"—but there's one great advantage in it, that one's memory works both ways."

"I'm sure *mine* only works one way," Alice remarked. "I can't remember things before they happen."

"It's a poor sort of memory that only works backwards," the Queen remarked.

"What sort of things do *you* remember best?"
Alice ventured to ask.

"Oh, things that happened the week after next," the Queen replied in a careless tone.[26]

In a sense, Arendt's description of the historian's or politician's relationship with facts, with reality, is even more apt for the futurologist than for the historian, because when it comes to facts, futurologists have the freest hand of all—who, after all, shall come from the future to testify against them?—and the rhetoric of "consensus" can be employed by them with greater impunity than by anyone else. When futurologists paint their little inventories of "likely scenarios," one never finds them advocating one that, in the context which they are addressing, would likely be regarded as extreme. In this respect, they give the appearance of being as reasonable as Aristotle, who exhorts the man who would be happy to steer his course along "the golden mean." Aristotle, however, respected individuality and the contingency of facts enough to assert that this mean will be different for each and every person.

Of all of the futurologists around today, perhaps none has demonstrated a more childlike aversion to the contingency of facts than Yoneji Masuda in his vision of a future society which he calls "Computopia." All of the age-old ideals of a humanistic utopian society exist in his vision, except, unfortunately, for the humans themselves, in any form which even the optimists among us would easily recognize. Masuda's Computopia is a future society in which the use of computers would be maximized, not only for the purposes of saving labor and increasing productivity, but also to "enhance" social relations and decision-making. For example, political negotiating, and, ultimately, political decision-making would regularly, daily, be made by referenda using universalized computer networking. In Masuda's vision, somehow or other the mere permeation of society with computer technology would bring out the best in everyone. But should a poor soul falter or change his mind, there is still always coercion to bring him in line, and Masuda, like Kahn, paints this all too human trait into his vision in a self-righteous and paternalistic way:

Let us consider some examples of this type of group futurization. One such might be venture businesses with a *new type of management organization*. A number of people who share the same business goal, might, for example, get together and set up a business venture. With shared risk, each would become responsible, in the activities of the enterprise, for one's own particular field. One might undertake the responsibility of providing capital; another might contribute specialized knowledge and experience. Each would have equal rights of participants in management; income from the enterprise would be distributed according to the agreement between all members, and each would agree to share the responsibility in case of loss.

Notice that up to this point he is merely describing, with the aid of a moderate amount of jargon, the type of arrangement that might be made even at present in a limited partnership agreement. It is ever the futurologist's way to project mundane present-day phenomena into the future and mystify them by dressing them up in fancy language. But then what follows after this is good old-fashioned domination:

In this type of venture all positions would be decided by the agreement of all participants which means that even the chosen president would be subject to the authority of the whole group, and failure to improve the performance of the enterprise would mean dismissal from such office. And if, for example, it was found that working for the enterprise conflicted with one's individual futurization, leaving the enterprise freely would be the only option. To carry out the responsibilities undertaken for a fixed period with the agreement of all would be the prime duty of such a person, *who would not be able to quit before the term of office ended.* (emphasis added)[27]

I ended the last chapter by observing that the psychology of futurology largely entails a sort of petty mastery of the self which finally boils down to self-avoidance. In the ideology of futurology mastery is extended also to others; predicting the future is part of the process, also, of trying to dominate it. Language is the key tool in all of this because with language one can do anything: with words anything is possible, and in the realm of action, language is always in the vanguard, is always forward-looking, is always supreme.

But finally, even in the context of this mastery of others, we also find *avoidance* to be the persistent theme in the ideology of futurology: not avoidance of the self so much—the individual hardly comes into the picture here at all—but of the disconcerting facts and values that do not fit neatly into the self-promoting future picture. The Soviet Union, which used to make a fetish of its own peculiar kind of futurology, has been avoiding facts and values in its culture for decades with some extremely detrimental economic and social effects that are only now being faced squarely. Futurehype in the West is more subtle than the Marxist variety, and certainly not as institutionalized, but it has had, and continues to have, adverse effects in all sorts of areas of our culture (some of which will be examined in the next section of this book).

It is always questionable to subordinate present realities to theories about the future because such theories can never properly be tested by facts. But when, as is often the case with prediction, the theories turn out to be projects for self-promotion, or the promotion of an elite or interest group, we have a recipe for ineffectiveness at best, disaster at worst.

As the reader will learn in Chapter Four on futurehype in the military, ideology is not just a matter of words with no consequences. All of the fiercest trappings of ideology are vested, in the end, in the military, and the way they are played out there can decide the fate of a civilization in an extraordinarily short period of time.

NOTES

1. Winston Churchill, "Fifty Years Hence," in *Popular Mechanics* (March 1932), p. 397.
2. See, for example, Annie Vinokur, "Malthusian Ideology and the Crises of the Welfare State," in Turner, Michael, ed. *Malthus and His Time* (New York, St.

Martins Press, 1986). Also, John M. Sherwood, "Engels, Marx, Malthus, and the Machine," *American Historical Review,* (1985), vol. 90, no. 4.

3. Georgi Shakhnazarov, *Futurology Fiasco: A Critical Study of Non-Marxist Concepts of How Society Develops* (Moscow: Progress Publishers, 1982), p. 7. See also, I. Bestushev-Lada, "Bourgeois 'Futurology' and the Future of Mankind," in A. Toffler (ed.), *The Futurists* (New York: Random House, 1972).

4. Marx's scientific pretenses run through the greater part of his work—in fact they were so important to him that Engels saw fit to mention them (though not as *pretenses,* of course) in his graveside eulogy. Perhaps Marx's most famous and powerful statement of the *inevitable* nature of future developments is contained in his Preface to *Capital* where he wrote: "Intrinsically it is not a question of higher or lower degree of development of social antagonisms that result from the laws of capitalist production. It is a question of these laws themselves, or these tendencies *working with iron necessity towards inevitable results.* The country that is more developed industrially only shows, to the less developed, the image of its own future." (emphasis added) Likewise, his most famous utopian vision is to be found in *The German Ideology,* whereas the idea of the necessity for a transitional phase of "revolutionary dictatorship of the proletariat" is spelled out in *Critique of the Gotha Program.* Marx was not the only nineteenth-century utopian who sought to harness raw power to effect his transformation to utopia—but his advocacy of a centralized, party-dominated power made him part company with other nineteenth-century socialists, particularly the anarchists who found this idea repugnant and anathema to their own more individualistic ideals.

5. Along with his critique of futurology, George Orwell is also notable for having written about the politics of language, how language is used to obscure ideology. We are all familiar with how he did this in his fiction, but one of his most famous essays was also on this subject. In "Politics and the English Language" he wrote: "It [the English language] becomes ugly and inaccurate because our thoughts are foolish, but the slovenliness of our language makes it easier for us to have foolish thoughts. Modern English, especially written English, is full of bad habits which spread by imitation and which can be avoided if one is willing to take the necessary trouble. If one gets rid of these habits one can think more clearly, and to think clearly is a necessary first step towards political regeneration." ("Politics and the English Language," in *In Front of Your Nose,* New York: Harcourt Brace Jovanovich, 1968, p. 128.) The heart of Orwell's argument was that politicians often use difficult or unclear language in order to obscure the meaning of what they have to say since, were they to say it clearly, it would be obvious to anyone who was paying close attention that what they were hearing was "a mass of lies, evasions, folly, hatred and schizophrenia," to use his inimitable expression.

6. Yujiro Hayashi, "The Direction and Orientation of Futurology as a Science," International Future Research Congress, Oslo, September 12–15, 1967.

7. Ben Bova, "Future Phones," in *Omni* (February 1985).

8. R. Buckminster Fuller, "Comprehensive Design Strategy," in *World Resources Inventory,* Southern Illinois University, December 5, 1967.

9. Herman Kahn and Anthony J. Wiener, *The Year 2000* (New York: Macmillan, 1967).

10. Paul Hawken, *The Next Economy* (New York: Henry Holt and Co., 1984). Alvin Toffler invented a term called "prosumerism" to define the same concept in *The Third Wave* (London: Pan Books, 1981). Fortunately they have not yet had a dispute about concept ownership.

11. Alain Gras, *La Futurologie* (Paris: Collection Clefs, 1976), p. 29.

12. R. Buckminster Fuller, *Utopia or Oblivion* (New York: Bantam Books, 1969).

13. Daniel Bell, *The Coming of Post-Industrial Society* (New York: Basic Books, 1973).

14. Herman Kahn and B. Bruce-Briggs, *Things to Come: Thinking about the 70s and 80s* (New York: Macmillan, 1972), pp. 244–245.

15. Herman Kahn and Anthony J. Wiener, *The Year 2000* (New York: Macmillan, 1967).

16. Henk A. Becker and Joseph W.M. van Doorn, "Scenarios in an Organizational Perspective," in *Futures* (December 1987), p. 670.

17. Ivan Illich, *Deschooling Society* (New York: Harper and Row, 1971), p. 2.

18. Cited by Joseph Weizenbaum in "The Computer in Your Future," *New York Review of Books* (October 27, 1983), p. 59.

19. See Russell Ackoff, *Creating the Corporate Future: Plan or Be Planned For* (New York: John Wiley & Sons, 1981).

20. W.H.G. Armytage, *Yesterday's Tomorrows* (London: Routledge and Kegan Paul, 1968), p. 49.

21. Jürgen Habermas, "Technology and Science as Ideology," in *Toward a Rational Society: Student Protest, Science and Politics* (Boston: Beacon Press, 1970), p. 113.

22. R. Buckminster Fuller, *Critical Path* (New York: St. Martin's Press, 1981), p. ix.

23. Fuller, p. xxxvii.

24. Hannah Arendt, "Lying in Politics," in *Crisis of the Republic* (New York: Harcourt Brace Jovanovich, 1972), pp. 11–12.

25. Daniel Bell, Foreword to Burnham Beckwith, *The Next Five Hundred Years* (New York: Exposition Press, 1967), pp. v–vi.

26. Lewis Carroll, *Through the Looking Glass and What Alice Found There* (London: Macmillan, 1927), pp. 99–100.

27. Yoneji Masuda, *Computopia: Information Society as Post-Industrial Society* (Bethesda, Md.: World Future Society, 1981), p. 138.

4

FUTUREHYPE IN THE MILITARY

War is such a risky business that, in a way, it is a wonder that it is ever undertaken. Of course there have always been defensive wars, and the motives for undertaking them are not too difficult to comprehend. But a remarkable number of wars throughout history have been started on the basis of the far more questionable and far less rationally compelling motives of nationalist fervor, the competition between ideologies, imperialistic ambitions and the imputed evil nature of the enemy. Because of the often dire consequences of war, it takes an extraordinary state of mind to contemplate, prepare for and undertake warmongering and war-making that is based on these motives alone. Even before the advent of the atomic age, it was possible, with great will and effort, to decimate an entire civilization and an entire epoch of building during the course of a relatively short war—now, it is easy.

Therefore it requires an extraordinary deadening of some parts of the mind and spirit and an inordinate enliv-

ening of others to undertake war. To prudent people, who
will first consult their common sense and comfort, this mind-
set does not come easily, and sustaining it is no trivial matter.
The individual's natural reluctance to go to war can be overcome only with compulsion, in the form of a draft, or with
words, that is, with propaganda. In fact, in the business of
war prophets are the most accomplished of all propagandists,
the most powerful purveyors of the words that produce the
mind-set that makes war possible. The power of these prophets is a consequence of their claim that they can predict what
warriors most want to know: how things will turn out.

Throughout recorded history, warriors have been desperate for guidance about how their war undertakings will
turn out, and prophecy has often been the only "advice"
that has been forthcoming. In fact, the relationship between
prediction and military affairs has always been so strong that
it is safe to say that if futurology did not now exist, the
military, in its characteristically determined way, would
probably be trying to invent it.

In every age wars have been both started and conducted,
at least partly, and sometimes even wholly, on the basis of
prophecy. "Force is the midwife of Progress," wrote Marx,
and in our century many revolutionary wars have been
started on the basis of Marx's theory that violence is necessary to beget change. The two centuries of Crusades were
also started in part because of the pervasive millennial prophecy about the coming end of the world that permeated tenth-
to twelfth-century consciousness. The undertaking of these
wars was more or less considered to be unfinished business
that would hasten the return of the Messiah.

And when prophecy per se has not been one of the main
factors that has helped to instigate a war, there has often
been some grand political theory with a great prophecy built
into it. One way of understanding the influential domino
theory, the roots of which go back to the time of the Athenian
Empire of the fifth century B.C., is to think of it as a prediction that if you lose one allegiance now you will inevitably
lose all of the allegiances there are to lose at some point in
the future. This is the kind of reasoning that Athens used
to justify its imperial adventures of expansion and subju-

gation during the early stages of the Peloponnesian Wars when it had the upper hand.

The role of prediction in warfare was particularly evident in antiquity when the domino theory was first contrived, and when soothsayers, oracles and other sorts of prophets regularly played a prominent and often very public role in personal, social and political affairs. In fact, though war futurologists now sit in offices and sometimes work in large bureaucracies, in the ancient world warriors used to take their prophets out onto the battlefield with them—so they could then be appropriately held accountable for their advice right on the spot.

But thinking of the role played by prediction in the wars of antiquity brings to mind a certain irony: the first casualty of the Trojan War was not a man, not a warrior, but a woman—and she was a victim, not of the fighting, but of the prophecy that preceded it. The legend of King Agamemnon and his hapless daughter, Iphigenia, speaks volumes on the theme of prophecy in that war, and it also has a great deal to say about our own time: in many ways, it epitomizes the pathetic and pathological relationship between forecasting and fighting.

According to legend, before setting out for Troy all of the Greek ships assembled at Argos, the city in Sparta from which Helen had been taken by the Trojan prince, Paris. The Greek allies then proceeded to have their war council. However, just before they were about to set out for Troy, the seas began to storm without letup. Hindered and troubled by this development, Agamemnon, king of the Argives and leader of the expedition, consulted an oracle by the name of Calchas. This prophet said the storms were caused by the goddess Artemis and predicted that she would stop them and allow the ships to depart only if Agamemnon would sacrifice his daughter, Iphigenia, to her. This the king finally decided to do. On the pretext of marrying her to the hero Achilles, he summoned Iphigenia to the altar at the Bay of Aulis, where the ships had been assembled, and sacrificed his daughter to the goddess. The storms stopped and the ships set out for their famous and fateful war.

In considering the role of prophecy in human affairs,

this legend has all sorts of fascinating implications. Calchas's prophecy was typical of Greek predictions—and of many modern ones too—in that it was extremely ambiguous. Not only could it be interpreted in more ways than one, but it was cloaked in mysterious innuendo. After all, this prediction was not simply a set of marching orders: on the basis of the information which Calchas gave him, and faced with the prospect of having to slay his own daughter in order to go to war, Agamemnon could have decided that what Artemis was really trying to tell him by bringing on the storms was that the war was ill-advised and that he should call it off. That Artemis did not really want Iphigenia's life is suggested by the legend which says that, just before Agamemnon struck her, when he had averted his eyes so as not to have to see his knife pierce his daughter's neck, the goddess quickly substituted a deer in Iphigenia's place and spirited the girl away to the Island of Tauris, where she eventually established a cult with Iphigenia as high priestess. But in the end the king did choose to sacrifice his daughter so that he could go to war. Needless to say, this was not the first, nor would it by any means be the last time someone would decide to sacrifice a family member in order to be able to go off to fight one sort of war or another. The core of the legend still contains the idea that on the mere basis of an ambiguous prophecy a king was willing to sacrifice his daughter in order to be able to go to war.†

The Trojan War lasted ten years, and though the Greeks eventually won it there was an enormous amount of suffering on both sides of the battlefield and on the home fronts, not only for its duration but for a great many years afterwards. And yet, in spite of the havoc which they helped create, the oracles were continually consulted during the course of this long campaign, so unwilling were the warriors to rely on their own judgment.

Wars may be long or they may be short, but planning for them, which is now extremely dependent on forecasting,

---

† A similar legend, in inverted form, is found in the Bible. When Jephthah, a leader of the Israelites, was about to make battle with the Ammonites he made an oath to God that upon returning home he would sacrifice the first thing that he saw from his household if he won. Tragically, this turned out to be his daughter and the sacrifice was duly made (Judges 11).

is interminable. This has especially been true in heavily militarized states like the United States and the Soviet Union. Not only is planning carried on during the periods between the wars, but it continues at an ever more frantic pace during the conflict itself. During the course of a war, the desperate military mind hurls itself forward to the next battle. If hope is lacking, the warrior looks for it in the future; if things are already going well, he looks to the future for victory and more security. The whole point of this kind of thinking is, quite simply, to envision scenarios of future encounters with the enemy by asking some form of the following question: What will be the outcome if, at some point in the future on a certain battlefield, the men and arms at our disposal meet with those at the disposal of the enemy? From this question follows a related urgent question: What do we have to do now to ensure that things will go our way then? This kind of thinking is the beginning and the heart of all strategic and tactical thinking.

In a limited sense, up to the present era, forecasting has been a reasonable and worthwhile enterprise for the armies of the world. After all, the military specializes in "controlling" events, and where there is control, prophecy is more capable of self-fulfilment, and so prediction is more likely to be accurate. It is not difficult to make a case that what will happen to purposeful, disciplined and motivated men under arms is somewhat predictable. In a way, prediction is built into the nature of fighting. Engaging in battle is an exercise in forward motion: it is a desperate striving for a favorable future. Bullets, missiles and all types of military projectiles have points and direction; flesh and armor are permeable by these points; force, hardness, resistance, persistence and all of the basic variables of war are measurable factors. And, most important of all, on the occasion of battle men are acting on the basis of orders, on compulsion. Loyalty, devotion and *esprit de corps* are exacting taskmasters, and what these are lacking can often be made up for by fear and desperation. Independent thinking and random behavior, subversion and working at cross-purposes, though not unheard of, are not the norms of behavior for warriors. Ideally, and, to a great extent even practically, the purpose of the individual is therefore closely bound to, almost completely merged with, the purpose of the group and thus, ultimately, of the state. Under these circumstances, why not make predictions?

On the other hand, even in the ancient world, long before the advent of the present period of rapid and hectic technological innovation, at a time when one could more easily make the case that war-fighting variables were far fewer and more easily understood, we have examples of false prophecies based on gross miscalculations. One has only to recall the fierce pride and determination which attended the Athenian preparation for the campaign against Sicily in the Peloponnesian Wars to be chastened about listening to prophets. At that time, Athens was by all accounts, especially its own, the most culturally and technologically advanced city-state in Greece, and certainly the richest. The idea of starting an imperial war to expand its empire to include Sicily and ultimately all of Italy was therefore, at least in principle, not incredible when it was proposed. Predictions of the success of this campaign were accordingly made by ambitious Athenian warmongers of many political stripes. But in the end Athens was badly beaten by the Sicilians whose territory it invaded, and great numbers of Athenian soldiers were consequently drowned in a foreign harbor whose waters were colored red by their own blood.

Aside from the determination to fight off aggression, among the factors that contributed to the victory of the Sicilian city of Syracuse and its allies over Athens were innovations in naval technique and technology, innovations that were actually accomplished during the very course of battle. These innovations, along with the fierce Sicilian resistance, were factors the Athenian prophets had simply failed to predict. According to Thucydides, the historian of the Peloponnesian Wars, the innovations that the Syracusans effected were to shorten and reinforce the prows of their ships. They then set poles into them and used them for prow-to-prow charging and ramming against the Athenian ships. The Athenians' prows were weak since they were accustomed to coming alongside rather than fighting prow-to-prow.†

† On the other hand, to cite a recent example of a successful innovation on the part of an invader, the Israelis were very successful in using drones as decoys for the purpose of knocking out the Syrian surface-to-air-missiles in the war in Lebanon.

Naturally, the desirability of forecasting becomes even more compelling during periods of technical innovation, when new weapons and techniques are being introduced into the war-fighting equations. However, as we can see from the above example, when innovation is involved, forecasting may be even more questionable than it usually is because unknown variables are introduced into the equation in the form of untried and untested new techniques and technology. And, since neither side has a monopoly on this type of activity, results can go either way. Therefore, to the old questions—How many men will we have available when battle is engaged? With what weapons will we furnish them? How will we effect resupply and care for the wounded?—are added a second set of more imponderable ones. When will the new weapons be available? How well will they work? How long will it take to train our warriors to use them effectively? And, most important of all: How will they affect the outcome of the next encounter given an enemy who will also be very motivated to counter our innovations and perhaps even devise others of their own?

It is difficult for us to imagine today that the second set of questions relating to innovation are relatively new, but this is certainly the case. The written description of a future war has been a genre for over two hundred years, but early versions did not envision, and therefore did not even try to predict, the effects of technological innovation in weaponry. The very first description to appear in print was written by an anonymous author in England in 1763 and was called *The Reign of George VI, 1900–1925*.[1] Briefly speaking, it is no more than an idyll of conquest and pacification of Europe by a future King of England. But what is remarkable about it to our ears, which are so accustomed to hearing about new developments in weapons technology almost every day, is that in this prophecy all of the weapons and tactics of the eighteenth century were simply projected to the twentieth *with no change*.

To understand the mind-set that made this possible, we need to remember that this scenario was written before the onset of the Industrial Revolution: it simply did not occur to the author, conditioned by centuries of relatively little innovation in warfare, to imagine new and fantastic weapons coming into play to alter, perhaps decisively, the outcome of future battles. Therefore, in conjecturing about this future war, the second set of questions pertaining to innovation were not even asked.

Given the present rate of weapons innovation, it is impossible to imagine anyone today writing a "credible" scenario of a future war that did not include, did not in fact highlight, the decisive importance of some hitherto unused, perhaps even unheard of, wonderful new piece of weapons technology. The change in conditioning that makes the thinking of modern war futurologists so different from that of their ancestors of the mid-eighteenth century occurred gradually with the development of the Industrial Revolution from the late eighteenth to the late nineteenth century. But the new genre of future war scenarios, which depends so heavily on weapons innovation, was born rather dramatically when Sir George Chesney, then an undistinguished military engineer who was about to begin retirement, published a scenario called *The Battle of Dorking*. It first appeared in the May 1871 issue of *Blackwood's Magazine* and was later published as a book.

The Battle of Dorking was written at the dawn of the arms race based on innovative technology that began with the introduction of iron-clad ships and breech-loading artillery in the Franco-Prussian War of 1870 and has proceeded incessantly and at an ever more hectic pace ever since. It was the innovations of that war that inspired Chesney. Since the Franco-Prussian War had dramatically changed the power structure of Europe, Chesney's article, which envisioned a future war in which Germany would conquer England by using new fighting technology, was not merely a fanciful exercise. As the English historian I.F. Clarke has remarked, "*The Battle of Dorking* episode was much more than a major publishing event of 1871. It was undoubtedly the most remarkable propaganda piece that had appeared since the Junius Letters."[2]†

The whole purpose of this predictive scenario was to show how decisive arms innovation could be, and it worked

---

† The Junius letters were a series of anonymous letters which appeared in newspapers in England in the late eighteenth century and were famous because they typically assassinated the character of the leading political figures of the time.

more effectively than anyone, including the author, was able
to anticipate. *The Battle of Dorking* was very widely discussed and immediately reprinted in several different languages all over Europe. Naturally it was rapidly followed by
alternative scenarios that argued for more positive outcomes.
These alternative scenarios had titles such as: *After the Battle
of Dorking or What Became of the Invaders?*; *The Battle of
the Ironclads*; *The Cruise of the Anti-torpedo*; *What Happened after the Battle of Dorking or The Battle of Tunbridge
Wells*; *Mrs. Brown on the Battle of Dorking*; and, *Chapters
from Future History*.

   In short, Chesney's article set the psychological tone for
the whole period of war speculation that followed. As Clarke
has commented elsewhere: "These apprehensions of wars to
come, by their very number, must have sharpened expectations if they did not modify strategy . . . it became common
practice to describe imaginary defeats or victories in some
future period in order to demonstrate the need for appropriate reforms in the armed forces, or to advertise the ad-
vantages of the measures and policies they recommended."[3]
But beyond this psychological effect, it appears as if Chesney
also demonstrated a number of other things by writing this
article, some of them perhaps unintentionally. The main
thing that he proved was what an extraordinary effect the
combination of a new warfare technology and the existence
of a long-standing "enemy"—in this case Germany—could
have on the imagination of literate masses. With hindsight,
it is easy for us to understand why the population of Europe,
still reeling from the social and economic turmoil created by
the Industrial Revolution, would be so greatly impressed by
the prospect that similar dramatic developments might be
repeated on the battlefield. But more than this, as Clarke
observes, articles of this sort make such a profound impression because "they spring from the universal desire to see
the enemy as contemptible, inferior and already defeated.
. . . The greater the passion, the greater is the element of
nationalistic fantasy. . . . Hope and fear, a desire to teach
and to warn, are behind all these tales of future warfare."[4]

   Furthermore, whether he intended it or not, Chesney
also proved what a great vehicle for self-promotion being a
prophet at the right time can be. Being an oracle during

times of national anxiety is a great step on the road towards self-advancement, which in Chesney's case, not uniquely for a prophet, meant becoming a politician. A little over a year after he wrote *The Battle of Dorking* this obscure colonel, just returned to England and about to retire after a tour of duty in India, managed to get himself elected to the British House of Commons.

In our time, as in Chesney's, playing the role of oracle has similarly proven to be a good vehicle for promoting a political career. One only has to think back to the presidential debates between Richard Nixon and John Kennedy to call up images of two politicians trying to outprophesy one another. They both predicted—Kennedy, as it would turn out, with greater effect—that the Soviet Union would eventually outperform the United States both economically and militarily unless the United States acted quickly and decisively to accelerate her own development in these areas. The famous "missile gap," which would eventually turn out to be nonexistent, appears to have had the same effect in galvanizing the public in 1960 as did the "ironclad gap" in Chesney's *The Battle of Dorking* in 1871. However, since both candidates in the American election used much the same rhetoric, other factors came into play to decide its outcome.

In the early 1980s Robert McNamara, Kennedy's defense secretary, blamed the misperception upon which Kennedy had based his pre-election rhetoric on misinformation stemming from a competition between two camps in the military intelligence community—military intelligence is, of course, a prime commissioner and purveyor of military prophecy. He then went on to describe the profound effect, in the form of an arms build-up, that this misinformation ultimately had. McNamara said:

Go back to 1960 when many in the U.S. believed there was a missile gap favoring the Soviets. With hindsight it became clear there wasn't any missile gap. But Kennedy had been told there was. What actually happened was this: In the summer of 1960, there were two elements in the U.S. intelligence community disagreeing on the relative levels of the

U.S. and Soviet strategic nuclear forces. . . . One
element greatly overstated the level of the Soviet
nuclear force vis-à-vis the other element. The first
element had data which they believed justified their
interpretation. When one looked over it, it became
clear the data didn't justify the conclusion. And
within two years of that time, the advantage in the
U.S. warhead inventory was so great vis-à-vis the
Soviets that the Air Force was saying that they felt
we had a first-strike capability and could, and
should, continue to have one. If the Air Force
thought that, imagine what the Soviets thought.
And assuming they thought that, how would you
expect them to react?[5]

They reacted, of course, by building up their own supply of
warheads and developing systems for delivering them.

McNamara's statement succinctly summarizes the ongoing dynamics of the arms race and the role that prediction
plays in the policy that has promoted it. Since the beginning
of the nuclear arms race in 1949, we have had several imputed "deterrent gaps" in the form of nonexistent "missile
gaps" and "bomber gaps," and, when the public got tired
of hearing about gaps, they were transformed, during the
Reagan administration, into "windows of vulnerability," *The
Battle of Dorking* mentality looms large behind every proclamation of a gap and, as in the case described by McNamara
above, the result of this propaganda is usually a massive
arms build-up. In attempting to "catch up" with the enemy
each side inevitably surpass them, either in quantity, quality,
or both. However, except for the launching of the first un-
manned satellite, an innovation in which the Soviet Union
took the lead for only one year, the United States has consistently led the Soviet Union in military innovation (see
Table). Reporting on the congressional testimony of Malcolm R. Currie, a past director of defense research and engineering, Robert Aldridge, a former high-level nuclear
weapons engineer who now spends all of his time as a disarmament activist, has described this nuclear weapons
rainbow-chasing in the following terms: "Currie's perspective conveniently slipped back and forth between present

Comparison of US-USSR
Technological Developments

	U.S.	U.S.S.R.
First deployed tactical nuclear weapons in Europe	1954	1957
First ICBM flight	1958	1957
First satellite in orbit	1958	1957
Acquired low penetrating bomber	1959	1975
Acquired supersonic bomber	1960	1975
Deployed solid propellant in missiles:		
SLBMs	1960	1977†
ICBMs	1962	1968
Placed satellites in geosynchronous orbit	1963	1974
Put MRVs on missiles:		
tested	1963	1968
operational	1964	1973
Put penetration aids (chaff and decoys) on missiles	1964	not to date
High speed reentry vehicles:		
tested	1968	1973
operational:	1970	1975
Put MIRVs on missiles:		
tested	1968	1973
operational:		
ICBMs	1970	1975
SBMs	1971	1978
Developed stellar inertial guidance (SIG)	1969–70	1972–73
Put on-board computers on missiles	1970	1975
Number of foreign military bases	hundreds	few

† Deployed 12 SS-N-17 SLBMs on one Yankee class submarine only.

From Robert Aldridge, *First Strike!*, 1983. The table illustrates the hectic pace of nuclear weapons innovation that has characterized the arms race for over thirty years. It is remarkable that the modern arms race began with the introduction of ironclads and breechloaders in the Franco-Prussian War which ended in 1871. The weapons have changed but the *Battle of Dorking* mentality which predicts victory in future wars through the introduction of new weapons technology has remained essentially the same.

and future tense to accommodate his preordained conclusions. When looking at the U.S. forces he spoke in the present tense of our inability to launch a preemptive first strike in an open society. But when referring to the Soviets he alluded to what may be possible at some future date and used that as evidence that the Soviets are upsetting some perceived stability in the nuclear balance. On this basis he argued that we need even more sophisticated weapons, thereby upsetting the current balance, in order to 'restore' a balance that might be upset by the Soviets at some future time."[6] How did we get into this rut of madly dashing towards the future in order to close fictitious gaps? One has to go to the beginning of the nuclear arms race to understand what is going on here; one has to look at the development of an illusion called "limited nuclear war."

After the United States dropped atomic bombs on Hiroshima and Nagasaki, World War II came to an abrupt and dramatic ending with the unconditional surrender of Japan. To most observers the atomic bomb appeared, quite rightly, to be the most revolutionary innovation in weapons technology in the history of mankind. And, as had been true in the wake of previous revolutionary developments, the prophets came out in number predicting its consequences for future wars.[†] The power of atomic bombs was so incredible that former soldiers did not even attempt, as Chesney had done, to describe scenes on the battlefields of the future. Instead, they focused on the aftermath of future wars, what the world would be like after a war with "the bomb." They thus became gloomy existentialists, brooding about the dark side of human nature and writing warnings in the form of depressing post-war scenarios like Nevil Shute's *On the Beach* and Aldous Huxley's *Ape and Essence*. Unfortunately, given their characteristically pragmatic bent, for a variety of reasons the

[†] After Alfred Nobel invented nitroglycerine in 1860 he predicted that, because its effects were so devastating, this would mean the end of wars forever. Similarly, in 1864 when lighter-than-air balloons were coming into their own, the famous novelist Victor Hugo wrote to his friend Nadar, a celebrated balloonist, that this meant the end of all war because balloons would effectively abolish all national boundaries—as if the boundaries themselves were the cause of wars.

soldiers were obliged to leave policy formulation and imagining what future wars would be like to abstract thinkers in government and private agencies. As one American historian has observed: "Current U.S. Strategic theory was thus born of a marriage between the scientist and the accountant. The professional soldier was jilted."[7]

What did these "scientists and accountants" who wrote prophetic military policy papers come up with? In 1945, when the United States had a monopoly on the atomic bomb, the mainstream of prognostication of its effects on future wars was, quite simply, that it would abolish them entirely. The destructive capacity of these weapons was widely understood even then to be so great that only a few would be needed to inflict enormous damage and, no matter how many one side delivered, it was thought that the enemy would also manage to deliver the few that were necessary to inflict what military theorists euphemistically call "unacceptable damage." The conventional wisdom that followed from this understanding was that if these weapons of mass destruction could not be abolished entirely they should be maintained at equal levels on both sides in order to create a stalemate. This was the theory of mutual deterrence, plain and simple, that was strongly argued by a group of academics at Yale in a book called *The Absolute Weapon*. And this was also the vision of Robert Oppenheimer who, in a famous article for the November 24, 1945, edition of *Saturday Review,* predicted that "in a world of atomic weapons wars will cease."[8]

Oppenheimer's vision, and that of the Yale academics, was also publicly echoed during his first term by President Eisenhower, who promoted it with the slogan, "there is no alternative to peace." As it turned out, however, just as Augustus had to contend with a rival school of prophecy led by Lentulus (see Chapter Three), a rival school of thought about the future of war began to develop by the end of the 1940s.

P.B.S. Blackett, a distinguished British physicist, contributed a great deal to what might be called the "verbal taming" of atomic bombs in a book he published in 1949 called *Fear, War, and the Bomb*. In this book he compared atomic bombs with conventional bombs simply, and solely, on the basis of explosive power. Noting that the U.S. Strategic Bombing Survey which had been conducted shortly after the war had demonstrated that conventional bombing had had little effect until the very end, on either German war production or morale, he argued that atomic bombs, with comparable explosive power, would also not be decisive in winning future wars between the great powers. In short, he predicted that nuclear bombing would be survivable, and therefore nuclear wars of the future, like other kinds of war, would be winnable providing one were willing to persist and follow through with conventional methods of occupation.

The idea that nuclear war would not necessarily lead to Armageddon, could be limited and was, in fact, winnable, was taken up and promoted in America as a justification for planning limited nuclear wars in the future as an alternative to "peace with no alternative." Many so-called cold warriors promoted this idea in the mid-1950s, but probably the most notable among these were the members of a study group in the Council on Foreign Relations, a private citizens' advisory group, which included a variety of people from different fields, among them such prominent future politicians as McGeorge Bundy, Henry Kissinger and Paul Nitze.

Their work should be understood in context: 1956 was, of course, an election year and some Democrats were trying to make political hay, just as Kennedy would in his debate with Nixon four years later, by taking Eisenhower to task for being "soft on Communism." Typically, one of the things they talked about then was what would turn out to be a fictitious "bomber gap." And, that year, in the January and April issues of the Council's influential policy journal *Foreign Affairs*, Paul Nitze and Henry Kissinger published what would eventually become seminal articles promoting their ideas about how, under certain circumstances, we could plan on having *limited* nuclear wars in the future.†

Bearing in mind the ideological basis for the arms race, it should be noted that Kissinger's point of departure was

---

† Kissinger at this time had not yet chosen his final political affiliation and was yet to work, in a minor capacity, for President Kennedy before finally becoming a Republican. He joined the study group late in its deliberations and came on board for the purpose of writing up their ideas. The year after the seminal article he published what was essentially the final report of this study group, his book called *Nuclear Weapons and Foreign Policy*, which became a bestseller and bible for cold warriors.

an ideological one: he began by questioning Eisenhower's proclamation, "there is no alternative to peace," by calling it not a policy but a "dilemma." He then went on to set the stage for his alternative perspective with a bit of the prophet's characteristic mystification, noting that "It is paradoxical, however, that so much hope should concentrate on man's destructive capabilities."[9] And then he continued in the characteristic manner of the oracle, as Clarke says, to teach and to warn: "If the phrase 'there is no alternative to peace' were to become accepted doctrine, it could lead only to a paralysis of policy."[10]

Before examining Kissinger's prescriptions in greater detail, it is instructive, by way of contrast, to compare his argument thus far with the one made earlier by Oppenheimer and the authors of *The Absolute Weapon*. As far as Oppenheimer was concerned, atom bombs, by their very nature, were too destructive to be used for "limited" purposes in any normal sense of this word. He wrote:

> There are people who say that they are not such very bad weapons. Before the New Mexico test we sometimes said that too, writing down square miles and equivalent tonnages and looking at the picture of a ravaged Europe. After the test we did not say it any more. Some of you will have seen photographs of the Nagasaki strike, seen the great steel girders of factories twisted and wrecked; some of you may have noticed that these factories that were wrecked were miles apart. Some of you will have seen pictures of the people who were burned, or had a look at the wastes of Hiroshima. That bomb at Nagasaki would have taken out ten square miles, or a bit more, if there had been ten square miles to take out.[11]

This was a very compelling argument against using nuclear bombs, especially coming, as it did, from the man who was known as the father of the atomic bomb, but Kissinger's rejoinder to it was typical of modern prophets who are enchanted by a recent technical innovation into thinking it will in the future solve a host of problems, even non-technical problems of incredible magnitude. The gist of Kissinger's argument was that the age of absolute nuclear weapons was basically over because the bombs that had been dropped on Hiroshima and Nagasaki were now "obsolete." There had been a new innovation, small nuclear bombs, "nuclear weapons of low yield" as he called them, and they could be safely used in a "limited nuclear war." And, continuing in Blackett's vein, he proclaimed: "A distinction based on the difference between nuclear weapons and 'conventional armaments' is no more fruitful. Apart from the fact that the distinction becomes increasingly nebulous as we develop nuclear weapons of very low yield, *it will be impossible to reverse present trends. The very existence of nuclear armaments on both sides seems to insure that any future war will be nuclear.*" (emphasis added)[12] And then he concluded: "If we build our whole strategy around 'absolute' weapons of megaton size, professions of limited objectives will be meaningless and any use of nuclear weapons is likely to touch off an all-out war. The possibility of keeping a limited nuclear war limited depends on our ability to extend the range of low-yield weapons of a kiloton and below, and to devise tactics for their utilizations on the battlefield."[13]

It is impossible to tell whether or not Kissinger's emphasis on the importance of technological innovation in policy-making was disingenuous, because he vacillated in the statements he made about the importance of technology for determining theory and policy. In 1960 he evidently believed in technological determinism when he predicted: "Every war henceforth will be nuclear to a greater or lesser extent, whether or not nuclear weapons are used."[14] Kissinger's argument at that time was simply that all future wars will be nuclear just because the potential for using nuclear weapons will always exist. However, in later years, having already contributed through his writing to promoting technological dependency, he appears to have changed his mind and proceeded to deemphasize technology. For example, in 1965 he wrote: "Strategy henceforth cannot confine itself to expertise in designing weapons systems, but must involve a close understanding of the opponent's calculations."[15] So in the end, if he did not always wholeheartedly believe in technological determinism, he certainly seems to have had a great deal of confidence in the ability of American leaders to understand and calculate the behavior of their enemies, to control it with threats of nuclear war and even to use nuclear war itself in "limited" doses.

In any case, after their introduction by the United States in 1954 and the Soviet Union in 1957, the small nuclear warheads upon which Kissinger based his calculations have naturally proliferated greatly on both sides. Today they represent perhaps the most unstable element in the constellation of nuclear weapons systems: because of their number; because they are, in certain cases, interchangeable with conventional weapons; and because their use is in some cases subject to the discretion of local commanders. And, as the physicist Freeman Dyson has observed, whenever computer simulations of battles are run using these weapons, the scenario always ends in chaos and utter destruction.[16]

Paul Nitze also shared Kissinger's view that the technical problems of fighting nuclear wars would be manageable, if not now, then at least at some point in the future. For example, with respect to one particularly touchy "technical problem," the close proximity of civilian population centers to nuclear installations, he wrote: "Is it possible to draw a distinction between industrial and population centers and air-atomic bases? Such a distinction presents real difficulties, but the importance of overcoming them is so great that it should be possible to do so."[17] It is extraordinary how strongly Nitze believed that, given sufficient necessity, any problem could be overcome. It is only because he was talking abstractly about the future that he could maintain such conviction. Were he discussing a persistently intractable matter of the present, it would have been much more difficult for him to make a case for such boundless faith. How could he argue, for example, that just because there is a compelling necessity to discover a cure for AIDS that a cure will in fact be discovered?

Given the enormous destructive capacity of nuclear weapons, and the desirability of using them only on soldiers and not civilians, Nitze's point of departure and emphasis was somewhat different from Kissinger's at this time. Instead of emphasizing the role that new technology would play in controlling and limiting future nuclear wars, Nitze placed

great emphasis on technique. But the technique that he promoted in his *Foreign Affairs* article was not battlefield technique but psychological calculation, the use of words to limit
wars. He noted, quite rightly, that words, especially the
words of belligerents, are ambiguous. Accordingly, he advocated developing a great deal of precision in talking to the
enemy so that they would have no doubt about our intentions
to keep these wars limited, and would likewise behave in
appropriate, self-limiting ways. His main point was very reasonable as far as it went: it was that our "declared" policy
(that is, our propaganda), and our "action policy" (what we
would actually try to do in the event that we started to fight),
should be as near to one another as possible so that the
enemy would always know exactly what we are up to and
what to expect.

Actually, both Nitze's and Kissinger's articles are full
of psychological techniques that were designed to ensure that
nuclear wars would, in fact, be limited. But not all of these
were to be directed at the enemy. The last two of three that
Kissinger mentions later in summing up his first paper are
self-directed psychological techniques. Echoing Herman
Kahn he wrote that we, that is, *our leaders,* must develop
"the ability to create a climate of opinion in which national
survival is not thought to be at stake in every issue," and
that our leaders should also develop "the ability to keep
control of public opinion should a disagreement arise over
whether national survival is at stake." In this vein he also
declared: "We cannot afford even the implication that nuclear weapons are in a special category, apart from modern
weapons in general, for this undermines the psychological
basis of the most effective United States strategy." In short,
in order to make these scenarios of future nuclear wars seem
plausible, Kissinger argued that politicians must learn to control not only the behavior of their strategists and those of
the enemy, but also the way the home front thinks about
such wars so that leaders would not be hindered in their
actions. And, in the end, this great exercise of control is
made possible, made reasonable, because somehow or other
it is exercised under the rubric of the then fashionable mental
artifacts called "game rules." He concluded: "The fact remains that the most fruitful area for current strategic thought

is the conduct and efficacy of limited nuclear war, the 'war gaming' of situations in which nuclear weapons are used by *both* sides, and a consideration of what would constitute victory in such a war."[18]

Considering their enormous influence, what is most re-markable about both Kissinger's and Nitze's scenarios is how calculating they thought one could be given the subject mat-ter with which they were dealing. They seem to have both set and reflected the tone of excessive abstraction, all in the name of rationality, which has come to characterize nuclear strategic thinking. Both of their articles are peppered with pronouncements of what would be the "rational" way to fight such wars. However, when they do get down to psy-chology, the realm where the irrational side of human nature might also come into play, we have only the most impov-erished psychology imaginable: the psychology of the ad-man and the modern business manager who avails himself of "gamesmanship" to prognosticate the outcome of market strategies. There are any number of psychological elements that should have been included in their visions in order to properly take into account the irrational side of human na-ture, a natural part of all wars. But missing from this psy-chology most conspicuously are not only a theory of aggression, aside from what is implied by self-interest, but also any theory of relationships aside from the mechanical ones contained in gamesmanship. Missing, too, are two other bulwarks of modern psychology which reflect the irrational side of human nature—the love-wish and the death-wish.

To his credit, assuming he was being sincere and not just cheering on the latest trend, four years after his paper was published in *Foreign Affairs,* Kissinger published an ar-ticle in which he largely repudiated what he had said earlier.[19] He did not however repudiate the idea of using force to gain political objectives, but simply declared that, in spite of all of the calculating with weapons and with words, things might get out of hand in a nuclear war anyway. There had already been war games to suggest the latter, but above all some logistical problems had come to his attention which he had not foreseen and factored into his own abstract war-fighting equations. These included military infighting among the var-ious branches of the U.S. armed forces branches (for some reason each branch of the U.S. military had its own pet theory about how to use these new small atomic bombs), the growth of the Soviet stockpile, and the long-range impact of arms control negotiations, all of which posed perhaps insurmountable problems for calculating and controlling the next war.

It was, perhaps, commendable that Kissinger should back off, at least formally, from championing an idea that he had worked so hard to promote, and this entire policy-propagating episode would now have no more interest than a historical footnote if his repudiation had been the end of the matter. It was not. Ideas have a life of their own, even bad ideas which are occasionally more or less disowned by their author. In fact, these ideas often have the unfortunate habit of getting worse with age: unanticipated conditions develop; other, perhaps less subtle minds take the ideas up; they become institutionalized and thus develop substance and meaning even more flawed than the original wrong-headed idea. As Hannah Arendt has observed in her essay "On Lying," the danger is that one eventually begins to believe one's own propaganda—if indeed propaganda is what it was originally meant to be. In any event, the idea of fighting limited nuclear wars worked its way into strategic thinking over the years and, far from fading away, eventually became an official part of U.S. military policy when President Carter signed Presidential Directive 59 (PD-59) a few months before he left office at the end of 1980.† By then, however, the Kissinger-Nitze calculus had worked its way into thinking and planning not only for limited nuclear wars with battle-field weapons, but also general nuclear wars using strategic weapons. It became the basis of the so-called nuclear war-*fighting,* as opposed to *deterring,* mentality.

Some of the circumstances attending the signing of PD-59 are worth mentioning because they reveal a great deal about the persistence of overly abstract thinking on the high-est levels of policy formulation and future war prediction. When PD-59 percolated up to Carter's desk from the De-fense Department eighteen months before he finally signed

† This directive changed official policy so that weapons would be used for fighting as well as for deterrence.

it, he equivocated about whether or not to go ahead with endorsing it. Even though others, besides Nitze and Kissinger, had made attempts to undermine it ever since the invention of the bomb, simple deterrence based on mutually assured destruction had been the only official doctrine up until then, and PD-59 represented the enshrinement of these war-fighting elements in that doctrine. So, by way of postponing his decision, Carter asked the Defense Department to commission certain "studies" to flesh out and legitimate this policy directive. There were a number of different "studies" commissioned for this purpose. One consulting firm, called the Analytic Assessment Corporation (ANASMC) of Marina Del Rey, California, was commissioned to "determine the nuclear weapon employment strategy that would eliminate the USSR as a functioning national entity . . . bring about the collapse of the government that now exists." Another firm in Vienna, Virginia, was asked to calculate "the viability of employing strategic nuclear weapons to achieve regionalization of the Soviet Union," as well as "strategic targetting against Soviet leadership."[20] Eliminate their leadership, destroy their government, repackage their national identity—simple objectives for future wars. These were the "limited" political objectives which by 1980 were to be solved by the now not so "limited" nuclear wars that were then being planned.

Most of this thinking was summarized by two disciples of Nitze and Kissinger, Colin Gray and Keith Payne, in a much-quoted paper which appeared in *Foreign Policy* just before Carter signed PD-59.[21] Their language and thinking are so similar to that of their mentors that one wonders why they were never sued for plagiarism. They wrote: "If American power is to support U.S. foreign policy objectives, the United States must possess the ability to wage nuclear war rationally."[22] But they carried the Kissinger doctrine even further when they declared: "To advocate LNOS (Limited Nuclear Options) and targeting flexibility and selectivity is not the same as to advocate a war-fighting, war-survival strategy,"[23] and concluded, apparently drawing from the think-tank scenarios that were commissioned by President Carter: "The USSR, with its gross overcentralization of authority epitomized by its vast bureaucracy in Moscow, should be highly vulnerable to such an attack. The Soviet Union might cease to function if its security agency, the KGB, were severely crippled. Judicious U.S. targeting and weapon procurement policies might be able to deny the USSR the assurance of political survival."[24]

What is most striking about the Gray and Payne doctrine, and very much in keeping with the Nitze-Kissinger doctrine, is its simplistic view of Soviet nationhood and society. The notion that the United States might be welcomed as liberators if they annihilated about twenty million Soviet citizens (Gray and Payne's estimate of the size of the so-called ruling elite) and largely destroyed the Russian economy is simply too fatuous to be taken seriously as insightful prophecy, but it certainly does speak volumes about the American military establishment's willingness in its collective prophetic mind to trivialize the integrity of Soviet nationhood.

In fact, this thinking is reminiscent of the prophetic fantasies that were being printed during the post–*The Battle of Dorking* period. The irony of this is particularly striking if one considers that in a French play published around the same time as Chesney's article, *The Invasion of England: A Prophecy in Two Acts,* one of the invading Frenchmen is made to say to the appreciative natives that have gathered round, "Englishmen! Now is your time to destroy the British Government which has caused all your misfortunes, desolated your neighbors, and set Europe on fire. It is time that the fate of the people should no longer depend on the caprice of an individual."[25] Substitute Russia for England in this passage, and Payne and Gray might have used it in their own prophecy.

The tendency to underestimate and caricature the enemy is typical of the thinking of futurologists, and is just another way in which they often tend to trivialize problems of every sort by projecting them into the future. If one is going to assume that a massive attack on the Soviet Union, if successful, will result in the attackers being welcomed as liberators, then one may as well also assume that certain "technical difficulties," like the close proximity of residential and military developments which Nitze was concerned about in developing his nuclear war scenarios, will undoubtedly also be solved. But nothing is more simple-minded in all of this than the enchantment with the so-called rationality of this most irrational of all enterprises.

When speaking publicly of PD-59, Harold Brown, Carter's defense secretary, justified this major alteration in official policy as being a mere adjustment to developments in the weapons procurement process, a supposedly rational accounting endeavor. Apparently, the number of strategic warheads had reached such a high level that the strategists had run out of targets. Another way of understanding PD-59, maintained Brown, was to think of it as merely offering a sort of release valve for targeting congestion. With this new policy, the new warheads that were coming on board could be targeted to suit the newly created military purposes not only to deter but to fight and win a nuclear war. No matter that the old warheads could just as easily be retargeted for this purpose, if the frightful occasion should ever arise. No matter that the two systems taken together were even more redundant than the system of deterrence based on mutually assured destruction alone had been. By a stroke of the pen, military planners could now plan two different kinds of nuclear wars at once, all the while protesting that they would probably only fight when provoked. And weapons procurement in this most "rational" system turned out to have been possessed of less rationality than a simple bucket brigade, which at least knows how to stop passing water when the fire is out.†

Since the recent arms reduction agreements have reduced the massive arsenals on both sides and, more importantly, eased up the horrifying dance of death between the United States and the Soviet Union, in some ways it is hard to imagine what our prophet-cum-policy-makers of the 1950s were thinking when they started putting into place all of

† The peacetime process of weapons procurement is riddled by innumerable irrationalities of other sorts. Perhaps most notable of all are procurements which tend to produce instability. One must remember that due to either a breakdown of interdepartmental communication or someone's malign intent, in the late 1970s, contrary to official policy, new weapons systems were coming on board that undermined the stability that is necessary for deterrence to work. (See Deborah Shapley, "Congress Seeks New Approach to Arms Control," in *Science*, February 9, 1979.)

their abstract nuclear war-fighting systems to fight the future nuclear war. At first glance it appears as if they were simply acting very impressionably—as their nineteenth-century predecessors had done in the war predictions business—on the possibilities which they believed were opened up by technological innovation. They also seem to have been characteristically very impressed by extremely abstract assessments of the situations they were confronting, and by their own rather worshipful approach to the power of reason. Reason, they believed, in spite of all history and practical experience, would continue to operate not only to avoid fighting, but even to control the situation once battle was already engaged. But one must also appreciate other more concrete conditions which may have inspired them. The war in Korea had recently been concluded—on an unsatisfactory basis as far as the American Right was concerned—and there was a great deal of talk of America's position in the world being "nibbled away" by the Soviet Union. Stalin's memory also loomed large then, and served well past his death as a symbol and constant reference point with which ideologues could caricature the Soviet leadership and the Soviet system. An ever present, supposedly implacable enemy; discontentment with how things had gone in the past; the promise of technological innovation: all of the icons that war prophets like to worship were abundantly present.

Another way of trying to understand their thinking is to bear in mind the old saying that soldiers are always prepared to fight their last war, the one which, with hindsight, they understand so well. Certainly the nuclear part of World War II—the bombing of Hiroshima and Nagasaki—could, on a certain level, inspire admiration and a desire to copy among leaders on the victorious side. After all the misery that had preceded it, the final phase of the war with Japan presented the Allied soldiers, after the testing of the bomb at Los Alamos, with a rather attractive situation: one side, America and her Allies, was in a position of almost complete control, the prophets favorite fantasy. Perhaps all of the postwar reasoning—with weapons and with words—concerning the nature of possible future nuclear wars has been no more than an attempt to recapture that moment in the past.

But perhaps more important than this consideration is

the fact that American isolationism was particularly strong right after the war. America had entered World War II reluctantly, and compared to the Russians had demobilized very rapidly as soon as it was over. This isolationism naturally fed the desire of some western leaders on both sides of the Atlantic that America help defend Europe against the perceived threat from Russia, but without at the same time acting as an army of occupation. One can almost see the attraction that tactical nuclear weapons represented to these naive and essentially technologically romantic but non-adept admirers of new military technology. Small-scale nuclear weapons appeared to them to be an elegant solution to all of the problems just mentioned: they represented the ability to fight a large standing army, like that of the Soviet Union, with a much smaller one. From the American perspective, this could be done almost by remote-control; by using these weapons America could do battle without directly risking its own people or nation. And finally, nuclear armaments were relatively inexpensive by then, and much cheaper to procure and maintain than huge standing armies—a consideration that was bound to have a broad appeal in a fiscally conservative administration like Eisenhower's.

In Chapter Two on the psychology of futurology, I noted that one can aptly apply to modern prophecy the Heisenberg principle, which states that you cannot observe a phenomenon without altering it; when you observe it, you are interfering with it whether you realize it or not, and therefore cannot claim to be viewing it with perfect objectivity. This principle should be magnified a thousand times for politics. The self-delusion of the cold warriors on both sides can hardly be exaggerated; whatever so-called objective facts the cold warriors of the 1950s may have pointed to in order to justify their policies, eventually they themselves became the most important factor in the belligerent confrontation between East and West—and a condition about which, needless to say, they could not even begin to become objective. But worse than this, if the maintenance of peace was ever really their aim—the epithet "cold warrior" is, after all, not one of their own choosing—their methods were extraordinarily self-defeating. The thickety jargon of these bedazzled prognosticators of future wars is really not that difficult to master, but as has often been said, it does numb the senses by mystifying a horrifying situation. Furthermore, it lends an air of mystery, mastery, science and rationality—all of the futurologist's arsenal—to a business which all ordinary people who are destined to fight and die know to be basically irrational and unpredictable.

During the decade of the American chapter of the war in Vietnam there were innumerable instances when reason was made to wither in the face of unpredictability; but these lessons seem to have been to no avail.† One of the most dramatic of these instances was reported by William Shawcross who, in writing about an early incident in the bombing of Cambodia, quotes one of the officers as saying, "We had been told, as had everybody . . . that these carpet bombing attacks by B-52 [were] totally devastating, that nothing could survive, and if they had a troop concentration there it would be annihilated. . . . We were told . . . that if there was anybody still alive out there they would be so stunned that all [we would] have to do [was] walk over and lead him by the arm to the helicopter." The American army then proceeded to do their worst, blitzing the area with a virtual blanket of bombs. But in the end they vastly overestimated the effect that their bombing would have and the effect of all of this devastating bombing was only to rile up the enemy, "to serve as taking a beehive the size of a basketball and poking it with a stick. They [the Viet Cong] were mad."[26]

Military futurology both reflects our obsession with trying to perfect the calculability of the incalculable and epitomizes the destructive, destabilizing, and paralytic role that futurology generally plays in human affairs. Because so much of our effort has been going into perfecting increasingly destabilizing weapons systems for the battlefields of the future, we have been unable properly to attend to the needs of the present, both for peace and for warfare of the conventional type. A few years ago Senator Sam Nunn conducted congressional hearings about a widely recognized crisis in America's

† Much of the same can be said of both the Israeli war in Lebanon and the war between Iran and Iraq, both of which were ostensibly started for limited objective purposes: Israel was trying to clean up its northern border of terrorist activity, and Iran wanted to change the Iraqi leadership for one more sympathetic to her own religious fundamentalist ambitions.

conventional forces: the acute shortage of ammunition.[27]
This issue was raised at a number of meetings of the Atlantic
Council which I attended in 1986, and the accepted explanation from the well-informed and high-ranking military men
present was that all of the money has been going into developing the weapons systems of the future, and therefore
there has not been enough to supply the weapons of the
present. The unspoken fact is, of course, that the armed
forces naturally do not feel inclined to purchase ammunition
for guns that will soon be obsolete.† To the extent that this
explanation is true, it implies that we cannot fight with conventional weapons any battles that are imposed upon us in
the present because we are preparing only to fight the wars
of the future. In any present battle we will quickly run out
of bullets and then be forced to resort to nuclear arms,
whether we want to use them or not.‡ In any case, in the
recent arms reduction negotiations the West's lack of conventional preparedness has persistently been cited as an important reason for not going along with Soviet proposals for
arms reduction.

  "No alternative to peace" may seem paralyzing to certain politicians—as it certainly did to Kissinger and his colleagues in 1956—but that is probably because at that time
the West was still so close to World War II and the Korean
War that we were no longer used to peace, in the sense that
we still had not learned to maneuver effectively within its
very broad "confines." Over thirty years after Kissinger
wrote his influential paper, in the future he was trying to
anticipate, the irony, of course, is that nothing has proven
to be more paralyzing than the arms race which he helped

† Richard Gabriel, a prominent military critic, has also argued that the munitions
shortage is due to logistical problems caused by an inefficient, infighting and top-
heavy military bureaucracy. This explanation is not, of course, mutually exclusive
with the one cited above, but actually complements the one I have most often
heard. If the United States does indeed decide to switch to a conventional rather
than nuclear deterrence, this inconsistency may continue to be a problem.
‡ Another theory holds that we are purposely keeping our stocks of conventional
ammunition low to tyrannize the enemy with the threat of imminent nuclear war
should they wish to fight one using conventional weapons, with which they will
supposedly be superior. If this is true, it is an institutionalized form of Dulles's
"brinkmanship" or Nixon's "mad dog theory of diplomacy," and in any case represents just another form of pretense with respect to being able to understand and
to calculate the opponent's every move.

to promote. The freedom that he and other cold warriors were trying to preserve has been severely undermined by the very methods they promoted. In the world that their thinking helped create, or at least perpetuate, until recently the choices for the leaders of both East and West were increasingly limited, to the point that they could choose only between one weapons system and another. And these are choices which were, and still are made not in tranquil forums, but in the context of partisan politicians and in the intense hard-sell atmosphere of military expos organized by defense contractors.

Writing about the atmosphere of arms promotion, engineering historian Joseph J. Corn has observed: "Defense contractors, in fact, often seemed to have the largest crystal ball when it came to envisioning the future. They had good reasons to foster rapid technological change and weapons obsolescence: Just as automobile makers depended on consumer dissatisfaction with present vehicles—and avidly cultivated it with "cars of tomorrow"—defense firms sought to keep the military hungry for new and improved weapons. Military contractors even exploited the techniques developed by auto makers to sell their future weapons systems. Believing in the adage of a picture being worth a thousand words, they hired illustrators to visualize futuristic weapons in action. These images have been promoted in trade shows and in the pages of periodicals such as *Army Information Digest*."[28] This hype has been the background to the clever and subtle reasoning about future wars which has been used by military policy-makers from the end of World War II to the present time.

But the irrationalities of the hyped-up military marketplace have perhaps amounted to little compared to the overarching fear that has justified so much military decision-making during the cold war years. Orwell's dictum that prophecy panders to fear can be true of no other area more than this one. Our age, of course, is a very fearful one, but it is also extraordinary that it is perhaps the first age in which fear is actually being promoted as a virtue. Some political analysts today have actually written about fear as if it were a virtue, slandering those who are unwilling to espouse it. For example, Richard Pipes, the émigré American historian and military consultant, has written: "In the United States, the consensus of the educated and affluent holds all recourse to force to be the result of the inability or unwillingness to apply rational analysis and patient negotiation to disagreements: the use of force is *prima facie* evidence of failure. Some segments of this class not only refuse to acknowledge the existence of violence as a fact of life, they have even come to regard fear—the organism's biological reaction to the threat of violence—as inadmissible." (emphasis in original) He then quotes with approval a distinguished colleague's prejudices along the same lines: " 'The notion of being threatened has acquired an almost class connotation,' Daniel P. Moynihan notes in connection with the refusal of America's 'sophisticated' elite to accept the reality of a Soviet threat. 'If you're not very educated you're easily frightened. And not being ever frightened can be a formula for self-destruction.' "[29] It is hard to tell who Pipes and Moynihan are slurring more—the educated, affluent elite, for not being fearful enough, or the uneducated lower classes, for supposedly being easily scared. In any case, this type of argument is wholly lacking in the kind of moral intelligence that can distinguish between courage, fear and recklessness. One can recognize and face danger without being fearful—in fact, that is precisely what courage is all about. But it is difficult to see the virtue of all of the reckless over-arming for the war of the future that we have been doing since the end of World War II. It is no wonder that Aristotle classified recklessness and fear as two extremes, two failures of virtue, both opposite from courage.

We have not yet experienced the unthinkable disaster that could result from the nuclear arms race, but recklessness in the present is still recklessness, even if it does not lead to a future disaster. In the election campaign of 1988, part of the Republican party's rhetoric was to claim that the reckless confrontational style of the first three-quarters of the Reagan administrations—a style which the party has preferred to call "dealing from strength"—is what led to the recent arms reductions. This is both absurd and vain. To realize how absurd it is, one has only to imagine what state the world would now be in were Brezhnev still alive and were Reagan's confrontational foreign policy not cooled off, as some have contended, because of the Contra-gate scandal. No one predicted, or could predict, that Brezhnev would die before the end of Reagan's terms, or that Andropov and Chernenko, his immediate successors and every bit the hard-liners that he was, would also die within months of assuming leadership of the Soviet Union. No one predicted or, given the entire modern history of Soviet succession, could predict that a reformer of Gorbachev's character and effectiveness would assume the Soviet stewardship. Even the deteriorating economic situation in the Soviet Union did not guarantee that economic, and certainly not political, reforms would be forthcoming: that nation, which both during the Napoleonic Wars and World War II has endured far worse without changing its course, is known for its tenacity. If not for these unpredicted developments, Reagan's confrontational style and Brezhnev's obduracy might very well have proven how truly reckless such posturing and massive arming can be.

One does not have to make a case for the fact that military futurology is driven by fear and the worship of power, the motives that George Orwell contended were at the heart of all prophecy; this much, at least, should be self-evident. But military futurology, more than any other area of modern prophecy, also exemplifies all of the other psychological and ideological devices which are contained in the futurologist's repertoire.

For example, very prominent in military prediction is the forecaster's characteristic tendency to minimize, or even trivialize, all problems which detract from his vision. But also rather common are the mystification of future problems and situations through the use of pseudo-scientific jargon, ambiguity and secrecy; the pretense of future mastery and control of complex environments like battlefields, usually on the basis of no more than mere visionary words; the tendency to caricature national and human psychology, particularly that of the enemy, but also that of the population that must be controlled at home. All of these ploys are designed to give the military forecaster an air of mastering the unfathomable irrationalities and complexities of future battlefields, the privileged leadership position that often follows from this and the protection of his forecasts from public scrutiny. Nowhere more than when it engages in the business of prophecy does the military behave like a cult. In fact, with the mystification of fact, the communication to the public by innuendo and the pretense to mastery of mind-boggling situations, the prophets and visionaries of war are cult-prophets *par excellence.*

It is difficult to think of the nuclear arms race without again recalling the story of Iphigenia, Agamemnon's wretched daughter. Many of the great Greek dramatists wrote plays about her sacrifice and the ensuing incidents that finally destroyed Agamemnon himself and his royal family. When he returned from the Trojan War, Agamemnon was assassinated by his wife Clytemnestra and her consort, and one of the reasons the queen gave to justify her action was that he had earlier sacrificed Iphigenia, their daughter. The great Greek dramatist Euripides wrote a sequel to the sacrifice called *Iphigenia in Tauris* in which he has Orestes, Iphigenia's brother, make the following remark about prophecy:

> The wisest men follow their own direction
> And listen to no prophet guiding them
> None but the fools believe in oracles,
> Forsaking their own judgement. Those who know,
> Know that such men can only come to grief.[30]†

Iphigenia's story symbolizes the present grace that is sacrificed for future glory. Had Agamemnon preserved his daughter's life, he would have at the same time been preserving innumerable other lives, including his own, and given his people the present opportunity to practice the arts of peace rather than those of war. Given the incalculability of the nuclear wars, limited or otherwise, that are now being planned, any politician who is really concerned about the judgment of the future would be far safer to steer in the

† Incidentally, Calchas, the futurologist who caused all of Iphigenia's troubles and for whom she openly expresses great hatred in Euripides's play, *Iphigenia in Tauris,* finally got his comeuppance. He is said to have committed suicide when he was outprophesied by a rival soothsayer by the name of Mopsus.

direction of peace, with all of its so-called constraints, instead of war.

NOTES

1. For this account, and for much of what follows about early war prediction, I am greatly indebted to I.F. Clarke's excellent book, *Voices Prophesying War 1763–1984* (Oxford: Oxford University Press, 1966).
2. Clarke, *Voices,* p. 10.
3. I.F. Clarke, *History Today* (1965), vol. 15, p. 110. To their credit, the English also displayed a great deal of humor about Chesney's predictive fantasy. For example, it was common banter during this period to say, when referring to any accidental injury, that it was a wound received in the Battle of Dorking.
4. Clarke, *Voices,* pp. 10–13.
5. Interview with Robert Sheer in *With Enough Shovels: Reagan, Bush and Nuclear War* (New York: Random House, 1982), pp. 218–219.
6. Robert Aldridge, *First Strike! The Pentagon's Strategy for Nuclear War* (Boston: South End Press, 1983), p. 268. Aldridge reports on Fiscal Year 1977 Authorization for Military Procurement Research and Development, hearing before the Senate Armed Forces Committee, March 11, 1976, Part 11.
7. Richard Pipes, "Why the Soviet Union Thinks It Could Fight and Win a Nuclear War," in *Commentary* (July 1977), p. 24. This argument is also made by one military critic as a primary explanation for the decline in effectiveness of the U.S. armed forces during the last quarter century. See Richard Gabriel, *Military Incompetence,* 1985.
8. Robert Oppenheimer, "Atomic Weapons and the Crisis in Science," in *Saturday Review* (November 24, 1945), p. 10.
9. Henry Kissinger, "Force and Diplomacy in the Nuclear Age," in *Foreign Affairs* (April 1956), vol. 34, no. 3, p. 349.
10. Kissinger, "Force and Diplomacy," p. 351.
11. Oppenheimer, "Atomic Weapons," p. 10.
12. Kissinger, p. 356.
13. Kissinger, pp. 360–361.
14. Henry Kissinger, "Limited War: Conventional or Nuclear?—A Reassessment," in *Daedalus* (Fall 1960), p. 800.
15. Henry Kissinger, "American Strategic Doctrine and Diplomacy," in Michael Howard (ed.), *The Theory and Practice of War* (London: Cassell, 1965), p. 275.
16. Freeman Dyson, *Weapons and Hope* (New York: Harper and Row, 1984).
17. Paul Nitze, "Atoms, Strategy and Policy," in *Foreign Affairs* (January 1956), p. 197.
18. Kissinger, "Force and Diplomacy," pp. 361–62.
19. Kissinger, "Limited War," pp. 800–817.
20. The following account was reported by Walter Pincus, "Thinking the Unthinkable: Studying New Approaches to a Nuclear War," in the *Washington Post* (February 11, 1979), p. A21.
21. Colin Gray and Keith Payne, "Victory Is Possible," in *Foreign Policy* (Summer 1980). Gray served as a top military adviser to the Reagan administration.
22. Gray and Payne, p. 14.
23. Gray and Payne, p. 19.
24. Gray and Payne, p. 21.

25. *La Descente en Angleterre: Prophétie en deux actes.* Cited in I.F. Clarke, *Voices.*

26. William Shawcross, *Sideshow: Nixon, Kissinger and the Destruction of Cambodia* (New York: Touchstone Books, 1987), p. 25.

27. See, "Where Did It All Go?" in *New Republic* (April 20, 1987).

28. Joseph J. Corn, *Yesterday's Tomorrows* (New York: Summit Books, 1984), p. 120. See also, John Markoff, "Welcome to the War Fair: Where the Hawks Hawk," in *Mother Jones* (July 1979), pp. 41–44.

29. Pipes, p. 25.

30. Euripides, *Iphigenia in Tauris* (trans. Witter Bynner), in *Greek Tragedies* (Chicago: University of Chicago Press, 1972), Volume 2, p. 137.

5

FUTUREHYPE IN EDUCATION

During the summer of 1985 the IBM Corporation launched an ambitious promotion scheme aimed at the education marketplace. With the help of a consulting firm called National Computer Training Institute (NCTI) and the Extension School at the University of California at Berkeley, they recruited two hundred teachers who had already had some experience in using computers in the classroom; the teachers were recruited in teams of two from cities located in every U.S. state. The recruitment brochure said that they were looking for "successful classroom teachers with organizational ability and entrepreneurial spirit." Through NCTI, who acted as middlemen, these teachers were brought to Berkeley, provided with room and board, and given a two-week minicourse in what the brochure called "educationally oriented technical training" at Berkeley Extension—all with the compliments of IBM.

After completing this training session, each of these teachers was provided with the use of fifteen IBM personal computers, along with the appropriate IBM software and instructional materials; they were then hired by the corporation on a part-time basis to pass their newly acquired skills on to colleagues at regional training centers which were established for this purpose. Between training sessions, these teachers-cum-entrepreneurs were allowed to keep a couple of computers for their own personal use, but told to bring the other thirteen to their schools for use with their students. Some of these teachers were otherwise unemployed or working at non-teaching jobs but, on the basis of the recruitment protocol described in NCTI's brochure, at least half of them were required to pursue these part-time jobs as educational computer-entrepreneurs as a sideline, along with the regular teaching duties which they were to resume in the fall. No mention was made of conflict of interest.

IBM is not the only computer company that has been promoting its products in the education marketplace with giveaways and training, but this scheme was unusual because of its scope. Undoubtedly it cost them a great deal to finance, but since the educational computing market is already large and lucrative, it takes little imagination to understand IBM's thinking behind this promotion scheme. For more than a decade there has been a great deal of talk in education circles about an imminent micro-computer revolution in the classroom. Not only did this corporation want to capture a large part of the present market, but it wanted to ensure that this revolution would, in fact, occur; the seeding effect of such a strategy was an attempt to hasten it on its way. From the corporation's point of view, this whole scheme was business as usual. They were pursuing the education marketplace in the same way they had earlier pursued the military and business marketplace before it: by trying to cultivate the present market and capture a large part of it, and by trying to insure their stake in the market of the future.

This is not the first time a revolution in education has loomed on the horizon. When I was a boy attending public schools in Toronto, I was at one time very taken by an article in a popular magazine about a great new innovation in education that was one day going to make learning virtually effortless. However, on that occasion, the revolutionary educational innovation was related not to computers but to subliminal suggestion, which was at that time a hot topic in the field of advertising. The theory behind subliminal suggestion is that a consumer can be induced to buy a product if its name or symbol is quickly and secretly flashed before his eyes on a movie or television screen, or if some other object of desire, usually sexual, is embedded, like camouflage, in a picture of the product when it appears in an advertisement on a billboard or in a newspaper or magazine. The article I read claimed that, in a similar way, you could learn anything in your sleep, ostensibly by suggestion, simply by listening to a tape recording of the subject matter while you were unconscious. Eventually, so the article predicted, we would be learning all sorts of things this way. Since school was insufferably boring and tedious for me at that time, this technique struck me as a perfect solution, a way of giving my courses precisely the amount and type of attention they deserved. Unfortunately, however, I could not afford to buy the system, and therefore had to continue to take a little precious time away from other activities in order to master my subjects.

The theory about learning in one's sleep was undoubtedly inspired by Aldous Huxley's then still very fashionable novel *Brave New World*. In Huxley's novel, this educational technique of the future was known as "hypnopaedia." However, it was forcefully rejected, along with other similar techniques of Huxley's visionary society, by John the Savage, one of the novel's principal protagonists, on the grounds that it contributed to what he called "civilized infantility." John the Savage believed that life was better if it had real challenges, and so he could not see the virtue of making learning and everything else in life effortless.

Hypnopaedia, as a disproven instruction technique, may seem droll or even outlandish at this point in educational history, but one thing it has in common with a great many modern educational innovations which are taken quite seriously and are supposed to be making our educational future, is that it is based on the premise that learning would be much more effective if only it could somehow be made at least effortless, and hopefully even enjoyable.

Of course the hypnopaedia of my boyhood turned out to be a groundless little fad, but as a fad, groundless or otherwise, it certainly has not been lacking for company. In ensuing years there have been a great many innovations in education, some of which were modest enough, and others which were supposed to herald a wonderful new age of teaching and learning. Because of this onslaught of educational innovation, I think my generation, the baby-boom generation, has been subject to more educational experiments based on both new techniques and technology than any generation before us.

All of us have been subjected to the parade of educational innovation of this century, from tape recorders, phonographs, and projectors, through educational television, teaching machines and now, finally, computer assisted instruction (CAI). Most of the mechanical innovations were designed to make learning and teaching a little easier, more effective and perhaps even more enjoyable. And though they were by no means revolutionary, many of these technologies, in fairly simple and straightforward ways, did indeed prove to be useful and effective when employed appropriately in the classroom.

Other techniques—like open classrooms, self-directed learning and schools without walls—made grander, more dramatic claims on our attention, and yet ended up producing very mixed results. But a special case has been made for CAI which, in its most recent incarnation on microcomputers, is still going strong: it is said to be both technology and technique, a new machine as well as a new approach to teaching, wholly different from everything that has come before it; it is said to be truly revolutionary, to be heralding the education system of the future.

Though the computer revolution in the classroom has loomed in the public consciousness only a few years, by some standards this talk about a computer revolution in our classrooms is getting pretty old. More than twenty years ago there was another flurry, minuscule compared to the scale of present activity, which predicted the same outcome. In those days, however, computer technology for educational purposes was less elaborate than it is today. Relatively inexpensive microcomputers did not appear on the market until the mid- to late-1970s, so these early computer assisted instruction systems required that students sit at time-sharing video-display terminals (VDTs) which were connected to mainframe computers. Naturally, time-sharing had to be carefully coordinated and this prohibited most spontaneous usage; computing capacity was much more limited and expensive; the terminals had none of the optional accessories like joysticks, digitized drawing pads, game paddles and light pens that make input into today's micros so varied and, to some students, so appealing; and when the mainframe went down, all of the terminals naturally went down with it.

Also, during this first round, educational software was more scarce and much harder to produce. Programmers who were producing it at that time had to use the earlier generations of machine languages then available, which are rather restrictive by present-day standards. They did not have the benefit of modern utilities programs, like authoring languages, which make programming much easier, or graphics utilities which greatly facilitate creating visual representations on the screen, or standard subroutines which simplify the correction of errors.

With the development of the micro, its accessories and these aids for producing software, many of the mechanical difficulties of introducing these teaching machines into our classrooms were solved, or seem to be imminently soluble. We have certainly arrived at the point where, if the money could be found today, we could quite easily and rapidly inundate our classrooms with vast amounts of hardware and software and give those of our teachers who are not yet using computers at least a minimum amount of technical training: IBM's promotion scheme is a perfect model for this.

But talk of a computer revolution in the classroom has been premature. An education revolution of the sort I have described, that is, by inundation, would be successful only in IBM's narrow marketing sense. In fact, in spite of the enormous amount of effort that has already gone into developing computing products for the education marketplace, the problems that have thus far been solved, largely technical ones, are trivial compared to those that remain, especially if one takes our forecasters' scenarios seriously. Given how little we know about the human issues involved here—the

real education issues—it is impossible at present to predict
even what a computer revolution might mean, much less
how it might turn out.

When one hears talk of imminent revolutions in our education system, it is important to bear in mind that, next to
the military, perhaps no other part of our culture is as susceptible to becoming the subject of propaganda as is our
education system. Although the two are obviously in many
ways very different, the one thing that our military and education systems do have in common is that they are both
major repositories of our individual and collective hopes and
fears. Our education system, like the military, is therefore
particularly susceptible to the propagandist work of our
modern-day prophets. Perhaps even more so because of the
pervasive and often pivotal role the education system plays
in our society and culture. However, if we consider this role
carefully, we begin to have some inkling of what an education
revolution might mean, and what our education prophets are
really about.

Just as the individual is reproduced in the family, the
education system has long been the formal center for the
reproduction and renewal of our society and culture: for
the transmission of knowledge, customs, and values, as an-
thropologists usually put it. It certainly does not do this job
alone. It is obvious that this business also happens in many
other places—in the home, on the street, in the workplace,
and in personal relations—but it is in the education system
that it is most clearly, unequivocally and formally vested.
Furthermore, as we continue to delegate more and more
authority and responsibility for all sorts of formerly personal
and private matters to professionals outside of the family, it
is in the education system, where so many family-serving
professionals tend to congregate, that the process of social
and cultural reproduction is increasingly carried out. That is
why we often say that, whatever else may happen to an
individual during the course of a lifetime, his educational
experience will have a great impact on shaping his destiny.
Because the education system is universal and compulsory,
it is a common path and a common place. Because it is a
staging ground for their future roles, it plays a major role

in renewing our society and has come to represent both our individual and common destiny. Hence its attraction to our prophets: anyone who can present a convincing picture of future society and show both that it will be significantly different from present society and that the education system is not producing the future citizens that will thrive in and foster that civilization can also make a strong and appealing case for radical educational innovation.

Because social and cultural reproduction are the main functions of our education system, it is naturally also a major center of transformation: what better time to change something than when you are making it anew? In the process of reproducing a civilization, there exists always the tantalizing possibility of renewing it, renovating it on the basis of a grander, finer design. This possibility may even present itself as an imperative when parts of the culture appear to be, or are said to be, rapidly becoming obsolete. You never want to reproduce something that is no longer useful, so you transform it while you are making it anew in the hopes that it will be better adapted to the future environment. Of course transformations may also occur unintentionally, like mutations, when the education system fails to carry forward a skill or some knowledge that society continues to value. An example of this in recent times has been the failure of our education system to maintain the rates and standards of literacy that were so painstakingly developed during the first two-thirds of this century. At other times, as I will presently show, the transformation may be intentional, as when the system is consciously used to try to create a new society and culture. At these times, changes may be of a most sweeping and radical nature, designed not only to improve the process of education, but to act as a major lever for changing a civilization. This is what happens during periods of revolution. In fact, no successful revolution or revolutionary plan can fail to give education anything less than a major place on its agenda, and no vision of a new society would be complete without an elaborate description of how the education system will be used for creating and maintaining it.

In this context it is worth bearing in mind that the oldest visionary description of a society, which was to be shaped and maintained by a revolutionary education system is Plato's utopia, the *Republic*. Plato envisioned a society that would be sorted and divided into different classes, and to achieve this goal he advocated incorporating into the education system a technique which was already well developed in his time and of which he must have had some knowledge: the technique of the "thoroughbreeder."[1]

Since he made use of allusions to some of the now more obscure parts of Greek mythology, the terms of Plato's vision may sound a little quaint and precious to modern ears, but his educational prescriptions for a utopian society are fairly clear. He imagined that the population of his new society would be divided into four different classes based on the four types of soul: *gold, silver, bronze* and *iron*. Merit in the *Republic* was to be based primarily on an aptitude for two sorts of skills: the ability to philosophize on the one hand, and, on the other, the ability to excel at the types of sports that were current at the time, that is, those geared towards the development of good war-fighting skills.

But here is where the thoroughbreeder comes in. In Plato's utopia, people with *gold* and *silver* souls would be encouraged by customs and rituals insinuated by their rulers (also selected from the class of *gold* souls) to breed prolificly, and thus have a disproportionate, and presumably beneficial impact on the population mix of their society. On the other hand, the *bronze* and *iron* classes would be encouraged to breed very little or not at all. The best souls would be separated from the rest and raised and educated communally by professional nurses and tutors.[2] This weeding process would continue at different stages of their lives until, at the age of fifty, those who had passed all hurdles would themselves be selected to join the circle of leaders.

Plato's description of an ideal future society also had some telling things to say about the role of women. Formally, women were to be selected on an equal footing with men and could rise just as high; equal opportunity, very narrowly conceived, was one of his basic precepts. In this limited sense, Plato's thinking was somewhat more egalitarian than that of most of his contemporaries. But social mobility for women depended strictly on their ability to prove themselves proficient at the conventional male skills of philosophical

abstraction and warfare. No other skill or craft—be it law
or business, weaving or pottery—no matter how highly developed, was esteemed in Plato's utopia to the extent that
it could act as a vehicle for the kind of upward social mobility
that would result in political leadership. And poetry and fine
arts were to be banished altogether because, as "imitative"
processes, they were removed from philosophical "reality";
they detracted from Plato's overriding philosophical project,
which was to try to discover the "essences" of things. So
obsessed was Plato with promoting the skills of war that in
his utopia women who aspired to positions of leadership were
required to exercise naked in the marketplace, as the men
did, presumably even into late middle age while they held
office,[3] while even little children were to be taken out into
the battlefield, on suitably safe occasions, and figuratively
given a taste of blood as part of their education.[4] In short,
the education system in Plato's new society was to be used
to create and sustain a community dominated by a culture
which heavily emphasized conventional male skills.

In our time, perhaps the closest thing to Plato's model
is the Israeli kibbutz. Of course the kibbutz strives to be a
classless society, and the values that have been created and
sustained in these communities are very different from the
ones Plato promoted. While Plato demeaned tilling the soil,
on the kibbutz this activity, especially at the outset, was
elevated to the highest level. And another difference between the kibbutz and Plato's vision is that in time, with
prosperity, it became possible to achieve distinction on the
kibbutz on the basis of art and poetry as well as agriculture
and industry. But what these modern utopian communities
do have in common with Plato's vision is that children raised
and educated in them are separated from their parents at a
very early age and raised by communal care-givers and teachers. Moreover, one of the main purposes of this separation
on the kibbutz, very much in keeping with Plato's idea, was
to create a new society by making a revolutionary break with
the past and to separate, or at least significantly decrease,
the influence of the family. Aside from the very real economic considerations which were particularly relevant in the
beginning, the founders of the kibbutzim wanted their chil-

dren to be freed from the debilitating neurosis of family and small town culture which they had brought from their Eastern European backgrounds.[5]

In more recent times, we have seen many other examples of the education system being used to create a brave new society. One is the ambitious scheme initiated by the United States to upgrade its science education system following the dramatic Soviet launch of the first man-made satellite in 1957; the aim was to produce scientists and technicians that would equal or surpass the Soviet achievements.† Another is the paroxysm of infighting between the old and new guard in China, commonly known as the Cultural Revolution, which closed the universities for a decade and sent intellectuals into the countryside to labor on the land. And a third is the literacy campaign launched in Nicaragua following the Sandinista Revolution in order to upgrade the skills of the population and get them into the mainstream of modern life.

But these movements, using only tools and techniques already in existence, have produced nothing compared to what some of our contemporary prophets have said will be the outcome of the present period of computer-based innovation in the education systems of the industrialized world. We have been told by its promoters that this revolution will change not only the way we learn but even the way we think, the very nature of how we work in science, and perhaps even lead to the very disestablishment of our school systems themselves. For example, Seymour Papert, a prominent computer scientist and psychologist at MIT and undoubtedly the foremost among these prophets, has written:

> I have described myself as an educational utopian—
> not because I have projected a future of education
> in which children are surrounded by high technol-

† The Soviet sputnik launch was really just another Texas Alamo. It did not signify that the Soviet Union was technologically superior to the United States. On the contrary, this innovation, in which the Soviet monopoly was very short-lived, was the first and only significant military innovation the Soviet Union has achieved during the entire post–World War II arms race. But the event had great symbolic impact, and could therefore be used by the military and those who wanted educational change to promote it.

ogy, but because I believe that certain uses of very powerful computational technology and computational ideas can provide children with new possibilities for learning, thinking, and growing emotionally as well as cognitively . . . many of which depend on a computer-rich future, a future where a computer will be a significant part of every child's life.[6]

Depending on one's taste, this vision of the future may or may not be appealing. But given the role that the education system plays in society, this vision, if it is to be realized, immediately raises a simple but fundamental question: If computers are to be used in the reproduction and renewal of our culture and society, exactly how will they do this? What is the nature of human society and what is the nature of machines, and how can the latter be used by the former to reproduce itself?

Since the Industrial Revolution, machines have played a dramatic and significant role in the production of *things*. What generally characterizes the production of *things* by machines is that they are all supposed to come out the same—in fact, our engineers have coined the now rather familiar phrase, "production to specification," to describe this goal. This sameness is precisely what engineers have striven for during the course of the last two centuries and continue to strive for to this day. It is the basis not only for uniformity but also for standards of a sort because, as far as machines go, quality is basically uniformity on a high level: an engine block with no cracks in it, a piece of fabric with high uniform density of fiber and dye, pistons that are sealed and seated with the precision that leads to uniform compression, and so forth. Those who have sung the praises of machines have praised not only their power but also their precision, that is, their uniformity and the uniformity that they produce. Indeed if *things* that are produced by machines do not, for some reason or other, come out according to specification, then this is usually considered to be a failure of the production system.

What characterizes people, however, is that they are not produced to specifications. We are different from one another because of the number and variety of traits in the human gene pool and the incessantly stirring and churning nature of genetic recombination which occurs when we reproduce ourselves. Though people have a great deal in common with one another (and in some ways this is just as important as the fact that they are different), the fact of diversity, of individual differences, is nevertheless one of the hallmarks of humanity, and ultimately of all of nature. In this light, perhaps the most fundamental question raised by the idea of an education revolution based on computers is this: How can machines both respond to natural human diversity and help produce a diverse future human society? Or put another way, how can that which is basically geared towards producing *sameness* assist in the production of those who are by nature *different?*

Perhaps it is not fair to put the question in these terms. Most computer scientists, especially those who belong to the artificial intelligence movement, would make the claim that computers are very special—Papert calls them the Proteus of machines.† Theoretically, what distinguishes computers from other machines is that they are very flexible, can perform different functions at different times, can simulate—or "imitate" to use Alan Turing's term—any function that anything or anyone else can do, providing it can be described in formal terms. This, at least, is the theory of computers and the battle-cry of the artificial intelligence movement. Therefore, not surprisingly, one of the major premises upon which the promotion of the computerized classroom of the future has been based is that computers actually have the capacity to optimize learning by tailoring instruction to the individual learner's abilities and idiosyncrasies.[7] The claim is made, in other words, that not only do students learn *individually* with the assistance of the computer—quite obviously this happens on other occasions too—but that their very instruction is *individualized,* somehow made to suit their particular natures as learners. In a sense, then, the CAI

† Poor Proteus! How easily this little god's name has been taken in vain. This minor Greek deity, the son of Poseidon, was known primarily for his powers as a seer who knew present, past and future, but was reluctant to talk. In order to make him speak one had to catch him, and he evaded capture by assuming different forms and shapes—hence Papert's allusion.

revolution has faced the question of human individual differences head-on, by claiming that much of its strength lies precisely in being ideally suited, perhaps even more so than human teachers, for dealing with this problem.

This is a very substantial claim, especially because a great deal of the appeal of computerized instruction and justification for the educational revolution rests on it. The educational philosophies of the western democracies place a high value on individual growth and development. But what does the CAI claim to individualized instruction actually mean? The best way to answer this question would be to look briefly at the development of this Proteus of teachers during the last quarter century in order to elucidate the meaning behind the myth of individualized CAI and thus put at least some of the hype about the coming revolution in education into perspective.

In spite of the fact that computers can supposedly simulate machines of any sort, in point of fact, most of the first computers used for teaching were simply designed to simulate B.F. Skinner's mechanical teaching machines. Masters often disown their disciples—even Marx, who loved to have a following, made a point of stating that he himself was not a Marxist—but it is nevertheless ironic when it happens. It was certainly ironic, for example, that Skinner himself expressed a rather dim view of educational computers when he first encountered them at the Seattle Exposition in 1961. He expressed this displeasure in an address to the French Psychological Association. In particular, he ridiculed the claim made by the boosters of these machines that the computer could be used effectively to individualize instruction:

> They told me with a great deal of pride that the machine [computer] was capable of addressing students by their given names. I have no doubt that in French they would address students by using the familiar form. In this way one adds the personal element to education! It is obvious that in all of these cases there is not one new idea, not one new conception of the processes of instruction. Such a machine serves only to perpetuate the most regrettable methods of education.[8]

However, the fact that Skinner, the father of programmed and machine-assisted instruction, chose to deprecate CAI did not prevent its proponents from using his learning theory and his model of programmed instruction for developing their own systems. So the first CAI programs, the linear programs, were based on the principles of conditioned learning, to the development of which Skinner himself had devoted most of his career.[9]

It is said that imitation is a form of flattery. To Skinner's credit—but obviously, from the above statement, against his best intentions—the majority of the first linear programs developed for CAI were no more than electrified and automated programmed learning books. In the simplest types of "tutorial" CAI, the subject matter is presented to the learner sequentially and systematically. All students are presented with exactly the same material, and whenever the student responds correctly to a question or problem, he gets a positive reinforcement, usually in the form of a message appearing on the video display screen saying that he is right. Because the learner is working on his own, and because, practically speaking, the computer is capable of presenting the material as fast as the student can handle it, the learning is self-paced.

In fact, given that every learner must go through all of the same material in exactly the same way, this self-pacing feature is the only sense in which the simplest linear educational software, or "courseware," can be characterized as being individualized. In other words, the learner who uses this type of linear program is treated as an individual by it, only in the sense that he is permitted to work at his own speed. But what does even this narrow form of individualization actually mean?

Consider two different hypothetical learners, both of whom would achieve the same credit for working through any given linear tutorial. The first learner is the kind who can anticipate very little or nothing at all of the material which is being presented by the machine, but nevertheless is able, in a reasonable amount of time, to comprehend and respond correctly to every question. The second is the learner who finds every question or problem immediately comprehensible and is able to anticipate some of these even before they are posed. This student is encumbered only by the speed at which he or she can physically transmit correct answers back to the machine.

Clearly, the learning experiences of these two very different kinds of students using the same "tutorial" will be very different, just as will be the experiences of two musicians, one of whom can sight-read only one note at a time, and the other of whom can sight-read a whole phrase, or a passage, or even an entire section at a time. Yet both students will get the same credit for completing the course, even though their experiences in doing so will have been considerably different. More important, insofar as these students do have different experiences—after all, scores certainly are not everything—it is because of what *they* bring to the computer, not what *the computer* brings to them. And as far as the product which results from this human-machine interaction is concerned, since all learners master the same material, then, for all intents and purposes, all come out the same. This is basically the kind of result that engineers hope for and expect from machine production. This is manufacturing to specification.

The obvious limitations of linear courseware were somewhat ameliorated by the development of a more sophisticated type called "branching tutorials." Branching programs are still based on Skinner's conditioning principles, but they do have some additional features which allow them to be flexible in their relationship to the learner's performance record. Corrective feedback, and thereby additional opportunities to learn the correct responses, are offered to students who fail to respond correctly at the beginning of each instructional sequence. (Conversely, this process is short-circuited or entirely eliminated for faster learners.) And, as another form of feedback, these programs are also capable of engaging the learner in highly structured tutorial dialogues—really only pre-recorded and pre-rehearsed sequences—and of posing questions in forms which are not explicitly multiple choice. However, *not explicitly multiple choice* is the key here, since these programs are capable of comparing a student's answer only with a set of pre-specified alternative responses which are invisible to the student but embedded in the program.

No one has more succinctly summarized the limitations of branching tutorials than Anthony Oettinger, an early critic of the movement towards computerization of education. Writing about them almost two decades ago, when the computer revolution in education was still in its first incarnation, he said: "Some claim that the advantage of a computer over simpler 'teaching machines' lies in its capability for practically infinite branching. But the real bottleneck is our inability to foresee more than a very few of the most common possible learner responses."[10]

Another variation of Skinner's basic linear tutorial which is worth a brief description is the so-called "generative courseware." These programs are capable of presenting wholly different problems to different students, generally at certain appropriate points in standardized routines. For example, in a drill-and-practice program in math, after a certain number of principles have been presented, each learner might be given problems that are different in the sense that the numbers in them are randomly generated. One learner might be asked to subtract 13 from 27, another 19 from 28, and so forth. But what is noteworthy and also ironic, about this type of computerized tutorial is that the *learner*'s individuality is generally defined, not with reference to the learner himself, but by the *computer*'s ability to generate random numbers. For example, if the object of the program is to present progressively more difficult problems, which is often the case, then "progressively more difficult" must be pre-defined, and it usually is, but on an average or random, rather than on an individual basis.

Yet another type of courseware is based on mathematically modeling learning behavior, and attempts to reduce learning based on the problem-solving model to mathematically describable situations, specifically to situations describable by game-theory.† Learning behavior is thus reduced to

† It is in the nature of game-theory to reduce complex behavior situations to a relatively small number of easily understandable variables based on simple human motives and simple probabilities of certain kinds of behavior. It is therefore not surprising that it has had a great deal of appeal to military strategists and has also been attractive to other kinds of strategists, including learning strategists. From the "gaming" of wars to the "gaming" of learning, this paltry theory certainly has got around for the purposes of trying to capture extremely complex situations in the simplest of terms. I shall have little to say about this type of courseware,

decision-making, based on a sort of game-playing, which is in turn based on a very mechanistic psychology and the rules of probability. The problem that game-theory encounters in education, however, is that aside from the fact that very few learning situations are well enough understood to be reduced to such terms, this type of courseware has been so strongly tied to its particular problem-solving theory that everything else has effectively been squeezed out. It turns out that, in practice, it has been forced to make a fatal trade-off: it has proven to be incapable of simultaneously both modeling the student's learning behavior and properly representing the subject matter at hand. The individual learner is defined by this type of program simply as a game-player, a "rational and normal" decision-maker, but *directly at the expense of the substance of the "game" he is playing,* that is, of the subject he is trying to learn. Because of this great shortcoming, one of the original theorists and authors of this type of courseware has commented on its well recognized failure that "the reason for stochastic learning models failing as models of instruction is *their lack of representing the content to be taught.*" (emphasis added)[11]

This brings us to the most progressive and probably the most famous type of CAI system, which also takes as its theoretical point of departure the notion of learner as problem-solver, but does not, however, burden itself by attempting to model the learning process on the basis of a mathematical formula. Essentially, what happens in this system is that the learner is taught, or teaches himself, a computer language, LOGO, and uses it in order both to set and solve problems, specifically *programming* problems. In other words, the student learns to program in a certain language and, since computer languages are mathematical constructs, he learns to pose and solve problems within the confines of these constructs.

It is interesting to observe that by the 1980s the rhetoric used to promote the LOGO system began to echo that used by the progressive education movement at the turn of the

---

however, beyond describing what it tries to do because it is generally regarded, even by its original proponents, as a failed system. It is therefore presently interesting only for what it tells us about another characteristic approach to individualizing instruction on the computer.

century. In 1982, Seymour Papert, the most prominent developer and promoter of LOGO, wrote: "My conjecture is that the computer can concretize (and *personalize*) the formal." (emphasis added)[12] This contention is part of the now familiar argument that computers are not merely a learning medium but an actual mathematical culture in which the learner acquires mathematical knowledge by programming in LOGO, by becoming, in other words, *acculturated* to what Papert calls "Mathland."

Papert's basic idea is really very old—older even than the progressive education movement—but has lost some of its familiarity since he embellishes it so much. It is therefore worth briefly unpacking here. He begins by asserting the theory that language is generally acquired rather effortlessly by most children, and attributes this phenomenon to the fact that children usually live in a language-rich environment. In this he is clearly a "nurturist" because he significantly does not likewise assert that the ability to acquire language has always been highly adaptive and, according to evolutionary theory, would therefore naturally be very widespread in the gene pool. Based on the questionable assumption that among humans the predisposition for learning math is just as strong as for learning language, his premise is that if we were to create an environment equally rich in mathematical as it is in verbal content, then mathematics would be acquired by our children with equal ease, and from this second conquest, somehow or other, the whole world of education would follow. A couple of years after publishing *Mindstorms,* his very influential prophecy, he described the future world that he envisioned in glowing terms.

> Then school, defined as a place where the three R's are imposed by force (or by the kind of subterfuge called "motivation" which is just as bad), will no longer be necessary. Society will be able to face the task of inventing environments in which children can develop as social, loving, honest human beings without distorting this goal by the crudely technical one of stuffing the multiplication tables into their heads.[13]

On the surface all of this may sound very romantic and appealing—perhaps that is why this school is often called the "techno-romantic" school of CAI—and there is no question that some children do indeed find it very appealing to learn certain mathematical concepts by programming with LOGO. But the theory does not stand up very well to close scrutiny, and, as scientists always insist, where theory is weak, predictions are bound to be wrong.

First of all, accepting Papert's claims at face value for the moment, it is revealing to probe some of their implications in order to see how this type of CAI relates to the individuality of the learner. If LOGO is indeed a *culture,* then one should ask the question: What is the process of becoming acculturated to it? One common way in which cultures are commonly characterized is as systems of shared values, symbols, customs and so forth. However, the process of sharing, almost by definition, entails some loss of individuality. In real cultures this is usually an acceptable trade-off. But consider what is lost in learning with LOGO.

Consider, for example, some of the earliest "lessons" in LOGO, in which the acculturation process is most manifest. Learning to "draw"—this is the term that Papert himself uses—with LOGO is tantamount to learning to program the computer to represent on its screen the figure one has in mind. To draw a circle the learner types on the keyboard: TO CIRCLE REPEAT FORWARD I RIGHT I, END; to draw a triangle: TO TRIANGLE, REPEAT 3 FORWARD 30, LEFT 120, END; to draw a square: TO SQUARE, REPEAT 4 FORWARD 30, LEFT 90, END. If one inspects these three programs, what is immediately striking about them is that they are all very much the same, that is, in form they are far more like one another than the figures in question. This observation is particularly true if one considers the great variety of ways in which individual learners might execute these drawings using other media or, sticking with Papert's terminology, I suppose one ought to say, in other "cultures."

Papert's ideas about drawing bring Plato to mind again. Plato dismissed art because it detracted from his great project: the pursuit of the immortal essences, which he called "the forms." He dismissed making art as a falling away from—worse, a negation of—his great project, which was to try to discover the essences of things. Plato felt that art removed ideas one step back from the essences rather than pushing them one step forward, as he hoped logic would do. The interpretive side of art would not have interested him because it is too ephemeral—precisely its virtue if one looks at art a certain way—while the creative side of art seems entirely to have escaped his notice. He would not have recognized it. To Plato, art was basically part of the false and deceiving world of flux, appearances and circumstances.

Papert's education program would probably have pleased Plato, his prophet predecessor, at least a little. By reducing art, as Papert's system does, to a kind of production which is based on a reductionist machine language, and by equating asymmetry, idiosyncrasy, deliberateness and all of the other marks of authentic, individualistic creation with the mere artifacts of duplication and randomization, two of the computer's most facile tricks, Papert trivialized art by emphasizing its merely imitative aspect and ignoring its creative, interpretive side, and reduced it to an essence, a symbolic machine language. In this way, he paid homage to Plato and at the same time tamed art by reducing it to production formulas. In this way, Papert also trivialized the problem of aesthetic creativity by obliterating not all, but a great deal of personality, context, individuality and judgment from the process. All this Papert—even given the most sophisticated of present developments—is logically willing to sacrifice in the future of education in pursuit of the power which the computer readily gives, and with which he is so obviously enchanted.

In the final analysis, individualization of instruction in the LOGO system consists, then, in the degree to which the individual learner can find ways of expressing himself within a formal, mathematical environment. After the preliminary stages there is indeed some freedom for individualized exploration in such a system, but the question arises: Where does all of this narrowly defined formal freedom ultimately lead? Consideration of this question points to a number of observations which throw light on how problematic the notion of individualized instruction really is.

Consider the following. LOGO, as its promoters claim,

is not a "tutor" but a "tool"; it is a system for exploring mathematico-logical ideas. However, practically speaking, this is not strictly true. In most LOGO teaching situations a human teacher will indeed be present to help formulate the next question or problem to be solved with LOGO, with the purpose of guiding the learner through what can rightly be regarded as a hidden curriculum of useful and perhaps systematic ideas. However, in the rare case when there is not a human teacher working as adjunct to the system and offering guidance as to its fruitful use, then there are two possible developments. Either the learner, in his own independent explorations, will be forced to reinvent the wheel; or, unless he can create an entirely new system which he can relate to old ones and/or share with others, he will lapse into solipsistic thinking. He may, for example, create a neat little geometric form, something like a butterfly, and use copies of these "butterflies" as building blocks to fashion more elaborate objects on the screen; if this works, he may well conclude that he has discovered one of nature's own building blocks. In the end, Papert's brave new world of learning turns out to be a precariously bare new world.

As it turns out, Papert has, in a sense, anticipated these troublesome outcomes, but decided to make a virtue of them. His vision is that you take whatever ideas you invent in your little computer environment to the marketplace and try to sell them. He writes:

> Increasingly, the computers of the very near future will be the private property of individuals, and this will gradually return to the individual the power to determine patterns of education. Education will become more of a private act, and people with good ideas, different ideas, exciting ideas will no longer be faced with a dilemma where they either have to "sell" their ideas to a conservative bureaucracy or shelve them. They will be able to offer them in an open marketplace directly to consumers. There will be new opportunities for imagination and originality. There might be a renaissance of thinking about education.[14]

But what can he possibly mean by an "open marketplace" when the product will be a computer program? What Papert neglects to mention in this clever formulation is that every marketplace must have a common coin. In Papert's marketplace the common coin would be a particular machine language, LOGO, the one he developed. This would, of course, be a logical perversion of individualization, and far from what any thoughtful proponent of progressive education might have in mind. So, in a somewhat different sense, for the LOGO learner, as for the learner who uses a program which models his learning behavior mathematically, the problem may arise that the system simply fails to represent the subject matter, the world of shareable knowledge.

The problem of adequately representing subject matter is persistent in all types of CAI programs, as is the problem of representing a model of the learner, or of learning, that can recognize the learner's individuality in more than one or two dimensions. Both of these problems are explicitly recognized in CAI that is informed with artificial intelligence (AI). This type of courseware, which is presently still in the developmental stages, is depending for its successful realization on the eventual solving of a number of formidable problems. They are worth listing because AI-informed CAI is the great hope of the CAI movement, and because they epitomize the problems which have always been faced by the entire field of CAI. First, in CAI knowledge must be representable as production rules and consist, therefore, of a reasonable number of related facts which can be logically extended. Furthermore, these facts must be comprehensible through natural and logical modes of reasoning. And finally, the computer must be able to engage the student in relatively open-ended dialogue and explain its thinking, that is, its decisions to him.

It is too early to judge how successful CAI informed by artificial intelligence will be. The task it has set for itself is clearly enormous. Simply representing all knowledge formally will itself present the greatest of difficulties, especially—it has become a commonplace by now—all of the humanities and most of the social sciences, where such knowledge is not "scientific," that is, does not come from a tradition which is already highly reductionist. As to the theory of learning that must be embedded in such programs, similar problems arise. All present theories of learning taken together present only a partial and sketchy picture of what learning may be. Even incorporating one of them in a CAI program presents great difficulties. After all, the work of Bruner, Piaget, Gagne, Atkinson and Skinner—to name only some of the major twentieth-century theorists that come to mind—are not parts of a puzzle, contributions to a general theory of instruction. No single learning theory, in and of itself, is nearly complete, but even taken together they are no more than distinct and loosely related approaches to a general theory of instruction. A general theory of instruction would be difficult if not impossible to devise, precisely because, among other things, learning is such an individualized process.

In the final analysis, then, it is characteristic of all educational software that the *learner*'s individuality is defined in terms of the *computer*'s capabilities. This is the hallmark of all people/machine interactions and a natural consequence of what Lewis Mumford long ago referred to as the "assimilation of the machine." In spite of appearances and claims to the contrary, even in computers the mark of the machine is very persistent. The malleability of this "Proteus of machines" is still largely a matter of theory; in practice it has been, and continues to be, greatly exaggerated.

It is impossible to say what the computerization of our education system will accomplish in the very long run, but, like the quest for a cure for cancer, there is no good reason, except for wishful thinking, to believe that in the foreseeable future it will accomplish even a small part of what it has set out to do. The reality of the present situation is that, after more than a quarter of a century of development, this ongoing project to revolutionize instruction with the use of computers continues to demonstrate persistent limitations based not only on the structural nature of machines and machine language, but also on the lack of imagination and skill among even the most talented programmers. But more important, it is also based on the individualistic nature of human beings and the indeterminate nature of a great deal of the knowledge contained in our culture, both of which are highly resistant to being captured in mechanical forms.

In the face of these enormous problems, and in spite of the predictions of the brave new world of education they will usher in, computers remain very machine-like in their instructional functions. They are indeed powerful in some ways, certainly as calculators, but the price of all of this much vaunted power is that they leave their mark on all knowledge and act as a sort of sieve through which, were the revolution ever completed, all knowledge would have to pass or run the risk of being discarded.

For elementary lessons Skinner's teaching machines and some computer programs have been very helpful and have made a real contribution. For these lessons the computer's sieve-like qualities do not matter very much because most of the knowledge at this level is simple enough to pass through the holes of the screen relatively unscathed. But beyond these elementary lessons the computer as an aid to instruction, be it in the form of tutor or tool, time and again keeps proving itself to be painfully literal, especially in instructional situations where this simply will not do, where ambiguity, context, and metaphor are not failures or aberrations of communication but simply the name of the game. At present, this includes the vast majority of learning situations, including those in all but the most elementary of sciences and mathematics.

This would be a merely cautionary observation if computers in education were usually used appropriately, as was largely true during the first phase of their introduction and development in the schools. However, because of the hype both from members of the "artificial intelligentsia" like Papert and corporations like IBM, there has been a rush to find uses for computers in the classroom, the vast majority of which are obviously inappropriate, in order to usher in the new era of education. The danger is that a great deal will be lost as the final consequence of all of this hectic activity. This is due to the fact that the computer's severe limitations in acting as bearer of culture are simply inadequate for the education system's enormously complex and critical role in reproducing our society and culture, even accepting the fact that that society and culture are changing.

Signs of this are already with us. Here are some typical examples. We now have an instructional program in geography that makes a logical game out of the founding of a city, based solely on simple geographical variables like access to water, transportation, resources. The city in the program in question happens to be my town, Toronto, a city which, in keeping with the severe constraints of this program, does in fact happen to lie logically on a sheltered harbor at the confluence of two rivers. But what if one were to consider the founding of cities that were established for ideological rather than rational reasons? How would one account in this program for the founding of Salt Lake City, which was established by religious refugees, or one of the large metropolises in Siberia which were built and populated by political prisoners? I know of another program which claims to teach something about poetry: the student is asked to input a list of words which are consequently made to appear on the screen in the form of a Christmas tree or some other designated object. Imagine how heartwarming such pyrotechnics of automated concretism would be to Apollinaire were he alive today! I also know of a project which is presently trying to develop software to teach the classics. With respect to the *Iliad,* one imagines such questions as: Why was the hero Achilles feeling sore? Did he miss his concubine Briseis? Did he want Agamemnon's job? Was he getting tired of Hector's hectoring? These examples should speak for themselves.

But even with respect to what computers are supposed to be best at doing, that is, teaching about themselves, there are other questionable practices going on, even in this "age of computers." In the cases that I now have in mind, however, these practices have to do with the all too human nature of people, and not machines.

The problem is that, in spite of the claims of future possibilities, the CAI system itself has already become somewhat stultified. Most software writers work within the confines of the instructional categories that were identified by Robert Taylor in 1980 in his well-known book, *The Computer in the School: Tutor, Tool, Tutee*—the title tells it all. But this stultification goes far beyond working in categories; it relates to the ongoing development of machine language itself. All machine languages have their strengths and weaknesses, but as this field is developed we are naturally working

out the flaws in some of the older ones in the new generations
that are coming on board. Nevertheless, one of the most
flawed of these older ones, the well-known pioneering language called BASIC, is still persistently being taught in our
schools in spite of all of its considerable shortcomings. John
Laski, a specialist in computer languages, has eloquently
spelled out the reasons, as well as the unfortunate, self-
defeating implications of this fact:

> How one thinks and what one thinks about are
> molded by the language one uses to express one's
> thoughts. Whorf originally proposed this for cul-
> tures and natural languages. It always surprises me
> that its analogue in programming languages and
> programs is not as widely recognized. For it ex-
> plains why people resist so passionately new
> programming language capabilities, and why pi-
> oneering languages like FORTRAN, BASIC and
> COBOL still flourish today.[15]

But Laski's argument can be taken even further. Why teach
the archaic machine-language called BASIC at all? What
stake is there in preserving this stepping-stone in the development of computer languages? Is it like Ancient Greek or
Latin, archaic languages in which great literature was written
and which served for hundreds of years as the communication
medium for entire civilizations? Little if anything has been
written in BASIC that could not be better written in a more
recently developed machine language, or in one of the others
that will be coming down the line in the future.

But beyond this, it is questionable whether we should
even be teaching programming universally. It is a skill which
for the purposes of most of the population is itself rapidly
becoming obsolete. Most people who are using computers
now are already using them more as clever appliances than
malleable machines. Clever appliances rather than sophisticated tools are precisely what most personal computers
have become over the last decade—after all, this is what
"user-friendliness" is all about. Why on earth, if they could
help it, which they now certainly can, would manufacturers
allow their potential sales to be constrained, as they were

even a decade ago, by the impediment of the consumer actually having to learn something even moderately difficult in order to be able to use their product? In the end, the rush to herald the new age of education by teaching languages like BASIC has been misguided and self-defeating, even if one takes the conservative view that most people will in the long run have to learn programming; it is simply wasteful and frivolous if one takes the more optimistic view that they will not.

Furthermore, whatever may be lost or constrained by allowing the computerization of education to turn our schools into a cultural sieve is exacerbated by the social losses that this process also entails. Creating an educationally rich environment out of a vacuum is far more complicated than what Papert in his facile talk about "computer-rich" environments and "Mathland" even vaguely begins to suggest. After all, we are not talking here about cultivating molds in a petri dish. The human population is extremely heterogeneous, and an environment that may be rich for one sector is bound to be adverse or poisonous for others. When Papert first introduced LOGO he was opposed to having it evaluated on the grounds that it was still in its developmental stages. However, now that it is finally being evaluated, there is evidence that suggests precisely the problem I have just described. We now have studies that suggest that female students, on the whole, seem to have less aptitude, less ability and, most important of all, less *interest* in learning with LOGO than do most male students.[16] These effects may be due to conditioning, or they may be due to innate differences—obviously this is an issue worth trying to sort out—but whatever the case may turn out to be, if such differences persist and this type of computer use becomes a significant sorting factor in our schools, it would have a very regressive influence on the academic fate of our female students—shades of Plato's *Republic*.

Furthermore, females are not the only part of the population being excluded by the cultural narrowing necessitated by the computerization of our education systems. A survey of 18,000 American students between the ages of nine and seventeen years indicated that a number of inequities exist in patterns of computer use among our school-age population.[17] Age, sex, region of the country and type of community are all factors which relate to the amount of exposure to the computer that students are getting. It is all too familiar by now, but those students from inner cities, from the American south and from rural areas are getting the least amount of exposure, while middle-class suburban white males from the northeast and southwest are getting the most—and since the first survey in 1978 this situation has worsened. Of course middle-class families are more likely to have a computer at home, thereby increasing accessibility. But beyond the accessibility issue, which is basically quantitative, is a much more important qualitative one: Arthur Luehrman of Computer Literacy Inc. has also reported that students in wealthier middle-class schools are given more independent access to their equipment and use it to develop new skills through exploration of its potential. In contrast, however, the passive and rather more limited use of computers for drill-and-practice is more prevalent in poorer schools.[18]

Finally, in addition to the software development problems and social issues, there are a number of health questions which an honest revolution should also be addressing. From our rapidly accumulating experience in using computers in commerce and industry have emerged a number of symptoms and syndromes associated with the use of or exposure to video-display terminals (VDTs). These include eyestrain, fatigue, headaches and anxiety. It is not clear what causes these and other symptoms. They may be brought on by radiation from the VDTs themselves or by other environmental factors associated with the use of micros, like room lighting, video brightness, air supply and proportion of negative ions. Unfortunately, our knowledge of the effects of low-level radiation is incomplete and controversial, but surely these effects, found in other places, cannot be dismissed with impunity when bringing computers into our classrooms. There is a great deal of conventional wisdom in the field of human development which holds that there are critical early ages in child development in which children are particularly susceptible to environmental effects. Since our children are being introduced to video-display terminals at ever earlier ages, we should be more circumspect than we are at present about exposing them to more low-level radiation.

Considering the pedagogical, social and health issues, it should be clear that there are no simple remedies for dealing with the difficulties and dangers inherent in the movement to computerize education—and the payoffs for doing so would seem to be rather questionable. So what does the future really hold in store for the computer revolution? It is surely impossible to say with any certainty. What is certain, however, is that in the rush to make this revolution happen, the future, rather than being broadened, has already been attenuated. Whatever has been gained by introducing computers into the classroom, a great deal has already been lost, all of it unnecessarily, and not just because of a further crowding of the curriculum. The machine's lust for uniformity is leaving its mark in many ways as our society and culture reproduce themselves and conform to the contours of this newly constructed educational mold.

The mechanical response to human individuality and knowledge, far from being liberating, has proven in all too many cases to be not only inadequate but actually stifling. This is the problem at the heart of the revolution, a problem that arises from the very nature of what it is trying to do: reduce humanity and knowledge to machine constructs. What is revolutionary about the CAI movement finally is not what it contributes but what it loses in the process of trying to simulate, to imitate people and knowledge. More than any other discipline or method, the computer's nature is not to coexist with but to transform every form of knowledge around it, to reduce to its own often paltry terms all of the diverse methods that have been developed to explore the diversity of knowledge that man has accumulated over the ages.

As far as prophets like Papert go, it is their lack of understanding of what the present is all about—particularly with respect to individuality and knowledge—that has made it so easy for them to recommend this impoverished future as if it were actually richer. Whatever the inadequacies of the present—and there is certainly no point in trying to minimize these—at least up until about twenty years ago the education system suffered from, among other things, an embarrassment of riches. Even as recently as two decades ago there was a greater variety of knowledge being pursued in

different ways with methodologies appropriate to each discipline than ever before in the history of the human race.
There have been serious problems, of course, with overspe-
cialization and the management of information, but the computer has merely trivialized them, not solved them.

This fact is masked, of course, by its power, power that
is often more apparent than real. Papert's writing is liberally
peppered with references to power. He speaks of computer
power, powerful ideas, empowering students by having them
learn to program, and so forth. Computers are indeed powerful, in a limited sort of way, but a great deal of freedom
and detail in life are lost by harnessing their power, just as
a great deal of freedom of another sort is lost in driving a
car rather than walking. If you break off the leg of an insect
and place it under a powerful microscope you can make that
leg appear many times larger than the original insect itself
and then claim to have gained a great deal, all the while
ignoring what you have really lost or discarded. Computer
power works in much the same way, and it is only an impressionable futurologist like Papert who thinks that computer
environments will inevitably be richer than the ones they
replace.

Knowledge is not the same as power. But if and when
we lose the ability to distinguish between power and knowledge, the computer revolution in the classrooms will be complete. (If Alan Turing's prophecy is correct, that will
probably happen around the same time as we lose the ability
to distinguish between simulated events and the reality they
are supposed to represent, between thinking and computing.) At that point our lives in the schools, as elsewhere,
will be simulated lives.

Earlier I observed that Papert's thinking about education,
with its abstract reductionist tendencies, can be traced back
to Plato. But Papert and Plato really both represent extremes. Plato's educational system, with its inbreeding and
selection, is elitist to an extreme, and Papert's, with its willingness to trivialize culture, is egalitarian to another extreme.
Plato wants education to be hard and unpleasant so it can
perform its selective function, whereas Papert wants it to be
easy and enjoyable so that no selection occurs, no one fails.

But Papert also shares common ground with a more modern futurist, Karl Marx. The common ground between Papert and Marx is that they both believe that the present state of affairs is somehow unnatural, somehow false, a degradation into which society has fallen. Both believe that the true potential of the individual has been greatly hindered by the growth and development of unnatural social arrangements based on social domination. That is why they both want a new start made possible by a revolution that will destroy these false and degrading relationships. Their analyses are compelling because they have a superficial humanistic flavor. But in the end their prescriptions, their cures, are at least as bad as the diseases they are attacking because each prophecy, a barely concealed call to arms, proposes to substitute one form of cultural domination for another.

This is not the first time an education revolution based on an ascendant form of cultural domination has reared its benevolent-seeming head. One does not have to go back as far as Plato to find an earlier example of this, although I have often referred to his vision because it is so distant and its prejudices are so obvious to our present-day eyes. This drama also played itself out in the nineteenth century in the growth of the high school and reform school movements. Writing about this period, the American education historian Michael Katz has remarked that "despite the intellectual's acceptance of cultural relativity, first apparent in the work of many of the intellectual reformers of the progressive era, the mentality of cultural absolutism has persisted."[19] The high school movement of the nineteenth century proved to be no more a panacea than the computerization of education will prove to be now. In the wake of its failure it did not, however, merely shrivel up and disappear. Katz later remarks that "as the ideology became ever more divorced from reality, as crime and poverty increased despite the extension of schooling, teachers turned inward, and within a couple of decades their growing network of bureaucracies became private worlds, sterile and rigid."[20] This has already begun to happen in the CAI movement, but it is not likely to do IBM any harm, aside from stabilizing its revenues from this field.

Beyond the fact that a great deal is being lost and squeezed out of the curriculum in the attempt to computerize it, and beyond the fact that the computer revolution in the classrooms is serving the purposes of one part of the culture which is trying to dominate the rest, what a tremendous distraction this revolution has turned out to be. In the meantime, what has now become a litany of educational problems still persists. Some of these, like declining literacy and increasing dropout rates, are getting worse. In the end the problem is not merely that the prophets like Papert are proving to be false, or that the movement they have promoted has proven to be a great distraction: this movement has also placed a great burden on educators who are having enough trouble mastering the system as it now stands.

As the U.S. Army learned in Vietnam, mastery does not simply follow from mechanization. This lesson is even more true for the more complex education system: if you get a person in your sights, given the best available technology in either field, it is much easier to kill him than to educate him. But one fortunate thing about the education system, compared to its military counterpart, is that in education field tests under real life circumstances usually occur very early on so that one does not have situations, like the present one in the military, where whole systems are developed and put in place without ever having had to face the test of reality. This means that the futurehype in education can be more easily refuted once it has bumped up against reality. This is already happening with the computer revolution in the classrooms, and indeed was already under way even when IBM launched its promotion campaign in the summer of 1985: damn the torpedos, full steam ahead! Meanwhile, Papert, ever the stalwart futurologist, has recently and characteristically not only claimed to be misunderstood, but has also attributed the criticism, which he calls journalistic backlash, to a conspiracy inspired by the media who are simply starved for another story.[21]

In spite of the hype about creating a master race of programmers by starting very early, computer programming can be learned at almost any stage of life, as many people who are now pursuing careers in this field have proven. And it should not be difficult, through the normal channels of graduate and professional training, to furnish our society with whatever number of higher-level computer scientists it may need without squeezing the whole education system in the process. But in the present, because learning is so much a mastery of the here and now, we would do well to devote our energies to taking responsibility by mastering rather than mechanizing the subtle arts of education.

NOTES

1. Winston Churchill was certainly no revolutionary but, in spite of its placid tones, his vision of the future, at least with respect to societal reproduction, certainly was. The reader will recall from the chapter on the ideology of futurology that in this vision the test-tube reproduction of babies, coupled with some sort of "expert suggestion," was to be geared towards radically influencing societal reproduction *at the source,* circumventing the usual social selection and sorting processes by producing two ready-made classes, one for "thought" and the other for "toil," Churchill said nothing of education in his prediction of the future, but the logic of his vision suggests that, in his new society, the genetic predispositions of these two classes would be so powerfully directed towards one or the other of these roles that education would then have the easy job of having only to reinforce and refine what was already set.

2. Plato, *Republic* (London: Oxford University Press, 1945), VII, 541a.

3. Plato, V, 457a,b.

4. Plato, V, 466e; VII, 537a.

5. See Melford Spiro, *Kibbutz: Venture in Utopia* (Cambridge, Mass.: Harvard University Press, 1975), p. 128.

6. Seymour Papert, *Mindstorms: Children, Computers and Powerful Ideas* (New York: Harper and Row, Basic Books, 1982), pp. 17–18.

7. For a distinguished educator's version of this claim see John I. Goodlad's article in *School, Curriculum and the Individual* (Waltham, Mass.: Blaisdell), 1966; for a more recent version emanating from the circles of "official" science see Stuart Smith, Chairman, Science Council of Canada, speech to Canadian Education Association on "Electronics in Education" (September 28, 1982).

8. (Author's translation) On m'a dit avec beaucoup de fierté que la machine peut s'adresser à l'étudiant par son prénom. Je ne doute pas qu'en français elle le tutoyerait. De cette façon on remet l'élément personnel dans l'éducation! Dans tous ces cas, bien entendu, il n'y a pas une nouvelle idée, pas une nouvelle conception des processus d'instruction. Une telle machine ne sert qu'à perpétuer les méthodes de l'éducation les plus regrettables. (B. F. Skinner, "L'avenir des machines à enseigner." *Psychologie Française,* vol. 8 (1963), p. 171.)

9. There is a certain logic behind the fact that Skinnerian learning theory forms the basis for this earliest type of CAI program. A quick glance at the historical context in which this courseware was born renders this logic very clearly. The earliest computers were used for military applications because this was the area which experienced the greatest amount of rationalization and also received the greatest amount of resources during both World War II and the Korean War. With the advent of a more or less real peacetime economy and the military market already having been captured, business and education, in that order, became the next logical areas to be captured by computer applications in the process of expansion of this field. As it turned out, programmed instruction by book experienced its heyday in the late 1950s and early 1960s concomitant with

Skinnerian psychology which, at least in America, was also at the peak of its esteem and prestige at this time. For a penetrating analysis of why the United States, above all, would have been hospitable to both Skinnerian teaching theory and CAI see Hannah Arendt's essay, "The Crisis in Education" (1968).

10. Anthony Oettinger, *Run, Computer, Run: The Mythology of Educational Innovation* (Cambridge, Mass.: Harvard University Press, 1969), p. 181.

11. J. H. Laubsch, "Some Thoughts about Representing Knowledge in Instructional Systems," Proceedings of the Fourth International Conference on Artificial Intelligence, Tbilisi, 1975.

12. Papert, *Mindstorms*, pp. 17–18.

13. Seymour Papert, "Tomorrow's Classroom?" in *The Times Educational Supplement* (May 5, 1982), p. 41.

14. Papert, *Mindstorms*, p. 37.

15. John Laski, "Basic Confusions," in *The Times Educational Supplement* (November 13, 1981), p. 30. This article spells out in laymen's terms exactly why BASIC should not be taught in our schools.

16. Studies executed by the Toronto Board of Education and Queen's University in 1985.

17. A. Anderson, reported at the American Micro Computer—Computer Literacy Conference, Baltimore, 1985.

18. Arthur Luehrman, reported at the American Micro Computer—Computer Literacy Conference, Baltimore, 1985.

19. Michael B. Katz, *The Irony of Early School Reform* (Boston: Beacon Press, 1970), p. 215.

20. Katz, p. 215.

21. See Seymour Papert, "Are Computers Bad for Children?" in Pat Campbell and Gieta Fine (eds.), *Young Children and Microcomputers* (Englewood Cliffs, N.J.: Prentice-Hall, 1986), pp. 172–179.

Parents are now able to choose personal characteristics for children, with very low incidence of selective abortion for defective (including wrong sex) children. . . . This has allowed expanded criteria for what is defective in children; what used to be considered merely unusual is now recognized as pathological. It also allows the design of special purpose humans. Some patriotic parents, for example, who wanted to maximize the United States' chance of winning Olympic gold medals were able to choose children with specific musculature potentials. (And there are even reports of the creation of rudimentary types of webbed feet for would-be swimmers).

—AMERICAN COUNCIL OF LIFE INSURANCE

FUTUREHYPE IN HEALTH

Of all of the realms of human existence in which our obsession with the future most clearly manifests itself, the one which seems persistently to retain the strongest hold on the popular imagination is health. Undoubtedly the popular concern about the "health future" stems largely from what is commonly regarded as a prominent characteristic of present-day western culture: the reluctance to accept sickness and death.[1] Almost every day there is a report in the news to the effect that scientists have made a major breakthrough in the treatment of one of the seemingly intractable diseases of our time, like cancer, cardiovascular disease, or mental illness, the cure for which is said to have appeared on the horizon and will be arriving in the not too distant future. These claims are often corroborated by testimony from a desperate patient seeking a cure. René Dubos, whose distinguished career as a microbiologist did not, however, include these kinds of press conferences, once observed: "There are always men starved for hope or greedy for sensation who will testify to the healing power of a spectacular surgical feat or a new miracle drug. They provide the testimonies of the new religions for which scientists with theories unproved or incomplete are always ready to provide the mystic language."[2] Undoubtedly the way in which health futurologists have come to play on our hopes and fears on a day-to-day basis is more stark than in any other area.

In spite of the many remarkable discoveries and innovations in medicine which have occurred during this century, and which might be used to justify the prophetic vision of our time, the tradition of prophecy in medicine is not new. In fact, it can be traced back to the famous Greek physician Hippocrates. It was during his time that western civilization witnessed for the first time a rapid and dramatic rise in medical science: a rise in which, it should be noted, he himself played a very prominent role. The ability to predict events on the basis of a deep understanding of the forces that shape them has always been regarded as one of the hallmarks of true science, and it appears as though this is the reason that Hippocrates advised his students and disciples to use forecasting to inspire confidence in their patients. He wrote: "I hold that it is an excellent thing for a physician to practice forecasting. For if he discover and declare unaided by the side of his patients the present, the past, and the future, and fill in the gaps in the account given by the sick he will be the more believed to understand the cases so that men will confidently entrust themselves to him for treatment."[3]

Plato was greatly impressed by the developments in medicine which had been brought about by Hippocrates and his followers, and therefore made extensive use of the metaphor of health, along with allusions to the physician's art, in writing about all sorts of philosophical questions. Like education, health also figured in Plato's vision of utopia. In fact, the health system which he prescribed for his visionary society can best be viewed as basically being an elaboration of the program of social selection which was to play a decisive role in the education system of that state. In Plato's vision, on the one hand, the state was to take it upon itself to encourage all citizens to take good care of themselves by following sound nutrition and practicing gymnastics to develop sound bodies. But, on the other hand, Plato also maintained that those who had poor constitutions, or were unwilling or unable to take care of themselves, should be left to die. He wrote:

> Then you will establish in your state physicians and judges such as we have described. They will look after those citizens whose bodies and souls are constitutionally sound. The physically unsound they will leave to die; and they will actually put to death those who are incurably corrupt in mind.[4]

Though Plato was in some ways very subtle when it came to thinking about justice, he was rather reluctant to temper it with compassion or kindness, especially when the welfare of the state as a whole seemed to be at stake. Today, many people would probably describe Plato's health policy as a form of "blaming the victim," but no matter how you look at it, Plato's position was definitely both a moral judgment and an ideological statement. And Plato's thinking is characteristic of the ways in which health futurology is tainted by the prejudices of our modern-day prophets.

Although Plato's vision of the health future is shared by some modern prophets, the ideological roots of modern medical futurology, as with military futurology, can be traced more readily to the nineteenth century, and especially to England, than to the world of antiquity. Around the same time that Sir George Chesney published *The Battle of Dorking,* one of his fellow countrymen, Benjamin Ward Richardson, also published a future scenario which is generally regarded as the first piece of modern health futurology. It is a description of a future society that is based on the precepts of health, and Richardson got his title, and the name of the society he envisioned, from Hygeia, the minor Greek goddess who served as one of the assistants to Asklepius, the Greek god of health.

A comparison between *Hygeia* and *The Battle of Dorking* is interesting well beyond the coincidental closeness of their dates of publication. Like *The Battle of Dorking, Hy-*

geia struck a very deep chord in the heart of its Victorian audience, a chord which has continued to resonate with ever increasing strength to our time. In the literature of prediction *The Battle of Dorking* and *Hygeia* also make a pair because, in some ways, the intensity of our interest in the health future stems from the same source as our intense interest in the military future. It originates in that part of us that feels, not that the future will be very much the same, but, on the contrary, that it may hold great danger or great gain.

Unlike Chesney's *The Battle of Dorking* which was, in a sense, a new prophetic genre, Richardson's *Hygeia* was in some ways akin to earlier English utopian thinking, as well as being a logical extension of the philosophy of the British Public Health movement of the late nineteenth century. Earlier, however, images of the health future had appeared only incidentally, in bits and pieces in fiction, and in the context of more sweeping visions. In 1516 Sir Thomas More had published his famous *Utopia,* in which he described a society that placed the emphasis in health care on the prevention of illness rather than on its cure, and in which temperate living, first-class hospitals and enlightened sanitary measures brought a great measure of health and longevity to the people of the land. On the other hand, in *The New Atlantis,* published in 1626, Francis Bacon, who idolized the powers of science, placed the emphasis on the cure rather than the prevention of disease in the health system of his visionary society. He described a society in which scientists performed remarkable feats of curing disease by the use of drugs and medicines, prolonged life by means of "artificial waters of Paradise" or "air chambers" and prevented infectious disease by means of a certain fruit which, to our ears, sounds strikingly similar to the orange. Bacon also advocated the establishment of a research and development system similar to the ones which exist at present in all advanced industrial nations. Finally, in 1872 Samuel Butler published his celebrated visionary novel *Erewhon,* which foreshadowed the collapse of the Victorian illusion of eternal progress. Butler, unflatteringly but logically following in the footsteps of Plato, portrayed a dark vision of a society in which illness was punished as a crime, sometimes even subject to capital punishment, in order to promote the propagation of a beautiful race; physicians in this society, on the other hand, were satirized as members of the underworld. But unlike all of these utopias and dystopias, *Hygeia* was a vision of a city of the future that would be based on health to the extent that all of its governance would be dominated by precepts of health. Before any other needs or considerations, before politics, before economics, before religion, before art, would come health.

The impression that Richardson's *Hygeia* made on his contemporaries is quite extraordinary, much like that made by *The Battle of Dorking* a few years earlier. In describing it, the historian James Cassedy has observed that "both British and continental newspapers reported it at length. . . . Uncounted numbers of young British doctors and sanitarians read it and were permanently impressed. Rich old ladies began to build 'Hygeian residences'; tradesmen advertised Hygeian goods. Busy Fabian reformers incorporated elements of Hygeia into their plans for national health services."[5]

There are several reasons why *Hygeia* captured the public imagination. First, since it followed on the heels of the passage of the British Public Health Act of 1875, on one level the publication of *Hygeia* was a sort of celebration of the triumph of the advocacy movement which had promoted the newly enacted public health measures. It was also a simple projection of continued progress along these lines. On another level, there were parts of *Hygeia* that undoubtedly appealed to the ideals of large sectors of the educated public because these parts pointed towards relief from the messy world in which almost everyone lived. Most of these measures are commonplace by now: in this city of the future garbage would be collected daily, streets would be well paved, properly graded for drainage and regularly hosed down, transportation would be underground, industry that was noxious or noisy would be located outside of town and hospitals would be clean, efficient, commodious, flexible and up-to-date.

But although on one level Richardson's vision was simply the embodiment of best practice in public health, he was certainly not content to stop there. Richardson published *Hygeia* in 1875, eighteen years after Louis Pasteur had published his first seminal paper on the germ theory of disease. It is no exaggeration to say that Pasteur's work was nothing less than revolutionary, but Richardson, far from being an easy or early convert, belonged to a school of thought which did not accept the germ theory as it was expounded by Pasteur and by Koch. In fact, Pasteur and Richardson are the intellectual ancestors to two of the most prominent schools of thought in health futurology. It would be worthwhile therefore to examine briefly the apparent connection between Richardson's thinking and that of Pasteur.

Although Pasteur was in many ways a very subtle thinker, the heart of his theory was decidedly mechanistic. Up until Pasteur began to publish his brilliant papers on the germ theory of disease, public health was based not on the notion that germs were the enemy, but rather on philosophical notions that were not strictly based on scientific proof or theory. These were notions to the effect that man must live hygienically, moderately and in harmony with himself and his environment. Many of the great triumphs of nineteenth-century public health, like Max von Pettenkofer's cleaning up of the city of Munich, were based on these kinds of principles, and not on mechanistic theories of cause and effect, like the germ theory of disease.[6] And, as far as the health of the individual was concerned, mid-nineteenth-century medicine generally maintained that it is the disturbance of a person's inner and/or outer equilibrium—with causes potentially emanating from any number of sources, sometimes several at once—that initiates sickness. Because they were so radical, Pasteur's ideas met very serious resistance in his time from both physicians and public health advocates, and Richardson was a part of the resistance.

It should be noted that the germ theory of disease, though based on good hard science, had effects other than merely promoting a dispassionate search for simple causes and simple effects. It also provided a basis for a philosophical posture of a different sort, in part because of other Victorian ideas with which it coincidentally became associated. René Dubos describes this association very well:

Pasteur's first paper on the germ theory, the *Mémoire sur la fermentation appellée lactique,* appeared

in 1857 just one month before Charles Darwin sent
to Asa Gray the famous letter stating for the first
time in a precise form the theory of evolution.
Through this historical accident the germ theory of
disease developed during the gory phase of Darwinism, when the interplay between living things
was regarded as a struggle for survival, when one
had to be friend or foe, with no quarter given. This
attitude molded from the beginning the pattern of
all the attempts at the control of microbial diseases.
It led to a kind of aggressive warfare against the
microbes, aimed at their elimination from the sick
individual and from the community.[7]

For followers of Pasteur and Koch, the enemy—microbes—
was clear, and the weapons—drugs and vaccines that would
destroy them—were either at hand or could be developed.
But for Richardson, the first health futurologist, the battle
for health was not simply a battle against germs. Like the
battle between men, it was naturally to be a struggle which
only the fittest would win. This battle, however, was to be
fought not only against germs, but against some aspects of
human nature as well.

Because of Richardson's zeal, his scenario went well
beyond best public health practice, and in doing so proved
that even such seemingly innocuous things as public health
measures can be tyrannical when carried too far. His future
health society simply did not respect any boundaries. It was
extremely prejudiced and flawed—in that it appears to have
neither known nor cared about human institutions, large
parts of human nature and areas of human life that have
little or nothing to do with health.

For example, he decreed that in this future city of health
the walls of all dwellings were to be devoid of pictures or
ornaments because these were deemed to collect unhealthy
dust and mildew, and indeed even wallpaper was to be
banned because of the supposedly toxic nature of the paste
used to hang it. Instead, he predicted a sort of bathroom or
laboratory architecture for the dwellings of Hygeia in which
all walls were to be made of glazed brick so that they could
be scrubbed down. And though at one point Richardson

suggested that the brick might be done in a variety of colors to suit the individual taste, at a later point he recommended that a uniform gray would be most suitable for everyone's purposes. (He made an exception, however, for the rich who he expected would have the means to adorn their walls in what he called fancy "Pompeian" brickwork.)

But more than assaulting the aesthetic lives of the individuals of this city, *Hygeia* prescribed a certain form of social intolerance of all "unhealthy" habits, an intolerance, it should be added, which in Richardson's fanciful mind would be enforced by socially ostracizing those who would or could not shake them. Richardson wrote, "Practically, we are in a total abstainers' town, and a man seen intoxicated would be so avoided by the whole community, he would have no peace of mind to remain." Where this person would go, Richardson neglected to say but he did go on to predict:

> And, as smoking and drinking go largely together, as the two practices were, indeed, original exchanges of social degradations between the civilised man and the savage, the savage getting very much the worst of the bargain, so the practices largely disappear together. Pipe and glass, cigar and sherry-cobbler, like the Siamese twins, who could only live connected, have both died out in our model city. Tobacco, by far the most innocent partner of the firm, lived, as it perhaps deserved to do, a little the longest; but it passed away, and the tobacconist's counter, like the dram counter, has disappeared.[8]

From the above it should not surprise the reader to learn that, aside from being a prominent public health advocate, Richardson was also an active member of the temperance movement of his time. Whatever merits the temperance movement may have had in its earlier and less extreme phases, by Richardson's time large parts of it had already become extremely dogmatic and intolerant. Richardson must surely have belonged to one of the more extreme factions of this movement because in his scenario of the future city of health he displayed no tolerance for even moderate uses of alcohol; according to his beliefs and those of the more zealous activists of this movement, all uses were, by definition, abuse. His description of the way alcohol would be treated in this society suggests that he believed that the cause of alcohol abuse was basically to be found in the substance rather than in the person.† For Richardson, a simple, technical problem requires a simple, technical solution: eliminate alcohol from the pubs and people's homes and they will no longer be alcoholics. There was no room in Richardson's rigorously logical society of health for the moderate, pleasurable use of any drugs.

Furthermore, for Richardson, not only was alcohol in itself an unmitigated evil, it was also the source of many others. Later in his vision he went on to predict that "in a city from which that grand source of wild mirth, hopeless sorrow and confirmed madness, alcohol, has been expelled, it could hardly be expected that much insanity would be found. The few who are insane are placed in houses licensed as asylums, but not different in appearance to other houses in the city. Here the insane live, in small communities, under proper medical supervision, with their own gardens and pastimes."[9] Even for a Victorian, Richardson had a blissfully ignorant way of skirting or simplifying the variety of sources of mental illness which come both from within us and from without us. In his future scenario all mental illness that was not the direct consequence of alcohol abuse would be treated as a form of mental retardation. One had either raving alcoholics or village idiots—nothing else and nothing in between.

But as a temperance-activist-cum-futurologist, Richardson was playing the part not of a religious, but of a technocratic fundamentalist. It is clear from his approach to alcohol abuse that he believed ardently in the efficacy of

---

† The temperance movement had its origins in religious fundamentalism in New England in the early nineteenth century. In its more extreme forms, aside from categorically opposing the consumption of alcohol it was also, among other things, anti-immigrant and anti-Roman Catholic. The idea that alcohol abuse is inherent to the substance rather than the person uses the same logic that is presently driving the American war on drug abuse, a movement that is focusing on trying to stop the flow of drugs rather than on restoring drug abusers to health.

technique and technology in solving all problems, even those that were not solely technical problems. But more than this, he believed that institutions that were not grounded in his very narrow view of nature were superfluous, much as alcohol and music are superfluous to the religious fundamentalist. Therefore, in his vision of the future city of health, Richardson opposed even profound religious practices, like the erection of tombstones, if they in any way undermined his precepts of health. In Richardson's completely rational mind the burial of the dead was to be little more than an exercise in replenishment of the soil. He wrote:

> The burial ground is artificially made of a fine carboniferous earth. Vegetation of rapid growth is cultivated over it. The dead are placed in the earth from the bier, either in basket work or simply in the shroud; and the monumental slab, instead of being set over or at the head or foot of a raised grave, is placed in a spacious covered hall or temple, and records simply the fact that the person commemorated was recommitted to earth in these grounds. In a few months, indeed, no monument would indicate the remains of any dead. In that rapidly-resolving soil the transformation of dust into dust is too perfect to leave a trace of residuum. The natural circle of transmutation is harmlessly completed, and the economy of nature conserved.[10]

Richardson's health prophecy, with its plethora of sterile and paternalistic precepts, was in some ways a sort of hypochondriac's heaven. Following ideals, this city of the future was to be constantly sterilized, or, to use the more modern term which has developed political connotations, it is forever being *disinfected*. It is not too difficult to imagine why *Hygeia* appealed to the educated and well-to-do Victorian public, but though parts of it may have appealed to their idealism, other parts must surely have appealed to the vanity and hypocrisy, rather than the logic, of those who actually read all of this little book.

What is most striking about this prophetic vision, now

that we have attained some distance from it, is that in this elaborate picture of a future city of health there are no recognizable, flesh-and-blood, all-too-human people—in a word, no individuals—except for the occasional caricatures of individuals which are so typical of the futurologist's portraiture. Richardson portrays the crazed and raving alcoholic but not the sometimes dull and sometimes witty, sometimes celebratory and sometimes silly, seldom inspiring but usually basically innocuous social drinker. Obsessively tied to precepts of health, Richardson's future society was prepared to expunge everything else of value in the human fabric from its midst. It was to be a society devoid of aesthetics, insensitive to religious sensibilities and unwilling or perhaps unable to distinguish between harmless little pleasures and harmful overindulgences. And, perhaps more important, devoid of choice and challenge. In the final analysis, Richardson's Hygeia is an extremely mechanical place, a sterile city in which the strongest emotions that one can imagine, if these can be called emotions at all, are contentedness and a feeling of safety. In the end, this little book reads more like a manual for good husbandry than a portrait of a human society.

Both *Hygeia* and *The Battle of Dorking* represent a battle fought and won. In the case of *The Battle of Dorking*, the battle was won by the wrong side, of course, but even this is as it should be because as warning this makes the prophecy even more salutary. In the end, whatever else it may be, *Hygeia* is also the story of a battle, the story of a victorious future war against all of the causes of disease. If the enemies are germs, then it is necessary to defoliate and eliminate their hiding places—even if these happen to be pictures on the wall or wallpaper. If the enemies are toxins, in whatever form or whatever quantity, in alcohol, tobacco, noise and pollution, then they too must be eliminated—*completely*. All of the precepts in *Hygeia* are based on the premise that the enemy is clear and obvious, can always be identified and, when identified, can be eliminated. These are the precepts of war.

We have seen how flawed and dangerous this kind of thinking can be in the context of war, and with respect to health it is, in some ways, just as flawed but not so obviously dangerous.† Yet this simplistic thinking is very attractive to futurologists. From their perspective we need above all to have a clearly defined enemy—in war as in the battle against disease—and on both types of battlefield it is always easier when we can persuade ourselves that the enemy is outside of us rather than within, that the enemy is another person or a thing rather than, as is often the case, ourselves.

Since Richardson's time, the war against disease has moved to new fronts. In our time there are three major schools of thought competing in the field of health care and, because modern prophecy is generally a projection of the present and usually likes to associate itself with some sort of power base, most of the innumerable health scenarios in the literature of health futurology represent one of these three. Characteristically, however, these scenarios are mere caricatures of the present. Whatever cooperation and tolerance may exist in the present complex health scene is banished from the future one, which is often portrayed as being both exclusive and intolerant. Ironically, therefore, along with the external battle against disease, we also have in the future world of health which these scenarios collectively portray a three-way civil war among the schools of thought. The three combatants in this civil war are physicians, purveyors of the so-called alternative therapies and health bureaucrats. Of course the seeds of all three schools of thought, along with the battlefront mentality, were already contained in germinal form in Richardson's future city of health, but there, at least, they did not compete. It took the modern rationalization and institutionalization of health care, with the accompanying growth of professional rivalry on the one hand and heavy pressure on national resources on the other, to create the present state of competition among the three sectors of the health care field. To end this rivalry and competition—which

---

† In our time we have even seen extreme and oversimplistic metaphors of health used to promote racism and applied to the most horrifying practices of war. As has been commonly observed, we have heard the term extermination applied to humans instead of to pests, all in the name of promoting the health of the fittest, who were eventually to become a master race. No more extreme form of social Darwinism is imaginable, yet it is easily enough buried in the metaphor of health.

naturally goes against the grain of most futurologists, who cannot bear to contemplate a "messy" world—what each of the three types of scenarios portrays, among other things, is the establishment of the domination of one school of health thought over all of the others.[11]

The first characteristic scenario is a description of the triumph of medical technology—the weapons in the war against disease—but also the triumph of physicians, the heroes who wield them. This scenario also, incidentally, describes the triumph of a basically unregulated laissez-faire marketplace for the provision of health care; somehow or other, physician heroes and the laissez-faire provision of health care services are deemed to belong together and destined to triumph together in the future world portrayed by this vision. The second type of future health care scenario has the patient as hero. He either eliminates disease by an act of will, metaphorically referred to by some futurologists as the "hospital-in-the-mind," or exercises his consumer sovereignty in what turns out to be a wonderfully varied health marketplace where he picks and chooses, at reasonable cost, the therapies he needs to heal himself. Needless to say, in this scenario the health consumer's completely rational approach to the maintenance of his health easily and naturally triumphs over any other drives that might motivate or defeat him. And the third type portrays the public health administrator in the role of soldier-hero. His weapons, not surprisingly, are legislation, public health programs and, as we shall soon see, the power to enforce them.

Unfortunately, over the years since Richardson published *Hygeia,* the mechanistic tendencies of health futurology have only increased—and, interestingly enough, so have its paternalistic tendencies. A brief glance at a fairly recent set of future health scenarios which are very representative of the three basic types I have just described demonstrate what I mean. The scenarios are published by the American Council of Life Insurance (ACLI) which sponsors an ongoing project called the Trend Analysis Program (TAP) to monitor trends in health care. The ones I have in mind are contained in a report called *Health Care: Three Reports from 2030 A.D.,* which is divided into three sections, each representing one of the three schools of thought in health futurology as well as in the field of health care in general.†

The first section, entitled "A Fifty Year Report from the American Association for the Advancement of Medical Technology 1980–2030," represents the school that believes that physicians and technology will continue to be the center of the health care system of the future just as they are today. Assuming the voice of the future historian, this section boastfully begins: "The stunning triumphs of the last half-century prove that most of our problems had technological solutions. Technology has extended man's medical prowess beyond the once-finite limits of cradle to grave. In the process, Americans have come close to eradicating disease, have created primitive forms of artificial life and appear to be on the verge of conquering death itself."[12] Many of the predictions which are made in this section of the insurance council report are just the sort of thing one might expect from a world view that feels that technology can and will solve any and all human problems. Human individuality in this view is not overtly avoided but, as was the case with the mechanical individualization of instruction, it is finessed in what are by now all too familiar terms: it is treated as a *problem,* a rationally definable problem with a mechanical solution. The report from 2030 A.D. glibly observes: "Preventive medicine has come to recognize that each individual is genetically and biochemically unique. This has meant that it is now routine to determine what occupational and lifestyle choices are optimal for newborn infants. . . . The use of computerized, problem-oriented record systems led to the creation and wide availability of model treatment profiles and higher standards for medical data. (Problem-oriented medical records noted *all the physiological, emotional, social and economic problems associated with a patient's life.*)"[13] (emphasis added)

Having trivialized the question of human individuality, both as problem and solution, by assuming it to be both

---

† Their methodology is the same as that used by Naisbitt to produce his newsletter and his book *Megatrends.* The way this project works is that over one hundred life insurance executives around the United States routinely monitor and prepare abstracts of relevant articles which may appear in any of a large number of designated publications. From time to time, these abstracts are summarized in reports to the life insurance industry and are then ostensibly drawn upon for the purposes of thinking about and planning for the industry's future.

comprehensible enough to be defined by rational terms and then simply absorbed into medical routine, the report then goes on to dispose of the physical problems of the human condition, large and small, with similarly unhesitating dispatch and with the neatest solutions: "The original breakthroughs in technologies for the handicapped were soon converted to augment the 'normals' who wanted, for example, to see in the dark, speak and eat at the same time, or regenerate limbs. . . . The computer in their 'hospitals on the wrist' can diagnose and suggest treatment for a disease before individuals even notice symptoms. . . . The recognition that senile dementia was caused by a virus and the ability to cure senility with anti-viral drugs saved many Americans from fear of aging. Initial tests of an anti-aging vaccine led to significant breakthroughs in 1997 and broad application by 2020."[14]

The elaborate pacemaker known in the health futurology trade as the "hospital-on-the-wrist" makes many appearances in the technology-driven model of future health care delivery. In some predictions, less constrained than the one above in describing its uses, these little machines get to make *automated* decisions. For example, Peter Goldschmidt of the Health Futures Project at the Policy Research Institute in Baltimore writes: "The hospital-on-the-wrist is the apex of medical technology. This device not only monitors body functions but also adjust them to maintain homeostasis."[15] How will the hospital-on-the-wrist adjust bodily functions to maintain homeostasis? This is spelled out in another version of this scenario by health futurologist Clement Bezold, who predicts that "such communications advances as the 'hospital on the wrist,' . . . monitors bodily functions and *administers appropriate doses of drugs and electrical charges directly through the skin*. (Remember when Dick Tracy's two-way wristwatch radio was science fiction?)" (emphasis added)[16] What is most striking about these hospital-on-the-wrist visionaries is that, aside from likening them to Dick Tracy radios, they seem unable to imagine how these devices might work out in real life situations, where even bodily states require context in order to be properly interpreted, understood and treated. It takes very little imagination to realize that, should these devices ever be developed for popular use, they would probably also be accompanied by newspaper accounts telling how hundreds of young people who had forgotten to reprogram their wrist-hospitals were carried out of rock concerts on stretchers, not on account of having fainted, but on account of having been oversedated by their sophisticated wrist-equalizers in reaction to the states of extreme excitation which are naturally produced at these events.

However, the reader should not imagine the American Association for the Advancement of Medical Technology to be naive in thinking that there will be no problems in introducing so much technological innovation into an ill-prepared society. It laments, for example, that "because technology has displaced so many health care workers, it has created a labor pool for services like the franchised Lov'n-Care stores. Clients now rent an older person for an hour or more to tell stories, soothe injured feelings, or just cuddle an ailing child."[17] It also observes that "problems with health care technology in the past often arose because society couldn't keep up with the hardware. Life and death ethical questions tended to overwhelm many proposed advances. Once we could directly modify and design organisms, new social forms were required to protect the democratic process. Today, of course, technology is being used to explore ethical questions more rapidly. It is possible for citizens all over the world to actively debate weighty social questions in a matter of hours."[18] The only thing that is missing from this scenario is that, given communication technology and the very short time frame allowed for these debates, they will undoubtedly be done with all of the incisiveness, conclusiveness and dispatch of a call-in radio show! Later on, this report also whimsically envisions that "parents are now able to choose personal characteristics for children, with very low incidence of selective abortion for defective (including wrong sex) children. . . . This has allowed expanded criteria for what is defective in children; what used to be considered merely unusual is now recognized as pathological. It also allows the design of special purpose humans. Some patriotic parents, for example, who wanted to maximize the United States' chance of winning Olympic gold medals were able to choose children with specific musculature potentials. (And there are even reports of the creation of rudimentary types of webbed feet for would-be swimmers)."[19]

The second section of the ACLI report, called "Comprehensive Report of the Cooperative Commission on Wellness 2030," describes a future scenario that ostensibly represents the philosophy of the alternative healing movement. It is not nearly as systematic or monolithic as the section reflecting the philosophy of the technophiles but is more of a hodgepodge caricature of New Age truisms. The great good that it promotes is the sovereignty and self-possession of the individual patient. It begins: "A cultural transformation has touched every aspect of Western industrial civilization, and as we all know, a change in the conceptual model of the world has an all pervading influence on the forms of human life and its institutions."[20] What is the nature of this "all pervading influence"? Well, for one thing, the report tells us that "trends in health care indicate that androgyny, or the realization of both masculine and feminine attributes in every individual, has become a cultural goal." A concept for explaining the sometimes ambiguous boundaries of sex will become a cultural goal? In that case, any state of being can become a policy goal, and so they do. Therefore, among the more enlightened members of this society, "it seems that human beings may have an innate biological awareness of their physical state down to the level of the single cell and that the human mind can intervene in and direct any physiologic function."[21] Furthermore, according to the philosophy of this school of future health thought, all disease is in the mind. For example, it observes that "comprehensive National Health Insurance bills failed to pass since the public had grown to recognize the ineffectiveness of such programs and place such great emphasis on individual responsibility."† For some reason or other, in this future nation of health, individual and collective responsibility for health are viewed as being mutually exclusive. If the individual takes responsibility for his or her own health, it simply leaves no room for the state, the natural enemy, to get involved even to facilitate individual decisions.

Of course this scenario, like its counterparts, also en-

---

† This view, of course, is a milder version of that stated by Plato in the *Republic*.

visions problems, but they are as much caricatures as the so-called solutions. The report observes that "professionals, particularly MDs, had an especially difficult time adjusting to the decreased reliance on professionals and more egalitarian relationships between professionals and consumers," and also that "research efforts were redirected because of the feeling that biomedical research could no longer rest on reductionist assumptions (e.g. separation of body/mind/spirit) which directed 20th century medicine. Throughout the closing years of the 20th century, researchers devoted themselves to finding techniques for *motivating wellness-enhancing behavior in populations that were not so inclined.*" (emphasis added)[22] Conclusion: since the mind is so important in controlling an individual's health, it is important that we discover ways of controlling the minds of those who are not inclined to control their own health as they ought to.

Of the three scenarios in this set, the one which is both the most direct heir to Richardson's *Hygeia,* and to Plato's relentless pursuit of "health justice" in the *Republic,* is the vision of the future in which public health triumphs over the other two as the dominant philosophy. It also happens to describe the most tyrannical future of all. Called "The National Health Caucus 2030 A.D.," this scenario begins, tamely enough, with the retrospective observation that "over the last half century, developments in two areas combined to create the enviable health care system we have today. Technology and political wisdom were those two areas, and it is our purpose now to briefly outline their simultaneous contributions to progress." But what passes for "political wisdom" and "progress" in this scenario, were it ever to come into being, would undoubtedly make a great many people in the year 2030 hanker for the good old days of political stupidity.

From this harmless little prelude the insurance council proceeds to sketch, in progressively more shocking terms, what can only be described not as "The City of Health" but rather as "The Third Reich of Health": "Perhaps the greatest administrative successes resulted from one simple Congressional directive issued in 1998. Everyone involved was to do whatever was necessary to find out which health care procedures really worked. . . . Model treatment data bases were set up describing those treatments which had been found effective, and were automatically triggered when the appropriate set of symptoms was entered into the computer. To reinforce the new system, penalties were imposed if it was discovered that model treatment plans had been ignored."[23] Presumably these penalties would be imposed even if, in certain cases, it could be demonstrated that a treatment other than the model treatment was more appropriate and effective. "Personnel in particularly hazardous occupations were monitored by remote control. Readings were then fed into a central data base and analyzed by personnel skilled in the early identification of actual and potential stressors. The unexpected success in the workplace led officials to conduct similar experiments in the home. Since, by 1990, many consumers used their two-way television systems to order goods, it became feasible to keep track of purchasing patterns. Hyperactive children who upset their biochemical balance by ordering candy bars, adults at high risk of divorce who placed numerous orders for sedatives and grandparents who were abusing recreational drugs could all be identified."[24] The authoritarian implications of this school of thought are inescapable: never underestimate the importance of knowing the enemy, even if it happens to be the unenlightened children, spouses and grandparents of the nation.

The report then continues along other lines that are still authoritarian but overtly more benign: "Citizens with criminal or anti-social tendencies can be monitored and prevented from doing themselves or others any harm. And there are hopes that by coordinating information about the gene pool, the government can help insure that only those most fit for a stressful environment encounter the challenges of today's world. One way to see that this happens is through the use of routine screening of the population for genetic markers. Counselors routinely use this information to help clients make decisions about how they should live. In some instances, of course, decisions have to be made for them." A simple program in eugenics to usher in the superior race, much as Plato hoped to do. "Everyone understood by the beginning of this century that health care costs were determined by the way people lived. To hold down costs and to promote public health, the government was forced to intervene in individual life decisions . . . it makes sense to ration potentially harmful substances and to treat people who pursue unwarranted risks as social criminals."[25] Rock climbers and hang-gliders, watch out!

The above scenarios all describe the future triumph of one school of health thought over the other two. However, in keeping with the social Darwinist tradition that originally set the stage for Richardson's *Hygeia,* some of our modern prophets even relish the struggle itself, that is, the competitiveness that reengineering and rebuilding our bodies ultimately implies. According to American health futurologist Jerrold Maxmen, the health future will hold some very interesting twists in the struggle for survival of the fittest. He writes:

> Despite nature's ingenious artistry, artificial devices may improve upon the human product, and eventually people may replace their organs freely. If so, humanity would enter a new stage of history in which the semiartificial man becomes a reality. Man and machine could be intermeshed so completely that the two would become indistinguishable. This hybrid, known as a "cyborg" (an abbreviation for cybernetic organism), would be capable of two-way communication between its human and mechanical parts. Computers and other sophisticated devices could be implanted in man to amplify his intellectual or physical powers. The potential implications are mind boggling. Pessimists fear that conflicts between men and cyborgs could lead to nothing less than a total annihilation of human culture. Conversely, optimists proclaim that eventually natural selection will allow cyborgs to dominate and enrich civilization."[26]

What is noteworthy about these two alternative scenarios is that whether the pessimists or the optimists are right does not really seem to matter in the sense that, in both cases, the "cyborgs" are predicted to be destined to win the struggle with ordinary human beings. In keeping with the mind-set of many forecasters in other fields, in this scenario the machine-human hybrids are once again expected to evolve further and be more successful than ordinary humans.

Later in this book, anticipating his critics, this prophet continues: "My opposition to social, legal, and theologically imposed restrictions of the development and use of biomedical innovations does not rest solely upon pragmatic considerations. If we are forced to follow absolute ethical standards that are not adjusted to historical change or individual need, our capacity to cope effectively with the future will be undermined. . . . We cannot and will not increase man's sense of free will by depriving him of the freedom to make his own ethical decisions."[27] Apparently this futurologist is unable to distinguish between freedom and license in medical ethics.

It is interesting, moreover, that for this modern-day prophet "coping effectively with the future" will necessitate, among other things, the adoption of Hobbesian postures of each against all. The apparent assumption behind this premise seems to be that those who are willing to buy into the new technologies deserve to triumph over their fellows. But the struggle for health supremacy is not always expressed in the graphic and vulgar terms of a war between ordinary humans and cyborgs.† Sometimes it becomes a simple class struggle and is expressed in the utilitarian terms of the dispassionate economist. This came out in a debate which was carried out at the National Heart and Lung Institute of the United States in 1973 on the appropriateness of developing a nuclear-powered artificial heart.

The program to develop a totally implantable artificial heart (TIAH), of which the nuclear-powered heart was the centerpiece, was initiated as a very large research and developmemnt program by the Johnson administration in the early 1960s shortly after Dr. Christiaan Barnard performed the first human heart transplant. The first artificial heart, designed by Domingo Liotta, was implanted in an American by the name of Haskell Carp in 1969, and sustained him for three days, whereupon it was replaced by a human heart

---

† One wonders what it takes to be considered a cyborg? Would an ordinary hip replacement do? When the warring factions are finally mustered at some point in the future, do people get to decide whether they want to be considered humans or cyborgs?

which sustained him for another thirty-six hours, and then he died. Carp's wife accused Dr. Denton Cooley, the surgeon who performed the operation, of making her husband "the unfortunate victim of human experimentation," and the FDA banned further artificial heart transplants until these machines and techniques for using them could be properly developed. The artificial heart that Cooley used had been privately developed. The NIH program, of which this device was not a part, was officially launched in 1964 with the establishment of the Artificial Heart Program Office. During one period in the artificial heart development project, the NIH collaborated with the Atomic Energy Commission in developing the nuclear-powered artificial heart, but bureaucratic infighting broke up this collaboration. NIH's program nevertheless grew very large, at one point being as large as the navy's program to develop the Trident missile. In 1973 dollars, a nuclear-powered artificial heart was projected to cost $25,000 for the appliance itself (mainly on account of the high cost of Plutonium-238) and another $15,000 for the surgical procedure.

Had the program succeeded, it would undoubtedly have ranked with the first moonshot as a great technological accomplishment. Several models of this mechanical heart were developed simultaneously, but the one which was at once most attractive to the NIH and most controversial was the nuclear-powered artificial heart. It was attractive because it would not require follow-up procedures for recharging the battery since, being nuclear, it would never require recharging. However it was controversial for several reasons: its production and dissemination would require supervision by the Atomic Energy Commission since it was to employ Plutonium-238; it presented a health hazard both to its user and to other people, especially potential offspring who would be at particular risk from radiation exposure; and it would be very expensive. A prototype was completed by Westinghouse by 1975, but it was abandoned because of its controversial nature.

Dissenting from the majority position of the advisory panel that rejected the nuclear heart, Prof. Clark Havighurst of Duke Law School began by accusing the majority of the panel of "moralizing." Then, after lamenting the fact that they had not come up with a set of "neutral values" upon which to make their judgment, he offered what he considered to be the following elegant solution to this problem:

> Sometimes, because the social arrangements being made today for the future do not benefit specific individuals at the expense of identifiable others, it may be possible to justify a pure utilitarian approach by viewing the stakes of individuals probabilistically, making each a possible gainer as well as a possible loser. Thus viewed, if potential gains exceed potential losses, the action might be deemed appropriate without concern for compensation of the actual losers. Difficulties remain, of course, if the advantages (disadvantages) are likely to accrue only to the more (less) affluent or to some other group to which all do not have a roughly equal expectation of belonging. But, even if compensation is impossible in such circumstances and injustice therefore inevitable, it may still be unjust not to take the action, since that would be to impose uncompensated costs (in the form of benefits denied) on the would-be beneficiaries. Justice demands not that perfect justice be done, for that is impossible, but that every effort be made to design public programs and the legal environment of private activities—if they are justified because the benefits outweigh the costs—so that uncompensated harms are minimized. It is hard to conceive of circumstances when it would not be wrong to require that a large benefit be forgone in order to avoid imposing a small harm.[28]

There is nothing original about Havighurst's arguments for developing the nuclear-powered artificial heart. Similar arguments were used to promote the development of nuclear power plants long before we knew anything about the effects of small doses of radiation. But by 1973, when Havighurst was writing the above dissent, there was already evidence that even very small doses were enough to cause cancer. This is spelled out in the report: the report acknowledges the fact that future recipients of nuclear-powered artificial hearts, although prolonging their lives by preventing heart failure, would nevertheless almost certainly assure themselves of later dying of leukemia or some other form of cancer induced by their appliance. If you unpack Havighurst's argument from its econo-legalistic wrapper and consider it in terms of real human beings, it is obvious why he stood alone against the rest of the committee.

Since Havighurst's was the dissenting opinion, this is partially a cautionary tale. But it is more than a merely cautionary tale because, although the project was eventually abandoned, the implications of its having been almost completely developed at great public expense, given how obviously ridiculous it was from the very outset, are rather disturbing. And, Havighurst's arguments are worth examining because they are so typical of the kinds of spurious arguments that are so often presented by our false prophets. In fact, his arguments are strikingly similar to the arguments offered by those who promoted the build-up of huge nuclear arsenals. These arguments are all calculation and probability, without taking into account either the enemies of calculability—human fallibility and irrationality—or the specific, real and palpable harm that can and will be done to the vast majority of vulnerable and uninformed people were the program put into operation.

What does it mean, for example, when thinking of the future that we should consider only probabilities and speak of small harms versus large benefits? It means that humans are, in effect, entirely removed from the picture. When you get cancer from low-level radiation, the severity of the cancer is not determined by the amount of radiation that started it, or by the probability that you might have got it in the first place, any more than the severity of a fall from a high precipice is determined by the strength of the push that sends the body plunging. Suppose the person to get cancer from exposure to radiation from someone else's nuclear heart were a child; it would most likely be the recipient's own child or grandchild. How would one weigh the value of the life that might be lost because of this exposure against the value that might be gained by the person whose nuclear heart is emitting the radiation? It takes little imagination to see how this new medical phenomenon, no matter what efforts were expended to regulate it, might play itself out in the singles dating scene, or in the context of nuclear terrorists who might be inspired to kidnap recipients of these nuclear-powered artificial hearts in order to steal the nuclear fuel that kept them going. But instead of these obvious considerations and a host of others, all that we get from Havighurst is a vain and sterile calculus of potential small harms versus potential huge gains.

Although each of the three factions in health futurology supposedly represents a different philosophy of health, in the final analysis they all have a great deal in common with one another and are also an elaboration of the world view expressed in Richardson's *Hygeia*. All three characteristically view the human population as being basically homogeneous, or if they recognize human individuality they either trivialize or depreciate it. They usually view the processes of staying well and healing as being basically mechanical— even the "hospital-in-the-mind" sounds more like an organization or a machine than a state of being. They typically display an unawareness of or insensitivity to the irrational side of human nature. And, just as classical economists assume that greed is the prime motivating drive in all economic affairs, they likewise assume that risk-avoidance functions the same way in the realm of health: they forget the side of human nature that might consider some risk-taking to be worthwhile, even essential to human existence, and the side that might consider self-sacrifice rather than selfishness appropriate human behavior; they forget even the great health *benefits* that may accrue from risk-taking and self-sacrifice. In the end, instead of celebrating the plurality of possible approaches to healing, health preservation and disease prevention that can concurrently exist, these futurist health scenarios are images of a future in which all approaches have been subordinated to one—either to the high-tech model, the public health model, or the self-help model—and that one is exaggerated to such a degree that it becomes a caricature of its present self, as well as a monster that preys upon all of the other approaches.

Yet some of our modern-day prophets seem to delight

in pushing the caricature which health futurology has become to ever greater extremes. For example, Stanley Lesse, a psychiatrist turned futurologist, seems actually to relish predicting the demise of individuality in his vision of the health future. In his book *The Future of the Health Sciences* he writes that "in some ways individualism may be antithetical to basic human nature," and predicts:

> Individuals, rather than being preoccupied with their personal selves, will find it necessary to change their orientation, to fit themselves as part of an integrated group, in order to be accepted by their society—indeed, to survive. It is likely that they will strive to become an integral and, paradoxically, an easily replaceable element of the group. They will be dependent members of the interdependent structure, for it is from this source that they will gain their main physical, psychological, economic and philosophic nourishment. In turn, they will probably, as a matter of course, perform specific functions and tasks. In this process, certain of their capacities, functions, and possibly eventually even some of their body structure will change, with some areas undergoing atrophy and others hypertrophy.[29]

For Lesse, a real neo-Malthusian in psychiatrist's clothing, the individuality of patients seems to get in the way of efficient and effective delivery of health services. His book is heavily spiced with carping on this theme; one gets the sense in reading it that in the war against germs the individuality of the patient is an unnecessary luxury with which we simply must dispense in order to fight effectively. In another attack on humans as individuals he predicts: "Since patients will be group rather than individually oriented, they will probably have far fewer individual expectations as to treatment. Most likely they will not object to a more impersonalized type of care. These trends are already poignantly evident in socialist countries. Emphasis will be focused upon the need for patients to integrate themselves into the group as quickly as possible. Indeed, they will be constantly reminded of their position as subordinate members of the group by the very fact that treatment will be group oriented."[30] For this health futurist, it appears that the war is between the hero physician with his high-tech weapons and the enemy germs; the individual patient is merely the battleground where all of this takes place.†

The other side of Lesse's anti-individualist coin is a sort of dark glamorization of the most exaggerated and caricatured types of professionalism. Here we have no Philistines of the ordinary variety—only Goliaths. But whereas Goliath had a superiority complex, the health experts in Lesse's future have far more interesting complexes of their own, complexes that Lesse considers to be indispensable to doing the job right. For example, writing about the future of health academicians, his own professional group, he declares:

> One of the main functions of the health academician will be to interrelate human values, both individual and social with technologic phenomena. As he or she scans information drawn from any computer-health technical expert terms, various factors will be given properly weighed values.
>
> This will require that health academicians have unique characteristics. Their positions [sic] should be one in which there would be guaranteed recognition and status. . . . They would ideally also have the capacity to "love" other beings and have a love of humanity, in general, coupled with appreciation and respect for themselves, requiring a capacity to be at one with the cosmos or allness.[31]

† This brings to mind E.O. Wilson's briefly famous dictum—borrowed from Samuel Butler—that the organism is merely DNA's way of making more DNA. The extent to which ordinary humans are regarded as mere battleground was starkly spelled out by the eminent biologist J.S.B. Haldane in response to the problem of evolving resistant microbes that are the consequence of the development of antibiotics, "I think there may be enough intelligent people to deal with the emergence of resistent bacteria and the like. I am very glad that it is going to keep us on our toes, but we shan't be able to do it all by means of computers; we shall have to start thinking. Even if it means that a few million people will die prematurely every year, it is worth it in order to keep biologists on their toes, in my humble opinion." (J.S.B. Haldane, "Health and Disease," in *Man and His Future*, G. Wolstonholme [ed.], Boston, Little, Brown, 1963, p. 234.)

Elsewhere, never losing touch with his self-professed humanism (although for some reason in the above passage he feels inclined to put the word love in quotation marks), Lesse calls the health academician a "humanistic cybernator," which is basically a master computer programmer or systems analyst. Another master in Lesse's health future is the health technical expert, who has a fascinating set of personal problems of his own. Lesse predicts: "The health technical experts, in common with today's super specialists, will be obsessive-compulsive personalities. The collecting of data is likely to satisfy their psychodynamic needs. In contrast to the health academician, the health technical expert is likely to react with anxiety, if bombarded with new information, particularly information reflecting a dramatic technical change. In a parallel fashion, he or she would likely be distressed by information coming from sources other than the health sciences.[32]

Jerrold Maxmen, on the other hand, sets his sights on eliminating even physicians in the battle against germs. In his book, *The Post-Physician Era: Medicine in the Twenty-first Century,* Maxmen predicts the demise of the physician sometime during the first half of the twenty-first century. He argues that physicians will disappear for a number of reasons but mainly because they will be too expensive to maintain. Furthermore, they will have outgrown their usefulness by then because technology will be able to perform most of their tasks better than they themselves can. But since, as we all know, technology cannot quite perform all of its tasks on its own, who then will replace physicians to perform, if nothing else, their mediating function between patients and machines? Well, for starters, technicians, of course, will help patients get into the space-suit type monitors that they will feel inclined to don from time to time to keep track of their health. But what about the other needs of patients, the human needs that are so often touted nowadays? Well, to satisfy these needs another kind of specialist will be introduced onto the scene. Asserting the futurologist's prerogative of renaming things in order to bestow novelty upon them, Maxmen calls this new professional a "medic," and has him specialize in two things. First, though his training will be suspiciously similar to the training of physicians today, the medic will make a point of not using the outmoded name "physician." And second, he will specialize in being human. What will this mean? According to Maxmen it will mean, among other things, that he will become a pro at cultivating what is commonly referred to as bedside manner—but not like an amateur, like a professional. He will be rather like a psychiatrist or clinical psychologist—like Maxmen himself—and he will master categorical formulas such as Kahana and Bibring's seven personality patient-types—presumably so that he can treat each patient like an individual human being![33]

Between the rampant anti-individualism of most health futurists and the worship of superspecialization of some, it is impossible to conclude that they are actually writing about a human society, one in which conscious individuals make decisions by the day, by the hour, and by the minute, and take actions, both rational and irrational, which ultimately affect their health. Instead they seem to be writing about a society of social bees, in which most members function merely as thoughtless drones while a few individuals, equally thoughtless but more exalted in stature, play the heroic roles like that of queen. Obviously, such a society would have little to commend itself to most people, but it has one advantage that must make it eminently attractive to the banal minds of these futurologists: it appears to be perfectible. That which is static, as all of these images to all intents and purposes are, can conceivably be perfected. That is the delusion, and that is the obvious appeal of these future health visions. René Dubos has observed:

> A perfect policy of public health could be conceived for colonies of social ants or bees, whose habits have become stabilized by instincts. Likewise, it would be possible to devise for a herd of cows an ideal system of husbandry with the proper combinations of stables and pastures. But unless men become robots, their behavior and environment fully controllable and predictable, no formula can ever give them permanently the health and happiness symbolized by the contented cow. Free men will develop new urges, and these will give rise to

new habits and new problems, which will require
ever new solutions. New environmental factors are
introduced by technological innovations, by the
constant flux of tastes, habits, and mores, and by
the profound disturbances that culture and ethics
exert on the normal play of biological processes. It
is because of this instability of the physical and
social environment that the pattern of disease
changes with each phase of civilization.[34]

One can immediately see how deadly these visions are by
simply considering what is happening in health developments
in the present. How is one to account, in these static visions,
for recent cultural developments that have already had, and
promise to continue to have, a profound effect on our health?
We are living during a period, for example, when exercise
has again become a craze; but it is also a period when sports
medicine has become a rapidly growing specialty. Speaking
more esoterically, we are also living during the beginning of
the age of space exploration, and during the beginning of
the development of a specialty in space medicine. These are
the sorts of changes that Dubos had in mind when he wrote,
"Free men will develop new urges, and these will give rise
to new habits and new problems, which will require ever
new solutions." All of these urges represent unanticipated
new experiences, and sometimes risks. They do not, however, represent utopia or paradise on earth. Yet in 1958,
following steadfastly in the steps of Richardson's childish
vision, Dr. Axel Hojer of the World Health Organization
(WHO) wrote that "man seems to have found out how to
make his dreams of a paradise on earth come true," and
around the same time Dr. M.G. Candau, Director-General
of WHO predicted that "if the great advances gained in
science and technology are put at the service of all the people
of the world, our children will live in an age from which
most of the diseases our grandparents and parents took for
granted will be banished. It may no longer be Utopian to
envisage a new chapter in the history of medicine."[35]
	Of course, notwithstanding all of this existential cheer-
leading, there are and always will be perils ahead. The sit-

uation remains much the same as Dubos described it in 1959 when he wrote: "Who could have dreamt a generation ago that hypervitaminosis would become a common form of nutritional disease in the Western world? That the cigaret industry and the use of x-rays would be held responsible for the increase in certain types of cancers? That the introduction of detergents and various synthetics would increase the incidence of allergies? That advances in chemotherapy and other therapeutic procedures would create a new staphylococcus pathology? That alcoholism would become widespread in the Western world? That patients with all forms of iatrogenic diseases would occupy such a large number of beds in modern hospitals?"[36]

Dubos is not a pessimist, but as a biologist, he has come to realize that medicine will never become a finished science like chemistry because, though the number of elements in the universe seems now to be finite, the number of things that can and will threaten our health is not, and as we evolve as a species, so do they. As we adapt to the microbes that threaten our health, new ones, like the AIDS virus, continue to emerge. As we eliminate some of the toxins we have created, we create, willy-nilly, others to replace them. As we eliminate or avoid some forms of stress, others emerge in our ever changing culture. And beyond this, we are constantly redefining what health is and how we should think of it. This is not a pessimistic view, but the human condition as it has ever been. Nor is it cause for despair, because the microbes are merely one type of thing that challenges us.

The alternative to the change and flux which is now, as always, largely of our own making, is a sterile, static culture. But a sterile, static culture is precisely what, in different ways, most of our health futurists are describing—when they are not too busy describing superman or superbureaucrat or some other sort of vain vision. Yet between their visions of doctors chasing germs, programs chasing people and people chasing therapies, all at an increasingly frenzied pace, there seems to be little room for the day-to-day individual decision-making which makes the greatest difference in all of our health futures. This is why Dubos wisely observed a quarter of a century ago:

While it may be comforting to imagine a life free of stresses and strains in a carefree world, this will remain an idle dream. Man cannot hope to find another paradise on earth, because paradise is a static concept while human life is a dynamic process. Man could escape danger only by renouncing adventure, by abandoning that which has given to the human condition its unique character and genius among the rest of living things. Since the days of the cave man, the earth has never been a Garden of Eden, but a Valley of Decision where resilience is essential to survival. The earth is not a resting place. Man has elected to fight, not necessarily for himself, but for a process of emotional, intellectual, and ethical growth that goes on forever. To grow in the midst of dangers is the fate of the human race, because it is the law of the spirit.[37]

Perhaps more than any other area of modern prophecy, health futurology from Richardson on down likes to envision what can only be described as the erasure of human decision-making from day-to-day life, delegating most of it to machines or experts. Therefore, more than any other field of modern prophecy, it envisions and promotes what Huxley called "civilized infantility," the infantilization of the human race. More than this, in the end these visions are all static and contain a belief that change is the great enemy that must incessantly be striven against. But that which is static is also sterile, and all three of the major schools of thought of future health are ultimately visions of sterility. They are decidedly not visions, like Dubos's, of healthy adaptation to, and struggle with, change. In fact, they are visions in which change, which must include some sickness, is regarded as being decidedly unhealthy. Therefore they are visions in which change, if not entirely abolished, is at least completely controlled. In these visions, the powerful medical concept of homeostasis (the way in which the body is constantly striving to regain its equilibrium) is transmogrified from the fluid concept which true scientists know it to be—recognizing that after any change nothing returns again to being exactly what it was before—to a caricature of itself, a static term, an icon

that wants to be worshipped in order to achieve . . . what?
At bottom, one suspects that the sterile and static concepts
that govern these visions of the health future, along with the
characteristic obsession with control of the mechanically regarded human body, are as close as these futurologists can
get to envisioning immortality.

NOTES

1. There are any number of books in the market today which cater to this mood,
   but probably the most popular recent one is *Life Extension* by Durk Pearson
   and Sandy Shaw. However, books like *Life Extension* are not uniquely twentieth-
   century phenomena that reflect the special nature of twentieth-century medical
   science. Rather, they are published whenever medical science seems to be gaining the upper hand. For example, at the end of the nineteenth century, when
   the most ravaging diseases were finally receding in Europe and medical science
   was once again beginning to feel confident in its powers, C.W. Hufeland published a similar book called *The Art of Prolonging Life.*
2. René Dubos, *Mirage of Health: Utopias, Progress and Biological Change* (Garden City, N.Y.: Doubleday & Company, 1959), p. 135. I am greatly indebted
   to this book, whose wisdom remains compelling even over a quarter of a century
   after it was written, for many of the perspectives I have gained about modern
   health futurology.
3. Hippocrates, "The Book of Prognostics," in *Hippocrates*, W.H.S. Jones and
   E.T. Whitington (ed. and trans.) (London: Heinemann, 1931), vol. 2, p. 7.
4. Plato, *Republic* (London: Oxford University Press, 1945), III, 410a.
5. James H. Cassedy, "Hygeia: A Mid-Victorian Dream of a City of Health,"
   Journal of the History of Medicine (April 1962), p. 226.
6. Max von Pettenkofer was a pioneer public health practitioner in early nineteenth-century Germany. He persuaded the city fathers of Munich to institute
   simple sanitary measures like street cleaning, and sewage and garbage removal,
   and achieved dramatic results.
7. Dubos, *Mirage of Health*, pp. 68–69.
8. Benjamin Ward Richardson, *Hygeia: A City of Health,* address to the Social
   Science Association, Health Section (London: Social Science Association, 1876),
   pp. 29–30.
9. Richardson, p. 38.
10. Richardson, pp. 43–44.
11. Or sometimes the future is regarded as a *terra sancta* for the sake of which all
    fighting parties must lay down their arms. See, for example, Susan Jackson,
    "Health Planning in Turbulent Times," in *Man-Environment Systems* (Septem-
    ber/November 1984).
12. American Council of Life Insurance (ACLI), *Health Care: Three Reports from
    2030 A.D.* (Washington: American Council of Life Insurance, 1980), p. 3.
13. ACLI, pp. 3, 5.
14. ACLI, p. 4.
15. Peter G. Goldschmidt, "Health 2000" (Baltimore: Policy Research Institute,
    1982), p. 12.
16. Clement Bezold, "Health Care in the U.S.: Four Alternative Futures," *Futurist*
    (August 1982), p. 17.

17. ACLI, p. 6.
18. ACLI, p. 5.
19. ACLI, pp. 5–6.
20. ACLI, p. 8.
21. ACLI, pp. 10, 11.
22. ACLI, pp. 10, 12.
23. ACLI, pp. 16–17.
24. ACLI, pp. 17–18.
25. ACLI, pp. 14–18.
26. Jerrold Maxmen, *The Post-Physician Era* (New York: Wiley, 1976), p. 181.
27. Maxmen, p. 214.
28. National Heart and Lung Institute, *The Totally Implantable Artificial Heart* (Washington: National Heart and Lung Institute, June 1973), pp. 235–236.
29. Stanley Lesse, *The Future of the Health Sciences* (New York: Irvington Publishers, 1981), p. 28.
30. Lesse, p. 28.
31. Lesse, p. 129.
32. Lesse, p. 131.
33. Maxmen, p. 223.
34. René Dubos, "Medical Utopias" in *Daedalus* (Summer 1959), p. 412.
35. Cited in Dubos, "Medical Utopias," pp. 413–414. Over a quarter of a century later, on the eve of the outbreak of the AIDS epidemic, and in light of the persistent intractability of certain diseases like cancer, cardiovascular disease, and mental illness, the WHO continued dauntlessly but somewhat more cautiously with this kind of forecasting, but by then the predictions were framed in a list of platitudes. Writing as true heirs to Richardson they predict: "Health for all does not mean that in the year 2000 doctors and nurses will provide medical care for everybody in the world for all existing ailments; nor does it mean that in the year 2000 nobody will be sick or disabled. It does mean that health begins at home, in schools and in factories. It is there, where people live and work, that health is made or broken. It does mean that people will use better approaches than they do now for preventing disease and alleviating unavoidable disease and disability, and have better ways of growing up, growing old and dying gracefully. It does mean that there will be an even distribution among the population of whatever resources for health are available. It does mean that essential health care will be accessible to all individuals and families in an acceptable and affordable way, and with their full involvement. And it does mean that people will realize that they themselves have the power to shape their lives and the lives of their families, free from the avoidable burden of disease, and aware that ill-health is not inevitable." (WHO, *Global Strategy for Health for All by the Year 2000*, pp. 31–32.)
36. Dubos, "Medical Utopias," p. 415.
37. Dubos, *Mirage of Health*, p. 230.

Our most serious problem, perhaps, is that we have become a nation of fantasists. We believe, apparently, in the infinite availability of finite resources.
—WENDELL BERRY

7

FUTUREHYPE ABOUT THE ENVIRONMENT

The most puzzling thing about the environmental movement, now that it has taken hold of the consciousness of vast numbers of the world's population, is that it was so long in coming. After all, predictions of environmental disaster have been around for centuries, and, in a way, their appeal would seem to be almost undeniable, having the logic and simplicity of the bathtub filling up. Yet it is probably fair to say that only since the dramatic discovery by scientists in 1986 of the development of a hole in the ozone layer has there been a large-scale popular awakening about environmental matters.

It is a commonplace to blame the late blooming of environmental consciousness on the all too common economic blinders of shortsightedness and greed, and there is undoubtedly a great deal of truth to this critique. But the world's earlier lack of consciousness about the environment

is due to flaws in modern economic thinking that are much
more profound than these two little demons suggest. Some
of the incompetence of modern economic thinking is reflected in the telling fact, which a number of critics have
observed, that pollution control is presently a greater priority
in national and international policy than resource conservation "because pollution affects the present generation immediately, whereas the global endowment of energy and
materials concerns future generations."[1] It is important to
understand the reasons for our recent lack of consciousness
about environmental issues, because if we do not understand
them we will probably go back to being oblivious to the
environment again after having made only a few cosmetic
changes in the way we live. As it is, environmental consciousness is already being anesthetized by political babble
and commercial cooptation. But, more important, it is systematically being undermined by modern economic thought,
which is inept at understanding the world of nature except
in the most superficial ways and therefore constitutionally
incompetent at planning for the future of the earth.

There is a memorable little episode in Tolstoy's *Anna
Karenina* that nicely illustrates one aspect of this ineptitude.
It begins when a Moscow aristocrat, Prince Stepan Oblonsky, goes to visit his friend, Konstantin Levin, who owns
and works a large estate in the country. Although the two
friends go hunting together, it turns out that the real purpose
of Oblonsky's visit is to sell a wood in the neighborhood of
Levin's property to a dealer called Ryabinin. But when the
Prince reveals the terms of the upcoming deal to his friend,
Levin immediately realizes that Oblonsky is going to be un-
derpaid by the shrewd dealer and bluntly tells him so. All
to no avail. It is obvious from their conversation that Levin's
good advice is going to be lost on Oblonsky because the
Prince is sure he knows what he is doing and is determined
to carry on. By the way Tolstoy describes their bantering
about this matter you can tell that the author is himself a
farmer. He writes:

"Oh, these farmers!" Oblonsky said jokingly.
"Your tone of contempt for us poor city dwellers!

But when it comes to business, we do it better than anyone. Believe me, I've taken everything into account," he went on, "and the wood has been sold for a good price. Indeed, I am afraid he may change his mind. You see, it's not standing trees," said Oblonsky, hoping by the term 'standing trees' to convince Levin of the unfairness of his doubts, "but mostly only good for fuel. And it won't yield more than about forty cubic yards of wood per acre, and he's paying me at the rate of seventy rubles the acre."[2]

In the end, Oblonsky does indeed go ahead with the deal and, from the way he portrays the transaction, Tolstoy makes it clear that the Prince really does get taken. But Levin, acutely aware of the relationship between wealth and natural resources, is tenacious—and perhaps also a little ungracious—in his attitude about all of this, so afterwards he will not let his friend live this foolishness down and continues to needle him. Finally, in utter exasperation, Oblonsky asks, "Well, what would you have me do? Count every tree?" To which the farmer tersely replies, "Certainly count them. You have not counted them, but Ryabinin has. Ryabinin's children will have the means to live and to get an education, while yours may not!"[3]

This little episode is, of course, the opposite of the usual tale of the country bumpkin being taken by the city slicker, but there is a lot more to it than a lesson in the difference between real and pseudo-sophistication. At one point in their conversation Levin calls Oblonsky "innocent," and, in a sense, he really is. Oblonsky's wood, as Levin wisely observes, is no more to him than a monetary asset whose value he calculates from clever, but in this case ultimately empty, economic abstractions—"standing trees," "yield," "cubic yards per acre." Now, one might like to think that Oblonsky's "innocence" reflects no more than his impractical nature or the inadequacy of his own economic training, but that would be taking too narrow a view.

Oblonsky, like most city dwellers, is not only out of

touch with the natural world, but alienated from it. But, more to the point, not only is *he* alienated from the natural world but *economics,* the discipline which he uses to try to understand the material world, is also alienated from it. Even though the world of nature makes up the largest part of our material world and is the ultimate source of wealth, economics, the social discipline which is supposed to improve our happiness by giving us insight into our relationship with the material world, has, at best, a very tenuous grounding in the natural world—and this is true of both streams of modern economic thought, neoclassical as well as the now beleaguered Marxist school.

Probably the most important reason the environment is such a late bloomer in modern consciousness is that it has for centuries been systematically excluded from our thinking about the world by modern economic theory. It is worth remembering that Tolstoy was roughly contemporary not only with Karl Marx but also, on the other side of the spectrum of economic theory, with Vilfredo Pareto, Stanley Jevons, Leon Walras and the other major originators of modern economic thinking. Tolstoy wrote *Anna Karenina* in 1870 when he was in late middle age, but by that time most of the elements of modern economic thought were already in place. However, although Tolstoy's fictional character, Oblonsky, was merely a silly snob about his citified, pseudo-sophisticated economic thinking, Marx went so far as to hold rural culture in contempt, assigning to it the famous epithet "rural idiocy"—in spite of the fact that it was only due to the high level of productivity of those who worry and toil in the country that city dwellers like himself were able to live free of the burden of having to raise their own food.

Because of the obtuseness of the architects of modern economic thinking about environmental matters, Nicholas Georgescu-Roegen, the famous economist and philosopher of science, has written that they "succeeded so well with their grand plan that the conception of the economic process as a mechanical analogue has ever since dominated economic thought completely. In this representation, the economic process neither induces any qualitative change nor is affected by the qualitative change of the environment into which it is anchored. It is an isolated, self-contained and ahistorical process—a circular flow between production and consumption with no outlets and no inlets, as the elementary textbooks depict it." And, to emphasize the almost complete alienation of the quantitative overview of economics from the qualitative world we live in, this economist then goes on to note, "Economists do speak occasionally of natural resources. Yet the fact remains that, search as one may, in none of the numerous economic models in existence is there a variable standing for nature's perennial contribution. The contact some of these models have with the natural environment is confined to Ricardian land,† which is expressly defined as a factor immune to any qualitative change. We could very well refer to it simply as 'space.' "[4]

It is an indication of the deeply flawed nature of modern economics that it does not even provide us with adequate terms and concepts with which to think about the environment. On the contrary, when economic theory is confronted with certain kinds of environmental problems it tries to deal with them by systematic avoidance. The extent of this pathology is reflected in a formal economic concept that epitomizes this avoidance, the notion of external economies or externalities.

Simply speaking, an externality is an unintended consequence of an economic process or transaction, and it may be negative or positive. To cite a classic example, a negative externality occurs when a train transporting goods across a farmer's field sets fire to the crops adjacent to the track with sparks from its engine. When this happens, the problem in classical economics is that then the railway, or an insurance company in the railway's behalf, is required to compensate the farmer, and the cost of this compensation, which was not anticipated by the original economic calculations, becomes an "added" expense of doing business. Now the compensation can be sorted out in different ways: the railway can either pay the farmer the value of crops that are actually

† After David Ricardo (1772–1823), an English economist who developed a theory of rent.

destroyed or pay him a lesser value, equal to his potential profit from these crops, to discourage him from growing them near the tracks in the first place. Obviously, however it does get sorted out, this additional expense would naturally make transportation more expensive—but the point is that it is *dealing with the added expense* that is considered the real problem in the theory of externalities, not that the transportation does damage to the environment and/or may result in removing food from the market.

Clearly there are countless negative externalities which are more general than crop burning and therefore more difficult to assess. In fact, in principle, every incidence of pollution can properly be considered an externality of our economic processes because someone must pay for it one way or another somewhere down the line. Not surprisingly, it is in terms of this kind of economic thinking, which is, quite obviously, heavily based on the precepts of private property rights, that many classical economists, especially of conservative tendencies, are presently trying to deal with the problem of pollution and solve it for the future.

For example, in a recent article in the *National Review,* Fred Smith and Kathy Kushner write, "The most common cause of environmental degradation is a lack of clearly defined and transferrable property rights in the resource in question. If a thing has no owner then no one has an incentive to care for it. Few will act to safeguard or enhance the property of others."[5] From this premise Smith and Kushner make an elaborate argument for privatizing everything from wildlife preserves to air spaces. They assume that everything will be cared for and protected once it is simply owned by private individuals. It is difficult to imagine on what they base this assumption unless it is the common orderliness of middle-class *domestic* life. However, outside the domestic sphere, and sometimes even within it, there is only very limited reason to assume that proprietors will always protect and preserve what they own—especially if protection runs into conflict with exploitation. One of the things that Smith and Kushner blatantly ignore in their vision are the effects of absentee ownership: why not clear-cut your tract of timber wood if you do not live in or beside it and do not have to look at it afterwards?

In the end, the theory of externalities, far from being a promising solution to the problem of pollution, is really no more than a striking indication of the ineptness of economics in dealing with the environment. The real point of a negative externality, from the point of view of the environment and not of economic theory, is that unless the economic actors can force each other to pay for an external damage, for all intents and purposes the damage simply does not exist. Smith and Kushner's view is that there is nothing wrong with the economic engine that expanding it cannot cure. They imagine that through increased appropriation and litigation the economic engine will eventually include all of nature and thus automatically cure all of our environmental ills. Their vision of privatizing the whole world and then settling all infringements through negotiation and litigation is mind-boggling. It begins with the impossible task of causally tracing and assessing all incidents of trespass and ends with the equally impossible task of knowing when, where, and what to privatize at any given point in history. (As far as the second problem is concerned we should not forget that when oil was first discovered gurgling spontaneously up from the ground it was considered a contaminant and a nuisance.) Clearly externalities is a paltry precept for dealing with the enormous and pervasive problem of pollution, but the inability of classic economics to deal with environmental issues goes much deeper than the theory of externalities can even begin to suggest.

The fundamental flaw in economic thought is its mechanistic nature.[6] Now, the basic characteristic of mechanics is that it cannot account for *qualitative* change, that is, for a change that not only has never occurred before but may be irreversible, like the development of the hole in the ozone layer. According to the precepts of classical mechanics, all of nature is an enormous machine in which everything that goes forward can also always go backward like a pendulum or water turning to steam and back to water again. Since the mechanistic nature of economics makes it incapable of properly understanding qualitative change, it also alienates it from the environment, because most changes in the environment, like the pollution of a body of water or the erosion

and exhaustion of soil, are manifestly qualitative. But until
the appearance of the hole in the ozone layer these changes
have, because of the narrowness of the economic perspective, been assumed to be susceptible to quantitative calculation. Higher interest rates, lower interest rates—the
environment gets a little dirtier and then a little cleaner—
the "economic engine" understands all operations only in
terms of thinking that holds that all processes are, at least
in principle, reversible. The development of the hole in the
ozone layer was the first qualitative change to demonstrate
dramatically and irrefutably that economic activity can have
irreversible results that are detrimental to human welfare.
Needless to say, precisely because it is a qualitative change
and out of the perspective of mechanistic thinking, no one
predicted it would happen.

Because no one predicted it would happen, the appearance of the hole in the ozone layer has lent the prognosticators of ecological doom, who have of course long been
with us, a great deal of credibility. This is not because it
vindicates their method, which is also decidedly mechanistic,
but because it vindicates their outlook, which is bleak. When
you look at them closely, the prophets of environmental
doom are little more insightful and no more spiritually attractive than their counterparts who predict that endless
rounds of technological innovation will solve all environmental problems that develop while the material standard
of living of the world increases without abatement. In the
end both kinds of environmental extremists, the doomsayers
and the optimists, like their counterparts in politics, have a
mechanistic view of the world and a childish view of human
culture because they believe either too much or too little in
the efficacy of human adaptation.

All of this was first brought home to me when I was a
tutor in graduate school and the faculty associated with my
residence convened a special colloquium to discuss Robert
Heilbroner's book *An Inquiry into the Human Prospect*,
which had just been serialized in *The New York Review of
Books*.[7] Heilbroner's book is a vision of doom and gloom
in the old tradition of Thomas Malthus and Stanley Jevons
and in the more current genre of the Club of Rome's *Limits*

to Growth.[8]† At this colloquium two of the three speakers stood up and advised the audience not to worry about Heilbroner's thesis. One of them, Daniel Bell, observed that although the prophets of doom have always been with us, they have never been right. On the other hand, Roger Revell gave us a talk about the earth's seemingly endless resources and the seemingly infinite ways we may potentially be able to tap them. At that seminar the so-called optimists outnumbered the so-called pessimists—and, in any case, if you did not probe into the matter any more deeply than our speakers did, the optimistic and pessimistic prophecies seemed to cancel each other out so we were still able to enjoy our after-dinner drinks.

But if you did probe into the matter more deeply this was hardly the case. Take, for example, the Club of Rome's report, *The Limits of Growth,* and look at its fate. Looking back at that set of predictions now most people who are not sympathetic with it will say that the model was all wrong; those who are sympathetic will say the model was right but the variables were wrong. This is the short of it—the longer critique of the report had a much more elaborate form and its fallacies are worth recounting because they reflect much of what is pathological in current thought about the future of the environment.

For example, in the March 1975 issue of *Science* Glenn Hueckel published a critical analysis of the limits-to-growth thesis called "A Historical Approach to Future Economic Growth," which illustrates two of three great myths that contemporary prophets have promoted to sully our thinking about the environmental future.[9] One of these myths is that the marketplace will solve our environmental problems as they develop, the other is that technological innovation will always have the power to do the same thing.

† Thomas Malthus (see page 83) was the eighteenth-century English economist who predicted that England would starve at some point in the future because the growth of population was outstripping the growth of food production. He was proven wrong first through the import of surplus food from the New World and later by technological innovation. Stanley Jevons was a nineteenth-century English economist who, in a book called *The Coal Question,* predicted the demise of English industry because of the depletion of coal. He was proven wrong in the short run by the discovery of vast new reserves in America and in the long by the switch to petroleum—although English industry did eventually decline for other reasons.

These two myths are, of course, related, and Hueckel cites a typical example to illustrate how this works. In 1920 the chief geologist of the U.S. Geological Survey reported that only seven billion more barrels of oil could be recovered using existing techniques. He then predicted that at the contemporary rate of consumption the U.S. would run out of domestic supplies by 1934. But by the time that fateful year arrived, due to increasing demand twelve, not seven, billion barrels had been pumped out of the ground and there remained another twelve billion barrels of proved reserves. How did this miracle occur? Quite simply. As consumption proceeded and diminished supply, prices naturally rose, making it economically feasible to initiate hitherto uneconomical technological innovation and to make possible further, more costly, exploration and recovery.[10]

It would be nice to think that all of this is as it should be, and indeed many people seem to think just that, but this is an insupportably narrow view. Rising prices may make all sorts of development feasible, but they do not have a neutral effect on the economy or the environment. As prices for any given commodity rise that commodity consumes an ever greater part of a nation's resources, often with diminishing returns. This is precisely what is happening now in the United States as rising health care costs each year consume a larger part of the GNP. But this problem is exacerbated in the case of the rising price of a commodity like oil because it figures in the manufacture of a vast number of other commodities whose prices also rise.

Now all of this may be all right or even a good thing in the short run in an economy like that of the United States which is heavily capitalized and can therefore handle some of this dislocation and reallocation of resources. Rising prices may also even entail the benefit of reducing pollution by reducing consumption. But consider the effect of rising prices on poorer, less developed economies.

It is easy enough for an economist like Hueckel to be complacent about escalating prices of non-renewable resources. The United States, where Hueckel does his thinking, effectively had the privilege of a subsidized development because it occurred at a time before there existed international market pressure on non-renewable resources which would later drive the price up. He can therefore ignore the fact that presently developing countries, which are, in some respects, living in the U.S. past, have to develop in the context of severe market pressure. But price rises—whether they result from increased production expenses due to the capitalization of technology or can simply be attributed to economic cartel—affect the poorer countries more than the rich ones, as has consistently been demonstrated ever since OPEC hiked its prices in the early 1970s. This fact is seldom properly appreciated in the developed nations. In some ways, the most difficult thing for a developing nation to do is accumulate the reserve of capital that will make it resourceful enough to be responsive to changing economic conditions. An advanced economy's solution to rising prices is based on vast capital reserves which make stockpiling and technological innovation possible, but the lack of these reserves is precisely the problem of developing nations in a world market.

In a sense the relationship between poorer countries and richer ones is the same as the relationship between present and future generations. The point is that the price of a commodity does not necessarily represent its true value, because only those living at present can bid for it. If the commodity is based on a non-renewable resource, like oil, whose price has risen and will continue to rise in the future, then the market would only work equitably if future as well as present generations could bid on the commodity. Similarly, the market for oil could only work equitably if poorer, less developed nations could buy it as cheaply now as the developed nations did when they were starting out.

As to the ability of technology to keep providing the world with new sources of power, the picture is also not nearly as rosy as the market/innovation school would lead one to believe. For one thing, we need to get out of our minds the notion that the necessary technology for retrieving and generating energy will, like calculators and computers, always decrease in price and to bear in mind the common fact that most nuclear power plants have come on line at prices far above those predicted—which is to say nothing of the long-term cost of nuclear waste disposal, which will be dearer to future generations than to our own. On the other hand, the idea that the development of nuclear fusion technology will solve all the world's energy problem from the point it is commercially feasible until the end of time is one of the most misleading notions of our time. As long as it is credible, it is bound to hinder the kinds of changes that entail a more sane and sensible approach to energy use. Ever since we left the period when wood and coal were our main sources of energy, there has always been a fantastic notion that there exists an infinite supply of energy somewhere. This futuristic fantasy is the modern counterpart in an age of disenchantment—or enchantment only with scientific things—to the genie in the bottle who can create infinite wealth out of thin air. In the nineteenth century electricity, which is itself, strictly speaking, not a form of energy but a method for transforming and transporting other forms of energy, was considered to be such a source—perhaps because one could not see it being used up as one can see coal or wood used up while one is burning it. In our time ordinary fission reactors were given the same attribute when they were first introduced in the 1950s, and then the so-called breeder reactors were endowed with it in the 1970s. Now it is the turn of nuclear fusion—but this time it is even before a single viable fusion reactor has even been built.

If it should ever come, the price of infinite energy promises to be very dear for any foreseeable future. Jeremy Rifkin has pointed out a few of the astounding difficulties entailed in nuclear fusion technology: (1) The deuterium-tritium model of the reactor, which is now the focus of development, is based on lithium, niobium and vanadium, all elements which are found in limited supply in the earth, and the first of which is dangerous to mine. (2) The hydrogen reactor, if it is ever developed, will have to operate at three billion degrees centigrade, and no known substance is able to contain such temperatures. (3) Fusion plants will still produce enormous amounts of nuclear waste every year. (4) The costs of building these plants will be enormous and capital intensive, which means not only that the energy will be expensive but its production will not happen on a really competitive basis because there will be very few players who can enter at such stakes.[11] This is what technological genies cost, and yet fusion is still being thoughtlessly billed as the latest panacea.

The third myth with which we have been anesthetized by thoughtless modern prophets is the notion that we are entering the age of post-industrial society. Supposedly we are about to enter or have already entered an age where information is the basis of economy, and in some versions of this vision because we are all, or will all be, trading in services rather than goods we will no longer draw on the earth's resources.[12] The notion of post-industrial society is based on certain trends in the industrialized nations and a very narrow view of what industrialization really is. The trends are very simple, but misleading, unless one looks at them in context. They entail, first, a shift of the labor force from agricultural work to industrial work, starting with the Industrial Revolution of the late eighteenth and early nineteenth centuries, and then, in the twentieth century, a further shift from industrial work to so-called service work, which ostensibly is low in resource and energy use. Second, information itself becomes the most common commodity and a component of all others.†

There is so much more to industrialization than this view implies. While it is true that industrialization, by definition, entailed a shift of labor into the industrial sector, it also entailed two other things which, far from abating, are actually increasing as time goes on. First, in light of mechanization, industrialization necessitated a substitution of non-renewable sources of power, like coal and oil, for renewable ones like human and animal energy, with the concomitant exploitation of other non-renewable resources that was driven by this shift. Second, it entailed a routinization and standardization of work processes in order to make them more efficient. Today the factory model has invaded all kinds of work, including a great deal of what is called information work, and has encroached on hitherto seemingly unen-

---

† It is interesting that just as modern economic theory was born in countries where resources were abundant and therefore could ignore the notion of "limits," the theory of post-industrial or information society was born in countries where automation was so advanced (and energy and resource use so profligate) that vast sectors of the population could be freed from industrial work.

croachable fields like the provision of health and education services. Most food production is now industrialized in factory farms, in processing plants, in "fast-food" eating places, and even in many specialized restaurants. Furthermore, in spite of modern efficiency and resource substitution, the per capita use of resources is extravagant and still growing to the point where it is more accurate to say that we are living in a hyperindustrial rather than a postindustrial age.† Though they may use very little energy while on the job, white-collar workers who drive automobiles in long commutes use more energy getting to and from work than their nineteenth-century counterparts used in order to get the job done. One need only add to this the enormous resources that are used for endless conferences and conventions attended by great numbers of privileged bureaucrats, consultants and academics, so many of which serve only as paid mini-vacations for those attending and produce, for all the energy entailed, far less intellectual payoff than a good correspondence or reading a good book, and the picture of the resource profligacy of the so-called post-industrial world is complete.

The information society would indeed be desirable if it meant that intellectual and spiritual goods were *substituted* for material ones. The telltale sign of what the information society really means is that it is symptomized by widespread rising illiteracy—which is just the opposite of what one would expect if it is ever going to really live up to its billing. As it is presently constituted, with its huge component of propaganda, advertising and bureaucratic blather, information exchange serves the purpose of intellectual and spiritual diminution, as well as serving as a catalyst and facilitator for material exchange.

As products of modern economic thinking—and especially the thinking of the developed nations—what all of the above myths have in common is their alienation from the world of nature: they all assume, in one way or another, that the laws of nature can be finessed. In the end, these future-minded myths about markets and innovation—and some ver-

† It is all too common to mistake high productivity for efficiency when labor and/or resources are cheap because efficiency is defined by economics only as the *cost* of producing each unit.

sions of the myth of post-industrialism—are all consumerist oriented. Therefore they all ignore the simple yet irrefutable law of nature that gives the lie to consumerism and demonstrates that if one takes a long view it can only hasten environmental degradation. This law is the second law of thermodynamics, commonly called the law of entropy.

When it was first formalized by the German physicist Rudolf Clausius in the nineteenth century, the law of entropy revolutionized the thinking of physicists as much as quantum mechanics did in the twentieth century because it severely undermined the hitherto universally accepted world view of a mechanical universe. On the contrary the entropy law entails that the universe continually and irreversibly evolves only in one direction, toward total degradation. In all of its technicalities the law of entropy is very complex, but in informal terms it is easily graspable by laymen, and indeed was intuitively understood for millennia before being formalized in the nineteenth century. We see it in action around us all the time, from the accumulation of dust in our homes to the more dramatic process that occurs when we burn wood in the fireplace. When we burn some logs in the fireplace we see them transformed to heat and to ashes and we recognize intuitively that this process cannot be reversed. In slightly more formal terms we convert the logs from a state of low entropy to a state of high entropy. The law of entropy states that all matter in the universe is constantly undergoing this irreversible degradation and, in the end, trillions of years hence, will result in a formless and lifeless universe. This ultimate end, being trillions of years away and preceded by the explosion of our sun, is almost unimaginable and would seem to be irrelevant to everyday life, but it is not, because the rate at which this degradation occurs in any given corner of the universe, like our earth, is crucial to our long-term survival and is to a significant degree in our control.

The famous physicist Erwin Shrodinger has observed that living organisms sustain themselves by hastening the entropic process in the environment around them, that is, by consumption, by converting parts of their environment from a state of low entropy to one of high entropy.[13] This is the ultimate existential meaning of consumption, and all economic activity, particularly that which encourages consumption of non-renewable resources, hastens the entropic process. As Georgescu-Roegen has written, "A living being can evade the entropic degradation of its own structure only. It cannot prevent the increase of the entropy of the whole system, consisting of its structure and its environment. On the contrary, from all we can tell now, the presence of life causes the entropy of a system to increase faster than it otherwise would."[14] What the law of entropy tells us about non-renewable resources is that their ultimate destruction cannot be avoided but only postponed; they exist on earth in finite supply and can only be used and/or reused a finite number of times. The sun, on the other hand, though not infinite, is a source of resources that is practically infinite for us to draw upon because, as has often been said, every week it beams towards the earth energy equivalent to all of the earth's non-renewable resources. The sun represents a flow of resources towards the earth that may, for all intents and purposes, be regarded as infinite and is the only effective check that we presently have or may ever have on drawing from the earth's finite stock of resources to sustain our lives.

In this context the ultimate question is whether we will draw our sustenance from an enduring flow, the sun, or from a decidedly finite stock, the earth. Before we switched to coal and oil and uranium for our power needs we were forced, by default, to live from this flow. Now, through technological and conservation techniques, we have the choice of adhering to it in other ways. Unless or until we transform our individual lives and the world economy in this way we will be consuming more than our fair share of stock resources and depriving future generations of their use. There is no getting around the law of entropy. However sophisticated we become at information transfer and transformation we will continue to live in an industrial or even a hyperindustrial age as long as material consumption remains the basis of our existence.

The law of entropy is what gives the universe direction and stimulates our thinking about the future and about time in general. If resources truly were infinite and if biological life did not entail irreversible processes like growth, aging and death—all manifestations of the entropic process—what would make us think about the future? Without the entropic process the universe would indeed be the perpetual motion machine that physicists once thought it was. What one must remember is that the perpetual motion machine not only goes on forever, but it goes on forever doing *exactly the same thing*. Because of entropy, life and even the lifeless universe are not like that but, on the contrary, are always changing and evolving in unpredictable ways.

Given the law of entropy and what it tells us of the limits of the natural world the only way that we can live in a way that is responsible to future generations is by reducing consumption. Future generations will not rightly be able to blame us for using resources to sustain our lives and to allow ourselves reasonable material comfort, but they will be able to blame us if we squander resources as we are now doing by living materially profligate lives. With respect to the environment, as in all areas of life, living responsibly for the future is a matter of living responsibly now. On the level of the individual, this is a matter of character, and on the level of society, a matter of culture. For at least the last half-century, the cultural development of the advanced industrial nations has largely consisted of trading the intellectual and spiritual bases of existence for material ones, and it follows that one of the logical environmental disciplines for our present time would be to reverse that process as much as possible.

It is interesting that historically there is a precedent for doing this, and, since the environmental movement is often enamored of seeking alternate cultural precedents outside the mainstream of western tradition, there is some virtue in the fact that the precedent I have in mind is found in the Judeo-Christian tradition. It is described in the Bible near the end of the Book of Leviticus and has to do with the convention of the sabbath of the land.[15] The law of the sabbath of the land is very complicated and is also described in slightly different terms in different parts of the Bible, but its basic precepts are simple. According to Jewish law, the people were allowed to work the land for only six years in a row; the seventh year was considered a "sabbath of the land" and during that year all the land had to be left untouched. During that year the people were to live off only what grew spontaneously from the land, sharing it equally among them-

selves and the animals. It was traditional that during the year
of the sabbath of the land the people were to occupy their
time in study rather than work, trading a material existence
for a spiritual one. In the Book of Deuteronomy (15:1–10)
the sabbath of the land was also a time when all debts were
to be forgiven, and in Hebrew the root of the word for letting
the land rest and for forgiving debts is the same and means
"to drop."

It is not clear how strictly ancient Jews adhered to this
law, but it is clear from historical records that for centuries
the sabbath of the land was in force to a great extent. It is
recorded in the First Book of Maccabees and also by the
historian Josephus that during a sabbatical year the city of
Beth-zur was forced to surrender to the Syrians because it
could not withstand a siege due to lack of provisions. Josephus also reports that Alexander the Great and Julius Cae-
sar were both sufficiently appreciative of these laws and
practices to exempt the Palestinian Jews from tributary taxes
during these sabbatical years.[16]†

The law of entropy is as fundamental as the law of gravity.
It may appear at times as if it can be beaten or finessed, just
as we appear to beat gravity by taking off in rocket ships.
But as far as everything we know or seem to know about
the natural world is concerned, it cannot be disabled. What
person who cares for humankind would stake the well-being
of future generations on the undoing of the law of gravity?
If, through our collective ingenuity, we should ever learn to
reverse the entropic process, then scarcity will be abolished
forever and humankind may, if it so wishes, adopt a course
of uncontrolled and unabated consumerism. Until such a
time, those who wantonly consume from the earth's stock
now deprive those who must make a living on the earth
tomorrow.

Whatever may be the virtues of stopping and controlling
pollution, if the environmental movement does no more than

---

† It is interesting to note that Jewish tradition also holds that if the sabbatical year
were not observed the earth would eventually make up the lost sabbaths by being
laid waste (Leviticus 26:34, 43), and that much of the hardship and suffering the
Jewish people endured in exile was considered punishment for not having faithfully
kept the sabbath of the land.

achieve this goal it will have failed in its obligation to future generations. Ultimately, the abatement of pollution through any method other than the reduction of consumption is largely a victory for consumerism because the consumer will no longer have to consume anything involuntarily but will not have to consume any less. In the long run the law of entropy is a no-win game, and for humans the only advantage lies in playing it as little as possible.

What seems to militate most against our accepting this fact and minimizing the material basis of our existence is our selfishness, our shortsightedness, and our lack of responsibility to future generations, all of which are enforced by fantastic tales of futurists. In 1965, at a conference on the prospects of genetic engineering, the biologist Kimball Atwood envisioned that "we could, for example produce an organism that combines the happy qualities of animals and plants, such as one with a large brain so that it can indulge in philosophy and also a photosynthetic area on its back so that it would not have to eat."[17] Similarly, in 1990, writing in *The New Republic,* Gregg Easterbrook fantasized that we will eventually be able to alleviate the strain of unecological human activity and at the same time bestow the blessing of human life in other parts of the universe by kindling other planets with life-supporting properties. "The prospect of expanding life into the heavens may sound too remote to be relevant to today's environmental debates. Hardly. It's far more meaningful than such details as unburned hydrocarbon gram level or delayed Subtitle D regulations."[18] Atwood's vision may be a little more down-to-earth than Easterbrook's, and it certainly contains the virtue of relying on the enduring resources of the sun, but their visions have two things in common: both reflect alienation, and neither is able to accept limits. It is no wonder that Wendell Berry has written, "Our most serious problem, perhaps, is that we have become a nation of fantasists. We believe, apparently, in the infinite availability of finite resources."[19]

The debate about the environment—present, past and future—begins and ends with questions about the extent of our alienation from the world of nature. What are we to think of the earth? Are we to regard it, ultimately, as a disposable launching pad, to be left in the custody of those who lack the means or will to leave it? And with all its joys and riches, what do we expect we will ever learn to love and cherish if, by the time we are able to leave the earth, we have not learned to love and cherish it? Though it will not happen until the very distant future, our destiny may eventually be to explore and inhabit other parts of the universe, but unless we can first learn to care for and cherish this earth and live within its limits, it will be only a wanton destiny to which we cannot be spiritually entitled.

NOTES

1. Joseph C. Dragan and M.C. Demetrescu, *Entropy and Bioeconomics* (Rome: Nagard, 1986), p. 167.
2. Leo Tolstoy, *Anna Karenina* (trans. David Magarshack) (New York: New American Library, 1961), p. 178.
3. Tolstoy, p. 182.
4. Nicholas Georgescu-Roegen, *The Entropy Law and the Economic Process* (Cambridge, Mass.: Harvard University Press, 1971), p. 2.
5. Fred L. Smith and Kathy H. Kushner, "Good Fences Make Good Neighborhoods," in *National Review* (April 1, 1990), p. 31.
6. This mechanistic perspective may partly be a consequence of the scientism inherent in modern economics, but, as Georgescu-Roegen has pointed out, it is surely also partly the result of the fact that modern economics was originally formulated in lands of abundant resources. Since both streams of thought have this origin in common, with respect to the environment Marxist economics is no different from neoclassical in its mechanistic thinking. Perhaps the Marxist position is even more attenuated because it places so much emphasis on class struggle and the labor theory of value. In this scheme the natural world does not fit in either as a legitimate source of wealth or as an appropriate antagonist.
7. Robert L. Heilbroner, *An Inquiry into the Human Prospect* (New York: Norton, 1974).
8. D.H. Meadows, D.L. Meadows, J. Rangers, W.W. Behrens III, *The Limits to Growth: A Report for the Club of Rome's Project on the Predicament of Mankind* (New York: Potomac Associates-Universe Books, 1972).
9. Glenn Hueckel, "A Historical Approach to Future Economic Growth," in *Science* (March 14, 1975), pp. 925–931.
10. This example is taken from Hueckel, pp. 927–928.
11. See Jeremy Rifkin, *Entropy: A New World View* (New York: Viking, 1980), pp. 112–113.
12. See for example Yoneji Masuda, *Computopia: Information Society as Post-Industrial Society* (Bethesda, Md.: World Future Society, 1981).
13. Cited in Georgescu-Roegen, p. 10.
14. Georgescu-Roegen, p. 11.
15. Leviticus 25.
16. See Gunther Plaut, *The Torah* (New York: Union of American Hebrew Congregations, 1981), p. 941. See also T.H. Hertz, *The Pentateuch and Haftorahs*, 2nd ed. (London: Soncino Press, 1981), p. 531.
17. Kimball Atwood, "The Revolutionary New Biology: Discussion," in

T.M. Sonneborn (ed.), *The Control of Human Heredity and Evolution* (New York: Macmillan, 1965), p. 37.
18. Gregg Easterbrook, "Everything You Know about the Environment Is Wrong," in *The New Republic* (April 30, 1990), p. 27.
19. Wendell Berry, "Word and Flesh," in *Whole Earth Review* (Spring 1990), p. 71.

. . . factual truth is no more self-evident than opinion, and this may be among the reasons that opinion-holders find it relatively easy to discredit factual truth as just another opinion.

—HANNAH ARENDT

8

TRUTH AND POLITICS IN DEBATES ABOUT THE FUTURE

Even in the best of circumstances debates about the future are never straightforward because they are always pulled in two directions at once. All debates about the future are likely to deal with two things: what *will* be, which is a matter of truth, and therefore should fall under the authority of science, and what *should* be, which is a moral matter, and in our time falls under the authority of politics. But since, outside of some aspects of the world of nature, science usually cannot say what *will* be, it often finds itself at a disadvantage vis-à-vis politics in such debates. Today, in any case, science and politics have become hopelessly muddled: not only do scientific debates have wide political ramifications, but what would otherwise be hopelessly shoddy political debates often manage to achieve a certain degree of legitimacy and respectability by assuming scientific airs. As a consequence of all of this, both scientific and political debates about the future tend at best to be obscure and confusing and at worst to be mistaken and misleading.

All of these problems were very apparent in a recent debate about artificial intelligence (AI). In January of 1990 *Scientific American* published a debate between some prominent members of the artificial intelligence community about whether machines will ever be able to think. As it happened, in this particular contest neither side made any really new points—but the argument was still very interesting, not so much because of its content as because of its style.

In scientific circles, where cold-blooded objectivity is supposed to be the name of the game, one should be wary whenever the style of a debate is more interesting than its content. Of course, there is a place for flair even in the somber halls of science, but it is also a commonplace that if you cannot win an argument with facts you may still be able to win it with rhetoric. It has always been true that a wilful debater, using nothing more than fanciful language, jokes, personal attacks and similar devices, can win over an unwary audience and deflect its attention away from the question at hand. And, if the rhetorician is skillful enough, while he is at it he may even manage to quietly introduce a different agenda.

In the *Scientific American* debate the differences in style were apparent from the very first sentence of each paper. John Searle, on the side of the doubters, began by simply restating the question in its classic and most familiar terms. "Can a machine think?" he asked.[1] Then, in the typical style of the philosopher, he proceeded to define the terms "machine" and "think" and went on to present a case against the possibility that computing machines, as we know them, will ever be able to think in the conscious way that humans do.[2] Until the very end of his paper Searle did not once deviate from sober analysis and simple logical statements. And when, in concluding, he did depart from this style, it was only to speculate as to why, in spite of the mounting evidence against it, some people still believe that computers will someday be able to think. Searle blamed the persistence of this belief on the lingering influence of behaviorism, and concluded that adherents to this school of thought were being unscientific and fighting a retrograde battle to protect theories that have already been discredited.

Now, whereas Searle began his paper by restating the question, Paul and Patricia Churchland, who took the affirmative side in this debate, began theirs by bragging. This tone was also apparent in their very first sentence, where they made the archetypal hyperbolic proclamation: "Artificial-intelligence research is undergoing a revolution."[3] From here they proceeded to recount the accomplishments of the artificial intelligence movement in the most glowing terms. They called it "a well-defined research program" based on "deep theoretical underpinnings" which has come up with "deepest reasons" for having confidence in its enterprise. Furthermore, not only did the Churchlands praise their movement, they also found it appropriate to slander their detractors, calling them, on different occasions, "ill-motivated," "ill-informed," "short-sighted," "unsympathetic" and, with apparent reference to Searle himself, "logic-chopping."

A little academic name-calling—fine. But what is particularly interesting about the Churchland paper is that when the authors finally did get down to addressing the question of whether the artificial intelligence movement will ever produce a consciously thinking machine they were almost as doubtful as their adversary. "We believe that the prospects are poor," they concluded, "but we rest this opinion on reasons very different from Searle's. Our reasons derive from the specific performance failures of the classical research program in AI."[4] Having made this concession, however, the Churchlands then went right on to describe some recent—though, if you look at them closely, by no means *revolutionary*—research developments in AI and to make a plea for more time to carry them forward.[5] So in the end, far from being a concession of defeat, the Churchlands' admission of serious doubt was only the prelude to a plea for more time in the hope that somehow it will all work out in the future.

On one level the Churchlands' plea for more time is perfectly reasonable and, naturally, it is constantly being echoed by researchers in every field of science, even in the face of the most frustrating results. Since frustration in the sciences is very common but is often enough followed by success, a plea for more time is perfectly understandable—and, in any case, one would instinctively want to give sincere and honest researchers the benefit of the doubt. In this spirit Stevan Harnad, an AI theoretician at Princeton, has observed: "Whereas Searle's thought-experiment and scepticism lead nowhere, there is every reason to believe that AI's toys will grow and grow, until some day they will begin to look like the real thing, and some of them may even begin giving the Turing Test a run for its money."[6]† Harnad's point certainly makes the suspension of judgment about future outcomes very appealing: what, after all, is the use of Searle's skepticism—except that it may give him the intellectual self-satisfaction of thinking that he really can foresee the results of the long and complicated quest for artificial intelligence?

A number of years ago Arthur C. Clarke, the famous British futurist and science fiction writer, wrote an essay called *Profiles of the Future: An Inquiry into the Limits of the Possible* in which, among other things, he tried to make a case for completely open-minded thinking about what science and technology will be capable of accomplishing in the future. At the same time, Clarke also attempted to put skeptics like Searle in their place. Yet, in spite of the fact that his book is written as a sort of tribute to science, what is interesting about Clarke's method in this essay is that it is patently unscientific.

He begins by giving a brief historical account of a number of technological feats which some skeptics believed to be impossible before they were accomplished. One could list any number of feats of this sort, but I will mention only a couple that Clarke himself cites to give the reader a feeling for what he was trying to do and how he was trying to do it. In the nineteenth century, after the invention of the locomotive, skeptics maintained that a person could not travel at the speed of thirty miles per hour without suffocating; in

---

† AI researchers commonly refer to their present, ostensibly provisional achievements as "toys"—partly as a matter of self-effacement, but also partly in self-assured expectation of achieving far greater results in the future. But the self-flattering nature of this terminology is evident if one compares AI to any other more vital field. For example, whatever their expectations may be for future results, cancer researchers would never refer to their present, provisional achievements as "toy" cures.

the early twentieth century, before airplanes were invented, many people believed that heavier-than-air-machines could not fly; and, after the airplane had become a reality, some skeptics continued to believe that these machines would never be able to carry many people or go very far or very fast and therefore would be impractical for commercial purposes. Of course, as history has shown, the skeptics in these particular cases proved to be wrong, but the conclusion that Clarke draws about skepticism in general, that it is useless in the short run and foolish in the long, is also wrong.

Good scientists are very reluctant to make generalizations about oddly assorted and/or carefully selected cases like the ones that Clarke cites. If a scientist feels inclined to draw conclusions about a number of cases he has studied he will tend to generalize to those cases alone and to no others— sometimes to the point where a layman, not understanding the spirit of this attitude, might even find it precious and laughable. The only conclusion that a sober scientist would draw from Clarke's cases is that in those *particular* instances—which he gives us no reason to believe are representative—the skeptics turned out to be wrong. But Clarke goes much further than this. He concludes, "Anything that is theoretically possible will be achieved in practice, no matter what the technical difficulties, if it is desired greatly enough."[7] From a scientific perspective such a sweeping generalization is almost meaningless, but it is worth looking at more closely because, in spite of its meaninglessness, it exemplifies the kind of thinking that forms a significant part of the background for all sorts of debates about what is possible.

The question of what is possible is an ancient one in philosophy and goes back as far as Aristotle, but the position Clarke has taken on it is closer to that taken by Descartes. Descartes believed that anything is possible provided that it can be clearly imagined and does not violate God's goodness. This is not the place to discuss Descartes' second condition, but an illustration of the first is that it might be possible to construct a round rectangle if only one could first get a clear picture of it in one's head. This is how Clarke thinks—he uses the term "theoretically possible" so loosely that it appears to be synonymous with "conceived" or "imagined."

Of course imagining something is certainly useful, and may even be necessary, to bringing it about, but Clarke would lead one to believe that it is also sufficient. Yet although he makes it sound simple and straightforward, the idea of theoretical possibility is actually fraught with problems. What, after all, does it really mean to say that something is "theoretically possible"? A couple of illustrations that countervail Clarke's argument will show how contrived his thinking really is.

Before they performed the first test of the atom bomb, Robert Oppenheimer and some of his colleagues on the Manhattan Project theorized that it was possible that when the bomb exploded it would set the earth's atmosphere on fire—perhaps even causing a worldwide conflagration. Presumably, the scientists who speculated about this astounding possibility were not idly conjecturing, but, as everyone knows, they went ahead with their test anyhow, and, in the event, the global conflagration did not actually occur. Since the bomb did not set the world on fire, what became of the theoretical possibility, which existed before the detonation, that this might actually happen? The simple answer is that presumably this possibility was obliterated, along with lots of other things, with the explosion of the bomb.

Of course, the conjectures of the atomic scientists about atmospheric conflagration was a bit of a sideshow: these speculations were not central to their main plan and purpose, nor did disproving the conflagration theory destroy the elaborate theoretical edifice which made the explosion of the bomb itself a possibility. Therefore my second example has to do with speculative theory that arose from the very heart of a long-standing scientific objective—this time in the field of biology—namely, cloning.

The idea of cloning, or exactly reproducing an individual, has been part of human fantasy for some time, but in the past it was generally regarded as a joke.[8] About a century ago, however, a German embryologist named Hans Driesch performed some famous experiments that showed that an organism may develop not only from a fertilized egg, but from an ordinary body-cell when that cell is taken from an embryo at the earliest stages of development. Half a century later a couple of experimental biologists called R. Briggs and

T.J. King pushed our practical and theoretical knowledge of cloning a big step further. They were able to pluck the nucleus from a single body-cell and use it to replace the nucleus of a fertilized egg, thus giving the egg the genetic material of the individual from whose body-cell the nucleus had been transplanted. Using this technique, in the early 1950s Briggs and King were able to clone reptiles from the body-cells of reptiles. Naturally, at that point in history, it seemed "theoretically possible" that one day we would also be able to clone humans, including everyone's favorite examples, Einsteins from Einsteins and Mozarts from Mozarts—if only some Einsteins or Mozarts managed to appear on the scene again.

However, one aspect of the Briggs-King experiments which did not appear to be particularly significant at the time of their early research but later proved to be crucial was that the nuclei they used for transplants had been consistently taken only from reptiles at the first stages of development. As it turned out, subsequent attempts to make clones using the body-cells of more mature organisms failed. For some reason—neither explained by nor anticipated by the theory as it then stood—the older the organism happened to be the less likely that the transplanted nucleus of one of its body-cells would make an egg develop into a similar organism.[9] With nuclei from mature organisms the process will not work at all. But until this was proven experimentally in the later investigations of Briggs and King and others there was no reason not to believe that it was "theoretically possible" that we would one day be able to clone humans from mature humans.†

The experiences of the Manhattan Project scientists and Briggs and King illustrate a little of what "theoretical possibility" actually means in science, and this meaning is obviously, to a greater or lesser extent, very contingent on new developments, on what is not yet known, unlike what Clarke's argument would lead one to believe. It should be clear from the preceding examples that Clarke confuses ap-

---

† Obviously, there would be little point in cloning humans from human embryos if this turned out to be feasible because, setting aside the problems of nurture, Einsteins and Mozarts are not identifiable at the embryo stage. One might as well use fertility drugs to induce identical multiple births.

parent but blind potentiality with real possibility. When we observe something in its earliest stages, be it an organism, an institution or a science, its potential seems unlimited, but this is largely due to our ignorance. The eggs of many species look superficially alike, and many species are superficially alike even at the stage of the embryo. It is not until development and differentiation have proceeded some way that it becomes obvious that one egg will develop only into a reptile and another into a human. What is left out of Clarke's equation is that development, be it of an organism, an institution, and even a science, along with being an expansive process is also a self-limiting one. The theoretical edifice in any science may lead to dead ends and blind alleys, some temporary, some permanent; it is more like a maze than like a long dark tunnel which will always and ever have a light at the end of it. The English philosopher R.G. Collingwood therefore once said of the development of science: "Natural science . . . consists of facts and theories. A scientific fact is an event in the world of nature. A scientific theory is an hypothesis about that event, which further events verify or disprove."[10] Because the hypothetical nature of theory, so central to science, is absent from Clarke's formula, it is certainly unscientific and almost meaningless. It does not describe real science, in which hypotheses are forever being proven or disproven, but an idealized, childish vision of science, as if it were a mechanical enterprise, a huge jigsaw puzzle in which all the missing pieces are somewhere to be found and their shapes will forever be discernible, a puzzle which we will always be able to complete simply by "desiring it greatly enough."

In debates about the future, misconceptions like Clarke's about the nature of scientific theory make for a lot of loose talk and wild speculation. Much of this could be avoided by simply bearing in mind what every scientist knows, that at bottom theory is only a shorthand way of representing and thinking about phenomena, both those that occur naturally in the world and those that result because of man's intervention but are still, of course, a part of nature. In a symbolic and economical way theory organizes and summarizes the world as we understand it at any given point in history, and, because we are curious, it does more than that:

it also provides a framework for speculating about what may be possible. This framework points to gaps in our knowledge and in our experience, and to the possibilities for filling them. But though theory allows us to speculate honestly about future developments, there is no scientific ground for assuming that all gaps can be filled and that all imaginable occurences will actually occur—and experimental developments, like the ones I have just described, demonstrate to the contrary.

Because of this, any statement about what is possible, especially about something that has never yet happened, cannot, strictly speaking, be taken as fact, but only as opinion. In particular the statement "anything is possible" is only an opinion—and a rather silly one at that, unless it is merely a way of stating the commonsense existential notion that all sorts of things may be possible that have not yet happened nor been imagined. But there is a world of difference between saying that "all sorts of things may be possible" when this is an existential position, and saying that "anything is possible" when this is meant to be a scientific statement reflecting the omnipotence of science when it is driven by imagination, human will and intelligence.

Whereas opinion is a necessary part of scientific speculation, it is a part of the scientific edifice about which scientists will always have mixed feelings. As long as science is driven by the quest for truth, its desire will always be to abolish opinions and get on to facts by proving or disproving a hypothesis one way or the other. Science thrives on facts and considers the opinion that is inherent in hypotheses to be no more than a necessary evil that will, it is hoped, ultimately lead to useful facts. But this places science, which thrives on "finding" truth, whatever it may turn out to be, directly opposite to politics, which thrives on "making" opinion—and often actually abhors facts either because they are dull or because their implications are threatening.

Yet, in spite of their uneasy relationship with facts, politicians will often seize on a fact in the form of an event if it will serve to shape opinion. Thus the fact of the recent arms reductions in Europe has been used by propagandists during the last year or so to vindicate the build-ups that preceded it, as if arms reduction were the only possible outcome of the arms race. Because a nuclear war has not happened as a result of the arms race, propagandists who wish to justify the build-up retrospectively would have us believe that nuclear war was never a real possibility. In this sense political rhetoric often tries to mimic scientific reasoning by claiming that a development either proves or disproves a given hypothesis. But in politics such a claim is always rhetorical because in human affairs nothing is "in the nature of things" and one can therefore always rightly say that "it could have been different in any number of possible ways." Yet this kind of pseudo-scientific rhetoric is very powerful because it is as true of human as of natural history that each development does, in fact, partially or wholly negate the possibility of others occurring—not because it reveals the true nature of things, as in science, but because each event in history exclusively occupies the moment in which it occurs. Once the Allied powers had won World War II it was then impossible for the Axis powers to do so. As Hannah Arendt has observed: "It is true that in retrospect—that is, in historical perspective—every sequence of events looks as though it could not have happened otherwise, but this is an optical, or, rather, an existential illusion: nothing could ever happen if reality did not kill, by definition, all the other potentialities originally inherent in any given situation."[11]

However, although present events may erode, or even kill, past potentialities, they do not kill future potentialities. The present does, of course, have a great deal of bearing on the future, but it is ridiculous to try to push historical logic forward in the way one can, with a great deal of wilful construction, more or less push it backwards, along a single path. From any given present innumerable futures are always possible, but this fact does not sit well with politicians who like to give the appearance of having completely mastered events by having chosen the right path, the path that leads to the best of all possible futures. In particular, when an event takes the form of an intervention like a program or policy, the instigating politicians will always attempt to prove that they have privileged insight into its logic and know its future outcome.

This kind of posturing was abundantly evident in Canada during the general election of 1988. The Canadian election of 1988 was fought on the basis of only one policy issue: should Canada sign a free trade agreement with the United States. However, by the time they called the election, the incumbent party, the Conservatives, had already begun negotiating the deal, so there was no question what their policy was or where their commitment lay. Naturally, during the course of the campaign, they predicted that great good would come from this treaty but economic hardship would be inevitable without it. The opposition parties, in turn, devoted their campaign energies to making opposite predictions based on the "studies" of their own hired forecasters. Needless to say, during these elaborate exercises in prophecy, no party cared to mention the commonsense fact that although trade treaties may prove to be important, as the EEC has demonstrated over the last two decades, they are not decisive to economic well-being. Even in the EEC there are winners and losers, countries that are better off or worse off with respect to certain aspects of trade. Trade treaties offer no more than opportunities and potential benefits that must be realized—or not—through innumerable individual decisions which reflect a nation's overall level of industriousness, intelligence, natural advantage and so forth.†

The prophetic propaganda which dominated the 1988 general election campaign in Canada illustrates how compelling debates about the future can be even when they are patently used as forums for making political hay. In politics, which is highly dependent on image-management and opinion-making, such debates are all too common, and the legitimating function of supposedly scientific forecasters is all too transparent within them. Increasingly, however, we live in a world in which it is difficult to separate science from politics because governments routinely initiate huge scientific projects as the embodiment of national policies. In these cases the transparency of pseudo-science working in the ser-

---

† Since the Canadian electorate were treated, on this occasion, to a one-issue campaign based entirely on "scientifically" legitimated fantasies about the future, it was not surprising that the polls swayed dramatically during the contest as politicians of all parties persisted in making melodramatic predictions. In the end the Conservatives were returned because their propaganda was better managed, but this was certainly one of those elections, all too common during the last two decades, where the electorate went to the polls holding their noses.

vice of political will is usually lost and instead we have debates about the future in which science, some real and some sham, is obscurely interwoven with political rhetoric.

Probably the best example in recent years of how this works is to be found in the American debate about the Strategic Defense Initiative (SDI), or Star Wars as it was commonly known. The most telling thing about the SDI debate was how rapidly and broadly its grounds and terms of reference kept shifting and becoming more vague at each step. When President Reagan first announced his plans to develop and deploy the SDI system he was unequivocal about its purpose: it would be an impenetrable defense shield that would make the nuclear weapons of the enemy impotent and therefore obsolete. Whatever their judgment as to its feasibility may have been, there is no question that for a long time the public as well as the media took this goal at face value. No sooner had Reagan finished proclaiming this incredibly ambitious goal, however, than the U.S. Defense Department began to "explain" to the public that in reality the purpose of SDI would be far more modest, that the system would be deployed only as an added component of the existing system of deterrence. Then, by the late 1980s, after the credibility of SDI had been seriously eroded by its critics, its proponents and defenders trotted out the old standby justifications that the goal of SDI was to be neither invincible defense nor even deterrence but to act as a vehicle for funding worthwhile research. Finally, some defenders of SDI even went so far as to argue that one purpose of deploying the system was to bankrupt the Soviet Union by forcing it to increase its military spending in order to respond to it.

Much as a reluctant striptease dancer, who remains forever alluring but never revealing, casts a spell on her audience, the shedding of a more ambitious—but clearer—purpose for more conventional and vaguer ones managed to keep the public in thrall for a long time. Of course political initiatives can legitimately have multiple goals, but when this is so each should be valid in it own right in case the others fail. What is most telling about the stated aims of SDI was that none of them alone could have stood up to scrutiny for very long. Only the shadow game of all four goals taken together could possibly have allowed SDI to persist as long as it did under public analysis.

Ironically, however, in spite of its incredibly ambitious nature, of the four justifications for developing the system, the scientists who wished to argue objectively about it could take only Reagan's original goal, to construct a completely invulnerable shield, as a proper point of reference—otherwise there would have been nothing to argue about. None of the other goals were scientifically testable. This is why when David L. Parnas resigned in protest from the advisory panel that was supposed to explore the feasibility of SDI he insisted: "I've taken my requirements from the very highest and most reliable source, Ronald Reagan."[12]† Sophisticates of realpolitik probably consider Parnas's statement to be hopelessly naive, but however "naive" it may have been, from the point of view of such cynics his position was anything but posturing because, from the perspective of a hard scientist, as lofty and ambitious as Reagan's goal may have been compared to the others that followed it, it was the only one that was susceptible to scientific analysis. Like school-yard morality in which children of a certain age will insist on constantly changing the rules whenever it is to their advantage, all of this ground-shifting may serve some fairly obvious political purposes but in the long run it can only be self-defeating, since it will prove to be extremely annoying to that part of the public that can see through it and confusing to the rest.

Unfortunately ground-shifting and rule-changing have become common traits of scientific as well as political debate.

---

† It should be noted that in making his assessment of whether it would be possible to write the software for such a system Parnas did not use perfection as his standard, but rather believable dependability. In his original papers justifying his resignation Parnas wrote, "The system has numerous technical characteristics that will make it more difficult than previous systems, independent of size. Because of the extreme demands on the system and our inability to test it, we will never be able to believe, with any confidence, that we have succeeded. Nuclear weapons will remain a potent threat" (in *Communications of the ACM*, vol. 28, no. 12, December 1985, p. 1329). And elsewhere he has written, "I have consistently used the work [*sic*] "trustworthy," explaining that what is required is a system with known, that is, predictable, effectiveness—one which we know, with great confidence is free of *catastrophic flaws*. That is far from perfection" (emphasis in original) (letter, in *Science* [July 25, 1986], p. 403).

Last year when the chemists Stanley Pons and Martin Fleischmann claimed to have created nuclear fusion at room temperature in a test-tube, they used the ground-shifting tactic to evade the ultimately devastating critiques of their colleagues. In commenting on the Pons-Fleischmann cold-fusion affair, Robert Crease and N.P. Samios, a philosopher and a scientist, compared the chemists to the French scientist René Blondlot, another famous ground-shifter, who imagined he had discovered n-rays, in the wake of the remarkable discovery of X rays by the German scientist Wilhelm Roentgen. Crease and Samios observed, "When someone claimed that it was not possible to produce cold fusion, the two Utah scientists would add more instructions—that the palladium cathode had to be prepared in a certain way, or the electrolyte had to be of a certain concentration."[13] (At least one can say of Pons and Fleischmann that they kept their shifting on scientific turf—some of Blondlot's followers eventually claimed that "only individuals of Latin descent had good enough eyesight to see evidence of the rays.")[14] Crease and Samios concluded that Pons and Fleischmann were self-deluded victims of "pathological science." Crease and Samios maintain that healthy science, far from trying to glorify new findings without first subjecting them to the rigor of peer replication and evaluation, will try to "kill the results" as did Roentgen, in case they should turn out to be only the consequence of experimental error.

Contrary to the schoolyard tactic of constantly shifting ground, those who are debating in good faith, be it in politics or in science, will always seek for common ground and common terms—in fact that quest alone is sometimes the substance of a debate. This makes for dullness at times, but it also makes for honesty. Ground-shifting is a sure sign that a debate about the future is political as opposed to scientific. Any side that uses the tactic is either deluding itself or not debating in good faith.

Unfortunately, in any debate, if one side is trying to argue from truth while the other is arguing from opinion the latter side will tend to have the upper hand, because factual truth is seldom self-evident. In fact, Hannah Arendt has gone so far as to claim that "factual truth is no more self-evident than opinion, and this may be among the reasons that opinion-holders find it relatively easy to discredit factual truth as just another opinion."[15] In this case the uses of skepticism, like John Searle's in the AI debate, should be obvious. Aside from the scientific use of trying to keep the debate as close to truth as possible, which honest skepticism always does, it brings to light the purely political aspects of such debates. If what might otherwise be scientific debates then become almost strictly political, at least we are in the position to insist that the other contingencies of political debate come into play, for example, that interests be spelled out and that any given interest be directly compared with competing interests. Getting back to the point of departure for this chapter, if the Churchlands insist on making the artificial intelligence debate a political one, then the claims of the artificial intelligence movement on the public purse should be weighed against the claims of other causes, like the educating of people, the cultivation of real intelligence. It would not do, after all, for any country to be a nation of smart machines and stupid people.

If politics were like science in every way one could say it was inherently "pathological." But part of the game of politics is forging consensus, and this may rightly necessitate shifting ground. We cannot expect politicians to have the integrity to try to "kill the results" the way honest scientists do before they publish them, because "results" in politics are always contingent, always created by forging consensus. But in the forging of consensus through the fostering of beliefs and opinion we can at least insist, as scientists will insist, that all the players stick to the facts as we know them and state their intentions honestly—otherwise, in our political culture, we will remain forever in the schoolyard.

NOTES

1. John R. Searle, "Is the Brain's Mind a Computer Program?," in *Scientific American* (January 1990), p. 26.
2. See John R. Searle, "Minds, Brains, and Programs," in *The Behavioral and Brain Sciences* (Cambridge University Press, 1980), vol. 3, pp. 417–457. Searle's refutation was, for the most part, a restatement of the famous rebuttal in the form of a thought-experiment that he had formulated for this purpose a decade earlier. In Searle's thought-experiment a person who does not understand a word of Chinese is sequestered in a room where he manipulates Chinese symbols

on the basis of a rule-book written in a language, like English, that he does understand. It follows in principle that if his rule-book is comprehensive and well written, he will give the appearance of understanding Chinese when in reality he does not understand a word. This thought-experiment was designed to show that a machine can display the appearance of thought by blindly manipulating symbols without actually thinking, that is, that computers have only syntax, the ability to follow rules, but not semantics, the ability to understand the meaning of the symbols which they manipulate. Searle's paper created quite a stir in the AI community when it was first published because it logically and directly countered Turing's thought-experiment, which had launched the AI movement. Searle's experiment demonstrated, among other things, what intentionality might mean even in the context of behaviorist psychology, and showed that, in spite of what behaviorists might claim, the "state" behind "appearances" can be very important. It was published along with comments from twenty-seven theoreticians and practitioners in the field. All but three of these comments were negative, but Searle refuted all of them with written responses. In any case the evidence that his paper has certainly struck a very raw nerve in the AI community is that it is still controversial and being debated over a decade later.

3. Paul M. Churchland and Patricia Smith Churchland, "Could a Machine Think?," in *Scientific American* (January 1990), p. 32.

4. Churchland and Churchland, p. 35.

5. At this point the reader finally gets to find out what the Churchlands mean by *revolutionary*. Apparently it is parallel architecture, a type of computer engineering which, although by no means new, is presently gaining a great deal of attention because it is superficially similar to the gross anatomic structure of the human brain. However, as Searle points out in his rebuttal, aside from decreasing computing time, there is nothing that can be done using this type of engineering that cannot likewise be done on the more common serial architecture. (See Searle, "Computer Program?," p. 28.)

6. Stevan Harnad, "Minds, Machines and Searle," in *Journal of Experimental and Theoretical Artificial Intelligence*, (1989) vol. 1, no. 1.

7. Arthur C. Clarke, *Profiles of the Future: An Inquiry into the Limits of the Possible*, 2nd rev. ed. (London: Victor Gollancz, 1982), p. 25.

8. In 1769 the French encyclopedist Denis Diderot published a satire which deals with this fantasy called *The Dream of d'Alembert*. Diderot imagined a room, like a large hothouse, which would contain potted people, pots of kings, of bishops, of stableboys, of courtesans and so forth. (See Denis Diderot, *La rêve de d'Alembert*, Paris: Librairie Marcel Didier, 1951, p. 54.)

9. See James D. Watson, *Molecular Biology of the Gene* (New York: W.A. Benjamin, 1965), pp. 416 ff.

10. R.G. Collingwood, *The Idea of Nature* (London: Oxford University Press, 1964), p. 176.

11. Hannah Arendt, "Truth and Politics," in *Between Past and Future* (New York, Viking, 1968), p. 243.

12. Quoted in M. Mitchell Waldrop, "Resolving the Star Wars Software Dilemma," in *Science* (May 9, 1986), p. 710.

13. Robert P. Crease and N.P. Samios, "Cold Fusion," in *The New York Times*, September 24, 1989.

14. Crease and Samios, p. 38.

15. Arendt, p. 243.

Actual life is full of false clues and sign-posts that lead nowhere. With infinite effort we nerve ourselves for a crisis that never comes. The most successful career must show a waste of strength that might have removed mountains, and the most unsuccessful is not that of the man who is taken unpreparedly, but of him who has prepared and is never taken. On a tragedy of that kind our national morality is duly silent. It assumes that preparation against danger is in itself good, and that men, like nations, are the better for staggering through life fully armed.

—E.M. FORSTER

EPILOGUE: EROS AND PLANNING: THE ANT AND THE GRASSHOPPER RETOLD

It is often said that we are living in the age of information, but insofar as this is true, it follows that we must also be living in the midst of a great deal of bad information, that is, misinformation, propaganda, nonsense and hype. In our time prophecy, in its various forms of prediction, forecasting, futurology and scenario writing, has become a major source of bad information—bad in the sense that it misleads us by distorting our regard for both the present and the future. It thereby brings out the worst in us, encouraging us to behave in narrow, selfish and self-defeating ways.

Because it so often works this way, notwithstanding the good that may sometimes come from trying to be mindful of the future, the role of prophecy today has become rather malign. Although our prophets like to tout themselves as being escorts along the avenues of salvation and exploration, all too often they act as legitimators of questionable schemes and programs that unleash the forces of abandonment, neglect, irresponsibility, destabilization and exploitation. But this is not surprising when you consider how simple-minded, self-serving and childishly impressionable most of our prophets are.

Yet the problem with modern prophecy cannot entirely be attributed to the fecklessness of our prophets; they are, after all, a product of our times and, as I have tried to demonstrate throughout this book, reflect the pathologies of their willing audiences. They exploit only that which is eminently exploitable. The problem with prophecy today and the source of our sometimes pathological obsession with the future is much the same as what Ivan Illich has said is the problem with medicine, that is, prophecy and medicine both represent major interventions in our lives that often cause harm.[1] They do not, of course, always cause harm, and if we wish to give them the benefit of the doubt we should say that they usually intend to do good. But they cause harm often enough and decisively enough so that we should be seriously concerned about the role they play in our lives, both unbidden and at our behest. And we should be particularly concerned because their malign side is not aberrant or accidental but part of their very nature, characteristic of the role these enterprises play today.

Illich's book *Limits to Medicine* is subtitled *Medical Nemesis: The Expropriation of Health*, and a large part of his argument is that, aside from any other harms the modern practice of medicine may entail, it also expropriates from individuals, with their consent, responsibility for their own health. Therefore, on the positive side, he argues that we should reappropriate the responsibility for our health, which we have both relinquished and had taken away from us, by learning to take better care of ourselves and relying less on health professionals. Modern prophecy, again with our consent, has also developed in such a way that it has come to rob us of an essentially human right and responsibility: the right to dream our own dreams and set our own goals; the right, ultimately, to exercise the freedom, individually and collectively, to make the decisions that will shape our destinies.

It is no accident that prophecy and medicine have both come to work this way; the same could be said of a great deal of present human endeavor. There are many areas in which we abdicate responsibility for our growth and development and for our regular duties and pass it on to professionals, to experts, thereby empowering them and at the same time rendering ourselves ever more irresponsible and helpless. On this level, prophecy today can be regarded as being no more than an attempt by self-appointed experts to rationalize the future. Rationalization today has become little more than an attempt to order and control just about everything by pressing it into the mold of formal logic, and into the paltry calculus of formal means geared towards the achievement of what usually turn out to be extremely narrow ends. In the process of trying to fit everything into this mold, we are constantly deluding ourselves about what can or cannot be done. We are ignoring a great deal of substance in life that cannot easily be fit into this mold, that cannot easily be defined as a problem to which an expert can apply a formal bag of tricks. In this way, we often avoid or ignore vast areas of human endeavor which rationalization cannot easily capture. Our tendency to ignore in the present that which cannot be easily defined and managed as a problem is the intellectual and spiritual precursor to the all-too-common habit of our prophets of trivializing the problems of the future.

The persistent themes of modern prophecy—including its penchant to trivialize and depersonalize all problems, its concomitant obsession with automated decision-making, its "gaming" of life situations, its anti-individualism and its view of the human population as being basically anonymous and homogeneous—are all extremely mechanistic ideas. They necessarily follow from our obsession with the mechanized world view represented by rationalization and the type of control that is supposed to come from it. However, individuality, diversity and heterogeneity are too difficult to capture and predict and therefore defy control. Notwithstanding their power and utility, all machines are a caricature of nature, and the mechanistic future is no more than a caricature of the present, that is, of life.

Yet the way we live is not in the nature of things. Our culture is of our own making, and the beginning of trying to ameliorate its faults is to try to become conscious of them. There are certainly alternative ways to look at the world and think about it than those suggested by our futurologists who, in addition to adopting a mechanistic view of the universe, often lack the imagination to envision a future world that is other than a mere extrapolation of the present, no matter how questionable some parts of that present may be, and who, as George Orwell rightly observed, so often appeal to our fears and our craving for power.

As a point of departure for exploring these alternative views, I will begin by trying to deal with a little unfinished business relating to the panic that so many people feel about the future, and which makes them turn to futurologists for guidance. Early in this book I made the observation that futurologists frequently justify their enterprise by making the claim that, because things are changing so rapidly, we need to be able to predict the future in order to be able, by anticipatory action, to adapt to it. To support this claim they usually refer to familiar slogans such as, "There are far more scientists and technologists alive and working to change the world today than in all the previous history of civilization," and, "The amount of information in the world is doubling every few years and increasing at a far more rapid rate than was previously imaginable." These commonplaces are said to be indisputable facts, and are supposed to portend revolutionary futures for everyone on earth.

However, if you scrutinize them closely, all such statements are questionable, if not simply false. For one thing, we should not mistake the hectic pace of modern life, which includes a great deal of wasted and duplicated effort, for rapid change, or even for forward motion. But even assuming, for the sake of argument, that all change is for the better, what does it mean, after all, to say that the rate of change is accelerating, and why should we assume that an accelerating—or even merely rapid—rate of change can and will be sustained indefinitely? There have been other bursts of scientific and technological activity followed by long or short lulls; is there any basis for assuming that our age will be different? Any number of developments can slow down or even halt the rate of technological innovation and the social and economic transformations that are said to follow it. These include: war; declining prosperity; a turning away of the human spirit from outer, materialistic matters towards inner, spiritual ones; and even a failure of intelligence and/ or imagination. Given the importance of mathematics, it is worth bearing in mind that in every age there are unsolved mathematical problems around. That most or even all of these will eventually be solved is highly probable; but exactly when any particular problem will be solved—no matter how important it may be to do so—is unpredictable. The serious decline during the Reagan administration in patent applications in the United States, a nation which prides itself on its innovative ability, is in and of itself evidence enough that these changes can happen to any nation, even during our age, which often likes to think of itself as being above the greater forces of history.

Furthermore, although social change is related to technological development, far less personal change is actually necessitated by such development than our prophets, who are typically so enamored with it, would like us to assume. This means, quite simply, that if we are only willing to exercise it, we can have much more control over our lives than is commonly supposed. To cite a crude example, just because televisions exist, and most of us are likely to bring them into our homes, does not mean that they have to be used as the centerpiece for social life in the family. Just because jet planes make traveling fast and relatively easy does not mean that any given married couple must keep houses in two cities at once in order to develop their individual careers, simply because it is possible to do so. There are perhaps difficult choices involved when a technological development makes a decision in personal life-style possible—many opportunities present precisely these kinds of difficult choices—but they are real choices nevertheless, choices which we can make to shape our own futures.

Now let me return again to the original question: How

fast are things really changing? The only way to answer this question is to compare our time with previous eras. Because we take electricity and mechanical power for granted, we have lost perspective on how dramatic was the introduction of these things in the world of the nineteenth century— dramatic not simply because the world at that time was technically naive, as our prophetic hucksters flatter us into assuming, but because these innovations were truly astounding. Perhaps what one considers to be earth-shaking is a matter of personal judgment, values and taste, but I know of no development in the twentieth century, including the computer and biotechnology, which has had and continues to have as dramatic and far-reaching an effect on our lives as the invention and development in the eighteenth and nineteenth centuries of the different kinds of mechanical engine and the electric generator.

In fact, it can be argued that, from the perspective of the power of its impact on our lives, technical innovation has been steadily slowing down during the entire course of this century. To understand what I mean by this statement, ask yourself which of the following innovations have had the greatest impact on your life: the refrigerator, which started making its appearance in the homes of the industrialized nations in the 1940s, or the microwave oven, which started becoming common in the 1970s? The automobile, which became common starting in the 1920s, or the home computer, which started to make its presence felt only in the 1980s? To assess the importance of these appliances, ask yourself the following questions: in each set, which would you sooner give up, the earlier or the later innovation? Which has made the greatest difference in your life?

As we press towards the end of this century, most innovations are no more than refinements of existing technologies: they enable us to do things faster or more neatly, in a glitzier fashion, or more precisely, but not *differently*. Furthermore, the existing technologies, upon whose development so much innovation depends, may themselves find their limits or be exhausted before they perform the miracles that our prophets tell us they will perform in the future. This has often happened in the past. For example, in the Middle Ages many communities in Europe competed with one another to see who could build the biggest and highest cathedral. Many of their accomplishments stand to this day as monuments to their ingenuity. Who has not heard of the cathedrals of Notre Dame, at Chartres, at Amiens and Rheims? But the biggest cathedral that was ever planned and erected was the cathedral at Beauvais. Sound familiar? It shouldn't, because this greatest of all cathedrals is no longer standing. Begun in 1247 and completed by 1557, this marvelous structure collapsed on Ascension Day of 1573. Its ambitious builders had pushed the technology of gothic architecture to the breaking point—and then beyond. This and similar lessons from history should teach us that we should not make predictions simply on the basis of extending present technologies; there is no basis for assuming that any technology is infinitely extensible.

Of course today, using the technologies of reinforced concrete and structural steel, we can build structures even higher and grander than the Beauvais cathedral. But when one technology reaches its limits, it is impossible to predict when a new one will be developed to replace it and push its logic forward. For example, the digital computer of today is based on the "analytic engine" which was invented by the Englishman Charles Babbit in the early nineteenth century. (The "analytic engine" was itself based on the Jacquard loom, the complete development of which, it should be noted, had to be delayed because of the advent of the French Revolution.) The theory of the modern digital computing machine is exactly the same as that of this early predecessor, so why wasn't the nineteenth century the computer age? The answer to this question is very simple: Babbit's "analytic engine" was completely mechanical and the mechanics, that is, the *practice* of the machine, simply could not do justice to its *theory*. There were no alloys in those days that were both light enough and strong enough to sustain the extremely rapid mechanical activity that computing with these machines required. The earliest computers used vacuum tubes and did present some problems with overheating, but the modern computer is basically electronic and therefore has very few mechanical parts so the problem of wear and tear caused by the extremely rapid movement of parts is no longer an issue, although other maintenance problems do remain.

Yet even the development of the modern computer has been limited by the development of software. In Chapter Five, I illustrated some of the software development problems that have now for a quarter of a century seriously limited the scope and effectiveness of the computerization of our education system. Admittedly, education is one of the most complex fields in existence for which one might try to develop software, but it is by no means unique. Similar problems are being experienced, for example, in the fields of meteorology and weapons systems.

These apparent limitations on innovation are not a pessimist's list of past and recent failures. Undoubtedly, with persistence, we will eventually be able to solve some, if not all, of the technical problems that now seem intractable. However problem solving, especially the way we practice it today, is not everything: not all of life's difficulties are reducible to these neat little things we call problems, and wishful thinking, intellectual dishonesty and half-baked answers solve nothing. Therefore we should not be basing human existence, including, especially, the existence of future generations, on premises and promises based on false predictions which stem from untried theories and claims of future mastery which may never exist.

It is much more effective, healthy and honest to recognize the complex nature of development as it occurs in this world and, as far as this pertains to definable problems, not to assume that anything can be solved until it has been solved—especially when there is an element of danger involved in failing to do so. It is, of course, morally questionable to create and bequeath any problems for future generations to solve when this is avoidable. But if we do convince ourselves that our development does indeed depend on this type of decision-making, we should ensure that problems that are created in the present will be solvable at some time in the future, and that we know how far in the future this will be likely to happen. The legacy of present problems that stem from the decisions of past actors who either did not care about the future—that is, *our present*—or assumed, conveniently, that we would be clever enough to deal with what, by disdain or neglect, they were preparing for us, is evidence of the importance of this care for the future. From crushing debt burdens—not only in the Third World but now also in the West—to exhausted and eroded soil, to unmanageable nuclear waste: there is ample evidence of this around us. The irony is that it was our prophets, who make the greatest claim to be mindful of the future, who encouraged us to get into these predicaments with their foolish, self-serving, dishonest and irresponsible predictions, and their assurance that if we pursued these paths to the future everything would turn out all right. It is all very well for a futurologist like Jerrold Maxmen to praise the virtue of making bold, optimistic predictions, but it is precisely these kinds of predictions that are likely to put us in greatest jeopardy if proven false.

Now let us look again at the premise that it is necessary to try to predict the future in order to adapt to it by anticipatory action. I said in the first chapter, and have illustrated throughout this book, that this kind of adaptation often has a bandwagon effect which can lead to making the prophecies in question self-fulfilling. On the other hand, why does one have to arrive in the future with, as it were, ready-made answers? Why does one have to predict to adapt? Do you have to know there will be a road in your future to be able to cross it? After all, it is not the prediction of the road but your eyes and legs, your intelligence and ability, that get you across. Likewise it is mastery of the present, which "living in the future" often makes us neglect, that will get us through the real future when it finally arrives.

Henry Kissinger has been the prophet of our time who, more than any other, has been enamored of the ready-made answer which can be persistently carried forward to the future. Characteristically, he likes to call this ready-made answer *doctrine*. Not surprisingly, therefore, he has had a strong aversion to, and very little patience with, real, that is, open-ended discussion. So he has written: "If there is no doctrine at all and a society operates pragmatically, solving problems 'on their merits' as the saying goes, every event becomes a special case. More energy is spent deciding where one is than where one is going."[2] And so obsessed has he been with where we are going that he has expressed great impatience with the sticky business of taking stock of where we presently are and where we are coming from. It is surprising that this kind of statement has been so appealing for so long in a country like America which prides itself on its pragmatism, which of course always entails dealing with issues "on their merits" and in context. Probably its sway and the closed-minded abstraction it entails have been major factors in America's decline, because in nations, as in individuals, there are few things that retard growth more than ready-made answers.

One cannot help but contrast Kissinger's penchant for ready-made answers with the views of Edmund Burke, the great English conservative statesman of the late eighteenth century. Burke once wrote: "In my course I have known and, according to my measure, have cooperated with great men; and I have never yet seen any plan which has not been mended by the observations of those who were much inferior in understanding to the person who took the lead in the business."[3] It is worth noting that, because of his willingness to consider all cases on their merits, and because he did not believe in approaching developments with ready-made answers, Burke was able in his time both to oppose the French Revolution on the one hand and to support the American Revolution on the other. Kissinger's statement may be appealing to foreign policy makers, but it would never appeal to airline pilots: they know the importance of knowing exactly where one is coming from and all of the other conditions of one's departure in order to be able to both depart and arrive safely. During the post-war years we have all been witness to how doctrine, precisely because of this aversion to open-ended discussion and the pragmatism that can flow from it, has degenerated to dogma; and we have all seen how this degeneration on both ideological fronts has prolonged and exacerbated the arms race.

The greatest development successes of this century have been based not on abstract goals or grand schemes, but on mastery of the concrete details relating to the situation at hand. This has often meant mastery of received technology, not of innovation. This was as true of the United States in the first half of this century as it has been of Japan in the second. No part of the automobile, except for the electric ignition system, was invented in the United States. But Ford and other pioneers in this industry were foremost at mastering quality control and efficiently producing mechanical systems that were invented in Europe, and thus they created the auto-industrial age. Similarly, Japan is not known to be an innovative country, but a masterful one. It is the high-level mastery of manufacturing technique and not innovation that has earned Japan her reputation for quality. By now it is a well-known fact that many of the things that Japan manufactures, from silicon chips to printed circuit boards, were invented in the United States and other countries; in fact even the much touted Japanese management techniques were invented in the United States.

For years after World War II, Japanese industry kept churning out the same dull and unimaginative models of everything from cars to transistor radios while they were mastering their production and quality-control techniques. In a sense, innovation would simply have been a distraction and an unnecessary luxury at that point. The Japanese were not concentrating on the model of the future, but on the one in front of their noses. Once they had complete control of the production process and were able to manufacture things exactly the way they wanted to, they began to introduce variety and to innovate on their own. By then their innovation was grounded in what they had already really mastered and could therefore do exceedingly well.

Likewise, the Soviet Union's remarkable accomplishments in space in recent years have been based on the mastery of received technology. It matters little whether they have stuck to the old technology out of necessity, that is, because of their relative technological backwardness, or out of choice. In 1969, when the United States won the race to the moon, all of the pundits predicted that the Soviet Union would never catch up in the race in space. And in the 1970s it appeared as if these prophets would be right. America surged forward with dazzling innovations and new programs to both broaden and deepen her lead, developing first the Skylab and then the Shuttle. Meanwhile the Soviets plodded on, using the same tried-and-true rocket systems over and over again, manufacturing them in large quantities and, with experience, with a high level of reliability. Needless to say, what has happened since then should embarrass the prophets of 1969. The Skylab came crashing down to earth and so too, tragically, did the American Shuttle. In the meantime, as they plodded on, the Soviets became very good at what they were doing. They logged an impressive number of man-hours, days, months and finally years in space so that now they are experts at dealing with the health consequences of prolonged stays outside of the earth's gravitational pull. This is acknowledged by observers in both the West and the East to be the type of experience that will be indispensable if a journey to Mars is to be undertaken, as it may be, towards the end of this century. The Soviets are also now close to the point where they will be able to build a space station, which could act as a stepping-stone for this proposed journey and would give them a permanent presence in space. Of course, any number of unanticipated things could happen to thwart the Soviet ambitions in space, but the point is that they are now universally acknowledged to be ahead in many of the most basic capabilities needed for getting to Mars, a development which no one could or would have predicted in 1969.

There are many races to the future going on now, cheered on by our prophets, and we are already beginning to see some of the consequences of the whole world chasing after the same goals. With more and more people and nations setting their sights on the same targets, the future is becoming like the small end of a funnel. One consequence of so many nations choosing the same developmental goals is that, with everyone heading for the same place, the way is very crowded and it is hard to find any standing room when one arrives. That is why it is said that we are living in such a competitive world. It is not because we are so masterful— too many of our goods, in spite of their glitz, are actually rather uninteresting and shoddy—but because there are too few goals being pursued by too many comers. Another consequence of the whole world chasing the same goals is that the globe is actually becoming increasingly homogeneous and losing some of its rich diversity. This has resulted, of course, in the boredom of finding the same sorts of goods and services all over the world; but it has also led to the loss of some invaluable cultural forms, from literacy to railways, that have been or are being abandoned in the process.

However, in the short run, just as bad as the sometimes harmful homogeneity that chasing after a narrow number of goals is imposing upon the world is the fact that the constant innovation upon which a great deal of futurology is based—and which it encourages—undermines our ability to act effectively in the present. Thinking about the past in moderation is a good thing and can enhance the present. That is why Goethe said that he who knows no history lives in darkness. But thinking about the past excessively, which is commonly referred to as "living in the past," is harmful because it undermines the present by halting human growth and development. The same can be said about thinking about the future: in moderation, it should enhance the present. But the modern obsession with the future is the same as "living in the future," and is simply the other side of the coin to "living in the past." It does not inhibit growth by fixing it at some stage in the past, as living in the past does; it inhibits it by limiting choice and paralyzing the capacity of individuals, communities and nations to maximize the discovery and creation which belong to the present. And it encourages us to live dishonestly and irresponsibly in the present in expectation of future redemption. Finally, living in the future undermines our ability to act effectively in the present because it forces us to constantly learn the "up-and-coming thing" regardless of its merits—sometimes even before the old one has been mastered.

Because of our obsession with the future, many of us have become innovation junkies, but this lust for innovation, often for its own sake, needlessly puts everyone, especially adults, who are often slow learners, into situations where they are periodically, sometimes permanently, being put off balance and rendered incompetent. And it puts children, who are fast learners, in the position of having to invest great amounts of energy in mastering ephemeral things, like rapidly obsolescing computer languages, while neglecting the proven and still necessary skills that would serve them in better stead in the long run. And the institutionalized lust for innovation often leads to institutionalized incompetence in all sorts of public and private organizations. When presented with proposals that are said to be our future salvation, we should always bear these problems in mind, and also bear in mind that today innovation is often no more than a racket. One student of this phenomenon, the educator Michael Fullan, has observed that, although few of the innovations in the education system have made any positive difference in the lives of students or teachers, they have made a great deal of difference in the lives of the innovators themselves; they help them develop their own careers. Just to get an idea of the magnitude of intervention which is here in question, one should bear in mind that in New York City alone there were no fewer than 781 innovative programs introduced into the education system between 1979 and 1981.[4]

Perhaps the best way to understand our obsession with the future and the lust for innovation which it engenders is to think of it as a trap in our culture into which our prophets have been able to lure us because of our fear. But there are other ways of understanding our susceptibility to being lured into this trap. In an illuminating study called *The Myth of the Eternal Return*, Mircea Eliade, the distinguished professor of comparative religion, discusses a phenomenon which he calls "the terror of history." The terror of history is an existential critique of the linear progress of modern history, and a way of comprehending why so many of its steps have been so horrifying. Eliade credits Hegel with formulating the existential position that accepts all historical developments, no matter how terrifying they may be, as being *necessary*. He writes:

> From Hegel on, every effort is directed toward saving and conferring value on the historical event as such, the event in itself and for itself. In his study of the German Constitution, Hegel wrote that if we recognize that things are necessarily as they are, that is, that they are not arbitrary and not the result of chance, we shall at the same time recognize that they *must* be as they are. A century later, the concept of historical necessity will enjoy a more and more triumphant practical application: in fact, all the cruelties, aberrations, and tragedies of history

have been, and still are, justified by the necessities
of the "historical moment." (emphasis in original)[5]

Hegel's sense of historical necessity should sound familiar
because the "necessary past" is basically just the other side
of the coin of the "inevitable future" with which so many of
our prophets are smitten. Both of these views are born of a
linear view of the passage of time; they both act as a rationale
for narrowing choice, for narrowing the scope of human
endeavor; and ultimately they both act also as an apology
for the loss of human freedom this entails. Therefore, Eliade
concludes this part of his argument with the following painfully ironic observation: "How could Hegel know what was
necessary in history, what, consequently, must occur exactly
as it had occurred? Hegel believed that he knew what the
Universal Spirit wanted. We shall not insist on the audacity
of this thesis, which, after all, abolishes precisely what Hegel
wanted to save in history—human freedom." (emphasis in
original)[6]

The attack on human freedom by modern prophecy is
perhaps the most disturbing aspect of futurology. Squeezed
between the "terror of history" and the "tyranny of prophecy" people today—in spite of the freedom that is much
vaunted, especially in the West—find that they have little
room to maneuver. No wonder our prophets appeal, as Orwell observed, to our fear and our craving for power: these
are precisely the drives that dominate those who feel
trapped.

The futurologists' arguments about inevitability and necessity are absurd. After all, what does the future represent
except a mental construct which contains possibilities? The
future seems ominous, not because it is rushing in on us and
forcing us to make decisions about an unknown time, but
because we are crowded by the failures of the present and
immediate past, many of which are based on the irresponsible programs of our contemporary prophets: over forty
years of failure to disarm, to properly end World War II;
over twenty years of decline in the education system; a health
system which in spite of worthy accomplishments still produces often questionable results and at an ever diminishing
return on resources invested in it. It is no wonder that our

failures haunt us. But why should we continue to make our disease worse by constantly returning to the same quacks who helped get us into trouble in the first place and letting them continue to mislead us and tyrannize our future?

What are the alternatives to these modern self-defeating habits of life? How can we avoid being terrorized by the past and tyrannized by the future? Eliade's study contains the beginning of an answer. It does not begin with the terror of history, but ends there. It begins with an appreciation of the pre-Socratic and non-western cultures which, he observes, sought consolation for the existential fear that springs from the remembrance of history and a dread of the future. The members of these societies coped effectively, not by trying to rationalize the future and control it, as we do, but by relating all events to religious and mystical archetypes and the cyclical view of time that they represent. In this world view, if a misfortune befell a person he would console himself by thinking that this was a repetition of the divine drama, that the same thing happened to a god at the beginning of time and was all part of a great drama that would lead, ultimately, to the making and salvation of the world.† Of course we cannot, and should not, try to reconstruct the world view and ethos of the so-called archaic societies, but it would be foolish not to recognize the fact that there is more scope for cycles and repetition in modern life, and more virtue in this than our modern prophets would allow.

The cyclical view of time is basically feminine, whereas the linear view, which appeals to virtually all of our prophets, is masculine. The cyclical view therefore sheds a very different light on human development than that which comes from our prophets. Nothing illustrates this better than Aesop's fable about the ant and the grasshopper. Though he lived in the sixth century B.C., morally Aesop had a great deal in common with our modern day futurologists—the

---

† Eliade has observed that there are signs that the cyclical view of time is gaining some currency in the modern world, and he cites as evidence of this the writing of the historians Toynbee and Spengler, as well as the literature of T.S. Eliot and James Joyce. More recently, Milan Kundera in his remarkable best-selling novel, *The Unbearable Lightness of Being*, has made a sustained allegorical argument for the goodness of repetition in life.

seeds of their thinking have always been with us. This fable is very short so here is the whole thing:

> One fine day in winter some Ants were busy drying their store of corn, which had got rather damp during a spell of rain. Presently up came a Grasshopper and begged them to spare her a few grains, "For," she said, "I'm simply starving." The Ants stopped work for a moment, though this was against their principles. "May we ask," said they, "what you were doing with yourself all last summer? Why didn't you collect a store of food for the winter?" "The fact is," replied the Grasshopper, "I was so busy singing that I hadn't the time." "If you spent the summer singing," replied the Ants, "you can't do better than spend the winter dancing." And they chuckled and went on with their work.[7]

Aesop's fable, which is told in the familiar retrospective mode of the forecaster writing the history of future time, speaks volumes about the world view of the typical futurologist. The ants, to be sure, had a prophetic vision: they foresaw a grim and cruel future in the coming of winter and, in anticipation, planned for it by stocking provisions. The grasshopper, however, who lived only in the present, failed to see this vision, failed to take the necessary adaptive measures and therefore, from the ants' perspective, was destined to "deservedly" perish. But when you think of it, these ants were not really that insightful; they were, after all, preparing not for an unprecedented future catastrophe, but for the change of the seasons, for the winter which they had seen before and were to see time and again as it was to recur during their lifetimes. They were only your typical extrapolating futurologists, feeling clever about pointing to the obvious. That is the key: they were motivated not so much by insight as by anxiety, and even when they had a full storehouse that only needed ordinary maintenance based on received wisdom about preventing spoilage, their fear and grim vision drove them on to create a very narrow little world, to cultivate a narrow little niche and live a spiritually impoverished life-style.

This is the most charitable interpretation that one can give to Aesop's fable, but by neglecting other issues it gives him, as a moralist, far more credit than he deserves. Bear in mind how nasty these clever little ant-prophets were when confronted by someone whose world view was different from their own. They were reluctant to stop work even to consider her plight. They did not merely tell the grasshopper to go her own way, they mocked her about her life-style and on account of her profession. They were the prophetic ones; they had vision; they knew the world of the future would be cruel to such as she; they had anticipated it, had made their plans and preparations, and were ready for it. But when you consider the matter more closely, were they not purposive and logical to an extreme? They consulted their heads in all things, including the plight of a fellow creature, but not their hearts. Finally, they denigrated her work, her profession, which was singing; there was no room for it in their world, not in the present and certainly not in the future, where it is represented as being no more than mere folly.†

To see how typical they are of modern prophets one has only to recall Feigenbaum's similar tirade, which I quoted earlier: "These intellectuals who persist in their indifference, not to say snobbery, will find themselves stranded in a quaint museum of the intellect, forced to live petulantly, and rather irrelevantly, on the charity of those who understand the real dimensions of the revolution and can deal with the new world it will bring about." By now this vision should also sound familiar from other prophetic sources. The reader will recall that Plato, who was one of Aesop's spiritual heirs, took a similar view. In the *Republic* we also have an idealization of narrowly purposive behavior, but there, instead of tilling the soil, an activity which is denigrated, we have the single-minded pursuit of philosophy and athletics relating to military skills. Plato also, as the reader will recall, had no room in his vision for the arts, especially the so-called imitative ones. Similarly Richardson, in his City of Health, where the single purpose was to gear all life to the promotion and

---

† Incidentally, Aesop really had it in for grasshoppers. In another fable called *The Grasshopper and the Owl* he describes another scene in which the head, Logos, represented by the Owl, literally devours the soul, represented by another grasshopper who knows no better than to sing in this owl's presence.

sustenance of health, also had no room in his vision for the aesthetic side of life and so he promptly banished all decorations from its households.

There is something very troubling about these visions and the plans and schemes they legitimate and promote—aside from their prissy and uncharitable views, and aside also from the fact that they leave no room for aesthetics. It is not just that they are purposive and spell out future goals, but that their purposes are so very narrow, and their goals are to the exclusion of so many worthwhile other ones. Aesop, falsely but characteristically, makes this single-minded purposiveness a matter of life-and-death necessity; this kind of falseness, at bottom, is what the tyranny of prophecy is all about. More than this, these visions that claim to be very wise seem very foolish when one considers how the world really does develop. The arts, for example, are not a matter of mere luxury, but of necessity, and by saying this I mean more than that music and poetry and fine arts and theatre are good for you—even the meanest agricultural laborer knows the value of a barn dance. Not all of the drive for development comes from science. From the arts come also the creative forces in life, some of which have had profound practical impacts on even our technological and economic development.

Cyril Stanley Smith, the distinguished metallurgist, has documented a great deal of the history of how art has aided in the development of industry. He notes, for example: "Metallurgy began with the making of necklace beads and ornaments in hammered, naturally occurring copper long before 'useful' knives and weapons were made. The improvement of metals by alloying and heat treatment as well as most methods of shaping them started in jewellery and sculpture. Casting in complicated moulds began in the manufacture of statuettes. Welding was first used to join parts of bronze sculpture together—none but the smallest bronze statues of Greece or ceremonial vessels of Shang China could have been fabricated without the technique."[8] I noted above that the precursor for the modern digital computer was the Jacquard loom, and in this vein Smith also notes that most minerals and many organic and inorganic compounds were discovered for uses as pigments; wheels first appeared on toys; lathes were used for making snuff boxes before they were used for heavy industry; rockets for fun came before rockets for military use; the chemical industry grew from the need for dyes and mordants used in fine textiles; and electric generation was developed in response to the need for electricity for electroplating silverplate tableware.

The above examples should illustrate that a great deal of innovation is not purposive but adaptive in nature: whereas for the economist innovation may be a wilful trick, for the artist and craftsman of the finest order it is a response to present need and a natural part of their creative intelligence. All of the above innovations and countless others came from play and from the cultivation of known techniques by those who were intimately familiar with them. They were not attempts to "invent the future," as Stewart Brand claims many scientists and technicians are trying to do at MIT, because these innovators had no fixed idea in their minds of what the future should be like; they were only trying to be masterful, or, what is much the same thing, to enhance their present abilities, but ultimately their innovations were all used in unintended and unexpected ways.

These are important distinctions. The research that is going on now at the Media Lab at MIT and in a similar vein in many of our research and development establishments all over the world is all based on a paradigm of planning that is itself largely based on the paradigm of war. These research endeavors are generally parts of grim campaigns to be the first to occupy a rather unimaginative and narrow future industrial-technological niche: the clever telephone, the artless but glitzy robot secretary, mechanized graphics, and so on. The alternative paradigm of development, which is based on the artist's methods of cultivation and of play do not, because they cannot, have a prophetic quality and therefore are treated with indifference.

War is a seductive paradigm because, in a sense, it is the ultimate act of subjugating substance to form. And it is surely the intellectual basis of a great deal of modern planning, especially the grandest and most ambitious schemes. It is therefore no mere coincidence that many futurologists of our time—perhaps Herman Kahn is most prominent among these—started their careers in military planning. Nor is it accidental that those "think tanks" that have specialized in military research, like the Rand Corporation and the Hudson Institute, have also been major centers for work in futurology. If there is a god of warfare, he undoubtedly serves double time as the god of modern prophecy. And, since influence works in both directions, a great deal of modern futurology is rife with the "campaign" mentality, and the paradigm of war has in turn even invaded the thinking of other areas of futurology, like economics and health.

Planning today is based all too often on the war paradigm. It depends on prior destruction, on the obliteration of a great deal, if not all, present context and detail in order to achieve its ends. Planning, which usually relies heavily on forecasting, has become something of a fetish in social and economic thinking since the end of World War II. In recent years it has been argued, particularly by economic theorists like Professor Lester Thurow of MIT, that the main advantage that Japan and Germany have over the United States is that the former countries have national industrial plans whereas the American economy is developed on an ad hoc basis.[9] But there is no magic in planning. Whatever merit there may be in planning per se, its meaning and effectiveness will vary greatly from time to time and from place to place. More than goals, materials or objectives, and far more than any elaborate or simple concepts, planning, to be effective, requires *context*.

This fact is well illustrated by an examination of the outcome of the Marshall Plan and its descendents, some of the grandest economic plans of this or any century. Although the Marshall Plan was devised by the United States to assist all of the nations of Europe that had been devastated by World War II in their effort to build themselves economically, it is well known that it was not equally effective everywhere it was applied. Jane Jacobs, an economist who has a rare understanding of both the uses and the limits of planning, has summarized the different effects of the Marshall Plan in Europe in this way:

> Some of the aided economies, such as those of the Netherlands, West Germany, parts of France and parts of Italy, did proceed to expand and develop

—as San Francisco did after its [1906 earthquake] disaster. But others did nothing of the kind. Britain received Marshall Plan equipment, as West Germany did, but this bounty did not make Britain's economy behave like West Germany's. Southern Italy received Marshall Plan aid, just as northern Italy did, but the sequels were strikingly different. Northern Italy, already the most prosperous and economically creative part of the country, proceeded to prosper, develop and expand further. Southern Italy, which had previously been persistently backward, poor and economically passive, stayed so. Insofar as Marshall Plan aid (or the much larger aid given later from the north of Italy) changed southern Italy, the changes did not transcend the gifts themselves, for southern Italy's economy did not take to expanding and developing on its own account or under its own steam . . .[10]

The gist of Jacobs's argument is that, in the different countries that were targeted by the Marshall Plan and by the subsequent Marshall-type plans that were aimed at Third World countries, these plans, in the form of economic and material aid, took hold only where there was context, where there were already enough people who had the necessary types of knowledge and skills to implement them, and in the context of networks and interactive systems in which this infusion of economic and material aid could take hold. In other places, like southern Italy, the Marshall Plan worked as effectively as sprinkling seed on rock or barren ground—in spite of the predictions.

My argument, of course, is not against planning per se any more than it is, in the final analysis, against being mindful of the future. Our experience with the Marshall Plan and similar enterprises has long demonstrated that, in spite of our fetishistic attachment to it, planning in and of itself is inherently neither good nor bad. Like regulation (a related process), planning can be either good or bad. The question is not whether or not one is to make plans. The question is, on what shall these plans be based? If plans are to be based on mere predictions then one must always ask: On what are these predictions really based? And whose interests will their fulfilment or self-fulfilment serve? But we should not delude ourselves into thinking that planning, per se, is always a good, always a virtuous thing to do. On the contrary, a significant part of planning is not only sterile, as was Marshall Plan aid to southern Italy, but often also debilitating, and even destructive.

Good planning should never unnecessarily limit choices; it should expand them. Ideally, good planning will not consist of that which is borrowed, but that which is bred. It will be a natural, concomitant activity, a by-product, if you will, of living as well as possible *in the present*; it will never be a substitute for it, which is often precisely what bad planning is about.

It is worth bearing in mind that the most effective method of combating the spread of AIDS has not been based on the war paradigm, so dear to the futurist. Even five years ago, the war paradigm dominated our thinking on how to deal with this challenge. Great cures were predicted. The disease would be knocked out by a heroic international research effort. But these predictions have so far come to naught. Meanwhile, the most effective means for coping with this disease have come from cultivation, which has led to changes in day-to-day habits of relationship. It is unfortunate that it has taken desperation for us to change in the present instead of continuing to wait for some future miracle to save us, but at least our experience with AIDS is teaching us that we can work effectively with present means, and that the present is the appropriate time in which to combat this or any future catastrophe. Unfortunately, in most other seemingly less desperate situations, we continue to wait for future miracles because we are told by our prophets that they will come.

The paradigm of war, which so many modern prophets invite us to worship, is also the ultimate depersonalizer of life, and therefore cares very little about relationships. It depersonalizes and trivializes all human relationships, all acts of nurturance and love that precede it and many that follow. That is why it is the ideal metaphor for our modern prophets—it fits perfectly into their psychology.

It is impossible to imagine a worse paradigm for thinking of the future, for growth and development, than the paradigm of war. One can say much against it, but basically it entails two main problems. The lesser of these is that it encourages us to put vast amounts of energy not only into preparation, but into overpreparation, to the point where our resources for other endeavors are sapped and we are never at ease to enjoy the fruits of our labor and the repose which should be the gift of everyday life. Those of us who think this is virtuous will stagger through life constantly pressed under the weight of their weapons; those who do not will simply retreat from life and try not to get trampled. No one has described this condition better than E.M. Forster in his novel *Howard's End*, where he writes: "Actual life is full of false clues and sign-posts that lead nowhere. With infinite effort we nerve ourselves for a crisis that never comes. The most successful career must show a waste of strength that might have removed mountains, and the most unsuccessful is not that of the man who is taken unprepared, but of him who has prepared and is never taken. On a tragedy of that kind our national morality is duly silent. It assumes that preparation against danger is in itself good, and that men, like nations, are the better for staggering through life fully armed."[11] Too many of us have completely forgotten the virtues of traveling light through life, relying on our character and inner resources rather than on externalities, on weapons.

The second problem with this mentality is, of course, that in any war there will be winners and there will be losers. In this context I have already mentioned the deadly dullness and homogeneity that results when all nations pursue the same goals; the world as a whole becomes the loser. The war paradigm, which has been a favorite among false prophets from Aesop on down, is not sometimes, but always, a recipe for disaster, if not your own than that of someone else.

The god of war has many attributes that have much to do with how we are today encouraged to regard the future. The god of war, the god of kill, is also the god of overkill, not only because fear of reprisal is a great motivator, but because relentless, blind pursuit is his nature. Even when the battle is going the wrong way, when the plan and the premises on which the plan were based are proving themselves to be useless, or worse than useless, the pursuit is relentless. Soldiers are told to ignore feedback that might distract them from their relentless course, and also to ignore details and context. Very rapidly, and increasingly, everyone becomes the enemy.

The alternative to the paradigm of war which has come to play such a great part in our contemplation of the future is Eros, who is commonly regarded as the god of love, but in this context can more generally be thought of as the god of connectedness. I will describe some of his attributes because they also belong to the alternative paradigm for thinking of the future. I have already mentioned two: repetition and the cyclical mode of living.

The uses of repetition are many in a world which strives for connectedness rather than merely for extension. It is used for gaining mastery and creating meaning, and repeated cycles serve the invaluable purpose of grounding life in the familiar rather than leaving it constantly subjected to the inherent strangeness of the novel. Open-endedness is another of this god's main attributes. Openness means that one never plans on arriving at a future encounter with the false prophet's ready-made answer, but alternatively on discovering the answer in the richness of exploring the new experience. But perhaps the most important attribute of this god which we must understand if we are to change our war-like mentality with regard to the future is cultivation.

Cultivation as an alternative paradigm to war for facing the future is different not only because it is ever constructive, but also because it is constructive by means of being respectful of context and paying close attention to detail. It is not like a moonshot, which is essentially an exercise in de-contextualization through the creation of a self-contained environment. Few things in life are like moonshots. Most things are not like that, cannot be made like that because they are too complex, too dependent for their success on paying attention to and interacting with context, to the external environment—including the needs of other people—rather than subduing it by blasting through it. Because it examines context, cultivation requires attention to detail and interaction with that which is being cultivated, be it a school, a child, a tree, a car, a factory.

There is much talk today of competitiveness, of excellence, and much of this talk is patently war talk. It is talk about grimly purposive actions, about heroic acts of will geared towards the achievement of some future goal. But most goals are not achieved by single acts of will, even heroic ones. They are achieved by *sustained acts of will*, that is, by a change of habit, of custom and of culture. That is why all failures in achieving goals, that is, in mastery, be they in our ability to build cars or to make love, are based on failures in cultivation, in nurturance.

Cultivation takes time. Its effect or its failure are cumulative, even though sometimes expressions of the success that comes from it may be dramatic, as when you make a breakthrough in your piano-playing technique, or a tree that has for years been carefully pruned one year bursts forth in blossom and fruit. Sustained acts are necessary because nature is generally forgiving in the short run but not in the long. An occasional inappropriate response to the needs of a child will not permanently damage him or her, but persistent abuse or neglect will. The failures of nurturance, of cultivation, are persistent failures; they are failures which result from persistent neglect of the present.

Neglect and abandonment of the present are symptoms and necessary results of our obsession with the future, and with the relentless pursuit of narrow goals that we think will make the future for us. The heart of all prediction is a correlation of means and ends, but one of the pathologies of modern futurology is to think that means *are* ends. That is why every little innovation—which is usually no more than a disembodied means—gets extrapolated and lionized by our prophets. The tendency to think this way is deadly because it entails the subjugation of ends to means, of questions to answers. The search for applications for the latest innovation becomes not an associative but an exploitative search. Means masquerading as goals, means looking for ends, answers looking for questions, are all agents of exploitation. On the contrary, between ends and means should be continual dialogue. A good answer always changes the question which elicited it, and the changed question requires then a different good answer, until answer and question, means and ends, are entirely different from what they started as.

Tadao Umesao, a Japanese cultural anthropologist, considers narrow goal orientation to be the deadliest form of cultural habit we can develop. He writes: "To say that a goal is clear is to say that it is functional. To say that it is functional is to say that it is 'unifunctional.' What I believe is that at some point our world became filled exclusively with such unifunctional things, and it is this that has led to our present state of confusion." He then goes on to ask: "Is it really so absurd to envisage a plan which does not take a single goal as its final end, a plan in which each successive goal emerges and grows from the process of planning itself—i.e., a process which is rather like a succession of makeshift expedients?"[12] Those who understand Japanese culture on the basis only of the caricature that is presented to the West may find Umesao's contention puzzling, because Japan is usually portrayed in the West as being single-minded. This is true to a point, but it is only a recent development born of the desperation that arose in the aftermath of World War II. Japan has been successful in part because of its single-minded goal orientation, but in larger part because of its ability, like Sweden, to act concertedly as a nation. Umesao argues, however, that in the process of overplanning, Japan has worked itself into a very narrow niche, and he thinks that this will be deadly in the long run.

Context is the enemy of our prophets who like to oversimplify and trivialize everything. The rich, sticky and stubborn nature of reality is their bane. That is why so many of them are so enamored with systems and mechanical precision—yet one must never underestimate how close the precise can be to the petty. So in thinking about future atomic wars Nitze worried not only about controlling the situation with precise language, but also about how atom bombs could be dropped precisely enough to avoid civilian casualties. It is certainly a high-minded goal if you accept the premise of such a war itself and allow for the vanity in such thinking. Similarly Papert wants to decontextualize the future. Not only does he want to introduce his LOGO system into the schools, but he has predicted the abolition of the school system itself—and even our system of knowledge which took

thousands of years to cultivate—in the process. That would
certainly be a great exercise in decontextualization.

If we continue to follow the lead of prophets who trivialize and depersonalize future life in order to make it manageable, imaginable, then our goals will become simple-
minded and we will continue to abandon the richness and
complexity that works, albeit with difficulties, for a narrow
future at best and an impoverished fantasy at worst. We will
be sacrificing reality to fantasy. Present reality must be sacrificed, will be sacrificed sooner or later, but then this should
be to a new reality, equally rich or richer—not to the impoverished visions of our prophets. There is room for any
amount of innovation in this world, but in introducing it we
should where possible follow the lead of our most sophisticated cultivators who are now practicing the art and science
of intersowing. We should make our gardens richer and more
diverse rather than always wanting to start with scorched
earth and the new unknown crop.

When those who have power avoid responsibility for making
the present work, those who are helpless suffer. The best
years of the lives of a large part of the population are frittered
away waiting for that miraculous time in the ever receding
future when the economy will be ready to let them be a part
of it; when society will be less alienating; the world will be
safe; the education system will work; a cure will be discovered for the latest disease. There is an enormous amount
that can be done with present knowledge, techniques and
technology to significantly alleviate these types of problems
now. Not to act now as best we can to deal with present
problems is simply irresponsible. We do not know, cannot
know, what will work to solve our problems in the future,
but we can find out what will solve them in the present by
working to solve them now, with proven means that are
already at hand.

By being so enthralled by the future we have made a
perversion out of what, when tempered with prudence, can
be a virtue, that is, the postponement of gratification. Even
on the level of the individual, decisions in which the importance of timing is fairly self-evident are very often indefinitely

deferred for the sake of waiting for the "perfect moment," which is always at some time in the future. Countless numbers of people delay marriage and having children to the point where it becomes improbable, if not impossible, to make these decisions sanely and soberly—let alone on the basis of love. Greater numbers refuse to enjoy the daily gifts that life has to offer them for the sake of first completing the dieting or fitness regimen which they have persuaded themselves will make them more worthy people at some point in the future. This kind of thinking has become so prevalent in our society that for many it has become an almost lethal sort of second nature. By adopting this kind of thinking we deny not only our bodies, but our very souls; we postpone not only gratification, but the quest for meaning and fulfilment that should be part of our daily lives.

Furthermore, when it comes to thinking about the future—largely due to the way it is incessantly hyped by some of the most influential leaders in government, business and the media—we have become like impressionable children at a carnival, wildly dashing from one huckster to the next, never finishing a thing before dropping it and running off to grab at the next marvel or treat that is dangled before our eyes. With children, such mad dashing about usually leads to exhaustion and sore stomachs. Is this really the way we want to develop our lives and culture?

This last question is a paraphrase of Tolstoy, who asked not, What does the future hold in store for us? but, What shall we do and how shall we live? If the futurologists who tell us that the future has endless possibilities are really right, we need not wait to hear from them what the future ought to be like. This, as Tolstoy suggests, is a question we should pose to ourselves. Unless we do so, unless we exercise the real freedom we have *at present* to shape our destinies according to the way we want to live, rather than acting on the basis of our prophets' versions of the good and the "inevitable," the less freedom in the long run we will have to exercise. Talk of the inevitable is cheap, but it is also insidious. When we hear it we would do well to ask ourselves: What does the promoter of a particular inevitable scenario have at stake in having it realized? What do they have to gain? And, perhaps more important, because there is no such thing as a neutral future, what do other, undoubtedly more helpless members of our society, have to lose?

In the Jewish tradition, waiting for the Messiah, that is, for the salvation of the future, is now considered to be morally corrupt. One must make the most of the present, not only because it is the given, but in order even to be worthy of the Messiah's coming. There are also similar precepts in Christianity (even though that religion believes the Messiah has already come), and in the other major religions of the world. These religions consider true prophecy to be the highest calling because they recognize that all questions surrounding the uses of prophecy are ultimately moral questions, questions that are concerned with what we want to become. In this sense prophecy that is not grounded in morality is always false. Far from being foresightful, it is myopic and evasive to forget that most questions that can be posed about the future can more meaningfully and forcefully be posed about the present. It is only at our peril that we forget that if we used only the knowledge we now have, and used it only for the good, we could have heaven on earth, without one further innovation or discovery, and thereby create a better world than any of our false prophets are capable of envisioning. This may be a truism but cannot successfully be evaded. It is a matter not of ingenuity but of character, and it is the key to any and all possible good futures.

NOTES

1. Ivan Illich, *Limits to Medicine: Medical Nemesis: The Expropriation of Health* (Harmondsworth, England: Penguin Books, 1977).
2. Henry Kissinger, "American Strategic Doctrine and Diplomacy," in Michael Howard (ed.), *The Theory and Practice of War* (London: Cassell, 1965), p. 277.
3. Edmund Burke, cited by Karl Popper in *The Open Society and Its Enemies* (Princeton, N.J.: Princeton University Press, 1966).
4. See Michael Fullan, *The Meaning of Education Change* (Toronto: OISE Press, 1982), p. 4. Fullan estimates there are tens of thousands of members of what he calls the "innovation establishment" working in the United States in the field of education.
5. Mircea Eliade, *The Myth of the Eternal Return* (New York: Pantheon, 1954), pp. 147–148.
6. Eliade, p. 148.

7. *Aesop's Fables* (trans. V.S. Vernon-Jones) (London: Heinemann, 1912), p. 125.

8. Cyril Stanley Smith, "Aesthetic Curiosity—The Root of Invention," in *The New York Times* (August 24, 1975).

9. Lester Thurow, *Zero-sum Solution: The Route to Economic Growth* (Harmondsworth, England: Penguin, 1987). Actually America does have a national industrial plan—but it is embedded in its military planning. It may not be a *good* plan, but it is national in scope and intervenes heavily in the economy.

10. Jane Jacobs, *Cities and the Wealth of Nations* (London: Viking, 1985), p. 8.

11. E.M. Forster, *Howard's End* (New York: Bantam, 1985), p. 101.

12. Tadao Umesao, "Soul and Material Things," keynote address to meeting of International Council of Societies of Industrial Design, ICSID '73 (Kyoto: Congress Report Japan Organizing Committee for ICSID '73), pp. 17–18.

INDEX

Evie looked up and sucked in her breath.

The man above her blotted out the sun. Evie could tell immediately that he and the girl she'd just met were related. But Faith's eyes were still warm with laughter. The man's were as chilly as the water lapping at her toes.

"I'm Evie McBride." She scrambled to her feet to retain her dignity. "Your daughter and I bumped into each other."

Sam looked from the slender redhead to his niece in disbelief. He'd been looking for Faith for the past hour—so he could ground her for the rest of her life. He hadn't expected to find her in the company of the uptight schoolteacher his dad had warned him about.

But somehow his father had forgotten to mention that Evie McBride was a *beautiful* uptight schoolteacher....

Books by Kathryn Springer

Love Inspired

Tested by Fire #266
Her Christmas Wish #324
By Her Side #360
For Her Son's Love #404
A Treasure Worth Keeping #436

Steeple Hill

Front Porch Princess
Hearts Evergreen
"A Match Made for Christmas"
Picket Fence Promises

KATHRYN SPRINGER

is a lifelong Wisconsin resident. Growing up in a
newspaper family, she spent long hours as a child
plunking out stories on her mother's typewriter and
hasn't stopped writing since! She loves to write
inspirational romance because it allows her to combine
her faith in God with her love of a happy ending.

A Treasure Worth Keeping
Kathryn Springer

Steeple
Hill®

Published by Steeple Hill Books™

STEEPLE HILL BOOKS

Steeple
Hill®

ISBN-13: 978-0-373-87472-9
ISBN-10:   0-373-87472-3

A TREASURE WORTH KEEPING

Copyright © 2008 by Kathryn Springer

This is a work of fiction. Names, characters, places and incidents are
either the product of the author's imagination or are used fictitiously, and
any resemblance to actual persons, living or dead, business establishments,
events or locales is entirely coincidental.

This edition published by arrangement with Steeple Hill Books.

www.SteepleHill.com

Printed in U.S.A.

But store up for yourselves treasures in heaven, where moth and rust do not destroy, and where thieves do not break in and steal. For where your treasure is, there your heart will be also.
—*Matthew* 6: 20–21

To Linda—
A fellow traveler on the writer's journey.
I'm glad we're in this together, friend!

Prologue

"Please think about it, Evie. You're the only one of us who doesn't have—"

At the sound of a meaningful cough, Caitlin's words snapped off and Evie McBride smiled wryly.

Who doesn't have a life.

That's what Caitlin had been about to say before Meghan, "Miss Tactful," had broken into the conversation. They were talking on a three-way call, the usual method her two older sisters used to gang up on her. Sometimes advanced technology made life easier, and sometimes it was simply a pain in the neck.

"What Caitlin was going to say," Meghan continued in an annoyingly cheerful voice, "is that you're the only one whose summer schedule is…*flexible.*"

Flexible. Nonexistent. Was there a difference? And if Evie had known how many times she'd be called upon to be *flexible* over the past few years since their father had retired, she wouldn't have chosen teaching as a career. She would have tied up her life with a neat little job that kept her working year-round, like her sisters had.

It wasn't that she minded helping out their dad. They were extremely close and she loved him to pieces. No, what drove her crazy was that Caitlin and Meghan always assumed she didn't have any plans for her summer vacation. And that just wasn't true. A neat stack of novels, the ones she hadn't had a chance to read during the school year, sat on the floor beside her bed. There was a miniature greenhouse in her backyard full of tomato seedlings waiting to be nurtured. And a gallon of paint in the hall closet, ready to transform her front door from boring beige to Tuscan yellow because she'd read somewhere that a front door should sport a friendly, welcoming color. And really, was there anything more friendly than yellow? Evie didn't think so.

"What if I have plans?" Evie asked. The sibling ambush had occurred at nine o'clock at night, interrupting her favorite educational program. There had to be some consequences for that. Unfortunately, stalling was all she could come up with.

"You do?" Meghan asked cautiously.

"What plans?" Caitlin demanded.

Now she was stuck. "Painting."

"Painting." Caitlin repeated the word like she'd never heard of the activity, and Evie could picture her rolling her baby blues at the ceiling.

"Is it something you can put off for a few weeks, Evie? Once I'm done with this photo shoot, I'll try to take some time off to help you." Meghan, bless her heart, let her keep her dignity.

Silence. Evie's cue to cave in. After all, that was her role. She sighed into the phone, knowing her sisters would accept it as the cowardly white flag of surrender that it was.

"All right. Fine. I can run Beach Glass while Dad goes on his fishing trip."

"Dad will be so happy." Caitlin's voice was as sweet as glucose syrup now that she'd gotten her way.

Evie resisted the urge to stick out her tongue at Caitlin's smiling face in the family photo on the coffee table.

"Evie, we *really* appreciate this," Meghan said. "And Dad will be thrilled. He didn't want to have to close up the store for two weeks."

"But he didn't want to ask you for help because he didn't want to take advantage of your free time," Caitlin added.

"Well, it's a good thing *you* don't have a problem with that, then, isn't it?" Evie said.

But not out loud.

What she said out loud was *good night,* allowing just a touch of weariness to creep into her voice. Hopefully enough to generate a smidgeon of guilt in her sisters' consciences. Not that it would matter when another crisis barked at the trunk of the McBride family tree. Why these crises always surfaced during the months of June, July and August, Evie didn't know.

Three years ago, Patrick McBride had officially retired from teaching and bought a small antique shop, whimsically christened Beach Glass by the previous owner. A quaint stone building, it sat comfortably on the edge of a lightly traveled road that wound along the Lake Superior shoreline. A *very* lightly traveled road. It wasn't even paved. The first time Evie saw it, she had a strong hunch why the previous owners had practically *given* it away. They'd probably cashed the meager check in nearby Cooper's Landing on their way out of town, anxious to rejoin civilization.

Evie had spent most of that summer making the year-round cottage that had been included in the deal suitable for her father to live in. The calluses still hadn't completely disappeared.

The following summer she'd been the one drafted to spend "a few days" teaching their dad how to use a computer so he could manage all the financial records for the business. The brief computer lesson had turned into a month-long project that had ended with Patrick's mastering of the power button and not a whole lot more.

The previous summer, Caitlin's tail had gotten tied in a knot when Patrick happened to mention a woman's name *twice* during their weekly phone conversation. A Sophie Graham. Evie had flatly refused to act as the family spy. Her dad was an adult and it wasn't any of their business if he'd found a friend. Less than twenty-four hours after Evie had drawn a line in the sand over that situation, Caitlin had figured out a way to tug her over it. Beach Glass needed to be landscaped and since the only thing she and Meghan knew about plants was that the root part went into the ground, Evie was the obvious choice to spend six weeks mulching and planting flower beds.

Suspiciously, her sisters were always too busy to help out but never too busy to call and check up on her.

But Evie loved them. Even bossy, tell-it-like-it-is Caitlin. And she knew they loved her. And really, was it their fault all she could find to fill up three months of summer vacation was painting her front door, transplanting tomato plants and living vicariously through the lives of the characters in her favorite books?

Evie had missed most of her program during the kissing-up portion of the conversation so she turned off the television and closed her eyes.

I want my own story, God.

Even as the thought rushed through her mind, she treated it like the mutiny that it was.

Your own story! What are you talking about? You're a junior high science teacher. Shaping impressionable minds. It's a high calling.

Wasn't she the first teacher who'd taken the Rock of Ages Christian School to first place in the science fair competition the past few years? While all the other schools had entered working volcanoes and posters labeling the parts of a rocket, her students had brought in *inventions*. Like Micah Swivel's solar-powered toaster. And everyone knew the reason Angie

Colson won the spelling bee with the word *bioluminescence* was because Evie had just finished a unit on insects. The day before, Angie had taken the chapter test and had chosen fireflies, a stellar example of bioluminescence, as the subject of her required essay. They'd shared the victory, celebrating with doughnuts and hot chocolate in the teachers' lounge.

Evie basked in the knowledge she had been loved by every seventh and eighth grader in her charge since the school had hired her. And if their test grades didn't prove their devotion, the number of cookies on her desk every morning did.

She had a story all right. It just happened to be woven into the lives of an age group most people ran, screaming, away from. She thrived between the months of August and May. The summer months made her feel restless. And lonely.

Maybe that's why she didn't fuss too much when her sisters rearranged her summer plans. It was nice to be needed. And she couldn't deny that their father, whom they affectionately referred to as the absentminded professor, needed a watchful eye.

Evie reached for the phone and pressed Speed Dial.

"Hello?"

"Hi, Dad. I hear you're going fishing."

Chapter One

Sam Cutter had driven almost twelve hours when an old joke suddenly came back to him. Something about a town not being the end of the world but you could see it from there.

Now he knew that place had a name. Cooper's Landing. And it was cold. No one had warned him that winter released its grip with excruciating slowness along Lake Superior's shore. The second week of June and the buds on the trees had barely unfurled in shy, pale shades of green.

He drove slowly down the main street and pulled over next to the building that sagged tiredly on the corner. The color of the original paint on the clapboard siding was only a memory, and the shingles had loosened from the roof, curling up at the ends like the sole of a worn-out shoe. A red neon sign winked garishly in the window. Bait.

He glanced at the girl slumped against the window in the passenger seat. Her lips were moving silently, showing signs that yes, there was brain activity. Since she hadn't talked to him for the past five hours, he'd been forced to watch for obvious signs of life. They'd been few and far between. Changing the song on her iPod. The occasional piece of candy being unwrapped. A twitch of her bare toes. Well, not completely bare. One of them had a toe ring.

He touched her elbow and she flinched. Sam tried not to flinch back. Once upon a time she'd been generous with her hugs.

"Faith? I'll be right back."

She frowned and yanked out a headphone. "What?"

"We're here. I'll be right back."

She straightened, and her gaze moved from window to window. She had a front-row seat to view Cooper's Landing, and Sam expected to see some expression on her face. Shock? Terror? Instead, she shrugged and pushed the headphone back in place.

He wished he could disengage from reality and disappear into another world so easily.

The warped door of the bait shop swung open when he pushed on it, releasing an avalanche of smells. The prominent ones were fish, sauerkraut and bratwurst. Sam's eyes began to water.

"Let me guess. Cutter. You look just like your old man."

Sam saw a movement in the corner of the room just after he heard the voice. Between the heavy canvas awning shading the street side of the building and the tiny row of windows, the sunlight couldn't infiltrate the inside of the bait store. Shadows had taken over, settling into the maze of shelves. The lightbulbs flickering over his head held all the power of a votive candle.

"Sam Cutter." Sam walked toward the voice.

He heard a faint scraping noise and a man shuffled toward him out of the gloom, wiping his hands on a faded handkerchief. By the time he reached Sam, he'd stuffed it in the pocket of his coveralls and stretched out his hand.

"Rudy Dawes."

Sam shook his hand even as he silently acknowledged that a long, hot shower and half a bottle of the cologne he'd gotten for his birthday weren't going to completely strip away the bait store's unique blend of odors.

"I wasn't expecting to see you so soon. S'pose you're anxious to get a look at her." Rudy squinted up at him.

"That's why I'm here."

Rudy started to laugh but quickly broke into a dry, hacking cough. "Come on, she's outside."

Sam followed him to the back of the store, and his boot slipped on something, almost sending him into a skid that would have taken out a shelf full of fishing reels. He didn't bother to look down, not wanting to know what was filling the tread of his hiking boot. In some cases, ignorance *was* bliss.

Rudy pushed the door open, and Sam found himself standing on a rickety platform that trembled above an outcropping of rocks. At the base of the rocks, a blackened, water-stained dock stretched over the water. With one boat tied to it. Sam stared at it in disbelief as it nodded in rhythm with the waves.

"There she is. The *Natalie*. She's a beauty, ain't she?" Rudy tucked his hands in his pockets and bowed his head in respect against the crisp breeze that swept in to greet them.

"*That's* the boat?"

Faith had materialized behind them, and Sam twisted around to look at her. She'd pushed her chin into the opening of her black hooded sweatshirt but the tip of her nose was pink, kissed by the wind.

"It can't be." Sam blinked, just to be sure the faded gray boat wasn't a hallucination due to the sleepless nights he'd been having. "When I talked to Dad, he said the boat was *new*."

"He's one of them positive thinkers." Rudy grinned and spit over the side of the railing. "It was new to him when he bought it. I can tell your first mate here knows quality when she sees it."

Faith's shy smile reminded Sam of his manners.

"I'm sorry, Mr. Dawes, this is my niece, Faith Cutter. Faith, this is Mr. Dawes."

"Aw, it's just plain Rudy." He smiled at Faith, revealing a

gold-capped front tooth. "Jacob said you wouldn't be here until mid-July. And he shoulda warned you we don't pack away our winter coats until then."

Sam glanced at Faith and noticed she was shivering. Instinctively, he wrapped his arm around her shoulders and pulled her into the warmth of his flannel-lined denim jacket. Instead of pulling away, as he half expected her to, she tunneled in farther. For a split second, she was six years old again, snuggled up against him with a copy of Dr. Seuss's *One Fish, Two Fish* book in one hand and a raggedy stuffed rabbit named Mr. Carrots in the other.

"Dad said the boat was available whenever I wanted to use it," Sam said distractedly. "June…worked out better for us."

"Doesn't matter to me none. I just keep an eye on it for him. Go on now. Get acquainted with her."

Faith skipped down the skeletal wooden staircase that spiraled to the water. Sam was tempted to yell at her to slow down and grab the railing, but one look at it made his back teeth snap together. It was probably safer *not* to use it.

By the time Sam hopped on board, Faith had already disappeared below deck. From his dad's description of the boat, Sam thought he'd be in a luxury cabin cruiser for the next few weeks. Now he simply hoped it was watertight.

"Sam!" Faith's muffled voice sounded more excited than it had in months. "You've got to see this!"

He ducked into the narrow stairwell and found her standing in the doorway of one of the cabins.

"Can I take this one?"

Sam peered in cautiously. A narrow bunk bed, a corner desk and a small table were the only furnishings in it, but even though they were old, everything was spotless. He exhaled slowly in relief.

"Sure. The desk will come in handy."

2 *A Treasure Worth Keeping*

Faith rolled her eyes in typical twelve-year-old fashion. "You had to remind me."

"That was the deal. Your mom let you come with me if you kept up with your homework."

"Mom would have let me come anyway." Faith lifted her chin defiantly, but he could hear the tremor in her voice. "I heard her. She told you that I've been 'too much' for her lately."

Sam closed his eyes. He had no idea that Faith had overheard his last conversation with Rachel. "Faith, it's not you. Your mom… Things have been hard for her the past few months."

"Well, here's a news flash." Faith's eyes narrowed and suddenly she looked years older. "Things haven't been easy for me, either…."

Her voice choked on the word and Sam pulled her against him. He wasn't sure what he could say to comfort her. Not when he hadn't discovered anything to fill in the fissures in his own heart.

"I miss him." Faith clung to him.

The knot of sadness forming in Sam's throat strained for release, but he kept a tight rein on it.

"I miss him, too."

"I thought you were only staying two weeks, Evangeline."

Evie saw the mischievous gleam in her dad's eyes and handed him another duffel bag from the trunk of her car. Patrick was the only person who called her by her full name, a gift from her parents to her paternal grandmother, the first Evangeline McBride, when she was born. "A person can't be *too* prepared."

"But what is it you're preparing for, sweetheart? A tidal wave? Or maybe an asteroid?" Patrick peered in the car window at the flats of tomato plants lined up across the backseat.

Evie was used to her dad's teasing. "Don't be silly." She handed him a large sewing basket embroidered with strawberries. And a stadium umbrella. "We'd have plenty of time to get ready if one of those things was going to occur. This stuff is just for…every day."

Her dad frowned as she handed him a bag of groceries. "There *is* a grocery store in Cooper's Landing."

"Do I need to mention that the expiration date on the can of corn I bought last summer coincided with the Reagan administration?"

Patrick winked at her. "You love it here."

He was right, but Evie wasn't about to admit that to Caitlin and Meghan.

A week after school had officially closed for summer vacation she'd packed up her car, locked up the house and driven away with her traveling companions—the box of books on the passenger seat beside her.

The closer she'd gotten to the adorable stone cottage her dad now called home, the more excited she'd been. When Patrick left on his fishing trip, Evie knew she'd be perfectly content just to stretch out on the wicker chaise lounge in the backyard and admire the lake from a distance. She loved watching Lake Superior change from steel-gray to vivid blue, depending on its mood. And Superior was a moody lake. The proof was in the hundreds of ships that slept below her ice-cold surface.

Evie leaned close and kissed her dad's bristly cheek. "You forgot to shave again this morning."

"I didn't forget," Patrick grumbled. "I'm retired. A man shouldn't have to shave when he's retired."

Evie looped the strap of a canvas messenger bag over her shoulder and headed toward the house. "Did you and your friend finally decide when you're leaving?"

"Day after tomorrow. Jacob's picking me up at five in the morning. And—" Patrick put up his hand to prevent her from saying what he knew was going to come next "—you don't have to get up and make oatmeal for me. The reason we're leaving so early is because it's a long drive to the lodge, and then we have to get to our campsite."

"Why don't you just stay at the lodge?" They'd had this conversation several times already, but Evie thought it worth repeating. Until she got her way. Patrick was only fifty-nine, but she didn't understand why he'd turned down a soft bed in the main lodge for a tent on a secluded island several miles away.

"Jacob's been camping for years," Patrick said. "He'll take care of me."

Evie snorted. "From what you've told me about Jacob Cutter, he's a daredevil. I don't want him to talk you into anything stupid. Or dangerous."

"You've been teaching the peer-pressure curriculum again, haven't you?"

Evie gave a weak laugh. "I'm sorry, Dad, it's just that I want you to be careful."

"Careful is my middle name."

"Stubborn is your middle name," she muttered under her breath.

The sound of tires crunching over gravel drew their attention to the vehicle creeping up the long driveway.

"Looks like you've got some customers," Evie said, watching a black pickup truck rattle into view.

"Maybe they're lost." Patrick grinned. "But I'll still try to talk them into buying a pair of seagull salt-and-pepper shakers."

Evie laughed. Beach Glass didn't have a single kitschy item like the ones he'd just described. Her dad spent the winter months combing estate sales to find rare objects—the ones that escorted his customers down memory lane. Patrick had told her more than once that everyone needed a connecting point to their past. Sometimes it was a book they remembered reading as a child or the exact twin of the pitcher their grandmother had used to pour maple syrup on their pancakes when they were growing up. Beach Glass was off the beaten path, but people still managed to find it. And when they left, it was usually as the owner of some small treasure.

"Just put that stuff by the door, Dad, and I'll take care of it in a few minutes." Evie couldn't help glancing over her shoulder at the truck idling in the tiny parking lot next to the antique shop. The tinted windows obscured the inside cab from view. She hesitated a moment but whoever was driving the pickup wasn't in a hurry to get out.

She went inside and finished unpacking her clothes, glad she'd tossed in a few sweaters. A person could never be too prepared and the breeze off the lake still had a bite.

When she peeked outside half an hour later, the truck was gone. She poured two iced coffees and headed across the yard to the shop. More than half the furnishings in her own home were compliments of Beach Glass, and she was eager to see the latest bounty her father had added since her last visit.

"What do you mean he's staying on the boat?"

Evie paused at the sound of Patrick's agitated voice through the screen door.

"Well, that's just one of our problems...." His voice lowered, ebbing away like the tide, and then strengthened again. "He stopped by a little while ago, insisting we bring him along. No, I don't trust him any more than you do, Jacob...but Sophie—"

Evie realized she was holding her breath. She'd never heard her dad sound so stressed.

"I suppose we can delay the trip but I'm afraid if we don't go as planned, Sophie is going to get... No, go ahead. Evie might be on her way over. I'll talk to you later this evening."

It suddenly occurred to Evie that she was eavesdropping. She backed away from the door, replaying the part of the conversation she'd overheard.

The elusive Sophie Graham again.

Evie had never seen the woman, even during the reconnaissance mission Caitlin had tried to set up the previous summer. In the interest of maintaining sibling harmony, Evie *had* dropped a few subtle hints to her dad that she'd like to meet Sophie sometime, but all she could get out of him was that the mysterious Sophie wasn't in good health.

"Evie?"

She froze midstep.

Her dad may have been a bit forgetful but apparently there was nothing wrong with his hearing.

Evie winced and caught her lower lip between her teeth. All the times she'd preached to her students that honesty was the best policy came rushing back. She pressed the glasses against her cheeks to put out the fire in them. The downside of having red hair and fair skin. She couldn't hide a blush to save her life.

"I brought you a reward for working so hard," she called through the screen door.

Patrick appeared on the other side and Evie could see the furrows in his forehead, as deep as stress cracks in a wall.

"So, did you sell some of those salt shakers?" Evie asked, deliberately keeping her voice cheerful to cover up the guilt nipping at her conscience.

Patrick's mouth tightened. "No. He wasn't interested in buying anything."

"Who—"

"Let's take this out to the garden, shall we? You can enjoy the fruit of last summer's labor while you take a break. Some of the plants are already coming up, and it's going to be beautiful."

Evie handed him one of the glasses and saw his fingers tremble as he reached for it. Worry scoured the lining of her stomach.

"Dad, is everything all right?" She tried to piece together the fragments of the conversation she'd overheard. It had sounded like someone else wanted to come along on the fishing trip. But why would that upset him? And what did Sophie Graham have to do with it?

"Right as rain."

"There's nothing right about rain unless you have an umbrella," Evie said promptly. It was an old joke between them, and she relaxed when he smiled.

Maybe her concern over the fishing trip was making her read more into the conversation she'd overheard. It was possible her father was simply a little uptight because he was taking a vacation for the first time in—Evie did a quick calculation—twelve years. Not since the year her mother was killed.

Chapter Two

Evie had her alarm set for five-thirty. Not to make sure Patrick ate his oatmeal but to make sure he didn't forget anything. Else.

She pulled on her robe and slipped into the kitchen, only to discover her sneaky father had already left. The coffee was on and he'd left a note taped to the refrigerator.

I'll call you as soon as I can. Relax. Love, Dad.

Evie snatched the note off the fridge and frowned. The faint smell of bacon and eggs lingered in the air. No wonder he hadn't wanted her to get up before he left. He'd wanted to eat his artery-clogging breakfast without a witness.

And what exactly did he mean by *relax*? Was she supposed to relax because she was on summer vacation? Or was she supposed to relax while knowing her dad, who thought one pair of socks per day was sufficient, was going on a two-week fishing trip with Jacob Cutter? A former Marine. The two men had known each other only six months, and already Jacob was pushing Patrick out of his familiar routine. Evie didn't like

Jacob Cutter. Her dad was a scholar, not an outdoorsman. A retired high school English teacher. What was Jacob thinking?

Her doubts about the trip had increased the evening before while Patrick packed his things. Evie had noticed an important piece of equipment missing from the gear piled by the door. When she'd called his attention to it, Patrick had laughed self-consciously and disappeared outside to rummage around in one of the outbuildings, finally returning with a fishing pole.

Shortly after watching her dad hook his thumb on one of the lures, Evie had had a burst of inspiration. She could go with them. As the cook. Keeper of the campfire. That sort of thing. When she'd brought it up to Patrick, he'd looked less than enthusiastic. In fact, he'd looked slightly offended and had reminded her that the reservations were for *two* people and they couldn't add someone else this late in the game. Which meant the owner of the black pickup truck who'd tried to coerce Patrick and Jacob into taking him along wasn't going, either.

No wonder Patrick had run out on her so early in the morning. Maybe he'd thought she'd stow away in the backseat.

Too bad she hadn't thought of that sooner.

If only her dad would have mentioned the fishing trip to *her* before he'd brought it up to Caitlin and Meghan, who'd both thought it was a great idea. Of course. They always had their passports ready to go at a moment's notice.

"Dad never does anything." Meghan had listened to her concerns and gently brushed them aside. "He loves to go to auctions and estate sales and putter in the store, but maybe he's decided he needs to expand his interests. You know, find a new hobby."

Caitlin, as usual, had been more direct. "Don't be such a worrywart, Evie. Dad wants to go fishing, not skydiving. If you see a parachute in the trunk of his car instead of a fishing pole, call me."

It was easy for her sisters to live their own lives and let their dad live his. Both of them had already moved away from home when Laura McBride had died unexpectedly. Meghan had been a freshman in an out-of-state college, and Caitlin a graduate student in France for a semester abroad. Evie had just turned fourteen and she'd been the only one left to take care of Patrick.

Lord, you'll take care of Dad, won't you? Keep him safe and comfortable, just like I would if I were with him? Don't let that reckless Jacob Cutter try to talk him into doing anything danger-ous. And help him remember to change his socks if they get wet.

Patrick had always encouraged her to talk to God, her heavenly Father, as easily and naturally as she talked to him. Some people might think she was crazy to talk to God about wet socks, but Evie figured if God knew when a sparrow fell to the ground, He cared about the details of His children's lives, too. No matter how small.

She opened her eyes, ready to start the day right. Beach Glass officially opened at ten o'clock, giving her time to weed the garden and go into town to pick up a gallon of milk and some eggs.

She'd just make sure to check the expiration date before she bought them.

Cooper's Landing was five miles from the antique shop, yet Patrick thought nothing of hopping on a rickety old bicycle and riding it into town. Evie kicked the tire with her toe, and when it wobbled back and forth like a toddler taking those first precious steps, she decided to drive her car instead.

Johnson's Market stuck to the basics—not bothering to cater to the tourists who used Cooper's Landing as a brief resting point to fill up their vehicles and stretch their legs a bit.

The sandy stretch of beach, strewn with sculptures of satin-smooth driftwood, drew Evie's attention when she stepped outside the store with her purchases. Ever since Patrick had moved to what Caitlin referred to as "the end of nowhere," Evie had been fascinated by Lake Superior. She'd grown up in a suburb of Milwaukee, where the only connection she'd had with water was the local swimming pool. But here, right in front of her eyes, the lake stretched across the horizon in variegated shades of blue. And even though today the water was a comforting shade of indigo, it could change with a turn of the wind.

A glance at her watch told her there was time for a short walk down to the dock. She tucked her groceries into the backseat of her car and headed toward the water. Picking her way down the rocky bank, Evie vaulted over a small ledge of rock and practically fell on top of someone.

"Hey!" A girl rose up from a crouched position. "What do you think you're... Oh, sorry."

"I'm the one who's sorry," Evie apologized. "I was staring at the water and didn't see you."

"That's okay." The words came out grudgingly.

She looked to be in the same age range as Evie's students, so Evie knew better than to take the edge in her tone personally. The girl hugged a sketchbook against her chest, and a metal case on the ground by her feet revealed a rainbow of oil pastels.

"You're drawing the lake? Or the boat?"

"The lake. The boat's kind of ugly."

Evie couldn't argue with that. The boat tied to the dock was as plain and drab as a cardboard box. And looked about as seaworthy.

"I admire anyone with artistic ability." Evie held out her hand. "Evangeline McBride. Science geek."

The girl's eyes met hers shyly and then she smiled. "My name's Faith. I'm a jock."

"What sport?"

Faith shrugged. "You name it."

"But Lake Superior inspired you, huh?"

"No, I'm being forced. It's art class." Faith peeked at the sketch pad and made a face. "It's terrible."

Evie knew better than to push. If Faith wanted her to take a look at her drawing, it had to be her idea.

"Okay. Tell me the truth." Faith suddenly flipped it over for Evie to see.

"It's…" Evie's voice trailed off when she saw the gleam of humor in Faith's eyes. She'd colored the entire page blue. "You captured it perfectly, I'd say. A closeup of the water."

"*Very* close up!"

Faith giggled and Evie joined in.

"Faith!"

The voice behind them startled Evie. Her foot slipped on the rocks, sending an avalanche of stones skipping down the bank.

"Hi, Sam." Faith's giggle changed to a bored monotone.

Evie looked up and sucked in her breath. The man looming above them blotted out the sun. Evie could tell immediately that he and the girl were related. Both of them had silver-gray eyes and thick, shadow-dark hair. Faith's eyes were still warm with laughter, but the other pair trained on Evie were as chilly as the water.

"I'm Evie McBride." She scrambled to her feet to regain her dignity, but it didn't matter. She barely reached the man's broad shoulders. "Your daughter and I sort of…bumped…into each other."

Sam looked from the slender redhead to his niece in disbelief. He'd been looking for Faith for the past hour—so he could ground her for the rest of her life. He was pretty sure he had the authority. Although Faith might not agree. The truth was, they hadn't been agreeing about much the past few days, and Sam was at the end of his rope. Moodiness he could cope with, but Faith had started to disappear whenever the opportunity presented itself. Like an hour ago.

They'd been staying with Jacob, who'd left early that morning on a fishing trip, and Sam had brought Faith into town with him while he got the *Natalie* ready to launch. This would

be the first time they'd had an opportunity to take the boat out.
While he'd checked the engine, his wily niece had pulled
another disappearing act.

He hadn't expected to find her in the company of Patrick
McBride's daughter. The uptight schoolteacher his dad had
warned him about. But somehow Jacob had forgotten to mention
that Evie McBride was a *beautiful* uptight schoolteacher.

And he hadn't expected to hear Faith giggling the way
twelve-year-old girls were supposed to giggle. The sound had
thrown him off balance. He realized he hadn't seen Faith smile
or heard her laugh for a long time. Too long. Dan's accident
had been like a scalpel—going in deep and removing the
laughter from all of them.

"I'm Sam Cutter—"

"He's my uncle, not my dad," Faith interrupted.

Sam exhaled silently. No one knew better than he did that he
couldn't fill Dan's shoes. His twin brother had been a great dad,
and all Sam could be was what he'd always been—a doting uncle.
But lately he found himself wondering if that was enough to keep
Faith from drowning in grief. When Dan had been injured, she'd
taken a leave of absence from school. Now she was so far behind,
the principal had said the only way she could pass to the next grade
level was by completing her homework over the summer. What
bothered Sam the most was that Faith didn't seem to care.

"Cutter? Are you related to Jacob Cutter?"

"I'm his son." Sam noticed the instant change in Evie's
expression.

"It's nice to meet you."

Sure it was. Jacob hadn't been kidding. Evie McBride *didn't*
approve of him. He wondered why. "Dad mentioned you're
minding the store while he and Patrick are fishing."

"I don't know a lot about antiques, but I do know how to dust
them." She glanced down at Faith and winked.

Faith grinned back.

Maybe Ms. McBride came across as a little stuffy, but she definitely had a way with kids.

"Faith, are you ready? We should be long gone by now." Sam stared his niece down, not ready to let her off the hook for disappearing on him.

Faith shifted uncomfortably and he saw a flash of good old-fashioned guilt in her eyes. *Good.*

"Are you house-sitting for your dad?" Evie directed the question at him, her voice polite but strained.

Sam suppressed a smile. With that tone, she sounded just like a prim schoolteacher. All she needed was a pair of horn-rimmed glasses and a bun. They'd go really well with the heavy cardigan she had buttoned up to her chin and the ankle-length denim skirt.

"We're staying on the *Natalie.*" Faith pointed to the boat nodding drowsily in the waves.

"You're living on *that?*"

Sam bristled at what sounded like an accusation. It scraped against the doubts he was already having about bringing Faith along. So the *Natalie* wasn't the best-looking boat in the harbor. And maybe she didn't have all the latest bells and whistles. But he'd checked her over, and she was sturdy. The engine had purred like a kitten before settling into a reliable, even hum.

"A few days on the water and a few days at the cabin." Sam lifted one eyebrow, daring her to comment.

Evie McBride's chin lifted, accepting his challenge. "I don't think—"

"You should come with us sometime," Faith broke in, leaving both adults momentarily speechless.

"That's sweet of you, Faith, but…" Evie turned and stared, almost mesmerized, at the water. "Beach Glass is going to keep me pretty busy over the next few weeks."

She was afraid of the water, Sam realized in surprise. His gaze dropped to the hem of her skirt, where the toes of a sensible pair of shoes peeked out. Not exactly the type of footwear designed for splashing in the surf. He hid another smile.

"I should get going, too. The shop opens at ten." Evie's expression softened when she looked at Faith. "Be careful when you're out on the lake."

Sam expected Faith to give Evie her signature don't-fuss-over-me-I'm-not-a-little-kid-anymore look, but his niece nodded solemnly.

"Sam knows what he's doing."

Sam's mouth dropped open at the confidence he heard in her voice. Before he had a chance to bask in the glow, she skipped down the rocks toward the dock. "I can't keep up with her."

He realized he'd said the words out loud when he felt Evie touch his arm. The warmth of her fingers soaked into his skin. When he glanced down at her, he saw a knowing look in her eyes.

"Don't try to keep up with her." Evie smiled. A genuine smile that sparkled like sunlight dancing on the water and had a curious effect on his pulse. For the first time, he noticed a dusting of cinnamon freckles on her nose. "The secret is to stay one step *ahead* of her."

On the way back to the cottage, Evie couldn't stop thinking about Faith Cutter. *And Sam.* Although she didn't want to think about him. Anyone who would take a child out in a boat on a lake as unpredictable as Superior for any length of time had to be a live-on-the-edge type of person. And in the end, that kind of person always hurt the ones closest to them, whether they meant to or not.

Just like her mother.

Growing up, Evie had loved hearing the story of her parents' romantic courtship. Her father and mother had met in the principal's office of the local high school. Patrick had been a first-year English teacher and Laura McIntyre—*Officer* Laura McIntyre—had been invited to talk to the students for career day. The principal had asked Patrick to give Laura a tour of the school before the assembly started.

They'd married six months later.

Growing up, Evie had been blissfully unaware of the dangers of her mother's career. By the time Evie was in middle school, Laura had been promoted to sergeant and spent the bulk of her time at a desk, scheduling shifts and taking complaints.

And then one day, Laura hadn't come home on time. Evie could still see the look on her father's face when the squad car pulled into the driveway and the chief of police had walked up to the front door.

Laura had been struck and killed by a drunk driver while assisting a stranded motorist.

Patrick's strong faith had never wavered, and he'd appealed to his daughters to lean on God, not blame Him for Laura's death. But in the following months as her family handled their grief in different ways, Evie had struggled with a growing realization. It wasn't God she was angry with. It was her mother, for choosing a career that had put her at risk.

Chapter Three

Evie's first customers of the day turned out to be newlyweds who spent more time exchanging loving glances than they did browsing through the aisles.

She felt a stab of envy as she watched the young man press a lingering kiss to his bride's cheek. The young woman, who didn't look much older than Evie, blushed and halfheartedly pushed him away. Evie pretended she hadn't seen the kiss. There were times she asked God why He was waiting so long to bring her future mate into her life. She liked to think God was working on a certain man's heart, making sure he was just right for her so when they met, she'd recognize him at a glance....

Sam Cutter's face flashed in her mind, and Evie fumbled the ironstone pitcher she'd been dusting. Fortunately, she caught it again before it hit the ground. *Sam Cutter!* Not likely. He wasn't exactly Mr. Personable. In fact, she'd sensed he'd found her...amusing. She hadn't missed his quick, appraising glance when she'd stood up. Or the half smile on his face when his silver gaze had lingered on her wool cardigan. It *was* chilly by the shore. Not everyone had an internal thermostat that made them comfortable wearing a T-shirt on a cool day.

Which brought to mind the tanned, muscular arms his T-shirt had revealed…

"Ah, Miss?"

The bride's tentative question zapped her back to reality. *Snap out of it, Evie.*

"I'm sorry. Can I help you?"

"We'll take this." She pushed a small figurine toward Evie. A ceramic horse with one ear missing.

"Did you notice it's chipped?" Evie wanted to make sure Patrick's customers were satisfied with their purchases when they left.

The woman nodded. "I don't care. It looks just like the horse I had when I was ten. And believe it or not, half her ear was missing, too."

Her husband hovered nearby while Evie carefully wrapped the figurine in tissue paper.

"Enjoy your trip," she called after them.

The store remained quiet for the rest of the afternoon, so Evie took advantage of the time by rearranging shelves and washing the leaded-glass windows in the store.

Solitude was wonderful during the day when she could see boats out on the water and the glint of the church steeple as it winked back at the sun. But as the sun melted into the horizon and shadows began to sift through the trees and creep toward the door, Evie realized it wasn't so friendly at night. To counteract the silence, she turned on her dad's ancient record player and curled up in a chair with one of the books she'd been waiting since Christmas to read.

It was just after eight when the motion lights in the front yard came on. Evie walked over to the window and peered outside. All she could see was the outline of a shadowy figure walking up the sidewalk toward the house.

Evie's breath caught in her throat until she saw the person's face briefly illuminated in the light.

Sam Cutter.

She hurried to open the door. His clothing looked rumpled from a day out on the water, and his hair was in disarray, combed by the wind. She didn't understand why he'd come for a visit so late in the evening, unless...

"Is Dad okay? Did you hear something?"

"I imagine they're fine. I haven't heard otherwise."

Relief poured through Evie. "Then why—"

"I'm sorry. I didn't realize you'd be tucked in for the night already." The faint smile had returned.

Evie didn't like his choice of words. He made it sound as if she were a chipmunk, hiding in a hole.

"Come in." Evie stepped to the side and he stalked past her. Her traitorous nose twitched at the pleasing scent of sunshine, wind and sand that clung to his clothes. "Where's Faith?"

"I didn't leave her alone on the boat, if that's what you're thinking."

That *had* been what she was thinking, and the warmth flooding into her cheeks gave her away. Evie ducked her head so he wouldn't notice.

"My father mentioned that you're a teacher, Miss McBride."

"Evie," she corrected, wondering where this was going. "That's right. I teach seventh- and eighth-grade science classes at a Christian school—"

"Faith needs a tutor."

The terse interruption reminded Evie of Caitlin. Her back stiffened like an irritated cat.

"A tutor." Evie repeated the words, giving herself a few extra seconds to process the unexpected statement. Was Sam simply stating a fact or asking *her* to be Faith's tutor?

"We're planning to stay in Cooper's Landing for...a while,"

Sam said. "We'll be out on the water most of the day, but in the evening we'll be back at the cabin. Faith needs to finish some of her classes before school starts in the fall and someone has to check her progress. Are you interested?"

Sam didn't bother to fill in the gaps. Originally, he'd planned to come to Cooper's Landing alone, but when Rachel, his sister-in-law, had found out, she'd insisted a change of scenery would be good for Faith. Sam had agreed reluctantly, not because he didn't love spending time with Faith but because he couldn't find a way through his own mixed emotions. How could he help Faith deal with something he wasn't dealing with very well himself? And then there was Faith herself. The happy-go-lucky little girl he'd spoiled since the day she was born had turned into a sullen stranger.

When Faith had laughed with Evie that morning, it had made Sam realize just how much his sweet-tempered niece had changed over the past few months. Maybe she needed someone outside the family to motivate her to get her school-work done. A tutor. And Evangeline McBride—with her funny wool cardigan and disapproving eyes—happened to be the perfect solution. She obviously liked kids or she wouldn't be a teacher. And maybe a woman would be able to navigate Faith's changing moods better than he could.

"I don't know." Evie perched on the edge of a leather chair and stared at him. "What exactly does Faith need help with? Did she fail a class?"

Sam walked to the window and stared outside at the darkness. "Not yet. She got…behind…a few months ago and didn't have enough time to make up the work she missed. Rachel, Faith's mother, talked to the principal and he said if she completed the work over the summer she could move on with the rest of her class."

Evie sensed there was more to the story than what he was

telling her. Questions tumbled over each other in her mind. Obviously, since Faith's last name was Cutter, her mother, Rachel, must be Sam's sister-in-law. But Sam hadn't mentioned his brother—Faith's father. Several things didn't add up. If Faith needed to catch up on her schoolwork, why was she vacationing on a boat with her uncle instead of working on her classes at home with her parents? Maybe Rachel and Sam's brother had divorced.

The possibility softened Evie's initial reservations. Losing a parent under any circumstances was traumatic, especially for someone in an already vulnerable age group like Faith.

"I'll only be here for two weeks," Evie reminded him. "And I have the shop to take care of."

Sam turned to face her again. "We'll work around your schedule. What time do you close for the day?"

"Four o'clock."

Patrick lived on his pension, so Beach Glass provided a supplemental income and gave him the luxury of flexible hours. He could open the antique shop late and close early, even take a day or two off if he felt like it. And her dad had encouraged Evie to do the same if necessary.

"I don't expect you to do this out of the goodness of your heart," Sam said. "I'm willing to pay you whatever you think is fair."

Evie wasn't sure why he put her on the defensive. She was usually a very easygoing person. "It isn't about the money."

"Then what *is* it about?" He crossed his arms.

If he could be blunt, so could she. "Why can't *you* help her?"

Sam's jaw worked, and for a moment Evie didn't think he was going to answer. He thrust his hands into the front pockets of his faded blue jeans. "She... I don't think she wants anything to do with me." It was clear the admission stung.

Evie remembered the change in Faith's tone when Sam had

joined them on the beach. Faith was at the age when she was beginning to assert her independence—to try to figure out just who Faith Cutter was and how she fit into the world.

Evie knew from experience the "tweenage" years had a tendency to put unsuspecting parents into a tailspin. Especially parents who weren't expecting the radical change in their homes when formerly cheerful, compliant kids entered the hormone zone. And if there'd been some kind of upheaval in Faith's life, the fallout could be even worse.

"She's been taking off a lot lately." Sam must have read the expression on her face because he quickly amended the statement. "She's not at risk as a runaway. Eventually she comes back. She either wants attention or time alone. I'm still trying to figure that out. But today—when she was with you—it was the first time I've heard her laugh in months."

Evie's heart, which had a soft spot for kids Faith's age anyway, melted into a gooey puddle. She remembered the glimmer of humor in Faith's eyes when she'd shown Evie her drawing of Lake Superior. Maybe she'd gone through a difficult time recently, but the faint spark of life—of laughter—hadn't been extinguished. It just needed tending. Evie gave in. Not because Sam needed her but because *Faith* did.

Okay, Lord, I'm going to assume this opportunity is from you. But did you have to include Sam Cutter?

"How about two hours a day? After I close up the shop in the afternoon?"

"We'll make it work."

"I thought you were going to live on the boat for a few days at a time."

"You'll only be here two weeks, but we'll probably be here longer. There'll be plenty of chances to take the boat out."

Even though Evie had agreed to tutor Faith, she needed to cover one more base. The one that would give her a clue whether or not the next two weeks were going to be a battle-ground. "How does Faith feel about this? Does she know you're here?"

Silence.

Uh-oh. Evie's eyebrow lifted.

"She knows I'm here," Sam finally admitted. "She didn't seem very happy about it but then she said, and I quote, 'Whatever.'"

"That's because it was your idea. The 'Whatever' meant she's not totally against it. Which makes my job easier." Evie hid a smile at the uncertain look on Sam's face. Obviously, he had no insight into the workings of an adolescent girl's mind.

As if his internal defense radar picked up on her smile, the uncertainty in Sam's eyes faded and it was back to the business at hand. Evie wondered briefly what Sam did for a living. Even in worn blue jeans and a faded black T-shirt, he oozed confidence. She could easily imagine him in an expensive suit, making important decisions in a high-rise office building, miles above the cubicle crowd.

Sam glanced at his watch. "Can you start tomorrow? We can hammer out more of the details then. Faith is spending the evening with a friend, and I promised I wouldn't be late picking her up. Sophie's one of those peculiar people who go to bed early."

Evie ignored the unspoken words *just like you* that hung in the air between them. "Sophie Graham?"

"That's right. You know her?"

"I've never met her, but Dad has…mentioned…her once in a while."

"Sophie's place is just down the road from us. Her dog had a litter of puppies a few months ago, and that's where I usually find Faith if she's missing."

Which gave Evie the opportunity she'd been hoping for. "If you give me directions, I'll come over to your place tomorrow."

"Are you sure? I don't mind driving Faith over here."

"I'm sure." Evie didn't hesitate. Maybe to break the ice between her and Faith, they'd take a walk down the road to see those puppies. And she'd finally get the opportunity to meet Sophie Graham.

Sam waited until he heard the lock on the front door click into place before he strode back to his car.

The antique shop really was off the beaten path.

He paused, scanning the trees that formed a thick wall between Evie McBride and civilization. Her closest neighbor was two miles away. As cautious as she seemed to be, he was surprised she didn't have any trepidation about staying alone on a secluded piece of property. Not that Cooper's Landing was a hotbed of criminal activity, but with the tourist season starting, the place drew a lot of people from outside the area.

None of your business what Evie McBride thinks or doesn't think, Cutter.

All that mattered was that she'd agreed to be Faith's tutor for the next two weeks.

Faith met him at the front door of Sophie's home, a drowsy puppy cradled in her arms.

"Sophie is going to let me name this one," she whispered, her eyes sparkling with excitement.

Sophie appeared in the doorway behind his niece. She was close to his father's age but still a striking woman, her beauty enhanced by the kind of smile that lit her up from the inside out. "I hope you don't mind, Sam. That puppy is Faith's favorite, so I thought it was only right that she be the one to name him."

"I don't mind." Sam was about to reach out and ruffle Faith's hair but caught himself. The last time he'd done that, she'd shrieked and disappeared into the bathroom, emerging only after she'd washed, blow-dried and styled her hair all over again. Later that day, they'd climbed to the top of an observation deck at Miner's Castle, where the wind had given her a new hairdo that made her look as if she'd been caught in a blender. She'd laughed. Go figure.

"I can't think of a good name," Faith fretted, rubbing the puppy's silky ear.

"Give him one to live up to," Sophie suggested, resting one hand on Faith's shoulder. "How did it go with Patrick's daughter? Did she agree to it?"

"Yes." Sam didn't bother to mention the split second when it had looked as though Evie would refuse to help Faith. The split second after he'd mentioned money. She'd looked offended he'd even brought up the subject, and he wasn't sure why. He didn't expect her to give up her time for free. "She's coming over tomorrow afternoon."

"Why don't you come in for a few minutes. Faith and I made cookies and we're just finishing up the last batch."

Sophie looked so hopeful that Sam didn't have the heart to say no. She ushered them into a small living room where the sparse furnishings looked old but well cared for. His gaze zeroed in on the man sitting at a desk in the corner, hunched over a computer keyboard.

Jacob had mentioned that Sophie had a son she didn't talk about very often. And now Sam had a hunch as to why.

"Tyson, would you like something to eat?"

Tyson looked up and scowled. His thin face was streaked with acne scars. Strands of dishwater-blond hair had been pulled back into a ponytail that trailed between his shoulder blades. "I told you I'm not hungry, Mom."

"You're going to ruin your eyes staring at that screen all night," Sophie scolded lightly. "At least turn around so I can introduce you to Sam Cutter, Jacob's son."

"Hey." Tyson barely glanced at Sam.

Sam saw the hurt look on Sophie's face before she murmured an excuse and disappeared into the kitchen. Faith followed her, still cuddling the puppy.

"That's a pretty nice setup you've got," Sam said, moving closer to see what Tyson was so focused on. He found himself staring at a blank screen. Tyson had shut down whatever program he'd been working on. A red flag rose in Sam's mind, especially when he noticed Tyson's shoulders set in a tense line.

"Thanks." Tyson's eyes glittered with resentment at the disruption. He yanked a pack of cigarettes out of his shirt pocket and shook one loose from the package.

"Outside with those, Ty." Sophie returned with a plate of cookies in one hand and a pitcher of milk in the other. "You agreed not to smoke in the house."

Tyson shoved the chair away from the desk and stalked out of the room.

"I'm sorry." Pain shadowed Sophie's eyes. "Tyson just lost his job last week, so he had to move back home while he looks for another one. He just got here this morning."

Sam didn't consider losing your job an excuse to be rude, but he didn't want to say so. Sophie looked embarrassed enough. "Those cookies smell delicious. How many am I allowed to have?"

Sophie brightened. "As many as you want. I miss feeding hungry men now that Patrick and Jacob are gone. I hate to say this, but Tyson is a picky eater."

Judging from Tyson's bloodshot eyes and sunken cheeks, Sam had a strong hunch the guy preferred to drink his meals.

He took a cookie from the plate Sophie offered and hid a smile when Faith reluctantly put the puppy on the floor. With her skinned knees and her mussed-up hair, she looked twelve years old again instead of twenty. Spending the evening with Sophie had been good for her.

"Faith and Evie will get along well." Sophie smiled at Faith as she handed her a glass of milk. "I feel like I know her already. Patrick brags about those girls of his constantly. Evie was voted Teacher of the Year last fall in their school district. According to Patrick, it was the first time a teacher at a Christian school won the award. From what Patrick says, out of the three girls he and Evie are the most alike."

Sam remembered the cardigan. *Poor guy.*

"Maybe he was referring to their adventurous streak."

Wait a second. He must have missed something. *Evie McBride? Adventurous?* Sam tried not to laugh. "I doubt it, Sophie."

And as far as Sam was concerned, a guided fishing trip at a cushy lodge didn't qualify as adventurous in his book.

"The whole trip was Patrick's idea," Sophie went on. "I only pray that Bruce Mullins can help them."

Mullins. The name sounded familiar. "Is Mullins their fishing guide?"

"He is a guide there, but he's not taking them fishing."

She'd completely lost him. "But that's why they went to the lodge. To go fishing."

"Oh, dear." Sophie bit her lip and set her glass down on the worn coffee table. "Is that what they told you?"

Every nerve ending in Sam's body sprang to attention at the odd inflection in her voice. "Dad said they were going on a two-week fishing trip at a place called Robust Lodge, which caters to retired businessmen."

"They'll probably do some fishing," she said weakly.

Sam took a deep breath. Judging from Sophie's expression, she was trying to figure out a way to explain without incriminating the two men.

"Sophie, it's all right. What's going on?"

"The whole trip is for me," she finally said. "Bruce is an old friend of your dad's, and they need his help."

"His help?"

"To find the treasure."

Chapter Four

From the roof of the cabin, Sam watched Evie get out of her car. He pushed to his feet, anchoring the hammer into a loop in the toolbelt around his waist. He didn't have time to retrieve the T-shirt he'd discarded earlier in the afternoon. It lay in a damp heap near the base of the chimney, just out of reach.

Evie lifted her hands to her hair, tucking in a few strands that had dared to escape from the sedate braid. Her slender frame stiffened as Jacob's flock of guinea hens charged around the cabin to greet her. The birds were as tame as dogs but as noisy as a squadron of fighter planes.

Sam expected her to dash back to the safety of her car. To his astonishment, a smile tilted the corners of her lips as the guinea hens swarmed around her feet, looking for a treat. Jacob always kept a handful of corn kernels in his pockets, a ritual Sam hadn't realized Faith had started to copy until he'd found a layer of soggy corn in the bottom of the washing machine.

Sam yanked the handkerchief out of his back pocket and swiped it across his forehead.

What was he supposed to tell her?

He wasn't sure Evie would take the news very well that

instead of fishing, their fathers had somehow gotten involved in a wild-goose chase to find a sunken treasure.

Evie took a few steps toward the cabin and spotted him on the roof. She stopped dead in her tracks, shading her eyes against the sun with her hand as she looked up at him.

"Isn't that dangerous?"

Now he was positive she wouldn't take the news well. Not if standing on the roof of a one-story building was her idea of dangerous.

Thanks for leaving me to clean up the mess, Dad.

After hearing stories about how overprotective Evie was when it came to her father, Sam could understand why Patrick hadn't told her the truth behind the trip. According to Jacob, Evie had even driven up to Cooper's Landing the previous summer, apparently suspicious of Patrick's friendship with Sophie. No wonder the poor guy had moved to Michigan's Upper Peninsula to escape her coddling.

Keeping Evie in the dark made sense, but what Sam couldn't figure out was why *his* father hadn't confided in *him.* But he had a strong hunch it had something to do with Dan's injury. As a carpenter, Jacob had spent the majority of his life after the Marines fixing things. Until he had come up against two things he couldn't fix. His wife's illness and…Dan. Now Jacob had been presented with an opportunity to help a friend and feel useful again.

Sam couldn't blame his father. Jacob coped with his feelings of helplessness one way and he had chosen another.

The conversation with Sophie the night before had been quite enlightening. And frustrating. Sam had spent half the night battling his conscience. Evie had generously agreed to help him by tutoring Faith. Didn't he owe her the truth? But if Patrick didn't want Evie to know what he was up to, was it his place to fill her in? And it wasn't as if there was any cause to worry. Jacob and Patrick were grown men, certainly capable of making their own decisions without getting flack from their adult children.

Sam had no doubt the men could handle themselves. It was adding Sophie to the mix that made the situation more difficult.

Her story wasn't his to share. She hadn't been able to provide many details because Tyson had slunk back into the living room, abruptly ending the conversation. It was obvious Sophie didn't want her son to overhear them. From the brief conversation, however, Sam had managed to put together a few of the pieces.

Sophie had been working on her family's genealogy when she was diagnosed with cancer. While searching through family archives, Sophie discovered diaries kept by her grandmother that exposed a skeleton in the Graham family closet. A scandal caused when a ship sank in Lake Superior and her great-grandfather, Matthew Graham, apparently saved himself and a young woman's dowry. No one else had survived.

At that point, Tyson interrupted them and Sophie had quickly changed the subject.

Sam buried a sigh and dodged between the boxes of shingles scattered on the roof, pausing long enough to scoop up his shirt. By the time he reached the ladder, Evie stood below him, holding the bottom of it.

"They do make aluminum ladders nowadays, you know," she called up to him. "They don't rot. They're splinter free. And they're equipped with multiple safety features."

Sam suppressed a smile. *You've got to be kidding me.* "I'll keep that in mind."

Sam bypassed the last three rungs of the ladder and landed on his feet beside her, light as a cat.

Evie averted her gaze as he pulled the damp T-shirt over his head and rolled it down over his abdomen. As if he knew exactly why she'd looked away, his eyebrow lifted in a silent question.

Better?

He was laughing at her again. Heat coursed into Evie's cheeks and she took a step away from him, knowing her freckles had lit up like laser dots against her skin. She took a deep breath and decided to focus on the reason she was there.

"Is Faith inside?"

"I think so. She was helping me but took a break about an hour ago."

The glint in his eyes told Evie he was deliberately baiting her. She took the bait anyway.

"I don't think that's a good idea—"

The guinea hens drowned her out as they recognized Sam's voice and charged. He sank his hand into the pocket of his tattered blue jeans and retrieved a fistful of corn, tossing it on the gravel.

"*Numida meleagris,*" Evie said without thinking.

Sam pushed his hand down his leg to wipe off the dust and looked at her. "What?"

"*Numida meleagris.* The Latin name for guinea fowl."

"I'll take your word for that, Miss McBride." Sam scraped a hand through his hair and ended up tousling it even more. "I should probably warn you. Faith doesn't really like science. Or math."

"She enjoys English? History?"

Sam shook his head and a few strands of dark hair flopped across his forehead. Evie resisted the urge to smooth them back into place.

"Gym class."

"She's into sports." Evie remembered that Faith had described herself as a jock the day they'd met on the beach. That didn't bother her. In a school like the one she taught in, the smaller ratio of students to teachers allowed her to focus on each individual child. Over the years, she'd found creative ways to tap into her students' natural abilities to make learning more fun.

"Don't get me wrong, she's a good student," Sam told her. "But she'd rather study basketball plays than sit down with a textbook."

"Is there anything else I should know?"

A strange expression flickered across Sam's face, but he shook his head. "I can't think of anything."

"Good, because I hate surprises."

Sam glanced at the canvas bag looped over her shoulder. "Here. Let me carry your…suitcase? You didn't have to bring your own books, you know. Faith's mother sent up an entire library."

"I've got it. And, just to set the record straight, it's a purse, not a suitcase."

"What do you have in that thing?"

"Oh, the usual stuff."

He studied the bulging bag. "Sleeping bag? Jumper cables? The kitchen sink?"

Evie saw the look on his face. "Of course not. Just the essentials." Her laptop computer. A miniature sewing kit. Tape measure. Collapsible umbrella.

"You must have been a Girl Scout."

Her eyes narrowed. Was he mocking her? "It's always good to be prepared."

The cabin door flew open, and Faith stepped onto the narrow porch. Evie guessed the reason behind the mutinous look on the young girl's face. Even though the two of them had connected over Faith's sketch of Lake Superior, Evie's role had changed. Instead of a kindred spirit, now she was the person responsible for making sure Faith kept her nose buried in the books.

Evie almost laughed. It wouldn't take long to put those fears to rest. "Hi, Faith."

"Hi." Faith studied her toes, refusing to meet Evie's eyes.

"Did you get your books out like I told you to?" Sam asked.

Faith shot him a look ripe with resentment. "Yes."

"Faith? Remember what we talked about this morning."

Judging from the edge in Sam's voice and the anger simmering in Faith's eyes, Evie doubted they'd talked at all. She guessed Sam had lectured and Faith had tuned him out.

"We don't need any books today," Evie said. "We're going on a field trip."

Sam and Faith both turned to stare at her.

"A field trip?" Sam sounded skeptical.

"For science class. We're going to study *Canis familiaris.*"

"Good. Great." Sam looked way too eager to escape. "I'm going back on the roof. I'll see you later."

"Sam?" Evie dug in her bag and pulled out a plastic bottle. "Here. Sunblock. The sun isn't as strong this late in the day, but you should still wear it. Or, ah, your shirt. That would work, too."

You aren't only a geek, Evie, you are officially their queen.

Sam stared at the bottle as if it were a live grenade and then at her. Evie braced herself, expecting to see amusement lurking in his eyes. She was used to it. Over the years her sisters had developed entire stand-up comedy routines based on her cautious ways.

We're not laughing at you, Evie. We're laughing with you.

To her amazement, Sam didn't laugh. But he did smile. A slightly lopsided smile that lightened his eyes to silver and warmed up her insides like a Bunsen burner.

"How can I turn down…SPF 50?" he murmured.

Maybe he *was* reckless but he knew his sunscreen.

Evie waited for Faith to join her, and they started down the driveway. Faith's plodding steps conveyed her unhappiness with the situation, but Evie didn't push for conversation or attention. When Faith wanted to talk, she would.

"What did you say we're going to study?" Faith finally asked. Evie hid a smile. *"Canis familiaris."*

Faith kicked a rock and sent it skittering down the lane. "I've never heard of that."

"It's Latin for the domestic dog," Evie said. "We're going to visit Sophie's puppies."

Faith grinned. "I think I'm going to like having you as a teacher, Miss McBride."

"This is summer school. Call me Evie."

By the time Sophie's modest, two-story house came into view several minutes later, Faith was still chattering about the puppies and how it was up to her to choose a name for her favorite.

"I've always wanted to have a dog, but Mom doesn't like it when they shed," Faith continued. "Sophie says she'll keep the one I name and I can visit it whenever I want to. That's kind of like having my own dog, isn't it?"

Evie thought it an extremely generous gesture on Sophie's part, which made her more anxious to meet the woman. And even though Faith's comment about her mother made Evie curious, she knew it wasn't the time to press Faith to talk about her family.

"There she is." Faith broke away and sprinted toward a woman kneeling in a patch of freshly turned soil. "Hi, Sophie!"

No wonder Patrick talked about her. Sophie Graham was beautiful. Blessed with classic features and smooth, porcelain skin, Sophie resembled an aging film star. Her faded housedress and scuffed gardening clogs couldn't disguise her natural grace as she rose to her feet and greeted Faith with a hug.

Faith pointed in her direction and Evie quickened her steps, hoping Sophie wouldn't mind they'd shown up without a formal invitation.

Before she could apologize, Sophie's warm smile put her at

ease. "Evangeline. I'm so glad to finally meet you. Patrick talks about you and your sisters all the time."

"Dad talks about you, too," Evie said, surprised to see a hint of rose tint Sophie's cheeks.

"Can I show Evie the puppies, Sophie?"

"If we're not interrupting anything," Evie added quickly.

"Not at all. You came at just the right time. I'm ready to take a rest." Sophie swept her straw hat off and used it as a fan.

Evie's breath caught in her throat as she saw the irregular patches of silver hair on Sophie's head.

"I'm in remission, praise the Lord," Sophie said simply, and then gave Evie a mischievous wink. "Now, let's get acquainted over ice cream and puppies, shall we?"

Chapter Five

When an hour went by and Evie and Faith still hadn't returned, it occurred to Sam that his niece may have tried to sweet-talk Evie into stopping at Sophie's house.

Which meant Sophie might inadvertently reveal the real reason behind Patrick and Jacob's fishing trip.

Sam winced as the hammer missed the nail and ground the tip of his thumb against the shingle.

None of your business, he reminded himself. If Evie had a problem with her dad, she should take it up with him. Sam had his own stuff to worry about. He was one hundred percent uninvolved in the situation.

Except that Evie was Faith's tutor. And for the next few weeks, he was committed to making sure she stayed that way.

Sam sat back on his heels, trying to convince himself it wasn't necessary to look for them. Evie would be a strict teacher—the kind who wouldn't waste precious minutes of a two-hour tutoring session playing with a litter of puppies. Hopefully the reason they were late was because the search for *Canis familiaris* was taking longer than expected....

A dim memory from Biology 101 struggled to the surface. Canis. Canine. *Dog*.

Sam's shout of laughter scattered the guinea hens in the yard below.

So maybe he'd misjudged her. But he knew one thing for sure. He had to get to Sophie before Evie did.

It didn't take Evie long to understand why Faith frequently "ran away" to Sophie's house. And it wasn't just to visit the puppies or because Sophie's home, filled with simple yet comfortable furnishings, created a peaceful retreat. Sophie was the reason Faith returned. The older woman radiated a warmth and inner peace that instantly made a person feel welcome. And accepted.

"I wish I could keep all four of them," Sophie said as Faith wrestled on the braided rug with two of the more active puppies while their mother, Sadie, kept a watchful eye from her wicker basket in the corner. "A few days after my diagnosis, Sadie showed up in the yard. I knew right away she was a stray—her fur was matted, and, even pregnant, she looked like she hadn't eaten for days. I called your dad and he came over and helped me bathe her. He even offered to take her home with him, but I'd already fallen in love with her. God must have known I'd need her." Sophie smiled. "She's a very good listener."

Was Sadie the only one you fell in love with?

Evie didn't voice the question that sprang into her mind. Whenever Sophie mentioned Patrick's name, her eyes sparkled with affection. The two of them had obviously become close. But had the friendship developed into something more?

And how would she feel if it had?

The previous summer, Evie had scolded Caitlin for her strong reaction to Patrick and Sophie's friendship. If Sophie Graham brought some happiness into their dad's life, shouldn't they be supportive?

She had to admit, though, that the possibility of making room for another person in her dad's life was a little unsettling. Especially when Evie had been the one looking out for Patrick since Laura died.

"I don't know what I'd do without Jacob and Patrick," Sophie went on. "They fuss more than they ought to, but I wouldn't be able to live out here if they didn't help me keep the place up. The Lord sent those two wonderful men. I was in the hospital with complications from pneumonia, worried I'd have to sell my house, when Patrick showed up one Sunday with a group of men from his church to read to the patients. Your father got stuck with me." Sophie chuckled at the memory.

"We had a nice chat afterward and found out that we both loved antiques. The next Sunday, he introduced me to Jacob. They brought Monopoly along and convinced me to play. I don't think I ever laughed so much in my life. By the time I came home from the hospital, they'd spruced up the place and every day one of them would stop by or call to check up on me. I think they adopted me like I was a stray—just like Sadie."

Evie hid a smile. Somehow, she doubted it was an accurate comparison!

"They were a reminder that no matter what the future holds, God's already there, preparing the way. Oh, He doesn't always smooth out the rough spots in the road ahead. Those are the places we have to exercise our spiritual muscles, you know. To build our faith, so to speak. But God always provides the strength I need to keep going."

The sincerity in the words touched Evie and explained the source of the peace in Sophie's eyes. Evie knew that the woman's deep faith, the fruit of years of walking with the Lord, was another quality Patrick would have been drawn to.

A sudden movement on the stairs caught Evie's attention. The man glowering at them over the railing looked to be only a few years older than she was, but the expression on his face made him look like a cranky toddler who'd just awakened from a nap.

"Evie, this is my son, Tyson." Sophie ignored Tyson's sullen look while she made the introductions. "Tyson, this is Evie McBride, Patrick's daughter."

"Hey." His hooded stare fixed on Evie. It reminded her of a crocodile. Cold and flat.

This was Sophie's *son?*

A shudder chased up Evie's spine, but she forced a polite smile. "It's nice to meet you, Tyson."

"Evie is taking care of Beach Glass while Patrick is away on his fishing trip," Sophie told him.

"There's not much to do around here." Tyson's gaze burrowed into her. "We should hang out sometime."

A shiver coursed through her. "I'm afraid I don't have much free time. I'll either be minding the shop or tutoring Faith."

Tyson shrugged and stomped down the rest of the stairs. "I'm going out for a while."

"Ty, where—"

The door snapped Sophie's question in half.

Evie's heart went out to her. It was hard to believe someone as rude as Tyson was Sophie's flesh and blood. With his unkempt appearance and surly attitude, Tyson didn't seem to be someone Sophie could depend on. No wonder she was so grateful for Patrick and Jacob's help.

Faith broke the awkward silence as she plopped next to Sophie on the couch, the puppy draped over her arm. It raised its head and tried to lick her cheek, igniting a fit of the giggles.

Sophie smiled but Evie didn't miss the pensive look in her eyes. Compliments of Tyson. Impulsively, Evie patted Sophie's hand before rising to her feet.

"We should go back, Faith. We still need to go over your homework for tomorrow."

"I'll have to do it on the boat. Sam promised we could spend the whole day on the water. And I get to make lunch." Faith launched to her feet and put the puppy back on the rug with his littermates.

Evie kept her expression neutral. She didn't want Faith to pick up on the fact she wasn't happy with Sam for taking her out on the boat. The thought of them at the mercy of Superior's changing moods made her uneasy.

It's not your business, Evie, and Sam Cutter would be the first person to tell you so.

"Come back soon." Sophie escorted them outside. "When I talked to Patrick this morning, he asked me if I had plans to stop by Beach Glass soon and introduce myself. I can't wait to tell him that you beat me to it."

"Dad called you? *This morning?* I thought they weren't going to be able to contact us until they got to the lodge."

Sophie looked away, flustered. "We talked only a few minutes. I think he called from a gas station and the connection wasn't very good.... Look, there's Sam."

Sure enough, Sam was striding down the driveway toward them. Seeing the uncomfortable look on Sophie's face, Evie got the impression Sam's appearance provided a welcome disruption.

She tried to squelch the tiny pinprick of hurt. Why had her dad checked in with Sophie first? It didn't make sense. Especially when Patrick knew she wanted to keep in close contact...

"Studying hard?"

The glint in Sam's eyes told Evie he was on to her.

"Don't you dare scold these sweet girls, Sam," Sophie said. "They're good company. And Sadie and the puppies love the attention."

Faith wrapped her arms around Sophie's waist and gave her a fierce hug. "We'll be back."

They said their goodbyes, and Evie and Sam fell into step together while Faith dashed ahead of them.

"*Canis familiaris,* hmm?"

Evie swallowed hard when Sam's breath stirred her hair. He was so close she could smell the pleasing blend of shower soap and afternoon sun. And a hint of coconut-scented sunscreen.

When she finally found her voice, it sounded a little breathless even to her own ears. "I thought Faith and I should take some time to get to know each other before we jumped into her lessons."

Sam slanted a look at her. "I think you know her already. It didn't take you long to figure out the way to Faith's heart is through those puppies."

Faith, several yards ahead of them, heard the word *puppies* and darted back.

"I thought of a name. I'm going to call him Rocky."

"Rocky?" Sam laughed. "Like the boxer?"

Faith nodded. "I watched the movies with Dad on cable last year. He said he liked Rocky because he never gave up."

Sam's throat closed.

Dan was giving up. The last time Sam had seen his brother, Dan had ordered the entire family to leave the room. When they'd hesitated, he'd thrown a pitcher of ice water at them. Along with a stream of angry words.

The man lying in the hospital bed had been a stranger, not the twin brother he'd wrestled, competed against and laughed with over the past thirty-two years.

Fortunately, Faith hadn't been there to witness her father's rage.

Moments before, the doctor had reminded Dan how lucky he was to be alive. But Dan had looked at him as if he'd just been given a death sentence.

Sam couldn't blame him.

Dan had been at the height of his career and the sole supporter of the family he loved. And he'd just been told he was facing months of painful rehab with no guarantee he would ever fully regain the use of his legs.

Responding to the doctor's meaningful look, they'd left Dan alone and gathered together in the family lounge. Sam had never seen Jacob look so defeated. And he'd never felt so helpless in his life. Even when Natalie, their mother, had died, he and Dan had stuck together. Leaned on each other. Found strength in their bond as brothers.

But not this time. Nothing Sam could say or do could change the reality of the situation. And he didn't know what to do with that.

Rachel, as emotional as Dan was easygoing, had clung to him. It would have been better if she'd been able to cry. At least tears could be dried. Sam had had no idea how to comfort a heart totally emptied by grief.

He had lain in bed that night, despair lapping at the edges of his soul. He'd tried to pray, but it had felt hypocritical. He wasn't sure if God would even recognize his voice. It wasn't as if they talked on a regular basis.

A week went by and Dan had still refused to see them. Faith had started to blame "the adults" for not allowing her to visit her father. Her close relationship with her mother had deteriorated, and she'd alternated between outright defiance and long, stubborn silences.

The hospital had transferred Dan to a private care facility to start rehab, and the doctor warned them that Dan's attitude would be a pivotal part of his recovery. The hospital social worker had told them Dan was battling depression and had compassionately suggested they give him a few weeks to adjust to his new surroundings before visiting again.

Jacob had reluctantly returned to Cooper's Landing. Sam

used up more vacation time and had stayed longer, watching in disbelief as Dan became verbally abusive to the nurses and refused to cooperate with his physical therapists. His bitter tirades had kept Rachel on the verge of tears.

Sam had always been able to encourage his brother. Even to bully him, if the situation called for it. But for the first time in his life, Sam had sensed his presence was causing more harm than good. The bitterness in Dan's eyes every time Sam visited had weighed him down with guilt. He was able to walk while Dan was confined to a wheelchair, and Sam couldn't find a way to break down that barrier between them.

When Rachel had overheard him talking to Jacob on the phone about taking the boat out for a few weeks, she'd begged him to take Faith along. Torn between meeting the needs of both her daughter and her husband, she'd said she needed time to concentrate on Dan and encourage his recovery.

Sam had balked. He'd wanted to be alone. His world had shrunk to the size of the hospital and he was tired of sterile white walls, the hum of machines and plastic tubing that kept a man alive but couldn't make him want to *live*. He struggled between feeling selfish for leaving Rachel alone with Dan and the overwhelming need to escape.

In the end, he'd agreed to take Faith with him.

He'd tried to talk to her about her dad but she'd refused. Somewhere along the way, Sam had become a member of the opposing team. An hour didn't go by when he didn't second-guess his decision to bring her along.

"I think Rocky is a great name. Don't you, Sam?"

With a start, Evie's voice and the touch of her hand on his arm pulled Sam out of the shadowy path his memories had lured him down. Faith hadn't voluntarily talked about Dan since they'd arrived in Cooper's Landing. She'd even rebuffed her grandfather whenever he'd tried to talk about her dad. Now, because of Evie's gentle prompt, he realized Faith was watching him, waiting patiently for his response. She wasn't just asking if he liked the name. There was another question in her eyes.

Is Dad going to be like Rocky? Or is he going to give up?

He couldn't answer her. It wasn't fair to give her false hope, yet he didn't want to be the one to crush it, either.

"I think you should take a picture of you and Rocky and send it to your dad." Evie bravely stepped into the silence.

"Really?" Faith glanced at him for affirmation. "The nurse told me the last time I called there was a bulletin board by his bed. She said Dad has my letter on it."

Sam had had no idea Faith had written to her father or called the rehab center. Guilt washed over him. He'd failed his brother and now he was failing his niece. He struggled to find his voice. "Evie's right. I think he'd like that."

"Does that mean we can study *Canis familiaris* again tomorrow?" Faith's tentative smile was like seeing a beam of sunlight peek through the clouds.

"You'll have to discuss that with your teacher."

Faith sprinted ahead of them and Sam held his breath, expecting Evie to hit him with a hundred questions now. And she'd be within her rights. He should have been honest with her the night he'd asked her to be Faith's tutor. He'd convinced himself Evie didn't need to know their family business but the truth was, he'd always kept a tight rein on his emotions and Dan's accident had stirred them up. Brought them to the surface. Even saying his brother's name had the potential to let those feelings loose, and he couldn't risk breaking down in front of a complete stranger.

Evie didn't say a word but one look at the set of her shoulders told him everything. He should have told her there was more to Faith's discontent than homework.

"Dan was...is...a police officer, and he was injured in

an…accident." It wasn't the whole truth, but Sam didn't know how else to describe what had happened. His jaw tightened. *Someone deliberately tried to kill my brother?* Too harsh. And it would only raise more questions.

"I'm sorry."

The simple words threw him off balance. He'd expected questions. Maybe even accusations. What he wasn't prepared for was the compassion he heard in Evie's voice. And it nearly undid him.

Sam retreated behind the walls he'd put up to stave off the pain of the past few months. He felt a rush of relief when the cabin came into view.

When Evie reached her car, she opened the passenger-side door and hoisted her gigantic bag inside. He caught a glimpse of a package of gum and a box of bandages.

Bitterness welled up, catching him by surprise.

So Evie McBride thought the contents of her duffel-size purse meant she was prepared for anything. It was too bad there wasn't something in it that could fix messed-up lives.

Chapter Six

I've been praying for Sam. And Faith.

The words scrolled through Evie's mind every time she woke up during the night.

In March, her father had asked her to pray for a friend and his family. He'd only shared a few details. The friend's son was a Chicago police officer who'd been shot while responding to a call. After surgery to remove a bullet near his spine, the doctors were still uncertain whether he'd ever walk again. He had a wife and twelve-year-old daughter. And a devastated twin brother.

"No one in the family is a believer, Evie," Patrick had told her. "They don't know how to comfort each other or how to *be* comforted. Instead of coming together, the family is splintering apart."

Evie had added them to her prayers even though she'd struggled with the circumstances. Another parent had chosen a dangerous profession and now a family had to suffer the consequences of that decision.

She'd had no idea the man she'd been lifting up in prayer for the past three months had been Jacob Cutter. And the child she'd asked God to comfort wasn't a nameless, faceless little girl. It was Faith. And the twin brother, Sam.

As daylight filtered through the sheer curtains, Evie gave up on sleep. She sat up in bed and wrapped her arms around her knees.

Lord, now I know why you brought me here. And why Sam asked me to tutor Faith. Give me wisdom to know how to encourage her. I wasn't much older than Faith when Mom died. I know what it's like to have your whole world turned upside down and not understand why.

Reveal yourself to them. Show them that even though the situation might seem hopeless, they can find hope in you.

Patrick had told her that none of the Cutter family were believers, but Evie had confidence God was at work. His timing was always perfect and there had to be a reason why Patrick's fishing trip and her arrival in Cooper's Landing had corresponded with Faith and Sam's trip.

Evie remembered Sam's expression when Faith had mentioned her dad. For a split second, the bleakness in Sam's eyes had reflected all the pain and anger and helplessness he felt.

Strengthen Sam, too, Lord.

Evie was closing up the shop for the day when a van pulled in and a stocky young man jumped out of the driver's seat, intercepting her on her way to the cottage.

Evie hadn't had many customers over the course of the day. If only his timing would have been better! When Patrick called, she wanted to be able to tell him she was single-handedly reducing the store's inventory. "I'm sorry. We're closed."

"Are you Evie McBride? Patrick's daughter?"

Evie paused. "Yes."

"I'm Seth. Seth Lansky? The computer tech? Mr. McBride hired me to install a new software program."

Computer tech? Evie's gaze traveled over the man's husky

frame. In a flannel-lined plaid shirt and heavy boots, he looked more like pictures she'd seen of the legendary Paul Bunyan than someone who spent his days at a keyboard.

"Dad didn't mention you were coming over." Not that it was unusual for her dad to forget something. The day before he'd left, she'd caught him wandering around the house looking for his glasses. They'd been tucked in the front pocket of his shirt the whole time.

"I couldn't tell him the exact day I'd be stopping by," Seth explained. "Emergency calls get priority."

That sounded legitimate. Evie glanced over his shoulder at the vehicle parked in the driveway. It didn't have a logo painted on it but that didn't mean anything. Sleepy little Cooper's Landing wasn't exactly on the cutting edge when it came to business practices. The local post office and Ruby's Beauty Salon operated out of the same building.

"I was just about to leave for a few hours."

Seth scratched a ragged thumbnail against the stubble on his chin. "If I don't take a look at it now, I'm not sure when I can come back around. Mr. McBride seemed pretty anxious to get it taken care of. Shouldn't take very long."

Evie glanced at her watch. Four-fifteen. She was already late for her meeting with Faith.

"I suppose it's all right."

"Great." Seth flashed an engaging smile and followed her inside. Evie led the way past the kitchen to the room her dad had converted into an office when he'd moved in.

"Here you—" Evie turned the doorknob and frowned. It was locked. "That's strange. Dad never locks anything."

"There must be a key around somewhere."

"I'll look in the kitchen."

When Evie returned a few minutes later with the ring of keys she'd found hanging on a hook by sink, Seth had his back to her, talking on a cell phone.

"I'm surprised you get reception. Half the time, mine won't work."

Seth gave a visible start and snapped the phone shut. "This one didn't, either."

Evie sifted through the keys, looking for one that might fit. "You'll have your work cut out for you. Dad hates computers. The PC my sisters and I bought him a few years ago when he opened the shop is already outdated. I tried to teach him how to use it but I'm pretty sure he kept his old typewriter as a backup. Here. I think this is the right one...." Evie choked as the door to Patrick's office drifted open.

"Looks like your dad got the hang of it," Seth drawled.

"I can't believe this," Evie murmured, studying the expensive flat-screen monitor she *knew* hadn't been part of the package they'd bought for Patrick. There was also a combination printer and—Evie blinked—*fax machine?*

Seth didn't answer as he sat down at the desk and pressed the power button.

Evie lingered, still uncertain whether she should leave him alone in the house. But Faith needed her. "I'll be back in a little while."

Seth chuckled. "Don't worry about me. Like I said, this shouldn't take long."

Evie slung her bag over her shoulder and made a quick detour to the garage before leaving for her afternoon tutoring session.

When she pulled into the Cutters' driveway, she was encouraged to see Faith sitting on the step, waiting for her to arrive. And relieved they'd made it safely back to shore.

Thank you, Lord.

Instead of saying hello, Faith greeted her with a gloomy announcement. "Sam says I have to work on my math assignments first."

"Really?" Evie opened the trunk of the car. "I hate to veto your uncle, but the teacher sets the schedule. We're having gym class first."

Faith peeked into the trunk and her eyes lit up when she saw the basketball hoop. "Is that for me?"

"It's for us. I warned you I was a science geek, right? You'll have to take it easy on me until I learn the rules."

"We can mount it above the garage door. I'll get Sam." Faith bounded away before Evie could stop her.

Evie's heart gave a strange little flutter when Sam emerged from the cabin. They must have recently come off the lake because his hair curled damply at the base of his neck. His casual clothing should have looked scruffy, but Sam wore the threadbare chambray shirt and faded jeans with casual ease. He could have graced the cover of any popular boating magazine.

Once again, Evie wondered what he did for a living. He'd walked across the roof with catlike grace the day before, but his skin didn't have the weathered look of someone who worked outside all day. Although his biceps could have been honed by construction work...

"Heads up, Evie!" Faith's cheerful warning rang across the yard.

The basketball sailed toward her, and Evie instinctively lifted her hands. And missed. The force of the ball against her abdomen winded her.

"Wow." She gasped the word. "There's a lot of power in that pass."

Faith grinned. "I'll get the ladder."

Sam stared after his niece in disbelief. "Who is she and what did she do with my niece? That is *not* the girl who was on the boat with me. The girl with me today refused to talk and deliberately left out the jelly on my peanut-butter and *jelly* sandwich."

Evie's soft laugh rippled through him. "You don't know how many times I've heard variations of that question at parent-teacher conferences."

The sound of her laughter never failed to surprise Sam. It was…young. Jacob had mentioned Patrick's youngest daughter was only twenty-six, but the serious blue eyes and conservative clothing made her seem older. Most women wore hats as a fashion statement, but Sam had a hunch that Evie had chosen the wide-brimmed straw hat to protect her from the sun. Probably because she'd given *him* her sun-block. Today she'd kept the cardigan but traded in her skirt for a pair of pleated khakis. And the flat-soled leather shoes on her feet weren't exactly the kind of footwear endorsed by the NBA.

Sam nudged Evie aside as she reached into the trunk of the car and wrestled with a rusty basketball hoop. "Gym class. You do have some interesting teaching methods, Miss McBride."

"Thank you."

Sam wasn't sure it was a compliment. They had two weeks to bring Faith's grades back up. So far the only books he'd seen were the ones he'd fished out of Faith's laundry basket that morning.

"I can play basketball with her anytime—"

Evie tossed the ball to him. "Great. Let's get this net up."

Not exactly what he'd meant. "Ah, maybe I didn't mention how much homework Faith has. She took it pretty hard when her dad got hurt. She stopped caring. About school. About…everything. You've got your work cut out for you over the next two weeks. To be quite honest, I don't know if there's time for puppies and basketball."

"Those are the things Faith cares about. We're going to *make* time for them. Everything else will fall into place. You'll see."

"You're the teacher."

Evie's chin lifted. "I'm glad we got that settled."

Sam expected Evie to sit on the sidelines. Maybe look over Faith's assignments while she had the opportunity. But no. She'd joined in the game with an enthusiasm that amazed him. The woman had two left hands and feet, but what she lacked in athletic ability she made up for in effort.

"You're going to have blisters on your blisters," Sam murmured as they crouched face-to-face in the center of the driveway in a battle for control of the ball.

Evie blew a wisp of hair out of her eyes. "Between the shin splints and the torn ligaments I won't even notice them."

Sam couldn't prevent the rusty bark of laughter that rolled out. And it surprised him. Maybe Faith wasn't the only one who had forgotten how to laugh over the past few months.

He had to admit Evie was a genius when it came to kids. Somehow she'd known exactly what his niece needed. Faith lived and breathed sports, but she'd quit the track team after Dan was injured. Not only had she walked away from something she loved, but she'd lost the physical outlet to deal with the additional stress on their family.

And he'd been totally oblivious to all that. Until now. For Faith's sake, he decided to trust Evie's unorthodox teaching methods.

"Ready, Evie?" Faith's eyes gleamed with the light of competition as she gave the basketball an impressive spin on the tip of her index finger.

"Ready, *Evie?*" Sam repeated in disbelief. "Haven't you ever heard the saying blood is thicker than water?"

"It depends on who's grading your papers," Evie retorted.

Feeling more lighthearted than he had in weeks, Sam knocked the ball out of Faith's hand and went in for a layup.

Evie came out of nowhere and stole the ball, lobbing it toward the net. It hit the backboard and swished through the hoop.

Faith whooped in delight at the stunned look on Evie's face.

"Beginner's luck," Sam muttered as he jumped up and caught the rebound.

Family loyalty aside, Faith gave Evie encouragement and advice as they played. Somehow Evie had reversed their roles. She looked to Faith to teach her the rules of the game. Trusted her commands. Accepted correction.

Her strategy, Sam acknowledged, was brilliant. Evie didn't expect to win Faith's trust and respect, she wanted to earn it.

Faith would have played until dark if Sam hadn't noticed Evie's slight limp and called the game. And he didn't miss the grateful look Evie shot in his direction.

"Sam, I'm going to shower and work on my math for a while, okay?" Faith took one more shot from the makeshift free-throw line and did a little victory dance when it swept through the net. "You played a great game, Evie. Don't let anyone tell you you're just a science geek." She gave her a cheeky smile and dashed into the house.

"Did my niece just say she was going to work on her math? Without empty threats or shameless bribes?"

"She did." Evie took a folded tissue out of the pocket of her khakis and blotted her forehead. "She's a great kid, Sam. You'll get through this."

Sam had a feeling she wasn't referring only to adolescence and her next words confirmed it.

"I know about your brother. Dad asked me to pray for your family when it happened, but I didn't realize it was *you*. Not until yesterday."

"You've been *praying* for us?"

"Since March," Evie confirmed.

Three months ago, and Dan was still on a downward spiral.

His lips twisted. "I wish I could tell you it's helped. Dan isn't walking yet."

"God is more interested in healing hearts than bodies," Evie said.

The simple words blindsided him.

"I'll be back tomorrow afternoon." Evie walked toward the car but Sam beat her to it and opened the driver's-side door.

"I'm going to toss some steaks on the grill. Why don't you stay for supper?" Sam had no idea which wire in his brain had short-circuited and disengaged his mouth from his brain.

Evie shook her head. "I can't."

No apologies. No excuses. Maybe he'd been impulsive to ask her to stay, but Sam still felt a stab of disappointment at her blunt refusal. He told himself it wasn't unusual to want to know a little more about the woman he'd hired to be Faith's tutor—but part of him chided himself for not being completely honest.

The truth was, Evie McBride intrigued him.

Sam reached the phone on the third ring. It was within Faith's reach but she was stretched out on the sofa with her eyes closed, headphones firmly in place.

After Evie had left, she'd retreated back into her shell. Lake Superior, for all its changing moods, had nothing on adolescent girls.

"Hello?"

A harsh crackle grated in his ear.

"Sam? This is...Patrick... Evie...needs help... Think we've...got a problem on your end." Static distorted the words and Sam frowned. "Take care...her."

"Patrick, I can barely hear you," Sam said. "What did you say about Evie?"

Patrick's voice broke up again and Sam felt a surge of frustration. "One more time, Patrick. The connection is terrible. Are you and Dad at the lodge yet?"

"Go…Evie. Might…danger." The line went dead.

"Patrick?" Sam hit Redial and got a busy signal.

Now what?

Sam tried to convince himself he'd imagined the word *danger.* But why had Patrick called him instead of Jacob?

Sam glanced at his watch. Seven o'clock. Evie had left half an hour ago. She'd think he was crazy if showed up out of the blue to check on her. And he'd have a lot of explaining to do if he told her Patrick had called *him.* He still hadn't found the right time to tell her what their fathers were up to. The truth was, he'd been hoping he wouldn't have to.

Ten minutes crawled by as Sam paced the living room, waiting for Patrick to call back. Finally, he shook Faith's knee to get her attention.

"I'm going to drop you off at Sophie's for a few minutes, okay? I've got an errand to run."

Faith, eager to play with Rocky, didn't question him.

When he got to Evie's ten minutes later, he saw a van parked close to the house. His stomach knotted. Beach Glass was closed for the day, and he doubted Evie had made friends in the short time she'd been staying at the house.

He knocked on the door but didn't wait for someone to answer it. Giving in to an overwhelming sense of urgency, he turned the handle and went inside.

Chapter Seven

"Miss McBride?" Seth poked his head into the kitchen. "Wow. Something smells good."

"Garlic bread." Evie wiped her hands on the old-fashioned pinafore apron she'd found in a box of linens at the shop. When she'd gotten back from Sam's, she'd found Seth still hard at work in Patrick's office.

Feeling a little awkward with someone else in the house, she'd reheated some leftover pasta from the night before and lingered in the kitchen, hoping Seth would finish soon. She wanted the house to herself to sort through the strange jumble of emotions she felt whenever Sam Cutter cruised the perimeter of her personal space.

She drew a deep breath. Even when he wasn't around, the man had the most unsettling way of creeping into her thoughts. "Are you finished?"

"No. As a matter of fact, I've got a little problem. Your dad gave me his password but he must have changed it and forgotten to tell me. Think you can take a look? Most people use familiar words. Birthdays. Names of children. That sort of thing."

"I can try." Evie followed him into the office and sat down in the chair.

"Here's what I've got so far." He pushed a piece of paper in front of her. "Charlotte. Sara. Jo. Do you see a pattern there? Are they middle names? Old girlfriends?"

Evie didn't think the last comment particularly funny.

"There's more than one password?"

Seth smiled and shrugged. "You know Patrick."

That she did. Her dad probably thought he needed a password to protect his password.

"They aren't middle names." *Or old girlfriends.* She studied the names a few more seconds and started to laugh. "I can't believe Dad remembered. We had an aquarium when I was growing up. Every time we got a new fish, my sisters and I named it after the heroine of a book we were reading at the time. Charlotte is from *Charlotte's Web.* Sara is in *A Little Princess* and Jo is one of the March sisters in *Little Women.*"

Seth leaned closer, his eyes strangely intent. "What's the next one?"

"Let me think…." Evie bit her lip. Nancy Drew? No, Caitlin had vetoed that one. It had been a blue Betta fish and according to Caitlin's logic, a fish named Nancy Drew had to be *red.* No wonder she'd started an image consulting business after graduating from college.

"Evie?"

The sound of Sam's voice startled her. She twisted in the chair and saw him standing in the doorway behind her.

"I knocked but you must not have heard me."

"Sam. What are you doing here?" Once again her first thought was for her father. She rose to her feet but Seth's hand snaked out and caught her wrist.

"I've got two more calls to make this evening, Miss McBride." The faint bite in the words surprised her. Seth hadn't mentioned other appointments. And he certainly hadn't seemed to be in a hurry to finish up before now.

Evie gently tugged her wrist free. "This will only take a minute."

"Sure." Seth's lips worked into a smile. "No problem."

Sam leaned against the door frame and stuck his hands in his pockets. "I forgot to give you Faith's reading list for her book reports when you were over this afternoon. I saw the lights on and decided to drop it off."

Not exactly an emergency, Evie thought. Maybe he'd had another argument with Faith and wanted to talk about it. "I'll be right back, Seth."

As soon as they were in the hall, Sam took hold of her arm and guided her toward the door. When Evie opened her mouth to protest, Sam tapped his finger against her lips, shocking her into silence.

Once they were outside, she pulled away from him and planted her hands on her hips. "What do you think you're doing?"

"Who is that guy?" Sam asked tersely.

"Seth Lansky. Dad hired him to install some software."

"Your dad set up the appointment? He told you about it before he left?"

"No. He forgot. But that's nothing new—"

"Evie. Think about it." Sam's eyes held hers intently. "Patrick wouldn't hire someone to install software. Not when he's got a computer-savvy daughter coming to stay at his house for two weeks."

Evie's mouth went dry. "What are you getting at?"

"What did Seth ask you to do?"

Evie noticed Sam Cutter had an annoying habit of answering a question with a question. "Dad isn't very knowledgeable about computers. He set up multiple passwords when one would have been sufficient." There. That should prove her point.

"Maybe he set up multiple passwords on purpose." Sam edged her into the shadows between the house and the shop. Evie squeaked as he backed her against the wall, angling his body so she was hidden from view and bracing a hand on either side of her.

"That's crazy. The only thing Dad keeps on his computer is his personal budget and the financial records for Beach Glass."

"If this guy is *installing* software, why does he need to access your dad's files?"

Evie stared up at him. "I don't know."

Disbelief and fear skimmed across Evie's face.

Good, Sam thought. Now they were even. The vehicle parked in the driveway had made him uneasy, but finding Evie sitting at the desk, with an all-star wrestler wannabe leaning over her, had shaved ten years off his life.

"When did this guy show up? Did you ask him for any identification?"

"Right before I left this afternoon," Evie whispered.

Her failure to answer his second question was an answer in and of itself. He'd lecture her about that later. Right now he had to determine if Patrick's phone call and Lansky's showing up was a big fat coincidence.

"I'm going to take a look inside his van." He took a step forward and so did Evie.

"I'm not staying here."

"Now isn't the time to be nervous. You missed that opportunity. It would have been when a stranger came up to the door and you let him in your house." He knew he'd already made his point, but he couldn't help it. His heart was still doing jumping jacks in his chest, and he blamed it on the naive redhead standing in front of him. Apparently, there were times when her warm heart overrode her cautious nature.

He took another step forward. So did Evie.

"You can't spy on him alone. What if he sees you and you get hurt?"

Thanks for the vote of confidence, Sam thought wryly. "I'll be fine. Stay here and make yourself invisible. I'll be right back."

This time when he took a step forward, she stayed put.

Sam sidled around the house, pausing to take a quick look in the window. Seth had taken Evie's place at the desk and it looked like he was trying to figure out the password himself. Sam watched long enough to see him engage in the good old "hunt and peck" method of keyboarding. If this guy turned out to be a computer tech, Sam moonlighted as a gourmet chef. And everyone who knew him knew he lived on takeout.

He worked his way over to the van and tried the door. Locked. That was interesting. Apparently Seth wasn't as trusting as the woman who'd let him into her house. Keeping a wary eye on the front door, he circled the van.

And bumped into someone coming around the other side.

"I thought I told you to stay put." Sam said goodbye to another ten years. Only catching a whiff of a familiar floral scent in the air had prevented him from tackling the person first and asking questions later.

"Will this help?" The faint glow of a penlight illuminated Evie's face.

"As a matter of fact, it will." Sam plucked the key ring out of her hand, not prepared for the weight of it. "What do you have on here? A hammer? Never mind. Let me guess. *The essentials.*"

He traced the interior of the van with the tiny beam of light. Crumpled potato-chip bags, soda cups and empty paper sacks littered the seat and floor.

"Where fast-food lunches go to die," Sam murmured. "Well, we know he's got high cholesterol. Let's take a look in the back and see what else we can find out about Mr. Lansky." He pressed the light against the back window and his blood chilled.

Okay, Dad, what have you and Patrick gotten yourselves into?

And more important, what had they gotten Evie into?

Evie stood on her tiptoes, her nose pressed against the glass as she peered inside. "What is all that?"

"Diving equipment."

Sam took a quick inventory and what he saw didn't make him feel any better. The gear wasn't amateur, weekend-warrior stuff. The front seat of the van might have resembled a college frat house, but the equipment in the back was practically arranged in alphabetical order. Expensive cameras. Oxygen tanks. Wet suits. And a very lethal-looking spear gun.

He lowered the light before Evie spotted it.

Sam's mind raced over possible scenarios and none of them included a computer tech. What he did have were two AWOL senior citizens with delusions of grandeur trying to track down clues to a sunken treasure. A frantic phone call from Patrick. A guy trying to access Patrick's computer files...and Evie somewhere in the middle.

The front door opened, tripping the motion light in the yard. Sam dropped to his knees, taking Evie with him.

She struggled against him and Sam saw the outrage and mistrust in her wide blue eyes. She didn't trust *him?* She let some guy into her house without asking for ID, and now *he* was the bad guy?

"Let me go." She struggled against him.

"Sorry." Sam eased away from her. "It looks like Mr. Lansky is done for the night and until we know if he's legit, I don't want him to catch us checking out his van. Time to work on your acting skills."

* * *

Sam did it again. He grabbed her hand, kept low to the ground and pulled her into the woods bordering the driveway.

"Play along," he whispered.

"Play along with what—" The words died as Sam rose to his feet, wrapped his arm around her waist and nuzzled her hair. Evie's feet melted to the ground, but somehow Sam managed to nudge her out of the shadows.

"He's watching." Sam breathed the words in her ear. "Let him think we were taking a romantic stroll."

Evie swallowed hard as she and Sam stepped into the light. Seth stood beside the van, scowling at them. When she'd met him that afternoon, Seth had reminded her of a teddy bear, but now his barrel-shaped frame and thick arms looked more menacing than cuddly.

Sam stiffened, as if he were bracing for a confrontation. Both men topped six feet, but even though Sam was muscular, he lacked Seth's solid bulk.

Evie had never been a flirt—she didn't even have a clue *how* to flirt—but she smiled playfully up at Sam and linked her arm through his. "Saturday sounds great.… Oh, hi, Seth. I'm sorry it took us so long but we had some things to…discuss."

She didn't have to pretend to be embarrassed that he'd caught them. She could *feel* her freckles getting hot.

For one heart-stopping moment, Seth stared at them, his fists clenched at his sides as he took a step closer.

"You two go ahead and finish on the computer, Evie." Sam tucked a strand of hair behind her ear and gave her a smile. "I'll make some popcorn and put in a movie."

Evie had never had a man look at her like that before— even if he *was* pretending. Her older sisters both had had their share of romances, but Evie had shied away from dating. In high school and college, she'd preferred reading to socializing and knew her serious nature turned off guys who wanted to have fun. Self-conscious of her pale skin, flaming red hair and gangly figure, Evie had discovered that even though she couldn't make herself physically disappear, she could get lost in the pages of a book. She could join adventurous people who didn't wear cardigans or carry dental floss in their purse.

"Honey?"

Honey?

Sam squeezed her hand and his eyes flashed a warning, reminding her to play her part.

Evie recovered and gave him an adoring look. "All right…dear."

Sam made a choking sound and Evie turned to Seth, giving him a bright smile. "Should we all go back inside? I'm sure I'll remember the password but I can always call my sisters. Maybe they'll know."

Seth looked as if he'd just swallowed broken glass. "I don't want to take up any more of your time. I'll finish the job when your dad gets back from his fishing trip."

He unlocked the van and climbed inside. As the van rattled down the driveway, Evie realized she was still clinging to Sam's arm. She let go and stepped away from him, crossing her arms over her chest.

"I think he bought it." Sam exhaled. "Or maybe he decided your house wasn't big enough for the both of us."

"What. Is. Going. On?"

Sam raked a hand through his hair. "I wish I knew," he muttered.

The man who'd given her the adoring, lopsided smile had disappeared. The man who replaced him looked as though he'd rather be treading water in Lake Superior than be with her. And it stung.

"You show up here out of the blue. Some guy is trying to access Dad's computer files. Why?" Evie's voice cracked on the last word. *Terrific.* She sounded like a hysterical female.

Sam pivoted and strode toward the house, leaving Evie no choice but to chase after him while he gave her a brief explanation. "I didn't show up out of the blue. Your dad called me."

"Dad? Why would he call *you?*"

"Believe me—I have as many questions as you do. The connection was bad but Patrick said you might be in danger. That's why I stopped by. And it's a good thing I did." He gave her a dark look.

"That's silly. You must have misunderstood him. Why would I be in danger?" A thought whisked through her, sending her heart speeding into overdrive. "Do you think Seth is planning to rob the antique shop? But why would he need Dad's password? Is *Dad* in trouble?" Fear spiraled through her. "I'm going to call the lodge and talk to him myself…."

Sam stopped so abruptly, Evie slammed into him. It was like running into a telephone pole.

"It might help if your dad was *at* the lodge."

"That must be where he called you from. According to my itinerary, they should have arrived there at six o'clock."

"Your *itinerary?*" he repeated.

"I plotted out their trip. Based on mileage. Number of stops. Packing the canoes and paddling to the island. My calculations could be off, but not by more than fifteen minutes."

Sam stared at her as if she'd spoken in a different language.

"That's it. We're going to Sophie's."

"What? Why?" She scrambled away from him when he reached for her hand. She was tired of being towed around like a piece of wheeled luggage.

"Because our fathers are having a delayed midlife crisis, that's why."

Evie managed to grab her purse as Sam took hold of her elbow and hustled her out the door.

Chapter Eight

"Oh, dear." Sophie took one look at Sam's face and put her hand to her throat. "Come in."

"Where's Faith?"

"She fell asleep on the couch. I think the puppies wore her out."

"We need to talk to you." Sam lowered his voice. "Is Tyson here?"

Sophie shook her head, casting an anxious glance at Evie. He didn't blame her for being concerned. If possible, Evie's skin looked more pale than usual. He'd expected to be bombarded with questions on the car ride over to Sophie's, but Evie had sat quietly, her hands twisting the straps of the gigantic purse in her lap.

"Come into the sitting room." Sophie bustled ahead of them. "We can talk there without disturbing Faith. Would you like something to drink? Tea? Coffee?"

"Sophie, I don't think—" Sophie speared him with a meaningful glance at Evie, who'd wilted into the worn velvet settee in the corner.

"Coffee." He had a feeling they were in for a long night.

He reined in his impatience until Sophie returned with a tray crowded with delicate china cups and a plate of paper-thin lemon cookies.

Sophie dropped two sugar cubes into Evie's cup before settling into a chair opposite them.

Sam had never been good at small talk, and he wasn't in the mood for it now. His stomach still clenched at the thought of finding Evie alone with the guy who'd managed to charm his way into Patrick's private office. Except Lansky hadn't gotten what he'd been looking for. Which meant he might come back.

"I got a call from Patrick tonight, Sophie. Before we got cut off, he said Evie might be in danger. When I went to the house to check on her, there was a man with her. A Seth Lansky. He told Evie that Patrick had hired him to work on his computer but it was clear he was really trying to get into the files." Sam watched the color ebb out of Sophie's face and felt a stab of guilt. Jacob would string him up for confronting her like this, but Sophie was the only person who might be able to explain Patrick's urgent phone call.

"You told me that Dad and Patrick were meeting with a friend about finding a ship that sank in Superior. Is there something you *didn't* tell me?"

Sophie's hands fluttered in her lap. "I'm afraid there's a lot I didn't tell you."

"We're listening." Sam softened his tone, reminding himself that Sophie had gone through a lot over the past year. But he had to make sure Evie was safe before he'd let her go back to the house alone.

"What are you two talking about?" Evie broke in. "Dad and Jacob are on a *fishing* trip. He never said a thing about meeting a friend…or searching for a…*ship*."

"He didn't want to worry you." Sophie sighed. "And the only reason I mentioned it to Sam the other day was because I thought Jacob had told him."

Evie leaned forward. "Told him what? Where *are* they?"

Sophie paused and closed her eyes. When she opened them, it was obvious she'd come to a decision.

"Shortly before I found out I had cancer, I'd started researching my family genealogy. I knew there'd been a scandal a long time ago. My grandmother always referred to it as the Graham family curse. It made me curious and I started contacting distant relatives, trying to find out what they remembered about it. Finally, I discovered a distant cousin who was thrilled to get rid of a box of old papers she'd had in her attic for years.

"My great-grandmother's journal was in it, along with letters she and her daughter-in-law, Dorothea, had exchanged. Dorothea and her husband had had a rocky marriage, and she blamed my great-grandfather, Matthew Graham. Apparently Matthew had been branded a thief and betrayed people who trusted him. Dorothea believed Matthew's actions had marked the family and no one would ever be free of them. I think that was why my grandmother referred to the scandal as a curse. But for me, it became a blessing. In the middle of reading through the journal and Dorothea's letters, I found out I had cancer. But I didn't feel hopeless because God had given me a purpose." Sophie paused and took a deep breath. "I decided to find out the truth. What really happened and if Matthew Graham was guilty or not."

"But what does this have to do with Dad? And Jacob?" Evie asked in confusion.

"They offered to help me."

Evie closed her eyes, relieved. "Dad is helping you research your family history? That makes sense. He'll spend hours sifting through books—"

"He's not looking through books," Sam interrupted. "He and my dad are looking for a ship. Or, to be more exact, something *on* the ship."

"That's impossible. Dad doesn't know the first thing about that kind of stuff." Evie looked to Sophie for reassurance, but the expression on the older woman's face caused a fresh crop of goose bumps to rise on her arms. Was she really supposed to believe that her quiet, scholarly father had gotten mixed up in a crazy hunt for a sunken treasure? If he had, she didn't blame Sophie. It had to be Jacob Cutter's fault.

"Sam is right," Sophie admitted. "They're looking for the *Noble.*"

"What do you know about it?" Sam asked.

"Not a lot. According to Dorothea's letters, a ship came over from England in 1890. Over the past few months, Patrick and I searched through dozens of old newspaper clippings. We found several references to the *Noble,* a wooden steamer that sank in October the same year. It went down in heavy fog and only one person survived."

"Your great-grandfather."

Sophie nodded. "Matthew worked in a logging camp and his boss had hired him to go to England and escort Lady Dale Carrington back to the United States. Lady Dale's father had arranged for her to marry Randall Lawrence, the son of a lumber baron. She brought a wedding gift from her family with her. A dowry, if you will. I can't find a specific reference as to what it was. Maybe jewelry. A family heirloom of some kind. Whatever it was, it must have been extremely valuable. The loss of it stirred up more of a fuss in the Lawrence family than the loss of a prospective bride.

"Matthew claimed Lady Dale's dowry sank with the ship, but they found her betrothal ring in his possession. It was all the proof Randall needed. He accused Matthew of saving himself and the treasure. Matthew denied it, but his reputation was ruined. A few years later, he married my great-grandmother but something had happened to him. He drank heavily and couldn't keep a job. They barely scratched out a living."

"Not exactly the kind of life a man harboring a treasure would choose," Sam said. "If he'd managed to survive and keep the dowry, he would have moved far away and put it to good use."

Sophie gave him an approving smile. "My thought exactly."

"Who knows about the *Noble*?" Sam asked suddenly. "Is it common knowledge there was something valuable on board?"

"I don't think so. No one in my family ever said a word about a treasure—I didn't even know what Matthew had been accused of stealing until I read Dorothea's letters. She was the first one who had mentioned a dowry. The newspaper articles only reported that the entire crew had gone missing, their bodies never recovered. Some of my distant relatives know I've been researching the Graham family history, but only Patrick and Jacob know specific details about the *Noble* and Lady Dale's dowry."

Listening to their exchange, Evie remembered the diving gear in the back of Seth's van and a knot formed in her throat. "Are there people who look for sunken ships that might have a treasure on board?"

Sophie hesitated. "There are laws that protect wrecks from being salvaged in areas designated as underwater preserves."

"But what if the *Noble* sank outside a preserve?"

"Permits would need to be filed." Sam answered the question. "But some people might bypass that little detail."

"But Sophie said no one knows for sure where the *Noble* went down," Evie reminded him.

"Jacob's old friend, Bruce Mullins, is a diver. He's been credited with discovering several important wrecks in the Great Lakes over the past decade," Sophie said. "He's familiar with Superior and would know if there's a possibility the *Noble* can be found. I know Patrick and Jacob made it clear to Bruce that everything they told him was to be held in the strictest confidence."

Sam scrubbed the palms of his hands against his face. "I'm pretty sure someone knows about it now," he said grimly. "Do you have any idea why they'd be interested in Patrick's computer files, Sophie?"

Sophie bit her lip. "The day before they left, Patrick said he had a surprise for me. Something to celebrate my six-month checkup. He wouldn't tell me what it was, but maybe he figured out where the *Noble* sank."

"He's been documenting your research on his computer?"

"Dad hates computers." Evie felt the need to point it out. Again. Patrick may have helped Sophie pore over old newspaper clippings, but if she knew her dad, he'd taken notes using his trusty ballpoint pen and paper.

Sophie slid an apologetic look in her direction. "That's not quite true—he's actually quite knowledgeable about them. He also scanned Dorothea's letters and pages from the journal into his files. I have everything locked up, but Patrick thought we should have copies. I let him handle that part of it. Tyson has a computer but I never bothered with one."

Evie didn't think her dad bothered with them, either.

Sudden tears stung Evie's eyes and made her nose twitch. It was bad enough that Patrick hadn't confided in her about his real plans. And it was possible that someone else was interested in the *Noble*'s cargo. But everything Sophie had shared with them shrunk in comparison to one simple truth.

Her dad had broken his promise to her. A promise he'd kept since she was fourteen years old when he told her that he'd always be there for her. That he wouldn't do anything to put himself at risk…like her mother had.

"What do you mean you can't get in touch with them?" Sam paced the length of the telephone cord and reversed direction when he reached the end of it. He lowered his voice, aware of Evie and Sophie in the next room and Faith asleep on the couch several yards away. "What if there's an emergency?"

"Our pilot flies into the camps once a week with supplies," the proprietor of the lodge informed him. "Even in an emergency, the earliest we could get a message to your father would be next Monday or Tuesday."

Not good enough. Sam had to warn Patrick what had happened to Evie and find out who else was interested in the *Noble*. He already had a strong hunch *why* they were interested. Legends of sunken treasure lured hundreds of divers to the Great Lakes. Even though Sophie was right about laws existing to protect areas designated underwater preserves, there were unscrupulous people willing to break them.

Bruce Mullins, if he remembered correctly, had served in the Marines with his father. Maybe all he'd done was mention the *Noble* to a relative or friend he thought he could trust and it had sparked their interest.

But how had Seth Lansky zeroed in on Patrick's computer files instead of going to Sophie—the source of the information?

"Mr. Cutter? Are you still there? What is the message you'd like me to deliver?"

"Ah…could you tell the pilot to have him call home as soon as possible?"

Silence.

Sam rolled his eyes at the ceiling. Right. *Phone home*. That sounded like a legitimate reason to send a pilot on an unscheduled flight to an isolated fishing camp.

"I'll pass the message on, Mr. Cutter. Was there anything else?" Her tone made it clear she hoped not.

"No. Thank you." Sam hung up the phone.

The grandfather clock in the corner of the room came to life. Ten o'clock. The past few hours had disappeared, absorbed by Sophie's story about her family and Matthew Graham. Under any other circumstances, Sam would have been fascinated. But not now. Not with Jacob and Patrick out of reach and Evie alone at the house.

Another wave of helplessness rolled over him. He'd come to the Upper Peninsula to take a break from his problems, not add to them. But Patrick had called him. Warned him that Evie might be in danger and asked him to look out for her.

He couldn't leave her unprotected, especially if whoever was interested in the ship was convinced Patrick's computer files held the key to the *Noble* and her secrets.

Hopefully the incident with Lansky would prevent Evie from giving another stranger access to her home, but anyone could show up at Beach Glass during the day, pretending to be a customer.

As much as he wanted Evie to continue tutoring Faith, he didn't want to risk Evie's safety. When he'd pulled her to the ground so Seth wouldn't see them, her slender body had stiffened in his arms, tight as a bowstring. She was fragile. Vulnerable. There was only one thing to do. Convince her to pack her bags, close up shop and go home. And it probably wouldn't take much convincing. She was such a cautious little thing....

Decision made, Sam padded into the sitting room and saw the two women sitting shoulder to shoulder on the old settee. Hands clasped. Heads bowed.

Praying?

He paused in the doorway, feeling like an intruder, as Evie's soft voice filled the quiet.

"...and heavenly Father, we turn to you for strength. And for wisdom. Protect the people we love and bring them safely home. For now, we trust they are in Your care."

The words sailed through the empty places in his heart. What was it like to be so sure Someone was listening? Someone who really had the power to give strength? Over the past few months, his had drained away. Punctured by the bullet wounds in his brother's spine. Dan had always come to him for advice. But now, when Dan needed him the most, Sam found he had nothing. Nothing to give. Nothing to say. Nothing that could reverse the clock or give his brother hope for the future.

Dan hated him for it.

And Sam hated himself.

Chapter Nine

Evie lifted her head and saw Sam standing in the doorway. The raw pain in his eyes burned its way through her before the shutters slammed back into place.

"I can't get through to them until next week," he said flatly. "Bruce Mullins took them to one of the more isolated camps."

Evie felt a flash of hope. "So they did go fishing?"

"I doubt it." Sam stalked into the room. "Maybe you should stay with Sophie tonight."

He still thought she was in danger.

Evie wavered, remembering the way Seth Lansky's massive paw had circled her wrist. Had he given up or was there a chance he might come back?

You will keep in perfect peace him whose mind is steadfast, because he trusts in you.

The verse from Isaiah that Sophie had quoted while they'd prayed cycled back through Evie's mind. Peace followed trust. That's what she had to remember. "I need to go home. Dad might call again and he'll want to know I'm all right."

"If we can't contact them, they won't be able to contact us," Sam pointed out.

"I have plenty of room," Sophie added, concern for Evie evident in the slight furrow between her eyebrows. "Tyson re-claimed his old room upstairs, but the sofa in the living room pulls out into a bed."

Evie had forgotten about Tyson. Even though he was Sophie's son, something about the guy creeped her out. "I ap-preciate the invitation, Sophie, but I still have to open Beach Glass in the morning. I'll be fine. I think Sam spooked Seth Lansky enough that he won't be coming back."

The thought occurred to her that maybe that was why Seth had boldly talked his way into the house. With Patrick gone, he'd assumed she was alone. Vulnerable.

"Can you take me home, Sam?" Evie ignored the hollow pit in her stomach at the thought of going back to the isolated house again. "I know you and Faith are going out on the boat to-morrow morning. She needs a good night's sleep."

I'll keep my mind on You, Lord, and trust You to provide the peace.

"Let me know the second you hear from Patrick and Jacob." Sophie's eyes clouded over. "I wish now that I'd never gotten them involved in this."

"It's not your fault," Evie murmured, unable to resist a pointed look at Sam.

"Once Patrick found out what I was doing, he begged me to let him help," Sophie continued. "That man does love a challenge."

"You mean Jacob," Evie corrected her gently.

"No. Patrick." A smile played at the corners of Sophie's lips. "I think he would have bought a wet suit and gone diving for the *Noble* himself if Jacob hadn't convinced him to contact Bruce Mullins first."

"Good old Dad. The voice of reason." Sam arched an eyebrow at Evie.

They *couldn't* be talking about Patrick McBride. The most challenging thing her dad tackled was the expert-level crossword puzzle book she bought him for his birthday every year!

The car's headlights barely made a dent in the darkness as Sam drove her home. Sophie had insisted he allow Faith to spend the night, and as Evie stared out the window at the thick stands of trees hemming the edge of the road, she wished she'd taken advantage of the offer now, too.

"Do you think Dad is in trouble?" Evie finally voiced the question churning in her mind since they'd left Sophie's.

"They're with an experienced guide," Sam said. "I'm sure they're fine."

Was it her imagination, or had he put the slightest emphasis on the word *they're?*

"I still can't believe Dad is involved in this," Evie murmured. "Helping Sophie is one thing but traipsing around, looking for a ship that may not even exist is totally out of character for him. And we have no idea who this Seth Lansky is. Or what he was trying to find."

"That's why you should go home."

Evie's mouth dropped open as the quiet force of the words vibrated in the silence. "Go home?"

"There's a real possibility you aren't safe here. Someone else is interested in the *Noble,* and they knew exactly who to go to for information. Patrick said you might be in danger. He would expect you to leave. Close up Beach Glass until I can make contact with them again and sort out this mess."

It was so tempting to grab hold of the suggestion. To put miles between her and whatever threat lurked around the corner. Would her dad want her to turn tail and run away?

You don't have to be here to talk to Dad, a logical voice in her head reminded her. *You can be at home just as easily.*

"The tourist season is just getting started," Sam continued in that calm, reasonable tone. "Even if you closed up the antique shop for a week, you wouldn't lose much business."

"I'm staying."

The announcement stunned Evie almost as much as Sam.

"There's no guarantee that you're safe," he said flatly.

Funny how those simple words shook her to the core. All her life, Evie had chosen *safe*. She'd built her life around it. Hadn't she learned that people who deliberately put themselves in dangerous situations eventually paid too high of a price? And so did the people they loved.

But what if her dad returned unexpectedly? Shouldn't she be waiting for him? And what about Faith? If God had brought them together, Evie had to trust she was under His protection and He'd give her the strength she needed.

"God brought me here for a reason," Evie said through dry lips. "I'm not leaving."

Sam didn't try to change her mind, but Evie had the feeling he wasn't happy she was staying. Or with the reason why.

"Hi, Evie."

At the unexpected greeting, Evie almost dropped the Depression-glass sugar bowl cradled in her hands.

"Faith." Evie looked at her in surprise before glancing at the row of whimsical cuckoo clocks mounted on the wall. Three o'clock. "Did you and Sam come in early today?"

Faith's face closed, reminding her of Sam's expression when he'd caught her and Sophie praying the night before. "Sam didn't want to take the boat out. It's supposed to storm later this afternoon."

The robin's-egg-blue sky, decorated with brushstrokes of wispy clouds, didn't look the least bit threatening at the moment, but Evie was glad Sam had chosen to believe the weather forecast over the clear sky.

"Is Sam with you?"

"Uh-uh." Suddenly, Faith became fascinated with the canning jar next to the old-fashioned cash register on the counter.

Warning bells went off in Evie's head. "Faith, does he know you're here?"

"What's this?" Faith avoided the question, studying the contents of the jar on the counter as if she'd never seen anything like it before.

"It's beach glass." Evie gave the girl an exasperated smile. Science lesson or lecture? She decided there was time for both. "The waves and the sand work together like a rock tumbler until the glass is smooth and polished."

"Cool."

Evie smiled. One word that equaled high praise. "Go ahead and take one. Dad won't mind. Banks give out Tootsie Rolls, and Dad gives out pieces of beach glass. He says they last longer."

As soon as her thoughts returned to her dad, worry scurried back, chewing at Evie's peace of mind like a nest of field mice. She'd managed to keep her fear under control throughout the long night and most of the morning, but there were times it snuck up on her. Like right now.

"Look at this one. It looks like a piece of bubblegum." Faith held up a piece of glass in a shade of deep pink and for the first time, Evie noticed the girl's red-rimmed eyes and the faint pleats at the corners of her lips. "Pink is Mom's favorite color. Every Christmas, Dad buys her something pink even though he says it's a girlie color. He bought me a pink baseball mitt as a joke for my birthday once."

Faith bravely cracked open the door to her heart to see if Evie really cared about what was inside. She did. But now she had to convince her.

God, please give me the right words to say.

"Have you talked to your Dad lately?"

"When I called this morning, Mom said he was asleep."

The uncertainty in Faith's voice told Evie she didn't know if she should believe her.

"You must miss him a lot."

"I do." Faith dropped the piece of glass back into the jar. "But I heard Mom tell Sam that Dad isn't the same person anymore. Maybe…he doesn't miss me."

Evie drew in a careful breath, but it still felt like a knife sliding between her ribs. Obviously Faith had listened in on a conversation not meant for her ears. No one had been honest with Faith about her father's situation, and while Evie understood that her family thought they were protecting her, it had forced Faith to try to make sense of it on her own. And without wisdom and experience to temper her thoughts, Faith had come to the wrong conclusion.

"I'm sure your dad misses you very much," she contradicted softly. "But he has to accept some major changes in his life and that isn't easy. It isn't easy for anyone."

"I want things to be the way they were," Faith admitted in a small voice.

"They won't be the same." Evie knew she had to be honest. "But that doesn't mean they can't be better." She retrieved the piece of glass and held it on her open palm. "Look at this. It's still a piece of glass, right? But it's changed. At one point in time, it would have been sharp enough to cut you. But the waves and the sand gradually rounded the edges. Softened it. I'm praying for your dad, Faith. That he'll open his heart and trust that God is big enough to bring something good out of this situation."

She wrapped her arm around Faith's shoulders and felt them stiffen. And then Faith melted against her.

"I'll pray, too."

"Good girl," Evie murmured. "Now, how about I call your uncle, who's probably tearing apart the forest looking for you, and tell him we're going to have school earlier today?"

"Field trip?" Faith smiled hopefully.

"English first. Then maybe we can fit in a short field trip."

"Look at this." Faith squatted down and pulled a chunk of rock out of the ground.

"It's quartz." Evie stooped down to admire her find and smiled when she saw Faith's bulging pockets. The girl already had a good start on a rock collection. Evie's own pockets were full, a testimony to the fact she had a difficult time passing up interesting rocks, too.

"I'll give it to Sam for his desk. Then he'll see it every day."

"He spends a lot of time in an office?" The words rolled out before Evie could stop them, and she winced. Talk about blatant curiosity! Faith, thank goodness, didn't think there was anything unusual about the question.

"Dad always teases him about being a paper pusher or something." Faith rubbed the rock against the hem of her T-shirt and left a trail of grime on the fabric.

Evie wasn't surprised at Faith's affirmation that Sam worked in some kind of corporate setting. And she couldn't help feeling a little relieved, although she didn't want to examine *that* too closely.

When he'd left the night before, he hadn't been happy with her decision to stay in Cooper's Landing, and he'd made it clear he thought she was making a huge mistake.

It isn't as if you've shown a lot of backbone up to this point, Evie admitted to herself. She'd shaken like an aspen leaf when she'd seen that diving equipment in the back of Seth's van. No wonder Sam worried about her being alone. Some witness for

God she was turning out to be. If Sam looked at her as an example of a believer, he'd think they were a bunch of wimps!

A raindrop splashed on the back of Evie's wrist. When she looked up, the blue sky had all but disappeared, filled with a slow-moving armada of dark cumulus clouds.

"Faith, let's get going. It looks like the storm that kept you off the lake is finally moving in."

A shard of lightning and a low growl of thunder in the distance underscored the point. Evie silently chided herself for being so focused on the ground that she hadn't paid attention to what was over their heads!

"We're going to get wet," Faith predicted.

Probably an understatement, Evie thought. *Soaked* was more like it. They had at least a two-mile hike back to the house. The beauty of the woods had enchanted them, luring them farther down the trail than Evie had originally planned.

She dug in her purse and pulled out her compact umbrella, popping it open and holding it over Faith's head. "Let's try this."

Faith grinned up at her. "You remind me of Mary Poppins. Remember, she had that great big carpetbag with a mirror in it? And a lamp?"

"I remember," Evie muttered as a gust of wind caught the umbrella and turned it inside out. "If I were Mary Poppins, my umbrella would behave."

They dashed down the trail as the light sprinkles, which must have been the opening preshow, became a pelting rain.

At one point, Faith slipped and fell. Rocks tumbled out of her pockets and she scrambled to gather them up again.

Evie quickly doubled back. "Don't worry, Faith. We can find more."

"I can't find the one I was going to give Sam." Faith had to raise her voice above the sudden screech of the wind.

Evie scooped a handful of soggy hair out of her eyes so she

could aid in the search. "Look. Here it is." Rivulets of muddy water coasted down her arm when she picked it up. Soaked *and* dirty. With a new story to tell her students in the fall.

Faith cocked her head, reminding Evie of Sophie's puppies. "I hear a car. Maybe Sam is looking for us."

Evie heard it, too. For a brief moment, hope burst inside her. Until she remembered. "The gate was locked. It has to be a government vehicle of some kind."

"Maybe they can give us a ride!" Faith whooped and sprinted into the woods separating the service road from the trail.

Through the trees, Evie caught a glimpse of a white van creeping along the road.

It couldn't be.

"Faith! Wait." Evie was no track star but the rush of adrenaline rocketing through her blood pushed her into high gear. She caught up to Faith just before the girl stepped into the road.

"Hey!" Faith squawked in protest as Evie pulled her down behind a clump of foliage.

"It's not a government vehicle." Evie tucked Faith tightly against her as the van rolled past them, so close she could have reached out and touched the tire. A shiver ripped through her as she read the license plate, which bore the same number she'd seen on the one parked in her driveway.

Seth Lansky.

Was he looking for her?

Evie bit her lip, thinking quickly. If Seth really was following them, he probably thought they'd gone to the scenic overlook. That meant she and Faith had a chance to make it back to the parking area before Seth realized they weren't where he thought they'd be.

Thank you, God, for watching out for us.

And bless Faith and her adventurous spirit.

If they'd stuck to the service road, Seth would have spotted them immediately. Not that he'd pursue them on foot…

Out of the corner of her eye, Evie saw the red glow of the brake lights and watched as the driver nosed the vehicle into a narrow clearing.

He was turning around.

"Come on." Evie caught hold of Faith's hand and pulled her back toward the trail, their progress hampered by the brush dragging at their clothing and a grid of exposed tree roots that stretched out like a minefield beneath their feet.

"Evie, you're scaring me." Faith vaulted over a fallen log and clutched Evie's arm as she slipped on a slick bed of decaying leaves. "Who is that?"

"I'm not sure." It was the truth. Evie had no idea if the man driving the van was Seth Lansky…but it couldn't be a coincidence the three of them had wound up in the woods together at the same time.

The wind swallowed Faith's shriek as a shard of lightning hurtled out of the sky, incinerating a nearby tree. The ground trembled under their feet. Evie trembled, too, but didn't want Faith to know she was afraid.

"Not too much farther, Faith. You can do it."

Through the sheet of water cascading over the brim of her hat, Evie saw the gate up ahead. As they veered around it, she tripped over something. The heavy padlock that secured the gate to the post lay on the ground. Clipped off by something a little sturdier than a pair of pliers.

"I see the restrooms," Faith gasped.

Evie gave the girl's arm a reassuring squeeze. Tourists would be in the parking lot, waiting for the rain to subside. And Seth Lansky wouldn't dare approach them in front of witnesses.

Just as the terrain changed from dirt to concrete beneath their feet, Evie heard the faint, muffled purr of an engine. Fear seared her lungs and she scanned the parking lot.

Empty.

Chapter Ten

Evie stopped, bending over to massage the stitch in her side. Should they stay on the trail and try to make it home or take refuge in the restroom? Maybe Seth had checked them already and wouldn't bother a second time.

She had about thirty seconds to decide before Seth spotted them in the parking lot. Evie's gaze darted to the trail and gauged the distance. A straight shot fifty yards in before it took a slight turn that would conceal them from sight.

They didn't have time.

"Restroom," Evie decided, lurching toward the tiny building. Faith remained close at her heels and they skidded inside just as the van rattled around the gate.

Evie collapsed against the wall and Faith slumped to the floor beside her. Outside, the van's engine idled in harmony with their ragged breathing.

Keep going, Evie silently urged the driver. It's pouring. You don't want to go out in this storm.

The snick of a car door closing sounded more ominous than the crack of lightning that had demolished the top of a tree.

"You don't happen to have a phone booth in your purse, do you?" Faith hopped to her feet.

The complete look of trust in the girl's eyes stunned Evie. And goaded her into action.

"We don't need a phone booth. We need a distraction."

Think, Evie.

The restroom had been equipped with the bare essentials. Paper towel holder. A soap dispenser on the wall. And a locked cabinet under the sink.

Bingo.

"Faith, there's a package of gum in my purse. Unwrap all the sticks and give me the foil." Faith looked at her as if she'd lost her mind and Evie managed a quick smile. "Trust me. I'm a science teacher."

While Faith tackled her assignment, Evie peeled off the cabinet hinges with the miniature screwdriver on her Swiss Army knife. Fear made her clumsy and she forced herself to take a deep, calming breath, praying the contents of the cabinet would yield what she needed.

"Here you go," Faith whispered.

Evie closed her eyes in relief when she saw the old bottle of drain cleaner stashed in the back of the cabinet with the rest of the cleaning supplies.

"Now I need you to look in the garbage for a large plastic soda bottle. Find one with a lid."

Faith wrinkled her nose but obeyed.

Evie licked her lips. Now came the hard part. She had to spot Seth before he spotted them.

"Faith, we're going to get out of here but we can't go home yet. There are some rustic cabins the Forest Service rents out on Porcupine Trail. Did you see them on the map?" At Faith's tentative nod, Evie patted her knee. "Good girl. We're going to head there and wait out the storm in one of them."

Hopefully by now, Sam would be looking for them, too.

Evie crept to the door and peered out. No one sat in the driver's seat of the van. Where was he? Evie edged out a little more and caught a glimpse of Seth's bulky frame near the trail. He had his back to them.

"When I give you the signal, head down the trail to the left."

"You're leaving me?" Panic flared in Faith's eyes.

"I'll be right behind you. I promise."

Faith's head bobbed. "What's the signal?"

"You'll know it when you hear it."

Evie filled the bottle with drain cleaner, shoved the foil into her pocket and sprinted toward the van. Seth had melted farther into the woods, and Evie knew she had only precious seconds before he realized they hadn't gone that way. Now she had no doubt he'd check the restrooms again.

Just as she skidded around the side of the vehicle, Seth appeared, lumbering back up the trail and heading straight for the restroom where Faith waited.

She shoved the foil wrappers into the bottle, screwed the lid back on, eased the door to the van open and lobbed it inside like a grenade.

Thank you Brian and Tyler for your science fair experiment. Let's hope it works on a smaller scale.

Evie made it to the woods just as an explosion burst over the sound of the rain.

Seth's startled bellow told her it had.

The chill settling in Sam's bones had nothing to do with the sudden drop in temperature as two weather systems collided in the heavens above him.

Evie and Faith were nowhere to be found. The front door of the shop had been locked up tight. So had the house. Which could only mean one thing—Evie and Faith had taken another unscheduled field trip.

Sam's back teeth ground together. "I can't look out for you when you disappear on me, Evie."

The rain sheeted the car windows and lightning still backlit the clouds, accompanied by the low rumble of thunder. Hopefully, they'd taken shelter somewhere until the storm passed. Sam didn't want to consider the alternative.

"This is crazy." Sam twisted around, searching the backseat of the car for a discarded hat or jacket. Anything to prevent an immediate soaking when he got out of the car. The only thing his search yielded was the crumpled copy of *Captain's Courageous* from Faith's summer reading list, a candy wrapper and a lime-green baseball cap. Way too small and not his color.

Evie's car was still parked by the garage, which meant they'd taken off on foot. If they'd stayed close to home, the storm would have pushed them back to the house by now.

Sam exhaled in frustration, wishing he knew the area better. He rifled through the glove compartment, remembering he'd shoved a bunch of tourist brochures into it on the drive up. A minuscule map showed a series of hiking trails less than three miles from Beach Glass.

Three miles. Judging from the map, he could drive in only as far as the rest area and then he'd have to hoof it from there. But he had to start somewhere. He wasn't a person who got rattled easily, but he'd feel a lot better knowing Evie and Faith were safe and sound. So he could chew them out for worrying him.

"What *was* that?" Faith's eyes were wide as Evie caught up to her on the trail.

"Just a little something I learned from the boys in my class."

"It sounded like a bomb."

"No, making homemade bombs is irresponsible. Reckless. I made a *distraction,* remember?"

"It was a good one."

"Thank you." The muscles in Evie's stomach cramped again, and she decided two miles a day on the treadmill didn't prepare a girl for running for cover over uneven terrain. "If my calculations are right, one of the cabins should be to the west of us about half a mile."

Rustic campsite didn't quite describe what they found at the end of the path, but at least it was a roof over their heads. Sort of. A one-room cabin fashioned from weathered cedar, equipped with screens instead of windows. A single bedframe complete with a questionable foam mattress. A fireplace layered with a thick coat of ash and a plank floor covered with droppings.

"Myotis lucifugus," Evie murmured.

"What's that?" Faith asked nervously.

"A bat." Evie scanned the ceiling to see if the culprit was still in residence. "Don't worry. All clear."

"I'm kind of c-c-cold." Faith wrapped her arms around her middle and perched gingerly on the edge of the bed.

Now that they'd managed to shake Seth loose, Evie had to concentrate on getting them dry. She rummaged in her bag and handed Faith a chocolate-dipped granola bar. "Here. Eat this. I'll try to start a fire." If she could find some dry kindling.

Faith read her mind. "We don't have any wood."

Evie poked at the ashes in the fireplace and turned up several chunks of charred embers. She wove her fingers together and closed her eyes.

"What are you doing? Did you get something in your eye?" Faith leaned forward.

Evie shook her head. "I was asking God for help."

"Starting a fire?"

"Of course. Have you ever heard the story of the loaves and fishes?"

Faith shook her head. "No."

"It's in the Bible. A huge crowd gathered all day to listen to Jesus talk. His friends told him to send the people away because everyone was hungry. Jesus asked what they had and all they could come up with was a few loaves of bread and some fish. Jesus blessed it and when his friends passed it out, those little loaves and fishes fed over five thousand people."

"Is that true?" Faith asked doubtfully.

"Yes, it is. And I'll tell you something else that's true. God cares about the small details of our lives as much as He cares about the big ones. I have the matches and few sticks and we'll let God handle the fire." She struck a match and held it against a splinter of charred wood, then blew carefully until a lick of flame chased up the length of it.

Another rumble of thunder rolled above them like a freight car, rattling the screens on the cabin.

"Look, Evie!" Faith stared in awe at the smoke curling into the air, born from the tiny flame that had begun to devour one of the chunks of wood.

"I'm going outside to make sure that smoke is going up the chimney like it's supposed to." Evie stood up and felt water squish in her shoes with every step.

Wisps of smoke emerged from the chimney, and Evie's gaze carefully moved from tree to tree. Maybe the heavy rain was a blessing in disguise. Seth didn't seem like the type of guy who carried an umbrella.

She eased back into the cabin and found Faith on her knees in front of the fireplace, hands splayed over the flames.

"Are we going to stay here for a while?"

Good question. And one Evie didn't have an answer to yet. She'd tucked some snacks into her bag before they'd set out but didn't normally carry a change of clothing! And both of them were soaked to the skin.

"Just until the rain subsides. Not that we can get any wetter."

Faith's eyes clouded. "Sam is going to be mad."

"He might be worried, but he won't be mad."

"It looks the same," Faith responded glumly.

"You might be right about that." Evie hid a smile. In spite of his annoying tendency to boss people around, Evie didn't doubt Sam's love for his niece. Not many men would take time off from work to care for a troubled adolescent, family or not.

"No one tells me anything." Faith stared into the fire, a frown puckering her brow. "I wanted to stay with Dad, but they didn't give me a choice. They made me come here."

They. It explained the tension between Faith and Sam. She blamed him for taking her away from her father. Evie didn't understand why Dan Cutter's family hadn't stayed to cheer him on during his recovery, either, but everyone had a different way of dealing with crises.

"Sometimes parents make decisions we don't understand," Evie said slowly. "But it's because they love us and want to protect us."

Faith's shoulders rolled in time with her heavy sigh. "So your mom did that, too? Did it drive you crazy?"

Laura McBride's face pieced together in Evie's memory like a tattered photograph. Her mother had loved her family but had chosen to protect everyone else. And where had that left Evie and her sisters?

"All moms do." Evie chose the safest response.

In a rapid change of moods, a mischievous sparkle lit Faith's eyes. "We need more loaves and fishes." She poked at the fire with a stick and it flared back to life. "Dry ones."

Evie doubted she could find a dry stick in the forest at the moment, but the steady drum of the rain against the roof had quieted. "It doesn't seem to be raining as hard anymore. We should be able to leave soon."

"Do you think *he's* still there? The man you didn't want to see us?"

"I don't know." Fear pinched Evie again as she imagined the long trek back to the house. And the very real possibility that Seth was still out there somewhere, waiting for them. His deliberate search for her brought back a rush of doubts. Maybe retreat was the best option. She didn't want to put Faith in danger.

Maybe you should go home.

"Maybe you should pray," Faith said simply.

"Thanks for the reminder." Evie choked back a laugh. Out of the mouths of babes! "Don't get too close to the fire. I'm going outside to check the chimney again." A flimsy excuse, but she couldn't tell Faith she planned to sneak up the trail and make sure it was safe to leave.

The storm had exhausted its power, and Evie saw patches of blue sky through the trees as she picked her way cautiously down the trail. What she wouldn't give for a hot shower and a cup of tea…

The crack of a branch turned her knees to water. Not more than fifty yards off the trail, a man moved purposefully in the direction of the cabin.

Seth?

Evie ducked behind the thick trunk of a white pine. Even above the sound of the rain, Evie was sure her ragged gasps of breath would give her away. Somehow, she had to get to the cabin before he did. Or, Evie thought with a flash of inspiration, draw him *away* from it.

Dropping to her knees, Evie scooted around the tree. "Okay, Big Guy. Let's see what you've got.…" The words died as she found herself face-to-knees with the man towering over her.

He hauled Evie to her feet so quickly she barely had time to process the long legs encased in blue jeans, black sweatshirt stretched over a broad, muscular chest. And a soggy, lime-green baseball cap.

Eyes as gray as the storm clouds captured hers.

For one heart-stopping moment, Sam pulled her against him, his fingers combing through her tangled hair with gentle roughness. And then he let her go.

"I've got trouble, that's what I've got," Sam said softly. "It's about five foot five with red hair, blue eyes and a habit of taking unscheduled field trips."

Chapter Eleven

"A man was looking for us," Faith announced from the backseat of the car.

Sam's foot pumped the accelerator, spewing gravel off the back tires. Neither Evie nor Faith had said much on the trek back to the parking lot, and he'd assumed they'd taken refuge in the little cabin to wait out the storm. Until now. "What man?"

"A man in a white van. But Evie made a—"

"*Distraction,*" Evie interrupted, shifting on the seat beside him.

"Uh-huh. A distraction." Faith nodded vigorously in agreement.

A white van. Seth Lansky again. Which could only mean one thing. He must have decided that since he couldn't get into Patrick's computer, he'd set his sights on the next logical source of information. Evie.

Sam had given in to her stubborn insistence to stay in Cooper's Landing once, but he wouldn't do it again. Not when Patrick had asked him to watch out for her. Evie had eluded Seth this time, but there was no guarantee she could do so again. Lansky might not be a physical threat, but Sam wasn't willing to take a chance.

"I'll drop Faith off to change clothes first and then I'll take you home." To make sure you pack your bags.

Evie didn't argue. Sam slanted a look at her, feeling an unfamiliar tug of *something* when he noticed the weary slump of her shoulders and the damp copper hair plastered against the nape of her neck. Hair he'd untangled with his fingers.

Sam's hands tightened on the steering wheel. He had no excuse for that. Maybe it was somehow connected to the relief that had slammed into his gut when he'd seen Evie scurry behind a tree near one of the Forest Service cabins. She'd looked as stunned by his unexpected embrace as he was. Immediately, he'd put some distance between them but that hadn't doused the confusing mix of emotions Evie always seemed to dredge up in him. And life was confusing enough at the moment, thanks, so now he planned to brush up on his grammar skills, take over as Faith's tutor and send Evie packing. For her own good. And maybe, Sam admitted, for *his*.

By the time they pulled up to the cabin, the sun was shining bravely again, gifting them with a spectacular double rainbow.

Faith propped her arms on the back of Evie's seat and gave them an engaging grin. "A rainbow is formed by the refraction and reflection of the sun's rays in the raindrops, right?"

Evie smiled. "That's true, but the Bible says it's also God's promise never to destroy the world with water again."

"Really?" Faith blinked. "That's in the Bible? Like the story of the loaves and fishes?"

Sam felt Evie's questioning glance and hot color crept into his face. The Cutters tended to live by the old Pull Yourselves Up By The Bootstraps motto. All his life, Jacob had impressed upon his sons that they had everything in them necessary for life. Courage. Strength. Discipline. All they had to do was mine it out and use it. If they didn't, they had no one to blame but themselves. Asking for help from an unseen God was never offered as an option. The closest Sam got to Him was at Thanksgiving, when they bowed their heads and offered a weak prayer of thanks under Grandma Cutter's watchful eye.

When Sam had walked in on Evie and Sophie praying the night before, he'd felt something stir the emptiness inside and wondered if it was too late to approach God. And if it was a sign of weakness.

Jacob would think so. When a friend of Rachel's had asked the pastor of her church to visit Dan, Jacob had intercepted the man and politely told him to tend to his own "flock" and he would see to his.

The image of Dan, confined to a hospital bed, sawed through Sam again like the serrated edge of a knife. His brother's career and favorite hobbies required the use of his legs. He could still see the hopeless look in Dan's eyes. Even his wife and daughter failed to move him toward recovery. And instead of being encouraging, Jacob's admonitions to Dan—that if he set his mind on recovery, he'd be walking in no time—had only made Dan pull further into himself.

"Do you have a Bible, Sam?" Faith asked.

"No." The word came out more harshly than he intended.

"I'm sure Dad has an extra one. I'd be happy to let you borrow it, Faith," Evie said carefully.

Faith looked at him expectantly, and Sam decided that even though it might not help, it probably couldn't hurt, either. "I'm okay with it." He hoped the rest of his family would be, too.

"As long as you don't test me on it." Faith giggled.

"I make no promises." Evie turned back to Sam. "I'll wait here in the car while you get Faith settled."

"We've got towels inside. You should at least come in and dry your hair." Sam saw the blush that rose in Evie's cheeks as she glanced away. Strange. Evie wasn't exactly shy. The night he'd urged her to pretend they'd been on a romantic stroll, her fluttering lashes and adoring look had convinced Seth they were a couple. Just when his cynical self decided he was seeing an unexpected side of Evie McBride, she'd struggled to come up with an appropriate endearment. *Dear.* His lips twisted at the memory. Straight from a rerun of *Happy Days.*

As Sam followed Evie up the path to the cabin, he found himself wondering if there was someone special in her life. Jacob had mentioned all of Patrick's daughters were single, but that didn't mean Evie didn't have a significant other. Someone who could overlook her exasperating tendency to preplan every step and carry a bag guaranteed to make a tinker jealous…and who would appreciate the sapphire-blue eyes that could take a man down like one of the hapless ships at the bottom of the lake.

Where had that come from?

Sam's heart locked up. No, thanks. Been there, done that, had the scars to prove it.

He'd been engaged at the ripe old age of twenty-five to a woman who'd confronted him a week before the wedding, asking him to choose between her and his career. He must have hesitated a fraction of a second too long because Kelly had walked out the door, taking the choice away from him.

Some deep soul-searching and a game of one-on-one with Dan at midnight had left him with a broken finger, a bloody nose and the conclusion he wasn't the marrying kind. Lucky for him that Dan was. Sam could focus on his career with the added bonus of hanging out with his brother's family unit several times a month, enjoying home-cooked meals from Rachel's kitchen and the chance to be Faith's doting uncle without having to change diapers or do that burping thing.

After a week in Faith's company, he'd begun to think diapers and walking around with a towel tossed over his shoulder to catch whatever didn't stay down had been easier than the stage she was in now. Earlier in the day he'd caught her on the phone, trying to sweet-talk the receptionist into letting her talk to Dan. The woman had refused to put the call through, but for some reason Faith had blamed *him*. And then she'd taken off. He'd been about to go to Sophie's when Evie had called him to let him know Faith was with her.

Sam felt a pang of regret. Faith wasn't going to be happy when she found out Evie was leaving. Hopefully, he could make her understand.

Right. Like she understood when you took her away from her dad and brought her here.

Sam pushed the thought aside, more comfortable with action than feelings. "Faith, get some dry towels for Evie, too, okay?"

"Okay." Faith disappeared up the stairs to the loft, leaving them alone.

"I'll stay here. I don't want to drip on the hardwood f-floors."

The faint chatter of Evie's teeth reminded Sam that she'd been soaked to the skin for several hours. "I'll be right back." He disappeared into the bedroom and came back with a pair of clean sweatpants and a long-sleeved T-shirt. "Here. The bathroom is down the hall on the left."

Evie balked. "You're t-taking me home, right? I'll be fine for a few more minutes."

"Just wear them and put me out of your misery," Sam told her curtly.

A smile danced in Evie's eyes. "Now I *know* I look as horrible as I feel."

Horrible? Not the word Sam would have chosen. With her wide blue eyes and tousled hair, she reminded him of a stray kitten who'd been left out in the rain. "At least you don't look like a raccoon."

"Th-thanks."

She looked confused, so Sam figured he should clarify. "You don't have those dark runny circles under your eyes."

Her laughter reminded him of the wind chimes on the deck. "Those are from mascara. And I gave up on makeup when I realized *nothing* hides f-freckles."

Sam frowned as another shiver rippled through her. "I'll change while you put these on, and then I'll give you a ride home."

"He's bossy, isn't he, Evie?" Faith called from the loft as she leaned over the railing and dropped two colorful beach towels.

"You're insulting me?" Sam couldn't believe it. "The guy who rescued you this afternoon?"

Faith gave him an impish grin. "I think Evie's *bomb* rescued us."

"Bomb?" Sam narrowed his gaze on Evie, who shrugged.

"Actually…it was a *distraction*." Plucking the clothes out of Sam's hands, Evie scooted down the hall to the bathroom. She knew what was coming next. He was going to try to talk her into leaving. Again.

She turned the lock and sagged against the door, unsure whether her bones were rattling because the storm had turned her into a walking sponge or in a delayed reaction to their close call with Seth.

Hands shaking, she managed to strip off her wet clothes. As she tugged the well-laundered T-shirt over her head, the familiar blend of soap, fresh air and forest teased her nose. She buried her face in the crook of her elbow and inhaled, comforted by the scent. Sam's scent. It was strange how they barely knew each other, yet she recognized it so quickly.

The black sweatpants puddled around her feet, but at least they were dry. Evie rolled up the bottoms three times and decided it was the best she could do. But when she saw her reflection in the mirror, she stifled a groan. Maybe she didn't look like a raccoon, but Sam had neglected to mention she looked like a drowned rat! Her hair sprang every which way and there were faint scratches on her forehead from being attacked by a low-hanging branch.

When she emerged from the bathroom a few minutes later, she found a drowsy Faith curled up on the couch, headphones in place and a cup of hot chocolate cradled in her palms. She yawned and pointed to the kitchen.

Sam stood at the breakfast counter, slathering peanut butter on a piece of bread. "Coffee or hot chocolate? No tea in this house. Dad doesn't think it's manly."

Evie hooked her thumbs in the waistband of the sweatpants and hiked them up as she sidled into the kitchen. "Coffee. Please."

Sam turned and his gaze swept over her. A smile twisted his lips. "I should have given you something of Faith's to wear."

"This is fine. Thank you." Evie pushed the words out, self-conscious under the weight of his quiet appraisal.

"Foil and drain cleaner," Sam murmured, padding over to her and handing her the peanut butter sandwich she'd assumed was for Faith.

Faith had taken advantage of her absence and spilled the beans. "Seth was about to search the restrooms and Faith was trapped inside. I had to do something to distract him so she could get away."

"Very ingenious." Sam's eyes warmed to liquid silver. "The woman has brains…and beauty."

Beauty? Evie instantly rejected the notion. Caitlin and Meghan reigned as the unchallenged beauties of the McBride family. Caitlin's classic features, sable dark hair and pale blue eyes may have contrasted with Meghan's exotic green eyes and untamed strawberry-blond curls, but both women drew their share of appreciative glances.

Her sisters, only two years apart in age, had been the darlings of Abraham Lincoln High School. The phone had rung off the hook on the weekends. Boys called to take her sisters to a movie or out for a burger. They called Evie when they needed a lab partner.

Sam was probably used to dropping compliments. The night they'd fooled Seth into believing they were a couple, he'd turned on the charm without missing a beat. And his rakish good looks and easy confidence guaranteed a watercooler fan club out there somewhere. He was a man comfortable in his own skin, something Evie had never quite mastered. Old insecurities seemed to hang on like a piece of tape stuck to the bottom of her shoe.

It was a depressing thought.

"I want to go home." Evie closed her eyes as a wave of fatigue swamped her. She didn't deserve any praise. Not when all she'd done was help Faith escape from the dangerous situation she'd put her into to begin with.

"Sit down and eat the sandwich." Sam didn't wait for her to comply, just took her by the elbows and steered her toward the kitchen table. "You look like you're ready to fall over."

Evie decided she was too tired to argue and nibbled at the corner of the bread as he stalked away. He came back with two cups of coffee and straddled the chair opposite hers. "So you're going home. I think you're making the right decision—"

A chunk of crust took an unexpected detour down the wrong pipe. "Not my home," she managed to choke. "Dad's *home*."

Sam stared at her. "You're still planning to stay after what happened today? Knowing Seth is still interested in whatever he thinks you have? Knowing you might be in trouble?"

When he put it that way…

"Yes." She cloaked the word in bravery, leaning on the passage of scripture she'd tucked in her heart.

You will keep in perfect peace him whose mind is steadfast, because he trusts in you….

Sam's chair scraped against the floor as he pushed it away and rose to his feet. "Brainy, beautiful…and bullheaded."

Chapter Twelve

Evie decided two out of three wasn't so bad.

Still, Sam barely said two words to her on the way home. But he insisted on checking to make sure Beach Glass was still locked up tight and no one had broken into the house.

If his intent was to make her nervous, he was doing a stellar job.

He circled the kitchen and paused next to the telephone. "Looks like you have a message."

"Maybe it's Dad." Evie punched the button and listened impatiently while the prerecorded message went through the standard pleasantries.

"Ah...Miss McBride?" She gulped when she heard Seth Lansky's familiar voice. And it didn't sound half as friendly as it had when he'd asked her to help him with the passwords! "I want to talk and I think you know why. I'll be in touch. Soon."

The worst part was, Evie *didn't* know why.

"Change your mind?" Sam growled.

Evie shook her head. Because she couldn't form a coherent sentence even if she tried.

"I'll be right back." He gave her a look that clearly questioned her sanity and finished his rounds. After he rattled the sliding glass doors, Evie stepped in his path.

"If you wait a few minutes, I'll give you your clothes back. Or I can give them to you tomorrow when I meet with Faith."

"Tomorrow's Saturday. Faith and I are going out on the boat for the weekend."

"Overnight?" Evie's voice raised a notch.

"I believe the weekend would include an overnight, yes."

Evie's back teeth clamped together. She knew he was being difficult because she refused to take his advice and leave.

"I'm sure Faith will enjoy it," she said sweetly. "She has fifty math problems to finish by Monday and I'd like her to read the next short story in her literature book."

"I'll see she gets it done." Sam pivoted away from her and headed toward the door.

"Sam! Wait a second. I forgot something." Evie disappeared into her father's office and returned with a small, leather-bound book. "Here."

Sam stared down at the book. "What's that?"

"A Bible. I told Faith I'd lend her one. Remember?" When he made no move to take it, Evie pressed it gently into his hands.

Sam's thumb grazed the words embossed in gold on the cover. "I suppose it can't hurt."

Evie's heart softened when she saw the shadows skim through his eyes. "Faith was fascinated by the story of the loaves and fishes. Tell her to look up Matthew, the first book of the New Testament, and go to the fifteenth chapter." *God, what should I say to him? He doesn't realize he's holding the power to change his life.* "I read one of the Psalms every morning."

"Why?"

Was he baiting her? Evie decided it didn't matter. She wouldn't pass up an opportunity to share the truth. "The

Psalmist, a man named David, didn't always understand God's ways but he wanted to know Him. And he wasn't afraid to ask Him tough questions along the way."

"Did God answer his questions?" Sam's voice carried an undercurrent of cynicism now.

"Not always," Evie said honestly. "But we don't find peace by having all our questions answered. We find it in God. He loves us and we can trust Him to bring something good out of everything that happens in our lives."

Pain darkened Sam's eyes. "Tell that to my brother."

"Faith? Are you ready to go yet?" Sam rapped his knuckles lightly against the fluorescent yellow Enter At Your Own Risk poster taped to the door.

He'd let Faith sleep away half the morning and then she'd holed up in her cabin again after breakfast. He hadn't minded being on deck alone to greet the sunrise. For the second restless night in a row, he'd watched the stars fade away one by one. Ordinarily he slept like the dead when they anchored the boat in one of the shallow bays for the night, lulled by the fresh air and the rocking motion of the waves. But not this time.

"You can come in if you want."

Sam gripped his chest with one hand and pretended to stagger. "Really? To the inner sanctum?"

There was a noisy exhale on the other side of the door. "That's what I said."

He chuckled and accepted the invitation before Faith changed her mind. "I'm surprised you aren't topside barking orders."

Reluctant as Faith had been to come to Cooper's Landing, she'd turned into a first-class first mate. She loved being on the water as much as he did. Not that Lake Superior provided an instant cure for the roller coaster of adolescence, but Faith seemed to be smiling a little more. And she'd even forgiven him for interrupting her unauthorized phone call to the care facility the day before.

Maybe it's Evie you should thank.

Sam shook the thought away even though he knew another one would replace it soon enough. That was the trouble. He couldn't *stop* thinking about Evie. The way she'd held it together and taken care of Faith when Seth had followed them into the woods. Her stubborn insistence on staying even though worry clouded her eyes.

He was starting to realize he'd underestimated her. Maybe she didn't laugh in the face of danger but she wasn't afraid to stare it down, either. And her faith was a wild card he had no clue how to deal with…

There you go again.

Sam yanked his wayward thoughts back in line and focused his attention on his niece, who lay on her back on the bunk bed, Evie's Bible propped against her knees.

"I wanted to finish reading something."

"Shouldn't you be doing homework?" As far as hints went, not so subtle, but the sight of Faith reading her Bible unsettled him. He still wasn't sure how Dan and Rachel would feel about it. He didn't know how *he* felt about it.

"I finished my math." Faith looked up at him. "Did you know Jesus healed people?"

"Uh-huh." Vague, but the best he could do on short notice.

"It says in here He healed all kinds of people. People who were blind and deaf." She paused for a second and sucked in her lower lip. "Even people who couldn't…walk."

It didn't take a biblical scholar to know where Faith was going with that. And Sam felt totally, completely out of his element.

He'd been there when Faith had let go of Dan's fingers and took her first wobbly steps. He'd taught her how to ice skate, slam dunk and do a mean imitation of a Tarzan yell. Although Rachel had never quite forgiven him for the last one.

Faith waited expectantly and Sam's throat closed. It was like seeing Dan all over again. Looking to him for answers. For comfort. For whatever.

You're wrong, Dad, Sam thought. You said all I had to do was look inside myself and I'd find everything I need to tackle whatever life throws at me. Well, I'm coming up empty here. I've got nothing. Nothing for Dan. Nothing for Faith. Nothing for *me*.

"Evie told me the Bible is true." Faith tested the silence when he didn't respond right away.

"A lot of people believe that." People who, according to Jacob, didn't have the strength and know-how to solve their own problems.

"Do you?"

Sam gave up and sat down at the foot of the bed. "I've never thought about it much." At least not until Dan was hurt. Ever since then he'd been bombarded by the same relentless questions. What happened when a man's life changed in an instant and he reached the end of his own strength? What took over?

"Evie told me I should pray for Dad. If I do…"

Sam winced, bracing himself.

"Do you think he'll laugh again?"

The question sucker punched him. He'd expected Faith to say she wanted her dad to walk again. But she hadn't. She missed hearing him laugh. Easygoing and fun-loving, Dan loved practical jokes. No one was exempt as a target, whether it was the guys who worked his shift at the police department or his immediate family. Sam had lost track of how many times his brother had set him up over the years.

Regret burned through Sam, leaving a bitter taste in his mouth. The last time he'd heard Dan laugh was the day his brother was injured, when he'd called to invite Sam over for the weekend to celebrate Faith's birthday. The phone call he'd received three hours later had been from a near-hysterical Rachel, telling him Dan had been shot while responding to a call for a domestic disturbance. He and his partner were walking toward the house when a guy, strung out on drugs, aimed a shotgun out the second-story window and opened fire. Diving for cover, Dan had been hit an inch below his Kevlar vest.

Sam tried to think of a way to encourage his niece without getting her hopes up too high. "Your dad is trying to find his way, Faith. And if you want to pray for him, go ahead."

Maybe God wouldn't listen to the prayers of a man like him, who'd always relied on himself, but Sam hoped He wouldn't turn a deaf ear to those of a young girl who wanted to hear her dad laugh again.

Faith turned her head away and Sam knew she didn't want him to see the tear sliding down her face. Too late. Now he'd do anything to see *her* smile.

Since they'd arrived in Cooper's Landing, he'd handled Faith's moods by retreating and giving her space because that's how *he* coped with pain. But Evie had shot that theory all to bits the day she'd brought over that rusty basketball hoop.

Surround Faith with the things she loves and everything else will fall into place.

He'd try it Evie's way.

"Why don't we stop by Sophie's when we get to shore and borrow Rocky for the rest of the day?"

"Really? Can we go now?" Faith sat up and hugged her knees.

"Sure." And maybe they'd stop by Evie's afterward. To drop off Faith's homework.

Sciurus carolinensis.

Evie groaned and yanked a pillow over her head to muffle the chatter of her alarm clock. Which happened to be the gray squirrel perched in the tree outside her window. At six o'clock on Sunday morning.

Fifteen minutes later, she gave up and tossed the covers aside. She peered at the squirrel through the screen. Now he sat on the empty feeder, his tail twitching with indignation. "Fine. You win. I'll replenish your corn supply."

Evie staggered to the kitchen in her pajamas, made a pot of coffee and poured herself a cup. Sunlight pooled on the hardwood floor, and in the distance the glittering surface of the lake looked as if it had been sprinkled with gold dust.

The heavens declare the glory of God; the skies proclaim the work of His hands.

The opening verse of Psalm 19 scrolled through her mind as she closed her eyes and said good morning to the Lord.

It's beautiful, God. You do all things well.

For a brief moment, she wished she could be out on the water. To feel the breeze brush against her skin. Have a front-row view of the towering sandstone bluffs. Watch the seagulls circling overhead in a graceful synchronized choreography. Experience...a severe case of nausea.

Evie decided she didn't have to be standing on the deck of a boat to enjoy God's creation. She could just be on a...deck. To prove her point, she took her Bible outside. Bypassing her dad's hammock, which, she noted critically, probably wasn't good for his back, she chose a cushioned cedar chair and flopped into it.

Curious black-capped chickadees landed on the railing to take a look at her, and Evie shared her bran muffin with them before closing her eyes and spending time in prayer. Armed with scripture she'd memorized over the years, she aimed a verse at every worry that crowded into her thoughts. She prayed for Patrick and Jacob. Sophie. Faith. Faith's parents. And for Sam.

Father, I think that Sam wants to talk to You but he doesn't know how. Reveal Yourself to him. Show him that he can find hope in You.

Thank You for watching out for me and Faith yesterday. I know You want Your people to be courageous and I fall so short of that. I'm tempted to go home but if You want me to be here for Faith, I'll stay and I'll trust You.

Evie kept her eyes closed for a few minutes, softly humming the tune to one of her favorite praise choruses. Within moments, a verse drifted soft as a breeze into her thoughts.

Trust in the Lord with all your heart and lean not on your own understanding. In all your ways acknowledge Him, and He will make your paths straight.

Thank you for the reminder, Lord.

That's what she wanted Sam to understand. If he turned to God even when life didn't make sense, God wouldn't let him down.

She glanced at her watch, calculated how much time she'd need to get ready for church and decided she had time to take a short detour.

Chapter Thirteen

"I'm so glad you called." Sophie smiled as Evie opened the passenger side of the door and waited for her to slide in. "I was just thinking how lonely church would be this morning without your father to keep me company."

Tyson could go with you.

Evie bit the inside of her lip to prevent her from saying it out loud. When she'd stopped by to pick up Sophie, Tyson had been sound asleep on the couch.

"I didn't want to go alone, either," she said instead.

"I made chicken salad and a loaf of banana bread last night," Sophie said. "Can you stay for lunch?"

"I'd love to." The older woman's offer of friendship wrapped around her like a warm blanket. Caitlin and Meghan would love Sophie if they had a chance to meet her. And Evie had a feeling they would.

She looked forward to spending a few more hours with Sophie but hoped Tyson wouldn't be at the house when they returned. Evie made a habit not to judge people by the way they looked, but the unease she felt around Sophie's son wasn't due to his hygienically challenged outward appearance. Something in Tyson's cool, flat stare made her question what was going on on the *inside*.

Evie started her car and maneuvered it out of the church parking lot. "I came here for worship services last summer when I stayed a few weeks with Dad, but I don't remember seeing you."

"That's because I didn't know the Lord last summer," Sophie said matter-of-factly.

Evie blinked. "I... The way you talked about God and the way you prayed... I assumed you'd been a believer for years."

Sophie chuckled. "I'm afraid it's been just the opposite! You can give your father the credit for introducing us. When everyone else brought bestselling novels to read to the patients at the hospital, Patrick brought his Bible." Her eyes twinkled. "I have to admit there were a few times I wanted to throw it at him, but I didn't have the strength! He had a captive audience and he knew it. I couldn't get rid of him, so I started to listen to what he was saying.

"One afternoon he read a story about a woman who'd been sick for years. She risked everything to get close enough to Jesus to touch his robe. She wanted a new life. I could relate to her. The one thing I'd always wished for was the chance to live my life over again. Growing up, my family wasn't the kind you read about in storybooks. I met Tyson's father and hoped things would be different, but he walked out on us when Tyson was ten years old. I'd been wallowing in the past, wishing things had been different. The day Patrick read that passage I realized I wanted God to heal me, too. Not physically, but from the pain I'd lived with on the *inside*." Sophie's face took on a radiant glow. "Your father prayed with me when I gave my life to Jesus."

Tears stung Evie's eyes. Patrick had always had a gift for pointing people to the truth. She wasn't surprised he'd known exactly what story would touch Sophie's heart. "I'm glad Dad was there for you."

"So am I. Me and the Lord, we have a lot of catching up to do. I wasted so many years trying to muddle through life on my own." A shadow momentarily dimmed the light in Sophie's eyes. "Like Jacob."

"Jacob *Cutter?*" Evie asked cautiously.

"I've been on my knees for that man so often, I'm going to have to sew patches over the worn spots on my slacks," Sophie said. "Just about the time Patrick and I sensed him softening, his son was badly injured and he closed up again. When he came back from Chicago last month, he was so bitter. He made both of us promise we wouldn't talk about God." Sophie's smile returned. "But we never promised we wouldn't talk to God about *him.*"

Evie laughed with her even as her heart ached for the Cutters. When Laura died, Patrick's unwavering faith had been a light that guided Evie through the dark valleys of grief. From the pain in Sam's eyes, it was clear he was stumbling through the shadows, looking for something to hold on to.

"Look at that." Sophie clucked her tongue as Evie turned the car into the driveway. "Tyson is almost thirty years old and he still forgets to shut the door when he leaves. It's a good thing I locked Sadie and the puppies up in the laundry room or they'd be in the next county by now."

Evie followed Sophie inside and heard Sadie whining behind a door off the kitchen. The puppies joined her in a chorus of frantic yips.

"Tyson?" Sophie called above the commotion. "Are you here? We have company for lunch."

The hair on the back of Evie's neck tingled suddenly. Something wasn't right. Other than the sound of Sadie's obvious distress, an eerie silence filled the house. And that open door…

"Sophie, wait."

"I'll be right back." Sophie disappeared into the den and suddenly a sharp cry pierced the air.

"What is it? What's wrong?" Evie bolted into the room and her vision blurred as she took in the scene in front of her.

The room had been ripped apart. Furniture overturned. Shards of what had once been the porcelain figures in Sophie's curio cabinet littered the floor like confetti. The rolltop desk had been hacked to pieces.

Evie couldn't swallow. Had to consciously remind herself to breathe. "Sophie—"

Sophie knelt in the middle of the destruction, sifting through the papers scattered on the floor. "They're gone, Evie. The letters. The newspaper articles. Everything."

"Look! Evie's here." Faith squealed in delight at the sight of the familiar vehicle parked in Sophie's driveway.

Sam barely had the car in Park when she unbuckled her seat belt and launched herself out the door.

Sam followed at a more leisurely pace, the relief of knowing Evie was safe and sound soaking into his subconscious. He hadn't wanted to admit his concern for her had been part of the reason he'd given up a beautiful day on the open water and come back to shore early.

After her near miss with Seth on Friday and the cryptic phone message he'd left, Sam thought for sure she would agree to leave. Not knowing what Seth wanted or how much of a threat he posed had to make Evie feel vulnerable. She'd said herself that she didn't like surprises and the structured way she lived her life proved it.

So why couldn't he convince her to leave?

God brought me to Cooper's Landing.

Sam remembered the reason Evie had given and he rolled his eyes toward the sky. Billions of people inhabited the world. Sam had serious doubts that God had noticed one twelve-year-old girl who was failing her classes and that He had sent

someone to help her. Even if he couldn't dismiss the fact that
Evie, with her unwavering faith and loving concern, had
somehow unlocked the key to Faith's heart.

Like she was trying to do to his.

When Faith wasn't paying attention, he'd snuck a look at the
Psalms, the book Evie said she read from every day. The brutal
honesty of the writer surprised him but what shocked him even
more was that God hadn't taken the guy out for hammering
Him with questions.

It eased the knot in his chest. He had a lot of questions, too,
but he still wasn't sure how to ask them.

Sam reached out to grab the handle on the front door just as
Faith blasted through it, almost toppling him back down the steps.

"Faith, for crying out loud—" The panic in her eyes
squeezed the air out of his lungs.

"Sophie," Faith gasped.

Sam didn't wait for a longer explanation. He pushed open
the door and met Evie on the other side.

"What happened? Is Sophie all right?"

"She's fine. But someone broke into the house." Evie's voice
wobbled and Sam took her hand. Ice-cold. Automatically, he
rubbed his thumb against her palm to stimulate the circulation.

"Where is she?"

"In here." Evie led him into the den and Sam exhaled slowly
as he took a quick inventory of the damage. Whoever had
broken in had had something specific in mind. And, judging
from the amount of senseless vandalism, an ax to grind.

Sophie occupied the same chair she'd sat in the night she'd
told them about Patrick and Jacob's search for the *Noble*. A
search that had gotten out of control. Maybe it had started out
innocently enough, like a trickle of water during a spring thaw,
but now it had picked up both strength and speed. And was
running roughshod over everything in its path.

"Have you called the police yet?" Sam recognized the shell-shocked look in Sophie's eyes and directed the question at Evie instead. She stood just inside the room, one arm looped around Faith, who'd wilted against her with Rocky cradled tightly in her arms.

"Not yet. We just got here."

"Evie and I went to church," Sophie added. "I don't know where Tyson is. When we walked in, we found this. Whoever broke in took everything Patrick and I collected about the *Noble*. It was all locked in a desk drawer. I don't know yet if anything else is missing."

"I'll be right back," Evie murmured. "I'm going to get Sophie a glass of water."

With a wide-eyed, fearful look at Sophie, Faith followed Evie out the door. After they'd gone, Sam dropped into the chair opposite Sophie and leaned toward her. "Was there any sign of forced entry?"

"No. But we never lock the door. There's been no need."

"And you said Tyson was here when you left?"

Sophie nodded. "He came home quite late. He must have been too tired to go upstairs because he was asleep on the couch when I came down this morning. I didn't want to disturb him."

Too tired or too drunk? Sam decided not to ask. The break-in was enough for Sophie to handle at the moment.

"I'll call the police and ask them to send over a deputy. They'll take photographs, so we can't clean up the mess yet. Have you checked the rest of the house?"

"No." Sophie closed her eyes. "I can replace the newspaper articles but not Dorothea's letters and my great-grandmother's journal. I can't believe someone would do this."

Sam could.

"The *Noble* would be quite a feather in a treasure hunter's cap," he said quietly. "Not only because it's a new find but because there might be something valuable on board." And Sam was more convinced than ever that whoever wanted to find the *Noble* wasn't going to bother obeying the salvage laws.

"I know Patrick and Jacob didn't say a word to anyone about the treasure. And according to Jacob, he and Bruce Mullins were like brothers when they served together in the Marines. You know your father doesn't confide in people easily—he wouldn't be meeting with Bruce about the ship if he wasn't sure he could trust him."

Evie returned and Sophie accepted the glass of water she gently pressed into her hand. "Do you think that man, Seth Lansky, did this?"

Before Sam had a chance to comment, a strangled sound came from the doorway.

"Mom?" Tyson hurried into the room, fear etched in his face as he dropped to his knees in front of his mother and took her hands. "Are you all right?"

"I've had better mornings, honey," Sophie said, a faint glimmer of humor returning to her eyes.

"What happened?" Tyson's gaze swept the den and his lips went slack as he saw the extent of the damage.

Sam speared Tyson with a look. Sophie might want to downplay the seriousness of the situation for her son but that didn't mean Sam had to make it all touchy-feely for him. "How long were you gone?"

He hadn't meant for it to sound like an accusation, but Tyson scowled, immediately on the defensive.

"Not more than half an hour. I went into Cooper's Landing to get a newspaper to check the classifieds for jobs."

Which meant someone had been hanging around, watching and waiting for an opportunity to get inside the house. Sam's fists clenched at his sides. Lansky must have decided breaking and entering was a quicker way to get what he wanted than lying his way in, like he'd tried to do with Evie.

"Tyson, after I call the police, why don't we check out the upstairs to make sure nothing else is missing," Sam suggested. "Your mom will need a list when she makes a claim to the insurance company."

Resentment simmered in Tyson's eyes but he pushed to his feet. "What did they take, Mom? The computer? The DVD player?"

Yeah, because life just wouldn't be the same without that stuff, Sam thought in disgust. The molecule of respect that had formed when he'd witnessed Tyson's initial concern for his mother evaporated like a drop of water on a hot skillet.

"I'm not sure yet," Sophie said vaguely. "But Sam's right. You go with him and see if anything is missing upstairs."

Tyson's gaze lingered on the demolished rolltop desk. "Did you have anything valuable in there?"

Sophie smiled sadly. "Valuable, no. Irreplaceable, yes."

Sam saw the confusion that skimmed across Tyson's face. Apparently the guy didn't realize there was a difference.

By the time the deputies from the sheriff's department left, Evie felt as if she'd been put through the spin cycle of a washing machine. One deputy snapped photographs of the den while another took statements from her and Sophie.

Sophie listed the missing items but didn't offer any reason as to why she thought they'd been taken. Some old coins locked in the desk were stolen, too, and Sophie didn't correct the deputy's assumption they must have been what the perpetrator had wanted.

Something about Sophie's reticence caused Evie to resist the temptation to tell the deputy about Seth Lansky. When it came right down to it, what did she know about him? He hadn't broken in and stolen her dad's computer. He hadn't even threatened her that day in the woods or on the message he'd left on the answering machine. Suspicions were the only evidence they had.

Sam and Tyson escorted the deputies to the squad car, and Evie shooed Faith and the puppies outside so she could tackle the mess in the den. She found a broom and began to sweep up shattered glass while Sophie collected the pieces of desk that littered the floor.

They worked in silence until Evie happened to glance at Sophie and saw tears tracking her cheeks.

"Sophie?" Evie scrambled over to her and put her arm around the woman's shoulders, mentally chiding herself for not banning Sophie to the living room with a cup of hot tea.

"Let me make you a cup of tea and something to eat." Evie guided her into the kitchen and into one of the wooden chairs at the table. She rummaged through the refrigerator until she found a block of aged cheddar cheese and some crisp apples and set to work cutting them up.

"As soon as we get in touch with your father, I'm going to insist he and Jacob come back." Sophie's voice barely broke above a whisper. "And I'm going to tell them to give up the search. Family is more valuable than any silly treasure that might be on board the *Noble*. What if Tyson had been home during the break-in? He could have been hurt. It's not worth the risk."

Ordinarily, Evie would have agreed. Maybe she *should* have agreed. But anger welled up inside her at the thought of people who didn't think twice about terrorizing a woman and destroying her property.

"I don't think Dad would want to give up," she heard herself saying. "And I don't think we should, either."

Chapter Fourteen

Had Sam really thought that Evie McBride, with her love of schedules and I-don't-like-surprises personality, was *predictable?*

Because she wasn't. In fact, she was turning out to be predictably *unpredictable.*

"What are you planning?" He could practically *see* the wheels turning in those big blue eyes.

"I'm going to call Caitlin and ask her if she remembers the name of the last goldfish Meghan forgot to feed, and then I'm going to access Dad's computer files and make new copies of the documents for Sophie so Dad will have them when he gets back."

It was worse than he'd thought.

"Are you out of your mind?" Sam whispered in her ear, matching his steps to Evie's as they walked to her car.

Evie adjusted the gigantic purse—probably to balance the amount of strain on her shoulder—and looked him right in the eye. "No."

"I'm sorry. Did you think that was a question? I meant it as a statement."

"Dad wouldn't give up."

"He might not give up, but that doesn't mean he wouldn't

want *you* to," Sam pointed out, feeling it necessary to do so. "He and my dad have no idea Sophie's place was broken into. Tyson is so freaked out he actually insisted Sophie stay with her minister and his wife for a few days."

"That's good. It shows he cares about her, although I don't think he's exactly bodyguard material."

Did she think he was? Because Sam was taking on the job whether he wanted to or not. He'd lost enough sleep over the weekend worrying about her safety. If he couldn't convince her to leave, there had to be some way he could keep a closer eye on her.

"I'll be over tomorrow afternoon to meet with Faith."

Faith heard her name and darted over, Rocky at her heels. "Can I keep your Bible a few more days, Evie?"

"Keep it as long as you like. It's an extra." Evie reeled Faith in for a hug, and Faith didn't squirm, kick or try to set Evie on fire with a glare.

Sam sighed.

Go figure.

Evie paced the floor for fifteen minutes, trying to decide which sister to call first. Caitlin had a memory like a steel trap and would no doubt be able to rattle off the names of all the goldfish the McBride sisters had nurtured throughout their childhood. But she'd also insist on knowing *why* Evie wanted her to remember them.

Meghan, on the other hand, wouldn't think to ask why, but she did have a tendency to be forgetful. Sticky notes wallpapered her apartment. And if Meghan didn't remember a cache of miniature chocolate bars hidden in her pillowcase—until after she put the pillowcase in the washing machine—Evie wasn't too sure she'd remember the name of the fourth goldfish that had taken up residence in the McBride household.

Evie took a deep breath and dialed Caitlin's cell. And got her voice mail.

"Hi, this is Caitlin McBride. I can't take your call right now but if this is Meghan, don't forget to mail out your car insurance. It's due this month. And if this is Evie, check your e-mail once in a while, would you? If you're a client, I'll get back to you as soon as possible. And have a nice day."

Check your e-mail.

Evie groaned. She hadn't booted up her laptop since she'd arrived. Patrick didn't have Internet service, although he'd mentioned the café in Cooper's Landing now boasted a wireless connection.

With only the songbirds at the feeder for company, Evie suddenly felt isolated and alone. And despite her confident words to Sam, she still felt a bit shaken from the break-in at Sophie's.

She'd called the lodge to find out if there'd been any word from Patrick and Jacob, but the proprietor had politely suggested she call back in a few days. Out of touch with her dad, Evie had a sudden longing to reconnect with her sisters. She decided it wouldn't hurt to drive into Cooper's Landing and get a cup of coffee while she caught up on her messages. At least that way, when she talked to Caitlin she could honestly tell her that she'd read them!

Evie didn't expect to see Sam and Faith until the next day, but when she got out of the car and paused to admire the sparkling sapphire water, there was no mistaking the tall, lean frame walking the shoreline. Or the puppy bouncing like a furry pogo stick at his feet.

Evie scanned the beach and relaxed when she spotted Faith, who'd staked a claim just out of reach of the waves to build a sand castle.

To Evie's astonishment, Sam flopped down next to Faith and

began to scoop handfuls of wet sand to assist her in the project. Even from the distance separating them, she could see him laughing at something Faith said. And then he picked up a plastic shovel and used it to catapult water at her. Faith retaliated by soaking him with the contents of the moat she'd dug around the castle.

He'll be a great dad.

Even as the errant thought took root and bloomed, Evie felt her cheeks glow underneath the thin layer of tinted sunscreen she'd applied before she left the house.

And the practical side of her nature immediately voiced its disapproval.

Sure. He'll be one of those dads who take the training wheels off too soon. Or let the kids play tackle football in the backyard without the proper padding.

And if his wife dared to express her concerns, she'd be labeled the family stick-in-the-mud. No fun. No sense of adventure.

No, thank you.

Still, she had to resist the sudden, overwhelming urge to forget about her e-mail and run down to the beach to join them.

She walked into the café and realized the rest of the world had decided to spend a beautiful Sunday afternoon *outside*. Every table was empty.

A teenage waitress wandered out of the kitchen. "You can sit anywhere you want to."

Mmm. A table with an unobstructed view of Cooper's Landing's quaint Main Street or a table with an unobstructed view of Sam?

She chose the table overlooking Main Street. Not as distracting. She put in an order for pie and coffee and opened her laptop.

The first three e-mails were from Caitlin. All of them began with a complaint about the lack of cell-phone towers in the "wilderness" and demanded to know why Evie was ignoring her. Evie suppressed a smile. Caitlin wasn't used to being ignored.

Meghan had written, too, accidentally sending her the same message twice, inquiring about their dad and expressing envy over Evie's "relaxing" summer vacation.

Evie rolled her eyes. She hadn't gotten past the dedication page on the first novel she'd intended to read, and the tomato plants she'd brought along were still waiting to be transplanted into their new containers on the deck.

Oh, it's relaxing all right, Meggie.

She erased some spam, skimmed through some general e-mails from the school administrator and came to one that said "Matthew 620" in the subject line. The sender's address wasn't familiar, and the last thing Evie wanted to do was set a virus loose in her hard drive.

Her finger hovered over the delete button. Some of her students had asked for her e-mail address so they could keep in contact over the summer, and she didn't want to inadvertently ignore one of them.

"Here goes." Evie clicked on the message and instantly a lithograph-type photo of an old map downloaded onto the screen. Along with a message from her father.

"But store up for yourselves treasures in heaven, where moth and rust do not destroy, and where thieves do not break in and steal. For where your treasure is, there your heart also will be." Matthew 6: 20, 21

Evie, please share this verse with Sophie. It's one of my favorites. See you soon.

Love, Dad

"Well, Patty McBride, aren't you just full of surprises?" Evie muttered, eyeing the verse superimposed over a sepia-toned map. "I didn't think you knew how to send an e-mail message let alone a background...."

Her heart slipped into the toes of her sensible shoes as she realized what she was looking at.

Seth Lansky had made a critical mistake. Patrick hadn't stored the latest information about the *Noble* on his computer.

He'd sent it to hers.

"Sam?"

It had to be a hallucination. One minute Sam was staring at the water, thinking it was an exact match to Evie's eyes, and the next thing he knew, he heard her voice.

"Hi, Evie!" Faith jumped to her feet, kicking a spray of golden, sun-warmed sand against his leg. "What are you doing here?"

For a split second, Sam thought Evie had changed her mind and accepted Faith's invitation to spend the afternoon with them on the beach. Until he saw her expression. A warning bell clanged in his head.

"Look at the castle we made."

"It's great." Evie's smile seemed forced as she bent down to examine it.

Sam frowned. More warning bells. Tension coiled in his gut. Now what? Something to do with Sophie? Or their fathers?

"I put the flowers on it and Sam put the rocks along the top. To protect it from invaders." Faith rolled her eyes.

"Hey, you thought it was a good idea at the time." Sam gave Faith's ponytail a playful tug.

She dodged away from him. "I'll be right back. I'm going to find some sticks and leaves to make flags. Can you stay for a little while, Evie?"

"A few minutes."

"Good." Faith grinned. "I can give you a tour of the *Natalie.*"

If anything, Evie's skin paled even more and she managed a jerky nod.

Sam waited until Faith was out of earshot. "Okay, what's up? I know you didn't come down here to build sand castles with Faith." He wished she would have. She'd stepped out of her comfort zone to play basketball, but the nervous little glances she directed toward the water, as if she were imagining a rogue wave rising out of nowhere and pulling her under, shot that hope all to pieces.

"Dad sent me an e-mail dated the day before I got here. The day he called Sophie and told her he had good news." She paused.

Okay, he'd bite. "What did it say?"

"I'd rather show you. I have my laptop in my purse. Can you take a few minutes and go to the café with me? I'll treat Faith to an ice-cream cone."

Was he imagining the faint glimmer of excitement in her eyes? "I doubt the owner of the café would believe Rocky is a service dog."

She gnawed on her lower lip. "Oh. I didn't think about him—"

"Do you want to see the boat now?" Faith returned, the puppy at her heels.

"Evie suggested ice cream." Sam stepped in, figuring Evie had already reached her quota of traumatic experiences for the day. "Why don't you keep working on the castle and we'll bring some back from the café?"

"That's all right." Evie smiled bravely. "I can see the boat first."

She continued to surprise him. He'd tried to let her off the hook, but once again she'd stepped out of her comfort zone for Faith. His respect for Evie went up another notch. Who was he kidding? Another ten notches. And suddenly Sam realized the needle gauging his emotions had somehow snuck past "like" and was hovering perilously close to…something else.

Sam's jaw locked. Attraction, maybe. That wasn't as scary. He wasn't blind. No one could blame a guy for getting caught in the depths of a pair of wide, sapphire-blue eyes. Or for knowing exactly how many cinnamon freckles dotted her nose. *Twelve.* But he didn't want to care about Evie McBride. Not that way.

Dan's injury had cut him loose from his moorings, setting him adrift in a sea of questions and doubt. The Cutter pride was the only thing keeping him from going under and who knew how long *that* was going to keep him afloat? Every time he remembered Dan saying that he wished he'd died on the way to the E.R., Sam felt his grip slipping a little more. The last thing he wanted to do was to pull someone else down with him.

Like Evie.

No, *not* just Evie. Not anybody.

"Okay, Faith, go ahead and lead the way." Evie marched stoically toward the dock as if she were going to have to walk the plank when she boarded the *Natalie.* Her purse bumped against her hip like unsecured cargo. Knowing how much stuff she had in that thing, she'd probably end up with bruises that wouldn't fade for a month.

"You don't have to do this, you know." Sam eased the bag off her shoulder and looped it over his arm, ignoring her look of surprise. He shrugged. "At least it's khaki and not pink with polka dots."

Her smile made a serious dent in the armor around his heart. "According to Caitlin, pink clashes with *this.*" She sifted strands of silky, red-gold hair through her fingers. "My wardrobe consists of greens and browns and golds. And I accent with pumpkin."

"You lost me." Because the way the sunlight played on her hair had his full attention at the moment. He scrambled to catch up. "Who is Caitlin?"

"My older sister. The *oldest* sister. And proof that everything you hear about first-born overachievers is true." Evie's eyes sparkled with obvious affection. "She works as an image consultant in Minneapolis and she has a lot of important clients. I surrendered my closet a long time ago, but so far Meghan, that's my other sister, refuses to be conquered."

"What does Meghan do?"

"She's a freelance photographer. She's in New England right now, working on a series of calendar photos for a private company. She and Cait are both pretty busy."

He detected a thread of wistfulness in her voice. "Which leaves Evie. A teacher with summers off. That must be nice."

"It is." She didn't sound very convincing. "I miss my students, but it gives me a chance to spend time with Dad. He gets lonely."

He *gets lonely,* Sam thought with a sudden flash of insight, *or* you *get lonely?*

He'd assumed from comments Jacob had made that Evie acted like a mother hen when it came to her father, but now he wondered if there wasn't another reason for it.

"Do you travel much when you aren't teaching?" *Way to keep your distance, Cutter. Ask her about her life.*

"No." Evie slowed her pace as they neared the dock. "I read. Garden. That sort of thing. I put in so many hours at school that I'd rather stay home when I have the chance." She paused and dug a half circle in the sand with the toe of her shoe. "What do you do in your free time? Besides boating?"

She was stalling. Sam suppressed a smile. "I do some rock climbing. Sailing. Fly fishing." And he'd done every one of those things with Dan. Regret rocketed through him again. He'd lost sleep wondering how Dan would cope if he couldn't enjoy his favorite activities, but until this moment, Sam hadn't looked at it from his own perspective. Would *he* still enjoy them?

"Sam? Are you all right?"

When he glanced down at Evie, he wondered why she

thought she'd needed to mix up a homemade bomb that day in the woods. The incredible blue eyes focused on him created enough of a distraction. She was five yards away from a dock that looked as if it had been built out of toothpicks, but the concern in her eyes was for *him*.

"I'm great." He lied through his teeth as he sealed up his emotions in a space marked by a sign similar to the one on Faith's door. Do Not Disturb.

Faith waved to them from the deck of the *Natalie*. "Come on, you slowpokes."

Sam hopped up on the dock and took three steps before he realized Evie wasn't following him. She stared at the boat, her complexion a bit green. She already looked seasick.

"She's tied up, Evie."

"*She's* still...bobbing."

Sam chuckled. "Boats tend to do that. Especially on the water." He retraced his steps, caught her hand and gave a gentle tug. She responded by digging her sensible shoes into the weathered wood and tugging back.

"I'm a coward," she murmured. "Ask my sisters. I don't like being on the water."

"In that case, you're good to go. You'll be on the boat, not the water." Still holding her hand, Sam urged her closer to the *Natalie*. He had to do something drastic to wipe the panicked look off her face. He remembered Evie's tendency to get defensive about her purse, so he let it go and it hit the deck with a dull thud. "We already have an anchor, but thanks."

"Very funny." Evie snatched it up but he noticed with relief that some of her color had returned.

Sam leaped across the narrow space separating the boat from the dock and stretched out his hand. "Ready?"

"Come on, Evie. You'll love it." Faith joined in the cheering section.

Evie cast another longing look at the beach.

"Come on, Evie. Trust me. I'm an expert at catch and release." Sam winked at her and Evie's burst of laughter went straight to his heart.

"That I can believe."

Chapter Fifteen

Evie focused on Sam's smoke-gray eyes instead of the enormous expanse of blue in the background. And jumped. True to his word, he steadied her and then promptly let her go. For a split second, disappointment outweighed her fear of the water.

"Faith, why don't you bring up a pitcher of lemonade. All that castle building works up a thirst."

"Sure." Faith disappeared down the short flight of steps that led below deck, and Sam motioned to Evie. "Step into my office and tell me about the message."

Evie perched in one of the captain's chairs, not sure where to begin. "Dad asked me to share a verse from Matthew with Sophie. That was strange enough, because he could have done that himself. But the background the verse is printed on is a...map."

"A map," Sam repeated.

Evie didn't take offense at Sam's skeptical look. It *did* sound a little far-fetched. She had her own doubts until she'd studied it more closely. "On the map, there's a ship just off the north end of a small island. It would make sense that the *Noble* would sail for the shelter of a bay if it got into trouble."

"You don't know if the ship depicted on the map is the

Noble. Patrick could have pasted in that image from an old book or a pamphlet from a tourist center. It might not mean anything."

"That's why I *know* it means something. The map isn't a copy—he drew it himself." And the lines he'd drawn over-lapped at the same point. On the tiny sketch of a ship.

"Even if Patrick has a general idea where the ship went down, don't you think if it sank that close to one of the islands, someone would have discovered it by now? Professional and recreational divers have combed this area for years." Sam scraped a hand through his hair in frustration. "And if by chance it is there and no one's found it, it means we won't, either. It's too deep or a reef smashed it to pieces and there's nothing left to find."

"Maybe. But that must be why our dads wanted to meet with Bruce Mullins. To find out if it was worth taking a look. When Sophie and I were on our way to church this morning, she mentioned Dad had found some old diary entries from a sawyer who had worked at one of the logging camps. He didn't have a chance to show them to her, but maybe Dad based the map on something he'd discovered written in them."

"You told Sophie about the map?"

Evie frowned at the sudden undercurrent of tension she heard in his voice. "I called her from the café. I thought she'd want to know that whoever stole the records didn't find the most important piece of the puzzle. She wasn't there so I left a message on the answering machine. Why? What's wrong?"

"I think—"

"I brought brownies, too," Faith interrupted them cheerfully, carrying a tray with a pitcher of lemonade and three glasses.

Evie smiled at the girl, glad to see that in spite of the scare they'd had at Sophie's house earlier that morning, she seemed to be fine. Or maybe Rocky had something to do with it. Faith and the puppy had become inseparable.

"Can I show her the rest of the boat now, Sam?" Faith asked hopefully.

"That's up to Evie. She might not have time."

A warm feeling trickled through Evie. Once again Sam was giving her an "out."

He had to be aware of her reaction to the water. And a man whose list of hobbies revolved around it probably wouldn't understand why she was afraid. She didn't quite understand it herself. When Faith suggested a tour of the *Natalie*, Evie had braced herself for a teasing comment or look of amusement from Sam. She'd been shocked when she didn't receive either one. In fact, the expression in his eyes when she'd agreed had stolen the breath from her lungs. It had almost looked like...respect? Affection?

Impossible.

Evie surged to her feet. At that moment, she would have jumped overboard and dog-paddled to Canada if it took her away from Sam's unnerving presence. "I've got time. Let's go."

"This is where I sleep." Faith clattered down the steps and moved to the side so Evie could peek into the tiny room, roughly the same dimensions as Caitlin's walk-in closet! The decor was strictly functional. A narrow bunk covered with a navy spread. A pair of vintage maps in mismatched frames that hung crookedly above a corner desk.

Maps. Fleetingly, she wondered if she'd convinced Sam that they might have the *Noble*'s location. She still didn't know why his gaze had narrowed when she'd told him that she'd shared the information with Sophie. Maybe he thought she should have waited until they were sure so it wouldn't raise Sophie's hopes.

"What do you think?"

Faith's question coaxed Evie back to the moment. "It's

cozy." And cramped. But if Evie kept her gaze from drifting out the window, she could almost imagine she was in a studio apartment. Almost.

"That's the desk Sam chains me to so I get my homework done," Faith confided.

"I heard that!" Sam called down from the upper deck.

Faith grinned. "He has ears like a fox."

"I heard that, too."

Evie's heart listed, and this time she couldn't blame the waves. She found herself wishing she could take Faith up on her invitation to spend the rest of the day with them. But the thought of being out on Lake Superior in a boat like the *Natalie* turned her knees to jelly. She'd gotten seasick just watching the boat bump against the dock. Imagine how she'd feel if she actually…

The engine roared to life and Evie clutched the door frame. "What's he doing?"

"Sam always checks everything before we go out," Faith said blithely.

"Oh." Evie felt foolish. Of course he did.

"Come on. I'll show you the kitchen." Faith raised her voice above the gargle and sputter of the engine. She led the way while Evie trailed behind, trying to concentrate on her young guide's knowledgeable monologue about the boat.

The tiny kitchen charmed Evie. Even though there was barely enough room to turn around, it was outfitted with a sink, stove, refrigerator and a row of open-faced cabinets crowded with a mismatched set of dishes. Someone had added a whimsical touch by stenciling cherries and cherry blossoms along the ceiling, and the colorful rag rug on the floor repeated the bright yellows, greens and reds.

"Look." Faith opened one of the cabinets and proudly pointed to an enormous jar of peanut butter. "Sam lets me do most of the cooking while we're on board, but you can help me if you want to."

"I'm not going to be here for…" The boat pitched to one side and Evie caught her breath. "Wow. For a minute there it felt like the boat was moving."

Faith's eyes widened. "It is."

Sam heard Evie's shriek above the sound of the engine.

Five, four, three, two…

Her feet thumped up the stairs and she appeared in front of him, hands planted on her hips. "What do you think you're doing?"

"Taking you somewhere we can talk." Sam turned the wheel slightly to the left as the *Natalie* chugged cheerfully away from the dock.

The color ebbed from Evie's face, highlighting the constellation of freckles sprinkled across her nose. *All twelve of them.* "We can talk on land."

"This is more private."

"You *planned* this."

"No." Sam liked to think of it as taking advantage of the moment. The minute she'd told him she'd left Sophie a message telling her about the map, he knew he couldn't let her go back to the house alone. And it conveniently solved his dilemma on how to keep tabs on her.

"You attract trouble like a magnet." There. Something a science teacher would understand. "I promised your dad I'd look out for you. This is the only place I can do it."

"Whoever wants the information on the *Noble* got what they were looking for. They'll leave me alone now," Evie argued, keeping her voice low so Faith wouldn't hear them.

"Except for the map. Which you now have."

Evie's mouth opened and closed several times like a beached whitefish. "The only people who know about it are you and

Sophie...." Her eyes darkened. "You can't possibly think Sophie had something to do with this. You should have seen her expression when she saw the damage and realized all the records were gone."

She was right. He hadn't seen Sophie's expression. But he'd seen Tyson's.

Guilt had been written all over the guy's face. Forget about innocent until proven guilty. When it came to Evie's safety, Tyson was guilty until proven innocent. Sophie's son or not, Sam didn't trust him.

"Faith will be happy to have someone to bunk with." Sam kept his eyes trained on the water so he wouldn't cave in and take Evie back to shore. "Think of this as a field trip."

"Bunk?" Evie gulped. "I'm not staying overnight on this...*leaky bucket*. You have to take me back. *Now.*"

"We should be able to put a call through to our dads sometime tomorrow. Until then, I'm afraid you're stuck with me. And, just for the record, the *Natalie* doesn't leak."

"This is...*kidnapping*." Her voice stretched thinly. "Sophie isn't going to tell anyone about the map."

He had to be honest with her. "Tyson might."

"Tyson?" The flicker of doubt in her eyes told him that she didn't trust the guy, either. "But he was upset when he saw the den and thought Sophie might have gotten hurt. He even arranged for her to stay with Pastor Wallis and his wife."

"He looked like a kid caught with his hand in the cookie jar." Sam's lips flattened. "I had a little talk with one of the deputies this morning. He recognized Tyson right away. He's been making the rounds at the local taverns lately and isn't choosy about the company he keeps. If he's out of a job and trying to support a drug habit, you can bet he's snooped around his mother's house. Maybe listened in on her conversations with your dad. He could have tipped off his so-called friends that Patrick had some interesting information about a sunken ship."

"You think Tyson knows Seth Lansky?" Evie slumped back down into the captain's chair and her purse slid to the deck. "Poor Sophie. When I saw the way Tyson reacted this morning, I hoped it meant he cared about her."

"I think he does." As cynical as Sam could be, the protective way Tyson had hovered around Sophie after the deputies left had seemed genuine. "Part two of my conspiracy theory? The break-in woke Tyson up to the fact that he's in deep with the wrong crowd and that's why he shuttled Sophie to her minister's house for a few days. He wants to keep her out of the way." *Just like I'm keeping you out of the way.*

As if she'd read his mind, panic flared in Evie's eyes. "If you take me back, I promise I'll check into a hotel."

Sam thought about it. For two seconds. The only way he'd get a good night's sleep was if he knew exactly where Evie was and who she was with. "Sorry."

"I don't have a change of clothes."

"Faith always keeps extra on board. And I have a spare pair of sweats." On cue, an image of Evie, looking adorably rumpled in his rolled-up sweatpants and T-shirt, downloaded into his brain. He shook it away.

"Beach Glass is open tomorrow—I can't just walk away from my responsibility."

"Neither can I."

"I'm not your responsibility." Evie folded her arms across her chest.

"Take that up with Patrick, okay? By this time tomorrow, we'll know if you're right about the map." And he'd find out if he was right about Tyson and Seth Lansky. And ask the deputy to run a check on Lansky, something he kicked himself for not doing sooner.

"You can't keep me—"

"You changed your mind about coming with us!" With what Sam considered to be an example of perfect timing, Faith rounded the corner and made a beeline to Evie.

And hugged her.

Evie's eyes met Sam's over Faith's shoulder. The smug glint in those smoky depths made her want to push him overboard. Except then no one would be driving the boat. And she'd actually been gullible enough to believe that Sam respected her fear of the water when all along he'd planned to lure her out into the middle of Lake Superior!

Her mouth felt as dry and gritty as the sand on the beach and Evie had to loosen her death grip on the straps of her purse in order to return Faith's impulsive hug.

For Faith's sake, she had to pretend to be a willing captive.

Her gaze shifted from Sam to the passing scenery as the *Natalie* cut a choppy path through the waves, like a pair of dull scissors through satin. The waning afternoon sun coaxed out the deep golds and crimsons etched in the sandstone bluffs, and in the far distance, Evie saw the boxy silhouette of a barge against the horizon.

Hadn't she wished she could be out on the water with Sam and Faith? Watching seagulls coast on the air currents over her head? Feeling the spray of the water against her face?

So not funny, Lord.

"Evie." Sam's husky voice sent shivers down her arms. "Come over here for a minute."

Evie's eyes narrowed suspiciously. "Why?"

"We're going to make you an honorary sailor."

Faith giggled and flopped down on the vinyl-covered bench that curved in a semicircle around the cabin. Evie shot her a look. "Are you an honorary sailor, too?"

"Yup." Faith nodded vigorously.

Sam held out his hand, and Evie automatically grabbed it. He pulled her gently in front of him and curved her fingers over the steering wheel.

"Oh, no." Evie took a step back and bumped into the solid wall of his chest. "Absolutely not."

"You can do it. It's not much different than driving a car."

"Sure. Except for the treacherous underwater reefs."

"Come on, Evie." Faith's eyes sparkled. "Sam's right."

"That's one for the books," he whispered.

Faith wrinkled her nose at her uncle. "I'm going to check on Rocky. I'll be right back."

"She's going to put on a life jacket, isn't she?"

Evie felt Sam's low rumble of laughter down to her toes. "This should be a piece of cake for a woman who can put together a bomb in a wayside restroom."

"It was a *distraction.*"

The movement of the boat had nothing to do with the nervous flutter in Evie's stomach. If she moved a fraction of an inch in any direction, she and Sam would be touching. She swallowed hard, aware of the corded muscles in the forearms braced on either side of her. And the warm strength of his fingers as they moved to cover hers.

She relaxed her grip and watched the blood rush back into her knuckles. She lifted her chin and felt the breeze cup her face and playfully ruffle her hair.

Okay, Lord, maybe this isn't so bad. After all, You created the land and the water and declared both of them good, right?

"It's different, isn't it?" Sam murmured. "To feel the movement of the waves instead of watching them from land. It gives you a whole new perspective."

Evie closed her eyes briefly. He'd not only read her mind, he'd just come close to describing her entire life. And lately she'd started to realize there was a difference between planning every moment of the day and actually living them.

"Hey." The tug of Sam's voice opened her eyes. Evie twisted slightly and looked up him, catching a glimpse of the half smile that tilted the corner of his lips. "Don't hit the island, okay? Rule number one—drive the boat with your eyes *open*."

"I'll remember that. *Captain.*" Evie raised two fingers to her forehead in a mischievous salute.

Sam's eyebrow arched. "Does this mean I'm absolved of all kidnapping charges?"

She tilted her head. "Maybe. But you have to promise me smooth sailing. And a blindfold wouldn't be a bad idea, either."

The breeze caught a few strands of her hair and blew it into her eyes. Before she could move, Sam reached out and tucked them behind her ear. He was so close she could see where the pewter-gray centers of his eyes deepened to charcoal.

Sunspots danced in front of Evie's eyes, and she felt curiously lightheaded. Probably the heat. Where was her straw hat when she needed it?

Sam shifted his gaze to a point somewhere in the distance. "I talked to Rachel before Faith and I left this afternoon."

Chapter Sixteen

"How is Dan?" The fragile thread connecting them gave Evie the courage to ask the question.

"It's not Dan." Sam's exhale stirred her hair. "There's been no change with him. It's Rachel…"

Evie held her breath and waited.

"You have to know Rachel. She's very emotional. Dan is easygoing but in their relationship, he's the strong one. I was afraid Rachel would fall apart when Dan got hurt, but she tried to keep it together for Faith. By the time the hospital moved him to the rehab facility, the stress was getting to her."

"I felt like Dad and I not only bailed on Dan, we bailed on her, too," Sam admitted. "Dan's doctor and the social worker…they didn't come right out and say it, but we were hurting Dan's recovery. He's bitter and angry and doesn't want to see me…*us*."

The edge of pain in Sam's voice sawed through Evie's defenses. She couldn't imagine how she'd react if one of her sisters turned her back on the rest of the family and refused to let them help her.

"I check in with Rachel at least once a day. The first few

times I talked to her, she couldn't make it through the conversation without crying."

"She's depressed?"

"I was beginning to think so. I even told her the last time we talked that I'd bring Faith back as soon as Dad got home, but today when I talked to her, she sounded...different. Better. She even made a joke about losing weight on the 'cafeteria diet.' I figured her good mood meant Dan was coming around, but when I asked if there was a change, she said no. I can't figure it out."

"Maybe she's decided she has to face whatever happens head-on."

Sam shook his head. "You don't know Rachel. She's not that strong. She has to hold on to someone. I think that's one of the reasons Dan is depressed. He knows how much Rachel depends on him. Now that we're not there, a friend of hers from work has been spending time at the hospital with her. Rachel mentioned she went to church with her this morning."

Evie thought about all the prayers being said on behalf of the Cutter family, and something stirred inside her.

Sam struggled with guilt for leaving Rachel and Dan alone but maybe he *hadn't*. Maybe God had intervened and cleared a work space at the rehab facility. And he'd started with Rachel.

God, You are so incredible.

"Maybe the change isn't in Dan," she offered tentatively, not sure how Sam would respond to her theory. "Maybe it's in *her*."

"What do you mean?" Sam frowned and adjusted the steering wheel.

"Maybe Rachel let God take over," Evie said simply.

"God?" Sam repeated.

"When you give God control of your life—and your heart—you don't have to muster up strength to make it through the day. He *is* your strength."

* * *

Sam stared at her, speechless.

It had to be a coincidence. Sam had taken Evie's advice and thumbed through the book of Psalms when he'd found it lying on Faith's bunk that morning. He had no idea where to start, so he'd randomly picked one out and started reading.

I love you, O Lord, my strength. The Lord is my rock, my fortress and my deliverer; my God is my rock, in whom I take refuge…

Sam hadn't expected the verses to lodge in his brain. Or brand his soul. He'd read the entire passage and remembered thinking that if God was everything a man named David believed Him to be, no wonder he'd loved Him. No wonder he'd turned to Him for help.

No wonder he'd trusted Him.

"So I should just let God take over? Not *do* anything?"

"Yes, you should let God take over. And no, I never said you don't have to *do* anything. The things we're responsible for— trusting, loving, believing—they're all acts of will. And they don't just happen once. We have to keep choosing them. Sometimes day by day. Sometimes second by second. Sometimes breath by breath."

Did he believe her? Evie wished Sam could see her in the classroom, confident and secure with her students, instead of worrying about Patrick and shaking like a leaf after her run-in with Seth Lansky. If she had half of Caitlin's fearlessness and Meghan's moxie, she knew she'd be a better example of someone who wholeheartedly trusted God.

"Hey, Evie!" Faith's muffled voice floated to the top deck. "Can you read through an essay I finished?"

"I'll be right down."

The corner of Sam's lips tipped. "Thanks, Evie."

Evie nodded mutely as she ducked under his arm and went below deck.

Had he thanked her for helping Faith? Or for something else?

"Do you want to help me make supper?" Faith closed her folder and with a twist of her wrist sent it hurtling toward the desk in the corner.

"I'd love to." Evie followed Faith into the kitchen to survey the well-stocked pantry. "Macaroni and cheese? Or ham sandwiches?"

One of the times she'd gone camping as a child stirred in Evie's memory. "Have you ever made shipwreck dinner?" she asked, trying not to wince as she said the name. Maybe they could come up with a new one. Like "safe-on-land dinner."

Faith made a face. "It's not raw fish, is it?"

Evie laughed. "I'll have you know that some people pay a lot of money for raw fish. But no, this has nothing to do with fish. We'll need hamburger, onions, carrots and potatoes. And foil."

"Okay. I think we've got all that." Faith gathered the ingredients while Evie kept one ear tuned to the sound of Sam's footsteps on the deck above them. As if by unspoken agreement, they'd given each other some space.

"Are you two ready to go ashore?" Sam called down.

Evie's heart bottomed out. "He's kidding, isn't he?"

"Sometimes we anchor and take the little boat into shore for a few hours."

"The *little* boat?"

"It's fun."

"If you say so."

Faith grinned. "I'll get you a life jacket."

* * *

"I look like a cross between the Michelin man and Santa Claus," Evie said, striking a pose in the bulky vest.

Faith giggled. "I think that one is Grandpa's."

"It is." Sam came up behind them. "Let me see what I can do to make it fit better." He yanked on the belt and cinched it tighter around her middle. "Can you breathe?"

No. Not with you so close. "Yes."

"Good." Sam tugged on Faith's jacket and adjusted one of the shoulder straps. "The boat's ready."

Evie peered over the side of the *Natalie* and gulped. The dinghy secured to a line off the *Natalie*'s bow was the size of a bathtub. And the peaceful cove looked *very* far away.

"Faith, you get in first and I'll hand Rocky to you," Sam directed. "Make sure you hold on to him."

"I will." Faith practically skipped down the ladder and reached out to take the puppy.

Evie, not wanting to deal with the raft until absolutely necessary, focused on their destination instead. The cove was a smooth notch carved from the rugged shoreline, its backdrop a canvas of sandstone stained by the iron-rich water that trickled down its surface.

Her gaze traced the curve of the shoreline to the narrow finger of land that pointed to one of the smaller islands. Farther down, Cooper's Landing sprawled at the edge of a stretch of golden sand.

"Evie? Ready?" Sam's husky voice momentarily distracted her.

"Not even close," Evie muttered.

Sam didn't try to take her hand as she turned her back toward the water, grabbed the rails and settled one foot on the top rung of the ladder.

He smiled down at her. "Don't worry. If you fall in, you'll float."

"That's so comforting." Evie's foot found the next rung. "You should be writing the inside copy of greeting cards."

Sam laughed outright, almost causing Evie to lose her balance. He didn't laugh very often, and this one swept away the shadows that lingered in his eyes, arrowing straight to her heart. "I'll keep that in mind if I ever lose my job."

Evie inched the rest of the way down the ladder, and Faith shifted to make room for her.

The word *sardines* came to Evie's mind as she wriggled into place and watched as Sam practically swung from the deck of the *Natalie* into the boat.

Show-off.

He unhooked the line and Evie linked her arm through Faith's.

"Everyone okay?" Sam asked over the gurgle of the motor.

"Yup," Faith sang out.

Evie was relieved Faith answered the question.

Within minutes, they left the *Natalie* behind and were skipping over the waves toward shore.

"Look! There's another boat." Faith pointed out a boat close in size to the *Natalie,* but the similarity ended there. Its chrome accents gleamed like the edge of a new razor while the sleek lines and onyx finish put it into a completely different league.

Sam's eyes narrowed. "I see it."

He turned the boat to the left and nudged the throttle up another notch. The dinghy agreeably picked up speed.

Evie kept her eyes trained on the speedboat. Was it her imagination or had it changed direction, too? And instead of taking a wide berth around them, it set a course that would put them directly in its path.

"Don't they see us?" Faith asked worriedly.

"I'm sure they do." The grim look on Sam's face belied his reassuring words.

Evie cast a panicked look toward the cove and then at the

boat rapidly closing the distance between them. Three-foot waves sloughed off her sides, gliding smoothly toward them like the dorsal fins of a school of sharks.

Sam shot a look at Evie. "Hang on tight. It's going to get bumpy."

Evie sucked in a breath and nodded. She could see people on the deck, but instead of witnessing a frantic effort to give them some space, the crew had lined up at the rail to watch.

To watch what? Their boat capsize?

Faith made a frightened sound and burrowed against Evie's shoulder as a wave slapped the side of the boat and tipped it. Before the boat had a chance to recover, a larger wave slammed against it. Cold water poured over the side and filled the bottom of the boat.

Evie closed her eyes and began to pray.

She prayed as she ground her feet against the floor of the dinghy and held tightly to Faith. She felt Sam's fingers grip her knee in an effort to keep her from pitching over the side.

Evie didn't open her eyes until the motor quit, and then she wished she hadn't. The sight off the bow squeezed the air out of her lungs. Instead of cruising past them, the black speedboat had cut its engine, too, positioning itself like a guard dog between their tiny boat and the shore.

It was close enough for Evie to read the name *Fury* scrawled across the bow, the red letters painted to resemble flames.

Sam half rose to his feet. "Are you insane?" he shouted at the man who came up to the railing and raised one hand in a casual salute.

"I like to think of it as *committed*." Seth Lansky grinned at Evie. "I thought it would be rude not to stop and say hello."

Sam wanted to keelhaul Lansky. Not for almost capsizing them but for the leering smile he aimed at Evie.

He moved to shield her from Lansky's view.

Seth looked offended. "What's the matter, Cutter? We're just being neighborly."

"By trying to drown us?" Sam called back irritably.

Seth shrugged. "Sorry. I guess I got a little close."

He was *still* a little too close, but Sam didn't bother to mention that. The waves had settled down into a gentle rocking motion, but they were still in a precarious position. Sam had no idea what Lansky was going to do next. His jovial greeting hadn't fooled Sam for a second. The guy was certifiable and, at the moment, they were sitting ducks.

"It's late in the day to be going out for a pleasure cruise," Seth mused.

"There's plenty of daylight left."

"We're doing some fishing this afternoon," Seth went on pleasantly.

"Good luck with that." Sam decided to dispense with the small talk and kept a wary eye on the *Fury* as he reached down and started the motor. It sounded like a Chihuahua growling at a Doberman, but Seth nodded to the man at the wheel.

The *Fury*'s engine roared to life, and Lansky strolled down the length of the rail, which gave him a bead on Evie again. "Miss McBride? Tell Patrick hello from me. And be sure to mention I'll see him around."

The *Fury* surged away, kicking up another row of waves large enough to swamp them. The little boat valiantly battled its way through them, but even when the water calmed, Sam's heart still hammered against his chest.

He didn't have to wonder anymore if he'd overreacted by keeping Evie close. If Seth had stolen Sophie's collection of records about the *Noble,* it meant he was getting desperate to find the location of the ship. And if Sam had to take a wild guess as to what that desperation stemmed from, he'd bet it had some-thing to do with Seth's fear he wouldn't get to it first.

"Why did they do that?" Faith scrambled toward him and Sam caught her against his chest. "And why was Tyson with them?"

"You saw Tyson?" Sam looked at her intently. "Are you sure?"

"I saw him looking out the porthole at us." Faith twisted around. "Didn't you see him, Evie?"

Evie shook her head, but the weary resignation in her eyes told Sam that she believed Faith had.

Sam's stomach knotted. Seth and Tyson. Teamed up and getting antsy. And how was he supposed to tell Sophie that her son had been involved in the break-in at her home?

"Shouldn't we go back to the *Natalie?*" Evie asked quietly. "All our supplies are soaked."

Over her shoulder, Sam watched the *Fury* drop anchor a mere hundred yards from the *Natalie.*

"Let's just stick to our original plan for now."

Evie could have cried with relief when the bottom of the boat finally scraped against a shelf of sand in the shallow water. Their clothing was almost dry, compliments of the wind, and Faith no longer clung to Sam like a barnacle.

Not that Evie blamed her. The stomach-churning boat ride reminded her why she avoided amusement park rides.

Sam rolled up the bottom of his jeans and hopped out of the boat. He reached for Faith, but she gave him an armful of wiggling puppy first. He deposited Rocky on the sand and reached for his niece. As soon as Faith's feet touched dry land, she and Rocky scurried away to explore.

Evie peeled off her shoes and socks and wrung the water from them.

"Sandals are a good choice for the beach." Sam returned,

eyeing the dripping socks with that familiar glint of amusement in his eyes.

She was glad he found something humorous about their near-death experience.

Evie stuffed the socks into the toes of her shoes. "You're forgetting one small detail. I wasn't planning to *go* to the beach today. And another thing…your methods of convincing me to *like* the water need some fine-tuning."

Sam's lips twitched. "Really? Because I thought you turned a much lighter shade of green this time." Before she could protest, he reached down and plucked her out of the boat and waded toward shore.

Evie smiled up at him. Which didn't make any sense. After what they'd just been through, and with the *Fury* looming like a specter right off *Natalie*'s stern, the last thing she should feel like doing was laughing. But she did. "That's all right, then. According to Caitlin, green is a good color on me."

"Evangeline McBride, you are…" Sam searched for a word.

Even without a thesaurus handy, Evie could have filled in the blank. *A worrywart*—Caitlin's personal favorite. *Organized*—Meghan's more tactful description. *Capable*—Patrick's loving moniker.

"Amazing."

That simple word would have been enough to render Evie speechless.

But then he kissed her.

Chapter Seventeen

He'd kissed her. Kissed her! And then apologized.

I'm sorry, Evie. I don't know why I did that.

At least afterward, Evie thought wryly, he hadn't asked her for her notes from her first class. The first kiss she'd ever received was from a boy who'd charmed his way through her defenses to bump up his ACT scores.

An hour had passed and she could still feel the warm press of his lips against hers.

Evie groaned silently.

She *couldn't* be falling for Sam.

She had a pretty good idea of the kind of man God would choose for her to spend the rest of her life with. Maybe a fellow teacher. Definitely someone who loved to spend quiet evenings at home and enjoyed home projects…

An image of Sam walking the roofline of the cabin, his T-shirt casually draped over his shoulder, came to mind. Evie shook it away. Replacing a roof wasn't the kind of home project she had in mind. Gardening. Painting a front door. They had to have some sort of common ground…some of the same interests and hobbies.

But more important, Evie knew her future husband's life had to be centered on Jesus' greatest commandment: *Love the Lord your God with all your heart and with all your soul and with all your mind…and love your neighbor as yourself.*

She sensed Sam's heart softening toward God, but it was obvious an internal battle waged inside him. She could tell he'd really been listening to her after he'd opened up about the change in Rachel, but Evie still didn't know if he'd put his trust in God.

Evie found herself frequently praying for Sam over the course of a day. And not only praying for him. Thinking about him. A lot.

When had she started to care so much?

Sam stalked the perimeter of Evie's personal space for over an hour after they came ashore, trying to figure out the best way to apologize. Because the way she kept avoiding his eyes told him that she hadn't forgiven him. She and Faith stuck together, making a private conversation with her impossible.

It wasn't until Rocky scampered down the beach and Faith chased after him that Sam had an opportunity to approach Evie. He followed the imprint of her shoes in the damp sand to a tangle of driftwood.

"Evie?"

Her shoulders tensed at the sound of his voice, but she didn't turn around. "Faith is doing really well in math. In fact, I think she might even be ahead of her classmates by fall. This week, we'll concentrate on grammar. She's still struggling a little with diagramming sentences, but she's smart. She'll get it."

Sam hadn't followed her to get an update on Faith's progress but the message was clear. *You hired me to be Faith's tutor.*

She put him firmly back in his place and the regret that weighted Sam down took him by surprise. That afternoon, when she'd told him about her sisters, he'd felt the first tenuous threads of *something* between them. And the threads had multiplied again when he'd confided in her about the change in Rachel.

He decided to try again anyway. "I'm—"

"Sorry. I know. You don't have to say it again." Evie sat down on a large piece of driftwood and stared at the horizon.

He didn't? Then why wouldn't she look at him?

Sam pushed his fingers through his hair. Maybe the fact she had to spend the night on the *Natalie* in the shadow of the *Fury* had her upset. "I know you don't like the water and I'm sorry I made it hard for you to go back to Cooper's Landing until tomorrow—" *Now* she looked at him. And it almost burned off the top layer of his skin. *Ouch.* "Okay…I made it *impossible* for you to go back to Cooper's Landing. But after what happened at Sophie's, I have to know you're all right."

"Why?"

The simple question ripped apart his prepared speech. Because she'd gotten under his skin? Because waiting to see what she was going to do next reminded him of trying to keep up with the changing wind currents when he sailed?

"I have no idea. You were just—"

"There. I know."

"No, you *don't* know. You make it sound like I would have kissed anyone," Sam said irritably.

Evie didn't answer.

Was *that* what she thought? That he made a habit of randomly kissing women standing within a five-foot radius?

Sam studied the faint blush of color on her cheeks in disbelief and realized that was *exactly* what she thought.

Maybe some guys' overinflated egos liked the idea of being labeled a "player," but it didn't sit well with Sam. "I don't play games like that," he said flatly. "Ever."

The confusion on Evie's face confused *him.* And then, almost as if someone turned on the proverbial lightbulb in his head, Sam knew. The day he'd told her she had brains and beauty, she'd totally shut down on him. He'd assumed she'd been reacting out of her fatigue, but now he wasn't so sure. Maybe her sudden retreat had been due to her rejection of his compliment.

The logical part of him, the part that was scared to death of giving Evie a weapon she could use against him in the future, urged him to go ahead and let her think he was some kind of Casanova.

But he couldn't do it.

"*You* were the reason I kissed you," Sam told her with quiet force. "You weren't conveniently in range. Or practice. Or a challenge. Or a chalk mark on the board. I kissed you because I'm attracted to you. And to tell you the truth, the only thing I really regret is upsetting you."

He rose to his feet and stared down at her. "Are we clear?"

She nodded mutely.

"Good. I'm going to find some wood to make a fire and try to concentrate on what to do about Lansky instead of kissing you again." Did he say that out loud?

Evie blushed.

Apparently so.

While Sam gathered driftwood for a campfire, Evie coached Faith through the dinner preparations. Which involved wrapping their food in tin foil and burying it in a hole they'd dug in the sand. It helped keep her mind focused on a task instead of Sam's stunning disclosure.

You were the reason I kissed you.

He'd stalked away, leaving her alone to sort out her tangled emotions. And to send up several fervent prayers asking for wisdom. She had a feeling she and Sam had just turned a corner. Instead of being nervous, she found herself actually looking forward to what would come next. Which made her more nervous. She didn't even *like* surprises.

"Earth to Evie." Faith waggled a stick in front of her nose. "When can we eat? I'm starving."

"In about an hour." Evie sat back on her heels and retrieved a handful of tiny packets of disposable washcloths from her purse. She peeled one open and wiped the sand off her fingers as Faith peered doubtfully into the makeshift oven.

"Does it really cook in there?"

"It'll be delicious. I promise." Evie handed her one of the packets.

"Who taught you how to make them?"

"My mom. We camped a lot when I was growing up." Funny how she'd forgotten how much time her family had spent camping and hiking through state parks over summer vacation. Laura saved all her vacation days for the months of June, July and August so she was free to travel with them.

Under their parents' watchful eyes, Evie and her sisters had learned how to bait a hook and clean whatever fish they caught. And cook it in the cast-iron skillet over an open fire. They'd also become expert outdoor chefs with gooey homemade "pies" cooked in a special iron and had copied Laura's famous recipe for "shipwreck" dinner.

Evie caught herself smiling. She and Meghan loved to fish but Caitlin hated it. The only way they could get her to join in was to make it a competition to see who could catch the biggest one.

She could still see her mother flipping pancakes on the griddle or rigging up an outdoor shower. During the day Laura brought their attention to wildlife camouflaged by the trees and after the sun set she'd spread out blankets on the ground and point out the constellations as they lay on their backs under the night sky.

Somewhere along the way, Evie had forgotten those summer

camping trips that had fostered her love for science. Her mother's passion and enthusiasm had been contagious—and out of the three girls, Evie had been the one who'd wholeheartedly embraced it.

As she let herself think about the past, Evie realized her memories had divided into two categories. "Life Before Mom Died" and "Life After Mom Died." And it occurred to her that she dwelled more on the ones in the second category. In many ways Laura's death had become the defining moment of Evie's life.

That day had drawn an invisible curtain between the past and the future and cast a shadow over the good memories the family had shared. And irrevocably changed how they created new memories.

After the funeral, Evie had made her father promise he'd always be there for her—that he'd take care of himself so nothing would happen to him.

Evie didn't even miss the camping trips the following summer. It would have been too difficult to enjoy them without Laura's presence. Patrick's hobbies changed from rock collecting to collecting antiques at auctions and estate sales. Evie spent her summers reading while Patrick remained close by, restoring vintage furniture to its original charm and then selling it to a local antique store.

Her dad hadn't seemed to mind staying close to home. And he'd kept his promise. Until now. Why had he broken it? Because of Sophie? His friendship with Jacob? Didn't he care that she was worried about him?

"Evie, can I ask you a question?" Faith dragged a path through the sand with the tip of a stick.

Evie took a ragged breath, still shaken by the bittersweet memories. Somehow she'd lost sight of the fact that Laura had been a devoted mother and not just a respected police officer. "Of course you can, sweetheart."

"How old were you when your mom died?"

"Fourteen."

"How did… What happened?"

Pain shot through Evie. It wasn't the question she'd been expecting, but it was the one she'd been dreading since she'd found out Faith's father was a police officer. "She died…at work."

Confusion clouded Faith's eyes. "Was she a teacher like you and your dad?"

Evie knew there was no way around such a direct question. "No. She was a police officer."

"Really? Like my Dad? And Sam?"

"Sam?" Evie's world suddenly tilted. "I thought you said Sam works at a desk all day."

"He does. He's a chief of police."

Sam didn't mean to eavesdrop. He'd gone to get more kindling and when he returned, Faith and Evie didn't hear him come up behind them.

Faith's first tentative question welded his feet to the ground. The second one nearly wrecked him.

Evie's mother had been a police officer? How could Jacob have failed to mention that? He and Patrick had been friends for months—he had to have known.

She died at work.

In the line of duty.

Sam's lungs burned at the pain he saw etched on Evie's face. *Fourteen.* She hadn't been much older than Faith when her mother died.

Because of Dan's injury, he had an idea what Evie's family had gone through. Sam had wrestled with the reality of losing his brother during the long surgery after the shooting. But even though Dan had survived, Sam discovered there were other ways you could lose someone you loved.

Just as he was processing how hard it must have been on Evie, Faith dropped her next question. And Evie's response ripped through him like shrapnel.

She thought he had a *desk* job?

Sam replayed conversations he and Evie had had since they first met and realized she'd never asked him what he did for a living. He'd assumed she knew. Apparently, their dads weren't the doting type that talked about their kids' accomplishments!

His law enforcement career had started at eighteen when he and Dan had applied to the tech school. But their careers had taken different paths. Dan loved being a patrol officer. He thrived in the middle of chaos and enjoyed dealing with the public. He had a reputation for being fair and even-tempered in the community while his zany sense of humor provided comic relief for his fellow officers during the course of a stressful day.

Sam had discovered his strengths rose to the surface while dealing with his peers and taking on roles of leadership within the department. While Dan had passed up promotion after promotion in order to stay on the road, Sam had taken every one they offered him. Eventually, he'd applied and been hired as chief of police in Summer Harbor, a small town in Door County. The rare opportunity to make it to the top of command at the age of thirty had forced him to make some difficult decisions, but he hadn't regretted it. Even when his dedication to his career had meant sacrificing his relationship with his fiancée.

But now Sam realized he must not have loved Kelly at all. Because he hadn't experienced a tenth of the pain when she'd walked out on him as he did now when he saw the look of horror in Evie's eyes.

She'd looked doubtful enough when he'd described his favorite hobbies. There was no way she would willingly accept his choice of career.

Especially a career responsible for taking her mother's life.

* * *

Everything suddenly made sense to Evie.

Sam's suspicious attitude when Seth Lansky had wormed his way into her dad's house. His take-charge attitude. His innate confidence. The way he'd reacted at Sophie's.

Evie closed her eyes.

Sam had practically processed the crime scene. The only thing he hadn't done was file a report. He'd asked Sophie the right questions. He'd warned them not to touch anything until the deputies had an opportunity to photograph the damage.

All the signs had pointed to his profession, and she'd been totally blind.

A police chief.

Up until that moment, Evie hadn't known how deeply her feelings for Sam had taken root. Until Faith's innocent disclosure about what he did for a living had ripped them out.

Chapter Eighteen

Evie wasn't sure what was more frightening: spending the night on the *Natalie* or spending another minute in Sam's company now that she knew what he did for a living.

No, not for a living, she amended. Dentists worked for a living. Lawyers worked for a living. Some people defined their lives by their careers, and some people's careers defined their lives.

Police officers, firefighters, soldiers…all of them fell into the second category. And Evie didn't miss the irony that every one of them put their personal safety at risk.

I guess that's it, God. You closed the door on a relationship with Sam.

At least Evie could be grateful she'd be going home in a week and life would return to normal. No more crazy stories about sunken ships. No more bad guys lurking around the corner. No more water. *No more Sam.*

So why didn't the thought of going back to her routine lift her spirits?

"Evie? Faith is ready for bed. She asked me to send you down to say good-night." Sam materialized beside her, wearing a navy-blue hooded sweatshirt. The department logo printed on the front slapped her with a reminder of what he was.

"Sure." Evie turned from the railing and averted her gaze. She'd managed to make it through supper and the trip back to the *Natalie* without talking directly to him. She could make it one more night. All she had to do was keep her distance....

"Evie? After you say good-night to Faith, can we talk?"

No, no, no.

She didn't want to talk to him. She didn't want to think about him. She didn't want to remember the look in his eyes when he'd told her she was amazing. Right before he'd kissed her.

"Please?"

She gave in. But only because she'd been raised to show good manners. And because there was nowhere on the *Natalie* she could hide. "All right."

Faith scooted over when Evie poked her head in the cabin, an invitation for her to join her on the bunk.

"Is the boat still gone?"

The worry in Faith's eyes told Evie she hadn't gotten over the scare of being caught in the *Fury*'s wake.

"Long gone." *Please, Lord, let them be long gone.*

Just when Evie had started to think they were going to be sleeping on the beach instead of the *Natalie,* Seth must have decided he'd toyed with them long enough. The *Fury* circled the *Natalie* several times and then roared away, disappearing around the rock peninsula.

Without a word, they'd taken advantage of the window of opportunity and immediately packed up the supplies so they could return to the boat. As quickly as possible. Sam had kept one eye on the peninsula and Evie knew he was wondering, too, if the *Fury* had temporarily anchored there, waiting for them to venture back out onto the lake.

"Why was Tyson with them?"

The question tugged at a loose corner of Evie's frayed emotions. She had no idea what to tell Sophie about her son and his involvement with Seth.

"They must be friends of his."

"I guess so." Faith didn't look convinced. "He's always nice to me when I visit Sophie. Sometimes we watch basketball and he makes hot-fudge sundaes."

That would have surprised Evie if she hadn't witnessed Tyson's reaction to the break-in that morning. And the panic in his eyes when he'd asked Sophie if she'd been hurt. His concern for his mother had seemed genuine but it would still break Sophie's heart to find out Tyson had been the one who had told Seth about the *Noble*.

"Will you pray, Evie?"

Evie answered the unexpected question by taking Faith's hand. For the second time, Faith had unknowingly reminded her how to deal with her turbulent thoughts!

"Dear Lord, thank You for watching over us today. Thank You for calming my fear of the water so I could spend the day with Sam and Faith on the boat. Take care of Patrick and Jacob while they're…away. And Faith's mom and dad. It's hard to be apart from the people we love, Lord, but we trust they're in Your hands. And so are we."

She was about to close the prayer with an "Amen," but Faith took a deep breath and attached her own request.

"And I want to go home, God. Can you do something about that? Thanks."

Evie reached out and pulled the blanket up, tucking it around Faith's shoulders as she asked God to answer Faith's heartfelt, innocent prayer.

"Are you coming back soon?" Faith murmured drowsily.

They'd fashioned a mattress for Evie on the floor next to

Faith's bunk from the extra blankets on board. Sam had folded one of his sweatshirts to make a pillow.

Practical. And thoughtful. Sam had proven himself to be both on so many levels since she'd gotten to know him.

"In a few minutes." She wouldn't spend any more time in Sam's company than absolutely necessary. "Sweet dreams."

"You, too."

The fragrant night breeze flowed over Evie as she made her way to the upper deck. Sam stood at the railing, his face tipped toward the sky. Pensive and…vulnerable.

The powerful rush of emotions that rolled through her reminded her of their hair-raising afternoon boat ride. She found it easier to guard her heart when Sam bossed her around, but it wasn't as easy when she caught glimpses of the sensitive man beneath the surface.

"It makes you feel pretty insignificant, doesn't it?" Sam asked without looking at her.

Even as a voice in her head warned her to keep her distance, Evie's feet moved on their own to join him at the railing. "No. Just the opposite. It makes me feel valued. And very…grateful."

"Grateful?" Sam slanted a look at her.

She didn't want to be near Sam, but she couldn't walk away from him when he was obviously searching. And just like Patrick's treasure map, she knew exactly where Sam could find the truth. She couldn't keep that to herself. If Sam was willing to listen, she had to be brave enough to talk.

"Because He not only created me, He loves me. When I look at those stars, I don't think about how small I am, I think about how *big* God is. And how much I mean to Him."

Sam didn't respond, and Evie was torn between wanting to say more and letting God fill the silence.

"Good night, Sam." She decided to let God take over.

Or maybe, Evie thought as she turned away, she was simply too much of a coward to stay any longer.

Sam watched Evie walk away, and it took every ounce of strength not to ask her to come back.

It was a good thing his officers weren't around to witness their chief totally losing his nerve.

He'd wanted to tell Evie he'd overheard her conversation with Faith. He wanted to talk to her about her mother and tell her he understood she fussed over Patrick because she didn't want to lose another parent.

He wanted to tell her he worked in a sleepy town not much bigger than Cooper's Landing. He'd leave out the part about living in a turn-of-the-century lighthouse only a stone's throw from Lake Michigan, but he could honestly tell her the most notorious crime his officers had solved was who'd put Jed Carson's VW Bug on the sidewalk on New Year's Eve.

But deep down, Sam knew none of that would matter to Evie. Whether he lived in a small town or a large city, police work always courted danger. The child of a cop, especially someone with firsthand experience of what the cost could be, knew it was the nature of the job.

Even if he told Evie what his life was like, there was no way he could convince her to embrace it. Or even to accept it.

And he had to face to truth. He *wanted* her to accept it.

Evie was a remarkable woman. Funny. Giving. Insightful. Patient. Beautiful. The kind of woman a man could imagine spending his life with. He'd started out thinking he had to protect her but somehow she'd become his *partner.* Watching out for Faith. Encouraging him to look outside of himself for strength. Facing her fears instead of running away from them. Finding humor in stressful situations.

Sam shook a blanket out and laid it on the deck. He wasn't going to sleep in his cabin and give Lansky another shot at them during the night. He stretched out on his back and folded his arms behind his head, staring up at the stars. The ones that made him feel insignificant and Evie, valued.

He didn't want to accept that the feelings stirring between him and Evie weren't as strong as their differences.

The engine wouldn't start.

Sam had planned to leave for shore right after breakfast, but the *Natalie* had a different agenda.

"Why did you decide right now to go temperamental on me?" Sam muttered, digging in the toolbox for a wrench.

Evie appeared in the doorway, looking annoyingly fresh in the wrinkle-proof khakis she'd worn the day before and Faith's favorite basketball jersey. "What's going on?"

"Something's wrong with the engine."

Evie moved closer to the engine compartment and watched him check the fluids. For the third time. Not that he was a slouch when it came to engines, but the *Natalie* had been around a lot longer than he had.

"It looks like the tube near the bottom is cracked," Evie said.

Sam couldn't believe he'd missed it. "That does pose a problem."

"You must have a backup motor on a boat like this."

"The key words are *on a boat like this.*"

"No backup motor?" Evie frowned.

Sam searched for the roll of duct tape every man stashed in his toolbox. Apparently every man *except* his dad. "Do I smell sausage?"

"Faith is making breakfast. Are you trying to get rid of me?"

"Not if you have something to fix this."

"I'll be right back."

Sam sat back on his heels and waited for her to return. When she did, it was with a roll of duct tape.

"You carry that around in your purse?" Sam saw her expression and rephrased the question. "Thank you for carrying that around in your purse."

Evie gifted him with a small smile and some of the tension between them dissolved. "Why don't you let me try. My fingers are smaller."

"Be my guest." He regretted the decision as soon as she knelt beside him and the pleasing scent of maple syrup combined with Evie's favorite brand of perfume played havoc with his senses.

"There. That should hold. I'll stay here while you give it a try."

He took advantage of the escape route she'd offered and went on deck. A few seconds later, the engine came to life and Evie clamored up the steps. "It's working!"

"We make a good team," he said without thinking.

Shadows skimmed through Evie's eyes and she backed away. "I'm going to help Faith with breakfast. It's almost ready."

Regret pierced him.

Or not.

Within an hour, Evie's feet touched dry land again. And she wished she was back on the *Natalie* with Sam.

You are out of your mind, Evangeline Elizabeth. You don't like the water. And you can't like Sam.

But she did. That was the problem. In fact, she had nothing to compare her feelings to, but she wondered uneasily if they'd moved past "like."

"Evie?" Sam caught up to her as she hiked through the sand toward her car. "I'm going to stop by and talk to Sophie. Will you come with me?"

Was he asking because he needed her help or because he wanted to keep an eye on her?

"Yes." No matter how anxious Evie was to put some distance between her and Sam, she wanted to be there for Sophie.

"Do you know where her pastor lives?" Sam's expression closed, reminding her of the man who'd come to her door the night she'd met him and told her Faith needed a tutor. A man whose career forced him to ignore his emotions while he helped people deal with theirs during difficult circumstances.

"In a house right behind the church."

"Good." Sam nodded curtly. "Let's go."

Pastor Wallis met them at the front door of the parsonage, dressed casually in twill shorts and a white polo. Only in his midthirties, his approachable manner and compassionate eyes seemed to have a way of immediately putting people at ease. Evie had liked him from the moment her father had introduced them when she'd attended Sunday-morning worship services the summer before.

"Hello, Evie." Pastor Wallis's lively brown eyes lit with a smile that encompassed both of them. "It's good to see you again. I'm sorry I didn't get a chance to chat with you yesterday after the service."

"That's all right." Evie had noticed he was in deep conversation with several teenagers and hadn't wanted to interrupt. "Pastor Wallis, this is Sam Cutter."

"It's nice to meet you." Pastor Wallis extended his hand and gave Sam's a vigorous shake. "Would you like to come in? Barbara took an angel food cake out of the oven a few minutes ago."

"Actually, we're here to see Sophie."

Pastor Wallis frowned. "She's not here. Her son and his friend picked her up early this morning."

"But I thought she planned to stay for a few days." Evie's heart picked up speed.

"She did." The minister frowned. "But after she talked to Tyson, she packed up her things and told us she had to leave. To tell you the truth, Barbara and I both thought Sophie seemed upset. I was planning to call her this evening."

"Did you recognize Tyson's friend?" Sam asked tersely.

Pastor Wallis shook his head. "He didn't get out of the car. I only saw him from the window, and he was looking the other way. Sophie told us about her house getting broken into. Do you think something else happened?"

Evie and Sam exchanged a glance. "We'll stop by her house and make sure she's all right."

"I'd appreciate that."

Sam was already turning away but Evie hesitated. "Pastor, could we ask a favor? Sam's niece, Faith, is in the car. Is it all right if she stays here for an hour or so?"

The man's eyes lit with understanding. "Of course. My daughter, Samantha, would love the company. She's been complaining since school let out that there's nothing to do around here."

"She must be a teenager." Sam's guess brought a smile to the minister's face.

"She's thirteen."

"I'll get Faith," Evie said quickly. "And Rocky."

"That's right. We have one of Sophie's puppies with us." Sam winced.

"Not a problem. Samantha loves dogs. Bring them both in. I'll tell my two favorite girls we have company."

Faith was hesitant to stay with the Wallis family until Samantha Wallis ran outside, a soccer ball tucked under her arm.

Within minutes Faith waved a cheerful goodbye and the two girls disappeared around the corner of the house.

"That was a good idea until we know everything is okay with

Sophie," Sam said. "I didn't even think about what we might be getting Faith into."

Evie tried to ignore the warm glow his words stoked in her heart. "I remembered they have a daughter close to Faith's age. Do you think Seth Lansky was the one with Tyson?" Evie murmured as they hurried back to the car. "Sophie will recognize his name if Tyson introduces them."

"I hope it wasn't him." Sam paused to open the car door for her before moving around to the driver's side. "I changed my mind about needing you to come with me. Do you mind if I drop you off at your house before I go to Sophie's?"

"Yes."

"Good. I'll—"

"Yes, I mind, not yes, you can drop me off. I'm going along."

Sam's lips flat-lined but he didn't argue. Until they got to Sophie's house. He stopped the car before the turn in the driveway and cut the engine.

"Do you mind waiting here for a minute?"

"Yes."

He flashed an impatient look at her. "Is that yes, you'll wait here or yes, you *mind* waiting here?"

"Yes, I mind waiting."

Sam's eyes narrowed. "Evie, I know what I'm doing and I won't be able to concentrate if you're with me. Please stay here while I evaluate the situation."

And let me do my job.

The words he didn't say hung in the air between them. Of course. Sam wasn't planning to walk up to the door and ring the bell.

Evie hesitated, not wanting him to go alone but not wanting to distract him, either. "I'll stay here." And pray.

Now he smiled at her grudging tone. "I'll be right back."

She watched as he melted into the trees instead of walking up the driveway.

As the minutes ticked by, Evie grew more concerned.

Why wasn't he back yet?

Sam, where are you?

Lord, please let him be all right.

The two thoughts collided as Evie slipped out of the car and followed the path he'd taken into the woods until the house came into view.

No sign of Sam. Or Sophie.

Evie's heart picked up speed as she stepped out into the open and crossed the bright green patch of yard. Should she knock? Or just go in?

As she hesitated on the porch, a hand grasped her arm. "Sam? Thank goodness. I was starting to get—"

Her voice died in her throat as she saw the bruised and bloody face of the man holding on to her.

Chapter Nineteen

"*D*ad!" Evie's knees turned to water.

"Hi, sweetheart." Patrick smiled wanly and then swayed on his feet.

Evie instinctively caught her dad before he fell over, and her frantic gaze skittered over him. Blood congealed over one eye and angry red scratches crisscrossed his cheek. His muddy clothing hung loosely on his frame and she noticed his glasses were missing. "What happened? Where's Sam? Who did—"

The door flew open.

"Evie." Tyson stepped to the side and motioned for them to come inside. "Come and join the party."

She found her voice and turned on Tyson, anger over Patrick's condition overriding her fear of Sophie's son. "What did you do to him?"

Tyson ignored the question. "Let's go into the kitchen."

Where he kept the knives? Not a chance.

Evie balked and Tyson made an impatient sound. Without ceremony, he nudged her away from her father and wrapped his arm around Patrick's waist.

"Let go of him." She glared at Tyson.

"It's okay, Evie," Patrick murmured.

Evie would have chosen a better word to describe the situation but because she couldn't exactly play tug-of-war with Tyson—with her dad in the middle—she gave in and followed him into the kitchen.

She took a silent inventory of the contents of her purse. If she could get to the travel-size can of hair spray in her bag, she could aim it in Tyson's face and get Patrick safely to the car. And then she could double back to find Sam…

"Oh, good, you found her, Patrick. Hello, Evie."

Evie blinked. Like watching a movie playing in slow motion, she tried to process the scene in front of her. Sophie stood near the kitchen table, calmly dabbing a washcloth against a jagged cut on Jacob Cutter's forehead while Sam knelt on the floor, holding a bag of frozen peas against his father's swollen ankle.

Sam glanced up and gave her a wry look. "I knew you wouldn't stay put."

Evie's face whitened alarmingly and Sam rose to his feet. His dad's sprained ankle could wait.

"Hey. It's okay." Sam drew Evie into his arms and she buried her face in his neck.

"I think we can take him," she whispered in his ear.

Sam choked back a laugh and felt Evie stiffen. "We don't have to take him," he murmured. "He's on our side."

"He's right, Evangeline," Patrick chimed in, wincing as Sophie turned her gentle ministrations to the scratches marking his face.

"But Tyson and Seth Lansky—"

Tyson hooked his foot around a chair, yanked it away from the table and dropped into it. "I can see I'm going to have to go over this one more time."

Sophie gave her son an affectionate smile. "I don't mind hearing it again."

Sam would have steered Evie toward a chair, too, but she took a protective stance near her father.

He didn't blame her. When he'd walked into the house and heard his dad and Sophie arguing over whether or not he needed stitches, he'd been ready to take Tyson apart, too.

And Tyson must have known it because he'd put the table between them while Sophie had intervened and explained the situation.

"It seems Tyson has a gambling problem," Jacob said, a little too jovially in Sam's opinion. "And he made some stupid mistakes. Go ahead and tell her, Ty."

Tyson didn't refute the accusation as he looked at Evie. "He's right. I needed money to pay off a loan from my friend, Gil. I heard Mom and Patrick talking about a sunken ship and I didn't pay much attention at first because I figured it was part of the boring genealogy stuff she's been researching. But when Mom said something about a ring, I got to thinking maybe there was something valuable on board.

"I was at the tavern one night and Gil started hassling me. Anyway, I'd had too much to drink and told him to be patient— that I was going to score some big money. But when I told him about the ship, he laughed and called me a stupid drunk. But the next day a guy called. Said he was a diver and maybe we could help each other out if I could tell him where the *Noble* went down. I did some snooping around here but couldn't find anything. I listened in on Mom's phone conversation and that's when I knew Mom had given Patrick the stuff about the ship." He drummed his fingers against the table and slanted a look at Evie. "I didn't think *she'd* be hard to get past. Seth was supposed to get the information off Patrick's computer without her knowing about it."

"But Sam came to her rescue." Jacob winked at Evie and her eyes widened. "That's part of his job, you know. Rescuing damsels in distress."

Sam groaned inwardly.

Dad, you are so not helping me here.

"Oh, I think Seth found out that Evie's pretty resourceful," Sam mused. "She's good at creating distractions."

There was a moment of silence as everyone in the room looked at Evie. But none of them looked the least bit surprised at his announcement. That seemed to fluster Evie more than anything else, and Sam smiled in satisfaction.

It was obvious from the expression on Tyson's face that he knew about it, too. With an encouraging nod from Patrick, Tyson continued. "When Seth didn't have any luck getting the stuff from Evie, he kept pushing me to find out if Mom had it. But I stalled, thinking Jacob and Patrick would get back and he'd leave her alone and focus on them."

"Tyson is sure Seth is the one who broke in." Sophie picked up the thread of the story calmly, as if she'd already forgotten the trauma of finding her den torn apart and months of precious research missing.

Sam couldn't quite understand that level of forgiveness but he was pretty certain it had something to do with a mother's unconditional love. And maybe her unshakeable faith.

"But I didn't have anything to do with that. I didn't know you'd locked the records in your desk. Seth took a chance and ended up finding them." Tyson looked quickly at Sophie, who smiled reassuringly at him. "I confronted him about it and he threatened me. Said he paid Gil off and now I owed *him.* He'd been watching Evie and was pretty sure she knew about the ship. When she got on the boat with Cutter yesterday, he thought they were going to the wreck site. So we followed you," he added, looking at Evie.

"And almost capsized the boat," Evie reminded him.

Tyson squirmed in the chair but didn't look away. "Yeah. But I didn't know he was going to do that. The guy's crazy, man."

"When Tyson got here, he found Jacob and I camped out in the driveway," Patrick said. "I wanted Sophie to patch me up before I came home, but Tyson told us you were on the boat. Jacob and Tyson picked up Sophie at the Wallis's and brought her home."

"Then we all sat down and had a little talk." Jacob leveled a mock scowl at Tyson.

"I don't care what Lansky does to me," Tyson said in a low voice. "I don't want anyone to get hurt."

"It looks like two people got hurt." Evie's fingers closed over her father's shoulder.

"Oh, Seth Lansky didn't do this, sweetheart." Patrick patted her hand. "It was Bruce Mullins."

Sam pulled out a chair and Evie slid bonelessly into it. Without a word, he poured her a cup of coffee and pushed it in front of her. He'd heard the hasty summary of Tyson's involvement with Seth, but he hadn't heard this part of the story yet.

"This is where things get interesting." Jacob looked smug. "Mullins double-crossed us. We figured it out after we got to the lodge—that's why Patty called Sam and told him to look out for Evie. We asked Bruce questions about how to go about filing for permits and organizing the dive, but he started pumping us for information about where she'd gone down. Got kind of cranky when we wouldn't tell him, too, right, Patrick?"

"Yup. Cranky." Patrick's split lip curved into a smile.

"He wanted to find the *Noble* and file for salvage permits before we had a chance to?" Sophie asked.

"Permits?" Patrick sighed. "We can't prove it, but we doubt they were going to bother waiting around for permits. I think the plan was to salvage the ship before *we* filed for them. We would have followed the rules and come up with a big empty nothing because they'd have gotten to it first."

"But I thought you and Bruce were friends," Evie said in confusion.

Jacob snorted. "So did I. But when you say the word *treasure,* men can get greedy."

"Seth mentioned Bruce Mullins's name once when he was talking about a dive he'd gone on near Whitefish Bay," Tyson said. "It didn't mean anything to me at the time, though."

"When Tyson told us about Lansky, we figured Bruce had sent him to nose around here," Patrick added. "Seth got lucky when Tyson's friend started making fun of him and his so-called treasure. We think Bruce's plan was to stall us until Seth had a chance to find out where the *Noble* went down, but he probably started to get impatient, thinking Sam and Evie would team up and go ahead with the search. We think he told Lansky to apply a little pressure."

"On Friday night, we waited until Bruce fell asleep and then we left. We spent the weekend trying to dodge him while we hiked back to the lodge. No tents. No food. Just the clothes on our backs, hey, Patrick?" Jacob reached out and cuffed Patrick's shoulder. "We were starting to worry about what was happening on the home front. Thought maybe you'd need our help."

The two men grinned at each other.

Sam saw Evie's expression. *Uh-oh.*

"Do you mean to tell me…" Evie said in a deceptively pleasant voice "…that you were lost in the woods for two days?"

"Not lost, Evangeline. We had the miniature compass you pinned to the pocket of my shirt," Patrick said.

It didn't look like Evie cared about the compass.

"No food. No tent. Just the clothes on your backs," Evie repeated.

"And we had a great time." Jacob lifted his coffee cup and bumped it against Patrick's.

"A great time," Patrick echoed. "I'd say all in all, the fishing trip was successful."

"What are you talking about?" Evie asked, exasperated. "We all know you didn't go fishing."

"Oh, your dad went fishing, all right," Jacob said wryly. "Fishing for men as the Good Book says. If it hadn't been for Mullins's double cross, I would have thought Patty planned the whole thing."

Sam tensed. *The Good Book?*

"Never underestimate what God will use to get a man's attention." A glint of humor brightened Patrick's eyes. "All He had to do was get us alone in the wilderness with no food or water…and a sprained ankle…and Mullins hot on our trail…to get this stubborn guy to listen."

"Well, I listened, didn't I?" Jacob said irritably. "Some of us take more convincing than others."

"It has a lot to do with the thickness of the skull." Patrick tapped his index finger against his temple.

"Dad, what are you saying?" Because it couldn't possibly mean what Sam thought it meant.

"I accepted Jesus as my savior. Got my life right with God out there in the woods." He looked at Patrick. "Is that how you say it, Patty?"

Patrick's eyes misted. "That'll do."

Jacob looked at Sam and laughed. "You look a little befuddled, son. I'll tell you all about it. And then, I'd like you and Faith to go back to Chicago with me. 'Cause your brother needs to hear it, too."

"I'm sorry I got you involved in this, Evie."

Evie stiffened when she heard her father's voice behind her. Under protest, he'd agreed to rest for a few hours at home before they met everyone again at Sophie's later. But when they got back to the house, Patrick hadn't rested. Instead, he'd printed out copies of Sophie's documents—something Evie had planned to do before Sam kidnapped her.

"I don't understand why *you* got involved." Evie still winced every time she saw the scratches on his face. Sophie had bandaged the cut over his eye but he still looked like a prize fighter who'd made it to the last round. "You promised—"

She caught herself. She hadn't meant to bring it up now that Patrick was home safe and sound. But she intended to make sure he stayed that way!

Patrick sighed. "The promise I made. I'm sorry—"

"It's okay, Dad. I forgive you."

Patrick gave her a gentle smile. "I'm not sorry I broke it, sweetheart. I'm sorry I made it in the first place."

"What?" Evie choked.

"I shouldn't have made a promise I couldn't keep, but you were young and we'd just lost your mother. I would have done anything to give you the security you needed. I said I'd never do anything that might take me away from you—even though I know our times are in God's hands—and that was wrong. Not only for you, but for me. I gave up things I loved because I didn't want to upset you…but I got restless after I retired. Your mother's been gone a long time but I found myself missing her more than ever. I needed some excitement. Something to make me feel alive again.

"When I met Sophie and she told me about her family genealogy and the scandal with Matthew Graham after the *Noble* sank, it gave me an opportunity to do something that mattered. Instead of selling people bits of the past, I could actually help Sophie connect with hers. She might have told you the search for her family history gave her a reason to live, but it gave me one, too."

Evie was speechless. She hadn't meant the promise to prevent her dad from enjoying life…or to make him give up things he loved, even if they were a little risky. She'd given them up, too. But she hadn't felt the void until she'd spent the day on the *Natalie* and relived the sweet memories of taking camping trips with her family.

She'd never known her father hadn't been as successful as her at forgetting those times. Or that he'd felt as though something were missing.

"Dad, I—"

Patrick held up his hand. "Just hear me out for a minute. Your mother was an amazing woman and I was blessed to have the years together that we did. Laura had a way of turning the most ordinary moments into adventures. She lived fearlessly and generously and she loved us the same way. I wouldn't have changed anything about her. Not even her choice of a career." Patrick gave Evie a tender smile. "You may think you and I are alike, Evangeline, but out of you three girls, *you* remind me the most of your mother. You're smart and curious and you care about people. Laura was that way, too."

All along, Evie realized with sudden, painful clarity, she'd been shaped by her mother's death instead of her life. And her father was right. Laura McBride had been an amazing woman. A dedicated police officer. And a loving mother.

"Some things are worth the risk." Patrick looked at her intently. "Friendship. Love."

Evie managed a smile as her heart struggled to recognize the truth she'd just discovered. "You love Sophie."

"Jacob loves Sophie," Patrick astounded her by saying. "And she loves him." He chuckled. "And he just might end up being worthy of her after all."

"Jacob and Sophie? Are you all right with that?" Unexpected tears welled up in Evie's eyes. She'd come to love Sophie, and she'd been ready and willing to welcome her into the McBride family.

"Oh, I'm more than all right with it. I've been asking God for months to give two people I care about a second chance at happiness."

Evie's lips parted. And no sound came out. She couldn't see

Sophie and Jacob together. Sophie was deep and insightful. Jacob Cutter was, well, *Jacob Cutter.*

"They remind me a little of your mother and I," Patrick went on. "Different, but we brought out the best in each other."

Evie forced her mind to take a detour around thoughts of Sam. She couldn't let herself think about him right now. "Is all this talk about adventure your way of letting me know you're not giving up on the *Noble?*"

"Absolutely. And from what Sam told me, it seems I sent the map to the right McBride daughter."

"I was right?" Evie was momentarily distracted. "That *was* the map showing where the *Noble* sank?"

Patrick smiled in satisfaction. "I knew you'd figure it out and that you'd keep it safe. But now that I'm back, the rest of us can take over from here."

"You're really going to look for the ship?"

"We can't give up now. We have to get everything in order so we can hire a dive team to go down and see if Lady Carrington's dowry is still there. Prove that Matthew wasn't a thief."

"But what about Seth?" Evie asked helplessly. "You know he can't be trusted. And he's still lurking around somewhere, watching you."

"We've got some ideas. That's why we're meeting at Sophie's later. To have a planning session. But you don't have to come along, Evie. You're probably exhausted." Patrick's eyes twinkled as he hobbled away, rubbing the hip that had collided with a tree stump.

"I'll come along," Evie said grimly. "Planning sessions happen to be my specialty."

And, she thought with an aching heart, it might be her last opportunity to say goodbye to Sam.

Chapter Twenty

"God answered my prayer, Evie. I'm going back to Chicago with Grandpa and Sam tomorrow."

Tomorrow?

Faith's exuberant greeting pierced Evie's heart but she reached out and hugged her. "That's great news."

"Grandpa called Dad and I got to talk to him. I told him about Rocky and sleeping on the boat," Faith went on. "And I told him about you, too. He said to tell you thank-you for helping me with my homework. And for playing basketball with me."

Evie tried to swallow around the knot in her throat as Faith towed her toward the people sitting around the crackling bonfire in Sophie's backyard. Jacob and Sophie sat shoulder to shoulder, toasting marshmallows over the glowing embers, while Tyson stood several feet away from them, sharpening the end of a stick with his pocketknife.

For some reason, the homey scene brought tears to her eyes. Maybe her dad was right about Sophie and Jacob being good for each other. And for Tyson.

Evie's gaze swept the yard but there was no sign of Sam anywhere.

"Sam didn't come," Faith told her, as if she knew who Evie was looking for. "He said he had too much packing to do if we're leaving tomorrow. He had to cover the boat and stuff like that."

Sam wasn't going to say goodbye?

Evie bit down on her lip to keep it from trembling. He'd barely spoken to her after he and Jacob had returned from their "talk" but she'd assumed it was because he was still in shock over his father's unexpected announcement. *She* could hardly comprehend that Jacob Cutter had surrendered his life to the Lord. She didn't know what it would mean for Sam and his brother, but she had a feeling that God had separated the entire Cutter family so He could work on them one at a time!

"Evie." Sophie rose to her feet and greeted her with a warm hug. "I was hoping you'd come over this evening with your father. Even though it might be kind of boring talking permits—"

"And strategy." Jacob chortled. "Tyson may have to pretend to be on Lansky's side for another few weeks so we can keep an eye on him and see what he's up to."

That sounded a little dangerous to Evie, but she saw the first real smile she'd ever seen on Tyson's face. "Boring? Are you kidding? Count me in."

Evie took a deep breath. "Me, too."

"Are you sure, sweetheart?" Patrick came up and linked his arm through hers. "I don't want to take up any more of your summer—you said you had plans."

Plans. Yes, she did have plans. To paint her front door and read through a stack of books. And do some gardening. And she fully intended to check off every one of those things on her list...

After they found the *Noble*.

"Special delivery for Evangeline McBride."

Evie heard the mischievous tone in her father's voice and set aside the box of china she'd been unpacking.

"I hope it's iced tea because I'm—" Her voice trailed off when she saw the huge bouquet of summer flowers in Patrick's arm. Daisies. Roses. Snap dragons. Lavender. All nestled together in a cloud of airy white tulle. "Where did those come from?"

"A florist, I suppose." Patrick smiled at her. "A deliveryman just brought them to the house." He transferred them into her waiting arms and Evie buried her face in the scented blooms.

"There's a card."

"I know." But she didn't want to read it. Already tears clawed at the backs of her eyes. It had been almost a month since the Cutters had left. She knew Patrick and Jacob kept in contact, but it was as if Sam Cutter had disappeared off the face of the earth.

Or maybe just from your life.

And hadn't she wanted it that way? There couldn't be a future for her and Sam. It was one thing to venture beyond the perimeters she'd put around her life, another to deliberately risk her heart by starting a relationship with a police officer. That was something she didn't think she'd ever be ready for.

"Why don't you put those in some water and I'll finish unpacking the boxes?"

Maybe the flowers weren't from Sam. Maybe Caitlin had sent them as a guilt offering for not being able to visit over the Fourth of July. Or Meghan. Sometimes she did things like send flowers or chocolates for no particular reason other than to "celebrate the day" as she called it.

Evie walked up to the house and let herself inside through the patio door. Vase first. Card later. She carefully unwrapped the filmy netting and the layer of tissue paper underneath it. The tiny linen envelope fell out, drifting gracefully to the table. Reminding her it was there.

"I'll get to you in a minute."

She put the flowers in water and took her time arranging

them in an ironstone vase. And then she wiped up the table and rinsed out the dishcloth.

With fingers that shook, she finally tore open the envelope and pulled out the small square of paper inside.

Therefore, if anyone is in Christ, he is a new creation; the old has gone, the new has come!—2 Corinthians 5:17

Evie sagged against the counter as she stared at the signatures.

Jacob   **Rachel**

   Dan   *Faith*

And Sam.

In the same tidy script he'd used to sign his name were two more words. *Thank you.*

Overwhelmed, Evie sagged against the counter.

All of them, Lord?

And then she burst into tears.

"He's a good man, Evie." Patrick draped her cardigan around her shoulders and settled down on the dock beside her.

"I know." Evie's gaze didn't shift away from the deep blue seam where the water met the sky in the distance.

Shortly after reading the card, she'd driven to Cooper's Landing and walked to the end of the dock. The *Natalie,* preening in a bright yellow canvas cover, bobbed a greeting. For a minute, she'd let herself remember the strength in Sam's hands as they'd covered hers while she steered the boat out of the harbor.

"Did I imagine it, or was there something happening between you and Sam?"

Something she'd walked away from. Evie drew a careful breath. "We're too different, Dad."

"Are you sure that's the real reason?"

She should have known her father would see through to the truth. "I was too young to realize how dangerous Mom's job was until she didn't come home that day, but now I do *know*. And I can't do it." Evie twisted her fingers together in her lap. "God brought me to Cooper's Landing to help Faith. I'm happy Sam is a Christian now but that doesn't mean we're meant to be together."

"I love you to pieces, Evie, but ever since your mother died you've tried to cocoon yourself from anything that might be painful. And I know I'm partially to blame for going along with it. You won't even go barefoot on the beach."

"That's because there might be broken glass in the sand," Evie muttered in her own defense.

Patrick smiled gently. "The last few weeks, I've seen changes in you. Good ones. And I'd like you to consider something. Maybe God didn't bring you here for Faith and Sam. Maybe He brought Faith and Sam here for *you*."

Tears spilled down her cheeks. "It might be too late, Dad. He didn't even say goodbye."

Patrick patted her knee. "Maybe because he hoped it wouldn't be."

"Hey, Chief. Mrs. Mattson called and wants us to check out a suspicious truck parked outside her house again."

Sam's chair creaked in protest as he leaned back. "Does this one happen to have the words FedEx printed on the side, too?"

Officer Tony Faller laughed. "I don't know. But I'll take care of it."

"Let me." Sam rose to his feet, once again battling a familiar restlessness that had dogged him the past few weeks. "I could use a change of scenery from the city budget right about now."

"Yeah." Tony made a face. "Sorry about that. It was one thing watching over the town, another one taking on the city council and all those numbers. All I can say is I'm glad you're back."

"You did a great job. At least now I know I can take a leave of absence if necessary." Sam suppressed a smile when he saw the panic in Tony's eyes, but he couldn't help giving the officer a hard time.

Tony had been employed at the Summer Harbor P.D. for only three years, and the mayor had questioned Sam's choice of men to take his place during the month he was in Cooper's Landing. But Sam had pushed and eventually got his way. In personality and dedication, Tony reminded Sam of Dan.

Thanks, Lord.

Every time his brother came to mind, it was the only thing Sam could say. Two simple words, but they came from the depths of his soul.

He still couldn't believe the changes in his family. In a lot of ways, he felt like Dan. Like he was starting from scratch. What had Evie said? Moment by moment? Breath by breath? He hadn't understood what she meant at the time. But now he did.

A hundred times over the past few weeks, he'd wanted to call Evie and fill her in on Dan's progress. But she hadn't made any attempt to contact him since he'd left Cooper's Landing, and that told him, more than anything, exactly where they stood.

Apart.

Even after he'd sent her a bouquet of flowers, she hadn't called or sent a note.

After that, he carefully avoided asking questions about Evie when Jacob called. He knew that, thanks to Tyson, Seth Lansky was being formally charged for possession of stolen property, while Bruce Mullins claimed Seth had acted entirely on his own. Sam even heard subtle references to Jacob's budding romance with Sophie. But Jacob didn't mention Evie, and Sam assumed she'd gone home, as planned.

It was clear that even though they now shared the same faith, Evie didn't see them sharing anything else.

"Not even a pizza," Sam muttered.

"You want to order a pizza?"

"No." He and Tony were friends but he wasn't ready to talk about Evie yet. "I was talking to myself."

"Michelle says you've been doing that a lot lately," Tony said, a glint in his eyes.

"Really?" Sam stalked toward the door, careful not to open it so quickly that Michelle, who probably had her ear pressed against it, would fall over. "What else does Michelle say?"

Tony followed him out. "That you sent flowers to someone name Evangeline McBride."

Sam stared at him in disbelief. "How does she know that?"

Tony shrugged. "She and the florist are second cousins."

"I should have stayed in Chicago."

Michelle, his loyal secretary and the department's efficient dispatcher, pretended to file papers when he rounded the corner.

"Cousins, huh?" He arched an eyebrow as he strode past.

"You weren't supposed to tell him!" She pouted at Tony, who winked at her.

"I'll be back. I'm going to check out the suspicious truck on Mrs. Mattson's street and then I'm going to stop home for a few minutes." Sam took his sunglasses out of his pocket and shook them open before reaching the door.

"Oh, that's right," Michelle called after him. "My mother's aunt Thelma reupholsters furniture and she said you can drop the recliner off anytime this weekend."

"Thanks." He planned to make his brother pay for the damages Rocky had inflicted on his favorite chair. In a moment of what Sam could only claim as temporary insanity, he'd offered to take care of Rocky until Dan came home. Rachel had changed her mind about having a dog in the house but the hours she and Faith spent with Dan at the rehab center weren't conducive to training an active puppy.

Neither were his, but he'd offered anyway.

Rocky missed his littermates and didn't like being cooped up all day, so he'd taken out his frustration on Sam's recliner. And a pair of boots. And the leg of a coffee table.

"I'll be back later. Don't call me unless it's an absolute emergency."

"Absolute emergency. Got it."

Sam glanced over his shoulder and saw Michelle curtsey and Tony salute.

Comedians. Both of them.

Sam rolled his eyes but tamped down the laughter welling up inside him. The price he paid for being the chief of police in a small town. And he loved it.

If only he could convince Evie that she would love it, too.

Chapter Twenty-One

"You knew about this, Lord," Evie said out loud as she read the bright blue, wave-shaped sign that greeted visitors at the city limits.

Summer Harbor.

Of *course* it was on the water. The little town Sam had promised to protect and serve curled around a sparkling, diamond-shaped bay like a contented tabby cat.

Evie tapped the brake as the speed limit sign suddenly took a radical drop from 55 mph to 25 mph. She didn't want to get picked up for exceeding the speed limit!

She refused to let herself be charmed by the tidy, old-fashioned main street with its brass light poles and wrought-iron benches. Or by the planters, overflowing with pink and white petunias, strategically placed at every corner. She could see the top of an old stone lighthouse jutting from the top of a hill that overlooked Lake Michigan.

There was no sense admiring a town she might only be visiting for fifteen minutes. Depending on how Sam reacted to her unexpected—and unannounced—arrival.

In a town of five thousand people, it didn't take Evie long

to locate the police department. One squad car was parked in front of the brick building with the engine running.

Evie's heart jumped.

Okay, God. I'm taking a risk here. Don't leave me.

She pushed open the door and the dispatcher, a young woman with spiky blond hair and jewel-studded glasses perched on her nose, smiled at her from behind the Plexiglas window. When she stood up and waddled over, Evie was surprised to see she was *very* pregnant. "Can I help you?"

"I'm looking for Sam Cutter."

"He's not here right now," the dispatcher said. "Would you like to speak with Officer Faller?"

"No, thank you." Evie gnawed on her lower lip as she tried to determine what to do next. Wait? Go back home?

The second choice was tempting, but she'd driven almost half the day to see Sam.

As she waffled, the door opened behind her and Evie's knees turned to jelly.

"Evangeline McBride?"

Evie turned toward the unfamiliar voice and saw a man in uniform standing there, looking just as surprised as she was.

"Yes?"

Behind the glass, the dispatcher gasped. "You're Evangeline McBride?"

Evie's gaze cautiously slid from one to the other. How did they know who she was? Was it possible Sam had *talked* about her? To the people he worked with? A flutter of wild hope took wing in her heart.

"I ran your license plate before I came in," the officer said cheerfully. "I'm Officer Faller, by the way."

"And I'm Michelle Loomis." The dispatcher grinned.

"It's nice to meet you both," Evie stammered.

"I told her Chief's not here." Michelle gave Tony a meaningful look.

"I can come back—" If she didn't lose her nerve.

"No!" Their combined voices drowned out her weak suggestion.

"He won't be gone long. Why don't you wait in his office." Officer Faller stepped in front of the door, effectively blocking her path.

Evie eased around him. "No. Thank you. Really. I'll come back…later."

Michelle and Tony exchanged skeptical looks.

"He said we should call him if it's an absolute emergency," Tony mused.

Michelle ignored Evie's strangled protest and nodded thoughtfully. "If she is Evangeline McBride, I think she definitely falls into the category of an absolute emergency."

Evie tried not to overthink Michelle's remark as the dispatcher scrawled something on a piece of paper and pushed it toward her through the narrow slot in the divider. "Here you go, honey. But don't tell him where you got it. I happen to like my job."

Rocky greeted Sam at the door, a tattered baseball cap clamped in his jaws.

"Found a new hat, huh, boy?" Sam held the door open and Rocky charged past him, on a mission to find the perfect spot to bury the hat. Just like he had the coffee table leg.

The July sunshine beat down on him and Sam loosened his tie as he followed Rocky's crooked trail down the beach.

The remnants of an elaborate sand castle caught his attention, and he immediately thought about Evie.

When *didn't* he think about Evie?

Given the short time they'd known each other, Sam was

amazed at how many things reminded him of her. When he looked out his living room window at the water, he remembered the afternoon on the *Natalie*. And her blue eyes. If he saw a woman on the street with a hair color similar to Evie's, his heart rate spiked in response.

Rocky let out a sharp bark and Sam lifted one hand to shade his eyes against the sun. The woman walking toward him on the beach wore a large straw hat. Just like Evie's.

There you go again.

Sam whistled but Rocky ignored him and made a mad dash for the woman, his stubby legs churning up sand like the wheels of a dune buggy.

"He's friendly," Sam shouted across the distance, hoping she wouldn't think his crazy dog was about to attack her.

"I know."

The laughter in the voice—even the voice itself—sounded like Evie. The heat was getting to him. No doubt about it.

As the woman reached down to pet Rocky, he saw the gigantic purse slung over her shoulder.

Somehow, Sam's feet kept moving. Even though everything inside had frozen solid.

"I can't believe he's gotten so big." The straw hat listed to one side and Sam caught a glimpse of sunset-red hair. And a straight little nose dotted with freckles.

Twelve of them.

He couldn't believe Evie was standing three feet away. Almost within reach. Sam blinked, just to make sure she wasn't a hallucination.

"What are you doing here?" He hadn't expected to see her, not unless circumstances forced them together. Sam had discovered his newfound faith meant trusting God when it came to his relationship with Evie. And that had become his greatest challenge.

As the days slipped by with no contact between them, Sam had started to lose hope that she could accept his career. And not only accept it, but support it.

Sam knew God was the only one who could wipe away the last barrier standing between him and Evie. But she had to *let* Him. Accepting that had been tough for Sam, especially when he wanted to crash through those barriers himself and *make* Evie see they were meant to have a future together. Sam had come to the realization that trusting God took guts, a lot more than trying to do things on his own!

"They got the permits." Evie smiled uncertainly. "Yesterday."

She'd driven all the way to Summer Harbor to tell him about the *Noble?*

"That's great. Sophie will be happy." He'd talked to Jacob the night before, but somehow his father had failed to mention the latest news. Maybe because they'd sent Evie to deliver it in person?

Why?

Sam was afraid to hope.

"The local news interviewed Sophie and our dads last night. They're celebrities now. Even a national network called to find out what was going on."

"Great." Sam tried to muster some enthusiasm. He was glad the months of research had yielded some results, but he found himself wishing Evie would have come to Summer Harbor for another reason other than playing messenger. "Have you been in Cooper's Landing the whole time?"

"I went home last week."

"How's the garden?" Sam winced. Okay, there'd been a grain of sarcasm in the question, but seeing Evie again had knocked him off center.

He stuffed his hands in his pockets, not sure how much longer he could hold out before taking her into his arms.

* * *

He wasn't making this easy for her. But then, this was a Sam that Evie didn't recognize. He'd had his hair cut since the last time she'd seen him and the five-o'clock stubble that shadowed his lean jawline was gone. He'd traded in his blue jeans and faded T-shirt for charcoal-gray Dockers and a crisp white shirt, paired with a conservative tie. The pockets displayed an assortment of pins. And his badge.

Sam didn't look like a windblown sailor anymore. He looked like a cop.

And she fell in love with him all over again.

From the minute she'd followed the path down to the beach and saw Sam walking by the water, she wondered why she'd let so much time go by. And why she'd let her fears control her future.

She'd put that control right where it had always been—in God's faithful hands. And she planned to leave it there.

Now she just had to convince Sam. If she hadn't waited too long already.

"It's a pretty town." Small talk. So maybe she wasn't as brave as she hoped to be!

"It's on the water," Sam pointed out.

Evie ignored the slight challenge in his tone. "I think it's prettier than Cooper's Landing, with the marina and the lighthouse."

"You like the lighthouse?"

Evie nodded.

"Come on. I'll show it to you."

Evie blinked. Had she imagined Sam's hint of a smile? "Really? I'd like that." She'd like anything that kept him with her.

Sam whistled for Rocky and this time the puppy bounded over and followed them up the beach. The stone lighthouse was smaller than others Evie had seen, but still quaint and well preserved. Probably due to being the target project of a local historical society.

Sam shocked her by following the uneven flagstone path right to the front door.

"You can go inside?" Evie frowned. "Is it open to tourists?"

Instead of answering, Sam turned the handle and stepped to one side.

"Are you sure?" She hesitated. "Don't we need permission?"

"After you." Now Sam did smile. And she would have followed him anywhere.

Evie decided the town must own the lighthouse and, as chief of police, Sam had permission to show it to visitors.

Rocky galloped over to them, his tail wagging proudly as he deposited a shoe at Evie's feet.

"Oh, no, you don't," Sam growled. "I happen to like that pair."

While he wrestled for control of the shoe, Evie turned in a slow circle and scanned the interior. Comfortable furnishings reflected a rustic, nautical theme and Evie realized the lighthouse had been converted into someone's...home. The truth suddenly dawned on her.

"You live in a lighthouse."

God, you knew about this, too! Are there any more surprises?

She hoped so. She was beginning to enjoy them.

"I bought it already fixed up. Over the years it's been a gift shop and an artist's studio, but the last owner put it up for sale within days after the police and fire commission hired me." Sam shrugged. "I couldn't resist."

Evie walked over to the circular staircase that wound up to the second floor.

"Do you want to take a look?"

"I don't like heights." A reluctant confession. Sam was going to think she was still afraid of her own shadow.

"Neither do I," Sam surprised her by saying. "But the view is worth it."

His cell phone rang and he flipped it open. "Excuse me, Evie. I have to take this."

So formal. So professional. When had Sam become the cautious one? And what was she going to have to do to prove to him that her perspective had changed?

"Of course." *I guess I've taken up enough of your time.*

While Sam stepped into the next room, Evie walked blindly outside into the sunshine.

Had she been wrong about Sam's feelings? Had she read too much into his unexpected kiss that day at the beach? Maybe he'd realized he didn't want to pursue a relationship with someone he thought couldn't accept his career.

Rocky followed her and made a beeline toward the lacey waves lapping against the shore. Without thinking, Evie peeled off her shoes and dropped them in the sand as she followed him into the shallow water.

He fished a wet stick of driftwood out of the surf and danced up to her. Evie laughed and tossed it into the water, unable to avoid getting splashed as he went after it.

They played the game for several minutes before Evie felt Sam's presence. She turned around and there he was, right behind her. Her shoes in his hand.

The warmth in his eyes took her breath away. And gave her the courage she needed.

"I'm sorry, Sam. I should've told you how I felt about you but I was scared and—" Evie decided words weren't enough this time. She stood on her tiptoes and reached up to frame his face with her hands. And kissed him.

Her shoes hit the sand with a thud as Sam drew her into his arms and looked down at her.

"Barefoot, Evangeline?" he murmured. "That's a little…adventurous, don't you think?"

She smiled up at him. "What can I say? I'm my mother's daughter. Do you think you can live with that?"

"I'm looking forward to it," Sam whispered in her ear. "For a very long time."

Epilogue

"Okay, Dad. Why did you call us all here? Did you find the treasure or not?"

Evie suppressed a smile. Leave it to Caitlin to cut to the heart of the matter. Several days before, everyone in the Cutter and McBride families had answered a mysterious summons to come to Cooper's Landing. E-mails flew back and forth but no one knew what was going on. When Evie called her dad to try to pry some information from him, all he told her was to pack her bag for the weekend.

So she had. And she'd picked up Sam along the way.

By mid-afternoon on Saturday, Sophie's backyard was crowded with people. Caitlin and Meghan had managed to get the weekend off, although Evie had a hunch their quick response had more to do with wanting to meet Sam than to find out what, if anything, had been discovered in Lake Superior!

Tyson was a quiet presence but Evie noticed Jacob was careful to include Sophie's son in the conversations. According to Patrick, Tyson had joined a support group for people with addictions. He still shied away from attending church services with Sophie, but he'd met Pastor Wallis several times for breakfast.

And it was good to see Faith again, too. And to finally meet Dan and Rachel.

Evie felt an immediate connection with Sam's twin brother and his wife. To her embarrassment, both Dan and Rachel made a point of seeking her out and thanking her again for tutoring Faith. When Evie tried to downplay her role, Rachel met her gaze evenly and told her it wasn't only the tutoring sessions that had put their daughter on the right track. The piece of beach glass on the table next to her bed proved it. When Faith had returned to Chicago with Sam and Jacob, she'd told her father about Evie's prayer asking God to bring something good out of the accident. And, Rachel assured Evie, He had.

It wasn't the only good thing God had done, Evie thought as she felt the warmth of Sam's fingers laced through hers. When Sam had time off, they'd been spending it together. Sometimes he drove to Brookfield to see her, and other times she made the trip to Summer Harbor. Each time she visited, it got harder to say goodbye. Not only to Summer Harbor, but to Sam. Once upon a time, she could never have imagined herself with a police officer. Now she couldn't imagine life without him.

"I agree with Caitlin," Dan said with a grin. "Not that we don't appreciate all this wonderful food you've provided, but we want some answers now."

Sam's fingers tightened and Evie gave him a reassuring squeeze. She knew what he was thinking. Dan was walking now with the use of canes, but the doctor was optimistic he could retire them in time for Faith's basketball season.

Jacob's laugh drew Evie's attention back to the moment. "We can all go in the house and then Sophie can tell you. She's the one who started this whole thing."

Everyone squeezed into Sophie's tiny living room and Sophie set a plain brown folder down on the coffee table.

"While the dive team was looking for the *Noble,* Patrick and I kept looking for more information about my great-grandfather Matthew. A few days ago, a retired pastor sent me something.

"The Church on the Hill was the first church in Cooper's Landing, started in the late 1800s by a circuit preacher at the request of the settlers here. It closed its doors about twenty-five years ago, but the original building is still there and so is the cemetery. The records of all the births and deaths were turned over to the local historical society. The pastor I contacted is a member of that society and he was very interested in Matthew's story. The name *Graham* caught his attention and he did some detective work for me."

Sophie hesitated and everyone in the room was silent, waiting for her to continue. Instead, Sophie removed a photograph from the folder on the table.

Evie looked closer and saw an image of an old headstone, pitted and scarred by the elements.

D. C. Graham
Beloved Wife
Born January 10, 1870
Died October 23, 1890

Sam frowned. "Another relative of yours, Sophie?"

"In a matter of speaking." Sophie's eyes misted over. "This headstone is in a section of the cemetery designated to remember people who died but weren't able to be buried. People who perished in blizzards and were never found. Or people who…drowned."

Judging from the confused expressions on the faces gathered around her, Evie knew she wasn't the only one having a hard time following Sophie.

"We think D.C. stands for Dale Carrington," Sophie explained softly. "While I researched our genealogy, I didn't find anyone in my family with those initials."

"But the last name is Graham. And it says beloved wife," Meghan said.

"Exactly." Patrick winked at his middle daughter.

Evie stared at Sophie and Patrick in amazement. "You think Matthew and Lady Dale were *married?*"

"We had a difficult time believing it, too," Sophie said. "But when we saw this photo, everything fell into place. It explains why Matthew had Lady Dale's family ring in his possession when he was rescued. He hadn't stolen it, she'd *given* it to him. According to relatives, Matthew was a changed man after the ship went down. Bitter. Burdened by guilt. But now I believe the guilt wasn't because he'd stolen Lady Dale's dowry—it was because he hadn't been able to save her."

"But wasn't she engaged to that lumber baron's son?" Rachel asked.

"Yes, but Matthew and Lady Dale would have spent a lot of time together, not only at her family estate in England but also on the journey over," Sophie said. "Stranger things have happened. The Lawrence family had a lot of money but lacked respectability. The Carrington family was just the opposite— that's probably why the marriage was arranged. It's possible Matthew befriended Lady Dale and offered her a way to avoid a marriage with a man described as selfish and hot tempered. Or they were simply two young people who fell in love. Whatever the reason, the ship's captain had the authority to perform a wedding ceremony on board the *Noble*."

"But if they got married, why didn't Matthew tell anyone? It would have saved his reputation," Caitlin asked, clearly skeptical.

"The proof went down with the ship," Patrick said. "The Lawrence family had a lot of influence in this area. Who'd believe a titled lady would give up everything for a lumberjack?"

Meghan gave the barest of smiles. "I would. God knows what He's doing when He brings two people together."

Sophie smiled up at Jacob and he turned red. "Yes. Well. I guess I can go along with that."

Evie felt the warmth of Sam's gaze. "So can I."

"So there's no treasure?" Tyson sounded disappointed. "All that work was for nothing?"

"The treasure is right here." Sophie tapped the photo with the tip of her finger. "For me, it was always about finding the truth."

"I suppose." Tyson sighed.

Patrick's lips twitched. "Maybe you should show him the other photo."

Sophie took something else out of the folder and slid it toward Tyson. "We turned these over to the underwater salvage and preserve committee yesterday. They were pretty excited, to say the least."

Tyson looked dazed. "Gold coins? There has to be at least—"

"Fifty of them," Patrick finished.

"Where—"

"Aw, that's up to the committee to decide." Jacob cleared his throat. "Doesn't matter to me what happens to them. Or even that we cleared Matthew's name. I think we found something a whole lot more valuable than a bunch of old coins."

Sam's eyes glistened as he brushed his lips against Evie's hair. "So do I."

"Did you see those two?" Jacob chuckled. "Who would have guessed?"

Patrick joined him at the window and saw Evie and Sam standing together in the moonlight, deep in conversation.

"We have a lot to be thankful for, my friend."

Jacob blew out a gusty sigh. "Isn't that the truth? But you

know something, now that we found the *Noble,* I am going to miss the excitement."

"Mmm." Patrick smiled slowly. "Maybe we don't have to miss it yet."

"What do you mean?"

"After we made the six-o'clock news last week, I got a call from someone."

"About what?"

"Let's just say it may involve another…fishing trip."

Jacob grinned. "Count me in. Partner."

* * * * *

Dear Reader,

Many stories are born from the simple question "What if?" What if a young woman who doesn't like to take risks is suddenly pushed into an adventure? And what if the things she views as flaws, or weaknesses, in her personality turn out to be strengths when they're put to the test?

I love that God created each of us with unique personalities. And I love that He puts us in situations guaranteed to stretch us beyond our abilities—so we learn to trust Him more.

I hope you enjoyed teaming up with Sam and Evie in the romantic adventure, *A Treasure Worth Keeping*. And be sure to watch for Meghan's story—we're not done with the McBride family yet!

Blessings,

Kathryn Springer

QUESTIONS FOR DISCUSSION

1. What is your first impression of Evie? Does it change over the course of the book? Why?

2. How did Evie's and Sam's childhoods differ? How did Jacob Cutter, Sam's father, influence Sam's faith (or lack of it)? How did Sam's childhood differ from the way Patrick raised his daughters? Think about the legacy of faith in your own family as you were growing up. How would you describe it?

3. Dan's injury caused Sam to question what he believed. Has anything happened in a similar situation in your own life? Describe what happened and how it changed your perspective.

4. Evie was a believer, but there was an area in her life where she struggled with totally putting her trust in God. What was it? What did it stem from?

5. When did Sam's opinion of Evie begin to change? Why?

6. What is your favorite scene in the book? Why?

7. Evie compares herself to her sisters and thinks she doesn't measure up to them. What is the danger in comparing ourselves to other women? Why do you think we tend to do this?

8. Have you ever researched your family history? Do you think it's important? Why or why not?

9. In what way did losing her mother affect the way Evie lived her life? How did it impact her relationships? Why do you think that Evie had to be the one to reach out to Sam at the end of the book?

10. What would you say is your greatest "treasure"? Why?

REQUEST YOUR FREE BOOKS!

2 FREE INSPIRATIONAL NOVELS
PLUS 2
FREE
MYSTERY GIFTS

Love Inspired.

YES! Please send me 2 FREE Love Inspired® novels and my 2 FREE mystery gifts (gifts are worth about $10). After receiving them, if I don't wish to receive any more books, I can return the shipping statement marked "cancel". If I don't cancel, I will receive 4 brand-new novels every month and be billed just $4.24 per book in the U.S. or $4.74 per book in Canada, plus 25¢ shipping and handling per book and applicable taxes, if any*. That's a savings of over 20% off the cover price! I understand that accepting the 2 free books and gifts places me under no obligation to buy anything. I can always return a shipment and cancel at any time. Even if I never buy another book, the two free books and gifts are mine to keep forever.

113 IDN ERXA 313 IDN ERWX

Name	(PLEASE PRINT)	
Address		Apt. #
City	State/Prov.	Zip/Postal Code

Signature (if under 18, a parent or guardian must sign)

Order online at www.LoveInspiredBooks.com

Or mail to Steeple Hill Reader Service:

IN U.S.A.: P.O. Box 1867, Buffalo, NY 14240-1867
IN CANADA: P.O. Box 609, Fort Erie, Ontario L2A 5X3

Not valid to current subscribers of Love Inspired books.

Want to try two free books from another series?
Call 1-800-873-8635 or visit www.morefreebooks.com

LIREG08

TITLES AVAILABLE NEXT MONTH

Don't miss these four stories in April

DRY CREEK SWEETHEARTS by Janet Tronstad
Dry Creek

They'd parted when his career took off, but musician
Duane Enger was back—and determined to win back his
high school sweetheart. Linda Morgan wasn't sure she wanted
to pick up where they left off, though Duane was the one person
who could make her heart sing.

HER BABY DREAMS by Debra Clopton

The Mule Hollow matchmakers were at it again, and this time
they had Ashby Templeton in their sights. Despite her hopes of
a family, she couldn't believe Dan Dawson was the right choice.
The flirtatious cowboy was determined to change that—and
make Ashby his bride.

A COWBOY'S HONOR by Lois Richer
Pennies from Heaven

Gracie Henderson's husband Dallas had been missing for six
years. Now he was found, but robbed of his memory by a tragic
accident. Gracie was relieved to have answers, but she had to
protect her child. Could a rekindled love heal her doubts?

MILITARY DADDY by Patricia Davids

They'd made a mistake that had led to an unexpected blessing:
Annie Delmar and Corporal Shane Ross were to become parents.
Shane wanted to be part of his child's life…and part of Annie's.
But getting Annie to give him a second chance would be the
greatest battle he'd ever faced.

LICNM0308